CW01431449

THE ART & MUSIC OF
JOHN LENNON

PETER DOGGETT

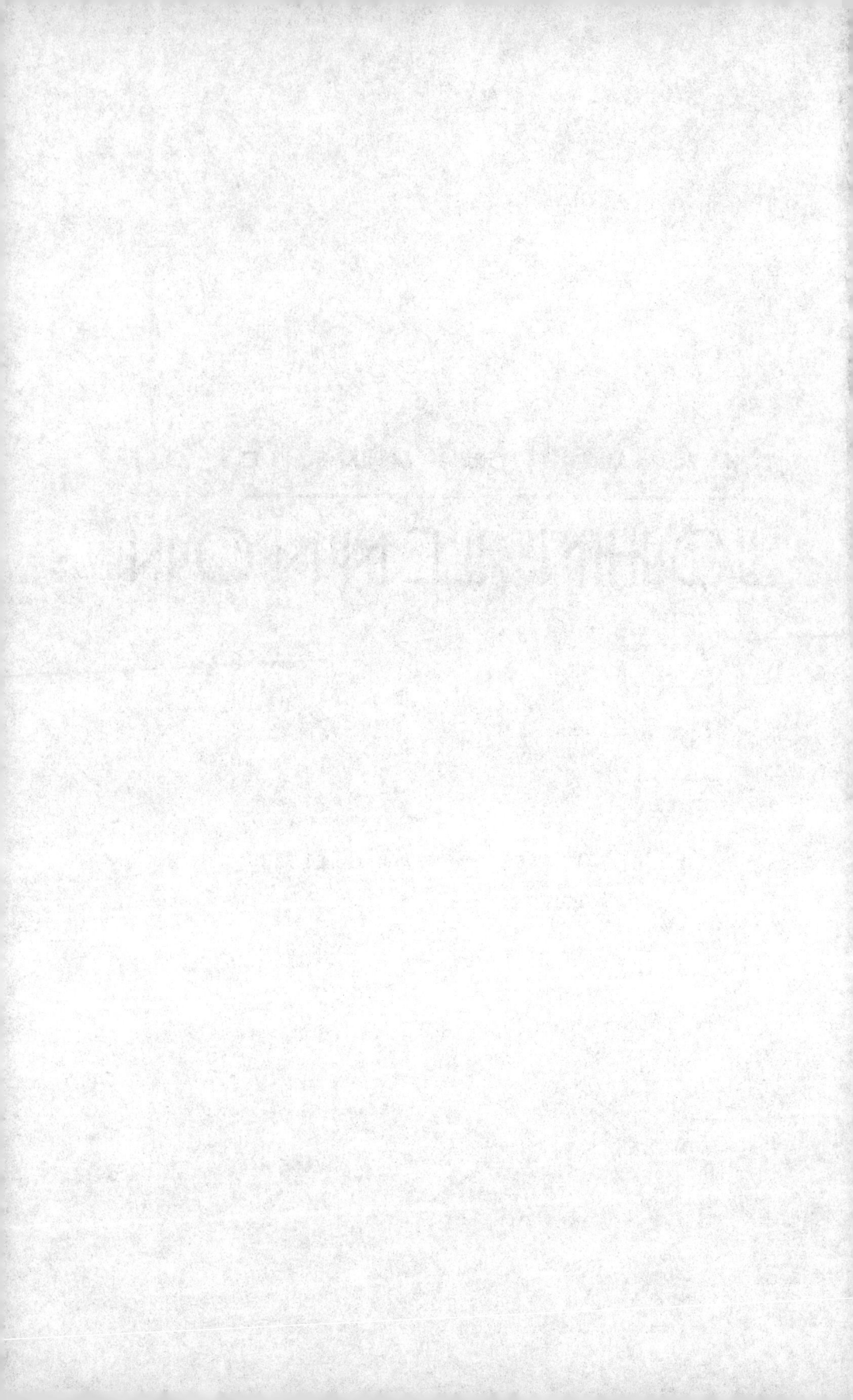

THE ART & MUSIC OF

JOHN LENNON

PETER DOGGETT

OMNIBUS PRESS

London • New York • Paris • Sydney • Copenhagen • Berlin • Madrid • Tokyo

Exclusive Distributors
Music Sales Limited,
8/9 Frith Street,
London W1D 3JB, UK.

Music Sales Corporation,
257 Park Avenue South,
New York, NY 10010, USA.

Macmillan Distribution Services,
53 Park West Drive,
Derrimut, Vic 3030,
Australia.

To the Music Trade only:
Music Sales Limited,
8/9 Frith Street,
London W1D 3JB, UK.

Every effort has been made to trace the copyright holders of the photographs in this book but one or
two were unreachable. We would be grateful if the photographers concerned would contact us.

Typeset by Phoenix Photosetting, Chatham, Kent
Printed by: Creative Print & Design, Ebbw Vale, Wales

A catalogue record for this book is available from the British Library.

Visit Omnibus Press on the web at www.omnibuspress.com

"For Rachel"

Contents

Acknowledgements

This book is the product of 35 years of listening to John Lennon's music, following his career through the Seventies as a fan and then chronicling his life and work as a journalist since 1980. It would be impossible to list all the source material that I have consulted over that period, or indeed name all the people with whom I have discussed Lennon, or who have offered titbits of information during that time.

The current edition could not have been written, however, without the assistance and generosity of Beatles scholar Pete Nash, who opened his collection and his considerable knowledge to me. Many thanks to him – and none of the blame if there are any mistakes, which are all mine. Meanwhile, check out Pete's website: www.britishbeatlesfanclub.co.uk

Otherwise, Mark Lewisohn has been an inspiration to me, as to anyone else who has written about the Beatles, both as a friend, a fellow journalist and as the author of three remarkable books: *The Beatles Live!*, *The Complete Beatles Recording Sessions*, and *The Complete Beatles Chronicle*.

As a teenager, I was amazed and delighted to discover Harry Castleman and Walter Podrazik's Beatles discography, *All Together Now*. The pages of my original paperback edition are now black with thumbprints, and their subsequent volumes, *The Beatles Again* and *The End Of The Beatles?*, were also vital in schooling me in The Beatles' recording history.

My favourite writer about The Beatles was Derek Taylor, whom it was a pleasure and a privilege to meet and to get to know a little in the last decade of his life. Although they weren't a prime reference source for this book, his volumes *As Time Goes By* and *Fifty Years Adrift* are highly recommended to anyone who cares as much about the Fab Four as he did.

The most remarkable book of Beatles scholarship published in recent years has been Chip Madinger and Mark Easter's *Eight Arms To Hold You: The Solo Beatles Compendium*. Although I don't always agree 100% with their findings, the sheer scope, depth, energy and intelligence of their research are quite astounding, and this book could not have been written without their help in guiding the way through the morass of Lennon home recordings and out-takes. If you don't have a copy of their book, buy it today. Also very useful was Kristofer Engelhardt's *The Beatles Undercover*, a superb chronicle of all the guest appearances ever made by the Fab Four on other people's records. And Keith Badman's series of books documenting what the Beatles did and said were another essential reference source.

At various stages of my life, I've enjoyed and learned from my discussions with people who knew Lennon and The Beatles, including Tony Barrow, Tony Bramwell, Bruce Bierman, Chris Charlesworth, Steve Gebhardt, Astrid Kirchherr, Alexis Mardas, Mike McCartney, May Pang, Ron Richards, Jurgen Vollmer, Bob Whitaker and, of course, Yoko Ono. Sean O'Mahony not only knew The Beatles as the editor of their official monthly magazine in the Sixties, but also gave me a unique opportunity to write about the group for more than twenty years, for which I shall always be grateful.

Friends with whom I've had fruitful discussions about Lennon since 1970 include Stuart Batsford, Debbie Cassell, Andy Davis, Andrew Dean, Spencer Leigh, Andy Neill, Mark Paytress, John Platt, Johnny Rogan – and no doubt many more, whose names I shall soon be embarrassed to have forgotten. Thanks also to Carey Wallace, Sarah Hodgson and Helen Bailey at Christie's in South Kensington and New York; to Andrew Sclanders, purveyor of rare books (www.beatbooks.com); and to my agent, Rupert Heath.

Finally, on a personal level, this book could not have been written without the love and support of Rachel Baylis. Much love in return to her, and to Catrin Mascall and Rebecca Mascall – and apologies to those two for preventing them from using MSN Messenger and Grand Theft Auto as often as they would have liked over the past few months.

INTRODUCTION

Forget 'Imagine' for a second. It's not my favourite Lennon composition; in fact, I wouldn't care if I never heard it again. But it *was* voted the greatest song of the last century, and it's become such a landmark in popular culture that it interrupts our view of the far more interesting man who wrote it.

John Lennon did far more, for good and for bad, in his forty years on this planet than composing a vague anthem of peace, love and humanism, and performing it on a white piano. In the same year that he released 'Imagine', Lennon also campaigned for a workers' revolution, for the overthrow of the US president, and for a victory by the IRA over the forces of British law and order. Suddenly this peacenik doesn't seem quite so cosy.

And that's the way that Lennon would have wanted it. The twin impulses of peace and war raged through his life and work, from his turbulent upbringing to the self-lacerating songs that he penned in his final months. In 1969, he compared himself to Christ and anticipated his own crucifixion. That same year, he willingly set himself up as a universal figure of fun, in the interests of world peace. He was often violent and cruel in his personal life, and in his encounters with the outside world. Yet he was also capable of extreme acts of kindness, heartwarming declarations of love, and an irrepressible sense of fun. Who was he? He was human, that's all, not an 'Imagine'-ary saint or a second Gandhi.

Every human life is too broad and too inexplicable to go down in history as anything more than a caricature. Caricaturists exaggerate; it's in the nature of the art. And so history rarely leaves us with complications: men of the past are either heroic or villainous. John Lennon's death on December

8, 1980 evoked both responses. To his fans and former wives, the deceased Lennon became little short of a martyr, sacrificed on the twin altars of peace and love. Yet his biographers countered with a dark portrait of a man who was tormented by demons, and transmitted his pain via his tongue and his fists. Their Lennon was apparently a bigot, a bastard, whose private life was some kind of obscene parody of the ideals he expressed in his work. Drugs, rape, murder, kicking his baby around the room – it was all in a day's work for the overgrown child who came to rule the world.

In the official histories, meanwhile, Lennon's tempestuous private life was ignored – or, at any rate, forgiven, as the inevitable backlash of major art. But what did that art consist of? Sometimes it seemed that the whole of Lennon's career could be condensed into one song – Lennon's naive statement of universal optimism, 'Imagine'. Which is where we began …

John Lennon – angel or devil? Well, that's a subject for another day, and another book. What both approaches ignore is the urge to create – and to perform – which pushed Lennon from Liverpool to Hamburg, London, and finally New York in the company of a radical Japanese artist who was anathema to Lennon's followers and friends.

It's that urge, and the dazzling variety of art which it produced, that is the subject of this book. Yes, Lennon was a Beatle; he also wrote 'Imagine' and a clutch of other counter-culture anthems. But although these are the activities for which he is most often remembered, they barely hint at the range and quantity of work he produced between the mid-fifties and the end of 1980.

Besides records, Lennon made home recordings – try-outs for new songs, romps though favourite oldies, and sound collages that were as outlandish as anything rock has produced. He published two books at the height of his fame, and left sufficient material for a third to be compiled after his death. With his second wife, Yoko Ono, he spent three years pushing at the barriers of rock stardom, creating a series of avant-garde, bewildering and often aggravating films, staging exhibitions, planning conceptual events, and dedicating their lives to the twin aims of world peace and artistic fulfilment. They also lent their names to campaigns for Marxist revolution, black power, feminism, gay liberation and a hundred other political crusades. Along the way, they lived up to one of the more extreme suggestions in Yoko's book, *Grapefruit*: the suggestion in *Shi* (*From The Cradle To The Grave Of Mr So*), that artists should capture their entire lives on film. In their certainty that, as artists, everything they did was a reflection of their art, John and Yoko came close to putting this ideal into practice, with the result that the initial years of their marriage were documented in more detail than the lives of any other public figures.

Most studies of Lennon have either ignored his non-musical activities, or else given them a token status as the bored ramblings of a self-indulgent rock star. What soon becomes obvious, though, as you examine his life and work, is that the art, the films, the books and the music are the product of the same imagination. Lennon wasn't, in his own eyes, a rock star who suddenly felt like making a film: both endeavours were personal statements. It may be true that his efforts in one medium were far more professional and innovative than in another; but that doesn't make them any the less revealing.

That was the initial impulse behind this book: the belief that you either take Lennon's art (he would have given it a capital A, of course) as a whole, or you misunderstand it. If nothing else, this book should ensure that you can never again consider his contributions to The Beatles' 'White Album' without remembering that at the same time he was recording the *Two Virgins* album with Yoko, chopping his furniture in half for a public exhibition, filming the slow rise and fall of his semi-erect penis, and launching balloons into the air in the quest for international peace. The 'White Album' was the event that attracted the most attention, but the films and the art exhibitions were equally important to Lennon.

Why has this work been ignored? Because it doesn't fit the myth – or myths, in fact: one for The Beatles, one for John and Yoko. The Lennons were as guilty as anyone of perpetuating myths, as we'll see along the way. The Beatles' myth was created for them, though, as soon as the media latched onto the four-headed hydra from Liverpool with the matching haircuts and quick line in repartee. The group tried to puncture the media balloon early on – to say, as Lennon put it in a memorable phrase, "This is us with our trousers down" – but it took John's relationship with Yoko, the failure of the *Magical Mystery Tour* movie in 1967, and the Lennon/Harrison drug busts for the 'boys' to return to normality.

Lennon effectively capsized The Beatles' myth in 1970, with his searing attack on his former colleagues in the *Lennon Remembers* interview with *Rolling Stone's* Jann Wenner. In its place he erected 'The Ballad Of John and Yoko' – eventually idealized as one of the century's great love stories, to be celebrated in films, a Broadway musical, and a host of 1980 interviews. The Lennons, by this account, were examples to us all: they were human, and they had fought their battles along the way, but love and destiny had eventually conquered all. They had a baby, and then Lennon retired from his work to concentrate on house-husbandry, not touching the guitar pinned

3

symbolically over his bed for nigh on five years, and re-emerging only to produce that *Double Fantasy* of hope for the over-40s in 1980. Lennon's almost immediate death gave the whole tale a tragic air of romance, which even the bitterest tales of drug addiction and antagonism that emerged later did little to tarnish.

Except: the myth of John and Yoko, polished to finesse in interviews given around the time that *Double Fantasy* was released, and supposedly the latest instalment of the Lennons' totally honest and public uncovering of their trials and tribulations, wasn't strictly honest after all. Lennon certainly didn't abandon music for five years in 1975; the songs on *Double Fantasy* weren't the overnight product of an idyllic holiday in Bermuda in 1980; and, if certain biographers are to be believed, the Lennons didn't spend their final years together ingesting nothing more toxic than French cigarettes.

Like the media freaks they were, John and Yoko were simply selling a story in 1980 – or using a story to sell an album. But the discovery that they had lied about something as trivial as the date that Lennon composed his *Double Fantasy* songs does suggest that their interviews should be treated as creative works of art more than expressions of absolute honesty.

Honesty was a Lennon watchword; it was the concept that he used to judge his own work and career. So The Beatles were honest in Hamburg, swearing on stage and pissing on nuns out of windows; dishonest when they wore suits, bowed and scraped before royalty and the establishment, and acted like trained poodles in their early movies. Lennon reasserted his honesty when he and Yoko became involved in 1968, began writing about personal feelings rather than romantic clichés, and then clinched the victory of truth over falsehood when he split The Beatles and asserted that he only believed in "Yoko and me, and that's reality". From then on, he equated honesty with Yoko, dishonesty with separation. More to the point, the Lennons' relationship seems to have become alarmingly out of focus: regardless of what he produced without her, their separation induced a state of panic. His celebrated 'lost weekend' of 18 months between late 1973 and early 1975 actually saw him record more music than the 18 months before and after combined; but in the Lennons' myth it was a barren period of depression and loneliness. Forget the fact that his reunion with Yoko coincided with his creativity being stymied: Lennon felt safe, and – if the evidence of much of his songwriting in the last 10 years of his life is to be believed – perpetually guilty, and in her debt.

So I make no apology (he said, apologising) for the fact that much of this book is concerned with 'Johnandyoko' rather than John. Lennon always needed cohorts and partners. At school there was fellow loudmouth Pete

Shotton; at art college the precociously talented and doomed Stuart Sutcliffe. In The Beatles, Lennon found a soulmate in Paul McCartney. And then, after 1968, there was Yoko.

What makes this relationship the most important of his life is not just its length: Lennon spent almost as long with McCartney. But McCartney didn't alter the way in which Lennon saw the world. For John, Yoko represented freedom from the past: her art didn't belong to the popular traditions in which John had always worked, but struck out for margins of culture that he had scarcely imagined in his dreams. And, for the first time, Lennon found a partner who was stronger than him: not as mercurial or brilliant, but with a unified vision of the world that didn't allow for criticism or restraint. Plus, she was a woman, and John found her irresistible.

So when John became Johnandyoko, it was on Yoko's terms. It was her concepts, not his, that fuelled their bed-ins for peace, their films, their avant-garde recordings. But the collision between cultures and souls also allowed Lennon the freedom to dig deep into his own psyche, and reveal the scars left by his troubled childhood and fishbowl existence as a Beatle. What resulted, in records like *John Lennon/Plastic Ono Band*, 'Cold Turkey', and 'Instant Karma!', was the finest work of his career. Without Yoko, it would never have been possible.

That brings us back to honesty, and deceit. What Yoko unleashed in Lennon was a ferocious spirit of self-examination, which would allow no pretence or fantasy. (In that light, the title of their 1980 comeback album takes on a new significance.) Having flung himself at the world naked, Lennon had to rebuild himself on new foundations, which is why little of his later work carried quite the same passion or conviction.

So it's possible to see Lennon's entire artistic career as a process of concealment and uncovering, a continual battle between honesty and self-deceit. That struggle powered his songwriting from 1963, when he realised that he could write songs about himself, through to his final confessional works of 1980. Maybe the Primal Therapy he underwent in the summer of 1970, which inspired the *John Lennon/Plastic Ono Band* album, actually did more than help John deal with his neurosis, and finally destroy his faith in father-figures. Maybe it also dampened down the creative fire that had propelled him from 'Please Please Me' to 'Cold Turkey' in six short years.

That's something to ponder while you read, or dip into, this text; in a way, it's the hidden theme. But it's not the reason you're here. Function number one of the book is to drag all of Lennon's work together, and try to pin down the creative urges that produced it. Function number two is more prosaic, perhaps, but none the less necessary: simply to catalogue the work, to place it chronologically in the context of Lennon's life and career, and to trace its evolution, through all the blind alleys into which he was led along the way.

Here you'll find full details of all his studio recordings; all the home recordings which are known to have survived; all his prose writings, from *The Daily Howl* in the mid-Fifties to *Skywriting By Word Of Mouth* and the enigmatic programme notes for his unfinished musical, *The Ballad Of John And Yoko*; his film work, from *A Hard Day's Night* to the controversial promo clips he was preparing for the *Double Fantasy* album; and his visual art, from boyhood paintings through the infamous *Bag One* lithographs to his final self-caricatures.

It's a long and winding trip, and the danger is that the major works – 'Strawberry Fields Forever', *John Lennon/Plastic Ono Band*, *Imagine* – will be overshadowed by the discovery of a rehearsal tape or a psychedelic doodle. The case for the defence is that Lennon scarcely did anything half-heart-edly: the same spirit invested his work on *Sgt. Pepper* and his avant-garde experiments with Yoko. In this theory, his drunken original take of 'Just Because' from the 1973 *Rock 'n' Roll* sessions tells us as much about the man as his finest creations – though *they* are the reason why we are here in the first place.

Although Lennon worked by himself, on songs, stories and drawings, from the mid-Fifties until his death, he also spent nearly a decade with a rock band called The Beatles. Their career has been examined elsewhere in enormous detail; we know exactly what time of day they recorded 'Twist And Shout', where they were on the evening of July 2, 1963, what colour jackets they wore for which live show in Tokyo in 1966. My initial impulse was not to write about The Beatles at all, but simply to concentrate on Lennon's solo career – beginning, perhaps, with his first collaborations with Yoko in 1968.

Then I realised how ridiculous it would be to write a book about the creativity of an ex-Beatle, without mentioning anything he did while he was in the group. I'm assuming, however, that anyone keen enough on Lennon to read this book is also a fan of The Beatles; and that they will at least know about, and in all probability have bought, some of the major ref-erence works on their career. Simply to repeat, verbatim, the information contained in Mark Lewisohn's books, *The Complete Beatles Chronicle*, *The Complete Beatles Recording Sessions* and *The Beatles Live!*, for example, would be an insult to you (and to Mark Lewisohn). So you'll have to look else-where for the complete Beatles studio log, and the complete Beatles gig list. Here I've chosen to concentrate on significant stages in The Beatles' career, and on Lennon's contributions rather than those of the rest of the group. There's one other reason for ignoring The Beatles' endless live work, and yet chronicling Lennon's solo appearances in great detail. The Beatles' concerts were simply part of the showbiz treadmill, the daily grind of a professional performer. Once Lennon had stepped off the merry-go-round, he never approached the stage without being conscious of himself as an artist, not a puppet.

As a recording band, of course, The Beatles survived for around seven years. Lennon was self-consciously creating art for around 25 years. Here is the complete story of that strange and hazardous journey: destination still unknown.

Peter Doggett
London and Hampshire, May 2005

CHAPTER 1

The Fifties to December 1961

Children create stories as a landscape for their play, and they love to express themselves visually on paper. The process of formal education gradually bends these natural instincts towards the need to pass examinations, with the result that no one creates 'art' after that without being conscious of what they are doing. So the birth of an artistic career has to be dated from the day when a child becomes aware of himself as an artist. John Lennon wrote stories and poems, and painted pictures, both at home and at school. But it was only in adolescence that he began to differentiate between what came instinctively, and what was the product of his unique vision.

c. 1954 to 1956: WRITING & DRAWING *The Daily Howl/ Treasury*

The earliest examples of Lennon's 'art' to have been exhibited in public are the schoolroom paintings that he reprinted on the sleeve and booklet of the *Walls And Bridges* album. Competent though they were, they told us nothing about John Lennon the individual. To find any evidence of *him*, we have to look at the handwritten pages of *The Daily Howl*, a vehicle for imagination and in-jokes that Lennon circulated among his friends and classmates.

The Daily Howl was not John's first pretence at being a journalist. Like many other budding authors, he had conceived grandiose plans for his own magazine, called *Sport, Speed and Illustrated*, while he was still at primary school in the late Forties. But *The Daily Howl*, with its mix of word-play, scurrilous invention and lightning pencil drawings, was the clearest ancestor of *In His Own Write* and *A Spaniard In The Works*. Written and crayoned as a mock daily newspaper, its contents were passed from hand to hand around Quarry Bank School in a book the size of a comic annual, when Lennon was in his early teens. Each single page bore a price ("1 onion", perhaps, or "1 wart") above its mix of cartoons and jokes.

Only fragments from Lennon's teenage scribblings have ever been published, though it's possible that some of the pieces in *In His Own Write* may date back to the mid-Fifties. They certainly shared a similar tone with the surviving pages of *The Daily Howl*, which was full of social satire, surreal nonsense, colourful caricatures, and the kind of Pythonesque humour that has been common currency in British grammar schools since the Second World War. There were contemporary showbiz references that are baffling to later audiences: "Hernando's Hideaway is a shed in our garden", ran a one-liner, referring to a mid-Fifties pop hit. Elsewhere, Lennon noted that "David Nixon is getting a Tony Curtis" (Nixon being a bald TV magician, rather than a relative of future US President and Lennon-persecutor Richard Nixon). A so-called 'Scotch Edition' of the suitably renamed *Daily Hool* would have failed all PC tests in the 21st century, but captured his verbal playfulness perfectly: "Some scotchmen live in caves, and are still canonoballs (wot eat men). They walk on their hands to save their shoos (not that their mean). They eat porrage, and something food also, to, as well. Some scotchmen have tarton hair instead of a kilt, silly niggers."

The very fact that Lennon chose to indulge himself in *The Daily Howl* – and in the poems and drawings captured in the *Treasury* illustrated obliquely in The Beatles' *Anthology* book (page 6) – was proof of a lively, restless imagination. His English language teacher in summer 1956, when Lennon was fifteen, noted that John was "an intelligent boy who could do very well", while a few months earlier he had come second in the class for his imaginative writing. The decision to prolong this teenage indulgence into his twenties was either a sign of profound immaturity, or else a recognition that within him burned a view of the world which didn't conform to the models that society had on offer. Eventually, music allowed him the option of twisting the world into his way of thinking.

Little of Lennon's literary imagination surfaced in his music until The Beatles had already become established as the most successful pop band in Britain. Playing music was a form of self-expression, and an even more basic need – a method of peer group identification as much as it was a burning desire to perform, and to be seen performing.

MID-1950s: DRAWING sketches

Several Lennon cartoon sketches have been reproduced in print, taken from a book believed to date from around 1955. They mostly featured caricatures of schoolboys (clad in the uniform of Lennon's school, Quarry Bank in Liverpool), all of them grotesquely exaggerated and distorted. These twisted, bloated, gargoyle creations became one of Lennon's visual trademarks, but at this early stage he was using this method to depict classmates or their parents. 'A Primitive Mrs Vaughn', for example, represents the mother of his close friend Ivan as a huge caveman, clutching a sperm-sized (and shaped) boy in his/her fist. It would be easy to read malice into these drawings, but they were undoubtedly intended to be humorous rather than cruel.

In the same sketchbook, Lennon drew 'Moi Dad (A Happy Man)'- a somewhat idealistic portrait of a father figure who looked nothing like his own estranged father, Freddie Lennon.

JULY 6, 1957: THE QUARRY MEN performing 'Putting On The Style'/'Baby Let's Play House'

The cultural influences on Liverpool teenagers in the mid-Fifties have been the stuff of legend since the Merseybeat boom a decade later. Liverpool was a seaport, a regular landing place for transatlantic crossings from New York. So the myth goes, sailors would return to Liverpool with new records they'd heard in the States, exposing a type of music that would otherwise have remained not only unheard, but almost unimaginable in mid-fifties Britain. Yet, as Merseybeat historian Spencer Leigh has demonstrated, 99% of the songs that were performed by the teenage Beatles and their Liverpool counterparts were actually available on British releases; the myth of the 'Cunard Yanks', sailing in with their treasure trove of rare rockabilly singles, has been greatly exaggerated.

Not that this alien music was on open display in 1955 Britain. The country was dominated by light popular music, much of it a watered-down replica of American idols such as Frank Sinatra, Johnnie Ray and Frankie Laine. Their British equivalents – Dickie Valentine and his ilk – had the sound but not the rhythm, or the sex appeal. The BBC Light Programme was the sole source of recorded music on the airwaves. It housed gentle dance-bands, crooners, novelty tunes and music hall routines, occasionally infiltrated by an invader from another planet, when a visiting American serviceman would request a tune by Hank Williams or Fats Domino on *Forces Favourites*.

Liverpool took the invasion in its stride; almost nowhere else in Britain was it possible to hear hillbilly music or rhythm and blues on pub jukeboxes, themselves a fresh innovation alongside the 45rpm single in 1955. "There is the biggest country and western following in England in Liverpool, besides London," Lennon remembered in 1970. "I heard country and western music in Liverpool before I heard rock and roll. There were established folk, blues and country and western clubs in Liverpool before rock and roll."

Folk-songs of the working man, the miner, the labourer; blues – the cry of the black man on a plantation, or stuck in an urban ghetto; country – the white man's blues: these were influences which Lennon and his contemporaries took on board. They provided a stern antidote to the optimistic, naive popular music that was otherwise the British staple diet. But as yet there were few musicologists to draw distinctions, and Lennon accepted both ends of the spectrum as music, nothing more or less. As a result, elements of both American blues, and Disney tunes and show songs, shaped The Beatles' music to the end.

For Lennon, as for teenagers across the world, Bill Haley's 'Rock Around The Clock' marked a turning point. Besides anything else, it introduced the world to the backbeat. No matter that Haley himself was a hillbilly at heart, performing music with a Negro flavour under duress; the song hinted at a more primitive excitement than anything Lennon had heard before.

But it was 1956 that brought the full-scale teenage revolution music to Britain. Elvis Presley's 'Heartbreak Hotel' – an echo-laden, almost incoherent mumble of despair – appalled traditional music lovers, but Lennon's generation recognised that Presley was speaking their language. Nearer to home, Scottish-born jazz musician Lonnie Donegan was putting a backbeat behind the classic folk tunes of Leadbelly and Woody Guthrie, and invented skiffle. At its strongest, on 'Rock Island Line' and 'Cumberland Gap', skiffle came close to pure rock 'n' roll; and as far as Lennon was concerned, it had the advantage that anyone could play it. Across the country, teenagers founded skiffle bands, learning three or four simple guitar chords and dragooning non-musicians to play the washboard or beat a dustbin for accompaniment. It was rough, raw and ready, and it appalled the hell out of their elders and betters. For Lennon, whose scholastic career seemed to be leading nowhere, skiffle equalled salvation. And so were born The Quarry Men – named after the Quarry Bank school in Liverpool that Lennon and his friends attended.

When Lennon founded his skiffle group in March 1957, he briefly named them The Black Jacks; but The Quarry Men was the name under which they played their first known public engagement, at a 'Starmaker' audition in Liverpool on June 9, 1957. A month later, on July 6, to be exact, The Quarry

Men appeared at a church fete in Woolton. Besides Lennon, who sang lead vocals and played guitar, the line-up included Colin Hanton, Len Garry, Eric Griffiths, Pete Shotton and Rod Davis. According to a review in a local newspaper, The Quarry Men allegedly performed Lonnie Donegan's skiffle anthems, 'Cumberland Gap' and 'Railroad Bill', plus a rocked-up adaptation of a Liverpool folk song, 'Maggie May'. Legend insists that Lennon also bull-dozed his way through Gene Vincent's 1956 rock hit 'Be-Bop-A-Lula' and The Dell-Vikings' 'Come Go With Me', improvising new lyrics to replace those he'd either forgotten or never been able to decipher.

Some of this speculation dissolved into disbelief when it was revealed in 1994 that a partial recording of The Quarry Men's evening performance had survived. Teenager Bob Molyneaux took his Grundig tape machine to St. Peter's Church Hall, and recorded extracts of the evening's entertain-ment. Just two songs by The Quarry Men were preserved on the tape: Lonnie Donegan's then-current skiffle hit, 'Putting On The Style', and the Elvis Presley rockabilly classic, 'Baby Let's Play House' (originally recorded in 1955 but not released in the UK until early 1957). The four-minute tape was auctioned by Sotheby's in London, and bought by EMI, who have kept it under wraps ever since. But a 30-second snippet of the Donegan tune was aired by Sotheby's before the auction. The sound quality of the recording proved to be so poor that it took most of the 30 seconds for the ear to dis-tinguish, first, that this was actually music, and second that the vocalist was indeed John Lennon. But repeated listening to this fragment revealed just how confident a vocalist the 16-year-old Lennon was. "He stood in the centre of the stage," Molyneaux remembered, "not a lot of movement, but during the instrumental break, I remember him dancing about and singing in a screechy-type voice." Small wonder that the 'Singing' section of his most recent school reports had been left blank, one might think.

Lennon certainly impressed 15-year-old audience-member Paul McCartney, who was introduced to him by their mutual friend Ivan Vaughn. The precocious McCartney immediately offered to join The Quarry Men. After a brief run through, 'Be-Bop-A-Lula' and 'Twenty Flight Rock' had convinced Lennon that the kid could not only sing, but also knew the proper words to both songs, McCartney was in.

c. 1958: CREATING untitled collage

In 2000, painter Peter Blake curated a fascinating exhibition, entitled *About Collage*, at the Tate Gallery in Liverpool. Among the artefacts he assembled was a paper collage credited to Lennon, which was on loan from an unidentified private collection. The artwork was a dense, deep-red mix of photos of women (mostly fashion or glamour models, but also several nuns), and painted grotesques. Some of the juxtapositions of images were provocative to the point of pornography, and throughout the piece there was a clear link between sexuality and blood. Meanwhile, a male onlooker with blank eyes and Lennon's long, thin nose lurked amidst the chaos. Freudian analysts would have found plenty to discuss.

The exhibition catalogue dated the collage as 'c. 1958'; but the pictures of fashion models, obviously snipped out of magazines, more probably dated from the early Sixties, throwing this attribution into doubt.

1958 to 1962: LENNON/McCARTNEY ORIGINALS

By the time that The Beatles issued 'Love Me Do' in 1962, their press agent Tony Barrow was able to boast that Lennon and McCartney had composed more than 100 original songs. McCartney would "sag off" school in the afternoons, while Lennon missed another art college class, and the pair would sit hunched over their acoustic guitars in the McCartneys' sitting-room reworking their favourite rock songs.

Of the legendary 100 songs, few were ever recorded. During the *Get Back* sessions in January 1969, Lennon and McCartney busked their way through otherwise unheard originals like 'Too Bad About Sorrows', 'I Lost My Little Girl' (revived by McCartney some 20 years later), 'Just Fun', 'Thinking Of Linking', 'Keep Looking That Way', 'If Tomorrow Ever Comes', 'Wake Up In The Morning' and 'Won't You Please Say Goodbye'. These 1969 renditions were humorous and nostalgic, and their composers made little effort to do their early compositions justice. Internal evidence suggests, however, that almost all of these songs were primarily McCartney compositions. It was Paul who immediately mastered song structure, and then married it to lyrics borrowed freely from the Tin Pan Alley clichés of the day. Lennon's forte at this point was lyrical improvisation, adding endless improvised verses to 'Ain't That A Shame' or 'Rock Island Line'. It is significant, meanwhile, that when The Quarry Men made their first recording, it was McCartney who contributed the only original song.

SUMMER 1958: THE QUARRY MEN recording 'That'll Be The Day'/'In Spite Of All The Danger'

In a home studio run by Percy Phillips in Liverpool, Quarry Men Lennon, McCartney, George Harrison, drummer Colin Hanton and pianist John

'Duff' Lowe recorded two songs on a portable tape recorder. The group paid a little under £1 for the privilege, and received in return a single ten-inch acetate disc. The five youngsters took turns to keep the record at home, and Lowe ended up as the effective owner – until he attempted to sell it at auction in the early Eighties, whereupon Paul McCartney stepped in with a legal threat and a cash offer. Neither Hanton nor Lowe remained with The Quarry Men for more than a few months after this session.

'In Spite Of All The Danger' was a McCartney composition, with Harrison given co-credit for his guitar solo. Lennon also took lead vocals on the cover of Buddy Holly's hit with The Crickets, 'That'll Be The Day'. What was apparent from the edited versions of these songs included on The Beatles *Anthology 1* album is that the teenage Quarry Men may have been naive, but they already possessed an air of confidence that overcame any musical shortcomings. Lennon's lead vocal on 'That'll Be The Day' was particularly striking, aping Holly's vocal mannerisms without quite managing to conceal his Liverpool rasp. 'In Spite Of All The Danger' was less impressive in musical terms, not least because McCartney's melody was little more than a copy of the early Elvis Presley recording, 'Trying To Get To You'. But it's telling that the lead vocal was once again handled by Lennon, with McCartney reduced to chipping in some rather strained harmonies. Clearly, there was only one leader of The Quarry Men in 1958.

1958/1959: COMPOSING 'Hello Little Girl'/'The One After 909'/'Winston's Walk'; possibly also 'I Call Your Name'/'What Goes On'/'Long Black Train'

Of the Lennon/McCartney songs written during the Fifties, these are the only survivors in which it is possible to see Lennon's hand at work. Lennon himself described 'Hello Little Girl' as "my first song," tracing its evolution back to the standard tune 'Delightful, Delicious, De-Lovely'. The more obvious influence is Buddy Holly, however. In fact, as it was originally written, it had a middle eight that borrowed clearly from Holly's 1958 hit, 'Maybe Baby'. Lennon was still performing the song as late as 1962, albeit in rewritten form; then he gave it to Liverpool band The Fourmost as their début single.

'The One After 909' is the best-known Lennon/McCartney song from this period, simply because it was revived for the *Let It Be* movie and soundtrack album. The 1969 Beatles were, for once, faithful to the spirit of the original, which was a simple 12-bar rocker with a stop-start chorus and a wonderfully naive rhyming scheme (station/location is a highlight), and a

14

line in American railroad clichés which must have entranced these English teenagers.

'Winston's Walk' was an instrumental, one of many in The Quarry Men's repertoire in the late Fifties. Unlike McCartney's 'Catswalk', however, it was never recorded, and all that remains today is the title. Likewise, 'Long Black Train', which was supposedly a Lennon original from 1959. Conway Twitty performed a song of the same name, however, and the phrase also cropped up in the lyrics of the Junior Parker song 'Mystery Train' which Elvis Presley recorded at his final session for Sun Records in 1955. It's likely Lennon rewrote one of these to fill out time at a Quarry Men gig. Of 'I Call Your Name', Lennon recalled: "That was my song, when there was no Beatles and no group – I just had it around. It was my effort as a kind of blues, originally, and then I wrote the middle eight when it came out years later. The first part had been written before Hamburg, even." i.e. before August 1960. 'What Goes On' was another attempt at a rockabilly song, which remained in the back of Lenon's mind until Ringo needed something to sing on *Rubber Soul* at the end of 1965.

c. APRIL 1960: THE QUARRY MEN rehearsing 'Hallelujah I Love Her So'/'I'll Follow The Sun'/'Hello Little Girl'/'You'll Be Mine'/'The One After 909' (two versions)/ 'Wildcat'/'Movin' 'n' Groovin' '/'I Will Always Be In Love With You'/'Matchbox'/'That's When Your Heartaches Begin'/'Cayenne'/'The World Is Waiting For The Sunrise'/'Some Days'/'Hey Darling'/'You Must Write Every Day'/'I Don't Know' plus various unidentified original songs and instrumental jams

With the benefit of hindsight, The Beatles' path from their first trip to Hamburg in August 1960 to the release of 'Love Me Do' a little over two years later seems direct and inevitable. Yet the two years between that debut visit to Germany and The Quarry Men's 1958 recording session in Liverpool had been anything but smooth and certain. At any of a dozen moments, the fragile partnership between Lennon, McCartney and Harrison could have been fractured – not by internal arguments of the kind that eventually broke up the band a decade later, but by the apparent lack of momentum that dogged their early career.

In Lennon's life, few events were ever as traumatic as the sudden death of his mother, Julia, on July 15, 1958. After a long period of irregular contact, mother and son had become closer than ever over the preceding months. "It was the worst thing that ever happened to me," Lennon remarked later. "I thought, 'that's really fucked everything. I've no responsibilities to anyone now.'" The tragedy tightened the bond between himself and Paul McCartney, whose own mother had died of breast cancer the previous year.

Meanwhile, The Quarry Men's progress was supposed to take second place to Lennon's activities at art college and McCartney's A-Level studies at Liverpool Institute. Their gigging schedule was so light during 1959 that George Harrison spent most of the year performing with a rival band. The three future Beatles did play the opening night of a new subterranean Liverpool venue, The Casbah Club, in August 1959, with Ken Brown augmenting them on bass. But Brown quit before the trio submitted themselves to another 'Starmaker' audition run by TV host Carroll Levis. They were briefly known as Johnny and The Moondogs at this point, but they'd become The Quarry Men again by January 1960, when Lennon invited his art school buddy Stuart Sutcliffe to fill the vacant bassist role.

Sutcliffe had cash on his side, and was able to purchase a new electric bass, but he couldn't actually play the instrument. A superbly talented painter, his musical talent was dubious, but Lennon insisted that he should remain in the group against the mild protests of McCartney and Harrison. And it was this line-up of The Quarry Men whose primitive musical experiments were captured on tape about three months later.

The first confirmation that pre-Hamburg recordings of The Beatles had survived came with the publication of Philip Norman's 1981 biography, *Shout! The True Story Of The Beatles*. He described having heard an hour or so of roughly recorded bedroom jam sessions, through which it was apparently possible to catch the first stirrings of The Beatles' magic.

Six years later, what appeared to be the same batch of recordings finally emerged on bootleg albums. Advance reports of the sound quality were well founded; and the musical stature of these rehearsals, recorded by Lennon, McCartney, Harrison and new bassist Stu Sutcliffe, possibly with Paul's brother Mike on percussion, were little more than impressive, making these by far the most amateurish recordings ever to have been issued on bootleg. But their historical importance was undeniable – our first extended glimpse of The Beatles at play.

Exact dating of the recordings – assuming they all come from the same month – is impossible. But the presence of three cover versions (Eddie Cochran's 'Hallelujah I Love Her So', Duane Eddy's 'Movin' 'n' Groovin' ' and Gene Vincent's 'Wildcat') that had all been issued in Britain in the early weeks of 1960 suggests that April that year is the most likely source. The Quarry Men had all witnessed Cochran (and another Lennon hero, Gene

Vincent) performing at the Liverpool Empire in mid–March 1960, just a month before Cochran was killed in a car crash.

The location of the session(s) is equally mysterious, although the liner notes to The Beatles' *Anthology 1* set, which included three brief extracts from these tapes, pinpoints McCartney's home as the site. (McCartney certainly had a tape deck at his disposal, as he and Lennon apparently used to make obscene recordings together in their teens, and then play them down the phone as prank calls.) Other sources suggest that the tracks were taped at the home of a mutual friend. Both suggestions may be correct, as the surviving recordings appear to come from at least two different sources, with virtually no duplication of material between the two tapes.

Disappointingly, the recordings tell us much more about Messrs Sutcliffe, McCartney and Harrison than they do about Lennon. This was supposed to be Lennon's band, as the 1958 sessions with Percy Phillips confirmed. But it was McCartney who took the lead vocals on everything apart from 'The One After 909', 'Hello Little Girl', Presley's B-side 'That's When Your Heartaches Begin' and 'You'll Be Mine', an original pastiche of the doo-wop ballad tradition, sung in wildly exaggerated style. Only on the last of these did any flash of the latter-day Lennon emerge, with a fleeting monologue reference to a "National Health eyeball." Four years later, it was National Health cows that inspired one of the contributions to Lennon's first book.

Instrumentally, it was impossible to identify Lennon's contribution to these tapes. Harrison took most of the dubious honours here, on almost endless blues instrumentals designed to show off his less-than-sparkling lead work. Certainly McCartney's Latin-flavoured 'Cayenne', debuted on *Anthology 1*, put Harrison's early efforts to shame. And with the exception of 'Hello Little Girl' and McCartney's surprisingly ambitious 'I'll Follow The Sun', all of the songs which sounded like original compositions followed standard R&B or doo-wop chord structures.

Over the next few months, both the group's music and its name were about to change dramatically. Stuart Sutcliffe had already suggested that they adopt the name of The Beatals, as a nod to Buddy Holly's backing band, The Crickets. Within a couple of months, The Beatals became The Silver Beetles, or sometimes The Silver Beats.

MAY 21, 1960: COMPOSING 'I've Just Fallen For Someone'

In April 1960, Lennon and McCartney were reducing to playing duo gigs as The Nerk Twins. But a month later, The Silver Beetles received what must have seemed like their biggest break to date: the chance to support recording artist Johnny Gentle on a nine-day Scottish tour. OK, it wasn't Cliff Richard or Billy Fury, though Gentle was (like Fury) managed by Larry Parnes, Britain's top pop entrepreneur of the time, who might perhaps be impressed enough to take The Beetles under his wing.

Still lacking a permanent drummer, Lennon, McCartney, Harrison and Sutcliffe persuaded Tommy Moore, the best part of a decade older than them, to accompany them on the trip. None of their fantasies were fulfilled: the pay and conditions were lousy, and they frequently fell out with Moore along the way.

Decades later, though, Gentle – who never quite became a pop star, despite Parnes' support – was still waxing lyrical about his times with The Beatles-to-be. In an interview with Radio Merseyside presenter Spencer Leigh, he revealed that he had once written a song with John Lennon. The number in question was called 'I've Just Fallen For Someone', and Gentle had released it in 1961 under the pseudonym of Darren Young. Back then, he hadn't given Lennon a writing credit, but now he revealed that John had helped him compose the song's hackneyed middle eight. And he could well have been right, though there's no aural evidence either way.

1961: COMPOSING 'Cry For A Shadow'

Recognisable new McCartney compositions surfaced throughout the early years of The Quarry Men and then The Beatles. Lennon's were far less obvious until the eve of their commercial success. From 1961, for example, the only Lennon song known to have been introduced into The Beatles' repertoire was this instrumental. It was inspired, as its title suggests, by Cliff Richard's backing group, The Shadows, who were the forerunners of a stream of tidy non-vocal groups in Britain during the early Sixties, stemmed only by The Beatles themselves.

'Cry For A Shadow' was actually a co-composition with George Harrison, the pair's only documented collaboration. It's a safe assumption that Harrison 'wrote' the melody on his guitar, while Lennon supplied the chord changes and the churning rhythm guitar accompaniment.

22-24 JUNE 1961: THE BEATLES recording 'Ain't She Sweet'/'Cry For A Shadow'; backing Tony Sheridan on 'Why'/'My Bonnie' (two versions)/'The Saints'/'Nobody's Child'/'If You Love Me Baby (Take Out Some Insurance On Me Baby)'

August 1960 found the newly renamed Beatles (Lennon's suggestion) performing in a seedy club in Hamburg's red-light district – part of an influx of Liverpool skiffle and beat bands who took the German seaport by storm during the early Sixties. For the trip, they had finally recruited their first ever full-time drummer: Pete Best, who was conveniently the son of Casbah Club owner Mona Best. Their musical education involved four months split between the Indra Club and the Kaiserkeller. That September, Lennon, McCartney, Harrison, Sutcliffe and Ringo Starr, the drummer from another Liverpool band, Rory Storm's Hurricanes, backed another member of The Hurricanes, Lu 'Wally' Walters, on an impromptu version of 'Summertime'. One copy of the acetate disc cut at the Akustic Studios in Hamburg on October 15, 1960 apparently survives, but it has never been heard publicly.

When The Beatles returned to Liverpool in December 1960, they had been hardened by booze, pep pills and a gruelling work schedule into a fully-fledged rock 'n' roll band. Stuart Sutcliffe elected to remain in Hamburg at the end of that trip, Paul McCartney shifted from guitar to bass, and The Beatles slimmed down to a quartet. They went back to Hamburg at the end of March 1961, to perform nightly at the Top Ten Club – besides occasionally backing up Norwich-born rocker Tony Sheridan, one of the unsung legends of the pre-Beatles rock scene in Britain. Sheridan moved and sang like Elvis, but never scored a hit in his homeland – not least because he was always working overseas. He had a record contract with Polydor in Germany, however, and when he was called in for a session in the early summer of 1961, The Beatles were recruited by producer and band-leader Bert Kaempfert as his backing band. Inevitably, Lennon was listed as the group's leader on the contract they signed with Kaempfert's production company.

The Beatles backed Sheridan on two rocked-up standards, 'My Bonnie' and 'The Saints', which were coupled on a single that was a Top 10 hit in Hamburg. Neither betrayed any Beatles trademarks beyond the unwarranted enthusiasm of the backing vocals. Likewise Sheridan's own rockaballad, 'Why', and the blues tune 'If You Love Me Baby', while 'Nobody's Child' might just as easily have featured The Shadows behind Sheridan's mournful lead vocal.

Listen to 'Ain't She Sweet', however, and you'll hear the unmistakable tones of the 20-year-old John Lennon as lead vocalist. Maybe he sounded a little short on vocal range, and overplayed his hand in his excitement at being recorded, but this was recognisably the same rasping voice that would be heard on *bona fide* Beatles records a year later. He'd borrowed the song from the repertoire of rocker Gene Vincent, but The Beatles' arrangement was markedly different to his 1956 recording. Also cut during the same sessions was 'Cry For A Shadow' – itself stunning proof of the distance The

Beatles had covered since their Liverpool rehearsals a little over a year earlier.

JULY 6, 1961: *MERSEY BEAT* publishes 'Being A Short Diversion On The Dubious Origins Of Beatles'

John's first appearance in print came in the début issue of a new fortnightly paper, edited by his college friend Bill Harry – who had met Lennon through their mutual confidant, Stuart Sutcliffe. Looking to capitalise on the burgeoning beat club scene in Liverpool, Harry planned a regular magazine that would feature articles about – and by – the local stars, plus photos, details of forthcoming concerts, and record reviews (contributed by local store owner and future Beatles manager, Brian Epstein).

For the first issue, Harry approached the acknowledged leader of the city's foremost beat band – The Beatles – for an account of the group's history to date. He expected to receive a straightforward account of names and places, but instead Lennon sheepishly turned in a goonish, pun-laden treatise that was the first outside evidence that the Liverpool rocker was also a notable wit. Like any comic writing, it loses all its humour in translation; best read the piece for yourselves, as it was republished in Bill Harry's anthology *Mersey Beat* in 1978. Cast as a mock fairy-tale, it unleashed Lennon's childlike delight in wordplay, and revealed a sense of fun that owed more to the spoken word than to what was normally accepted as written humour.

Besides references to major events in The Beatles' career – the trip round Scottish ballrooms backing Johnny Gentle, the clashes with German police which halted their first Hamburg residency – the piece also introduced a line in self-mythology which the group repeated for several years to come. "Many people ask what are Beatles? Why Beatles? Ugh, Beatles, how did the name arrive? So we will tell you. It came in a vision – a man appeared on a flaming pie and said unto them, 'From this day on you are Beatles with an A'. Thank you Mister Man, they said, thanking him." The article garnered attention beyond the local rock'n'roll scene. When the *Liverpool Echo* newspaper reported on The Beatles' first recording session, they singled out Lennon for special mention, noting that he "writes articles in beat language".

Mersey Beat's first issue was published just three days after The Beatles returned from their second trip to Hamburg. It had presumably been several months in the planning, as Lennon's contribution was handed over to Bill Harry before the group left for Germany in late March.

AUGUST 17, 1961: *MERSEY BEAT* publishes 'I Remember Arnold'

Lennon quickly realised that *Mersey Beat* might prove to be an outlet – maybe the only possible outlet – for the bizarre poems and stories which he was still occasionally committing to scraps of paper from old school exercise books. Luckily, Bill Harry was intrigued by what Lennon had already shown him, and continued to publish Lennon compositions at irregular intervals over the next three years. Lennon appears to have given Harry a selection of pieces for safe keeping; but almost all of these – the stuff that John considered to be the best of his writing since the days of *The Daily Howl* in the mid-Fifties – were lost when the magazine moved to a new office sometime during 1962.

By then, Harry had already published this Lennon poem, later to appear as the final piece in Lennon's *In His Own Write*. This time it was the epitaph that was the literary form in the firing line of Lennon's zany humour, with a subject who not only changed name but also sex, and then met a sticky end under a train. As with much of Lennon's early written work, his pre-cursors are easy to spot. There were hints of the wordplay of Lewis Carroll, the inventiveness of Edward Lear, the anarchy of Spike Milligan. But what was essentially Lennon was the cruelty, the matter-of-fact attitude to death and destruction, and the quick descent from bathos into gibberish which carried the poem to a kind of conclusion. And like the well brought-up Beatle he was, Lennon remembered his manners: the final lines read:

"Bumbleydy Hubledy Humbley
"Bumdley Tum (Thank you)".

In that same issue of *Mersey Beat*, Lennon contributed the first of a series of parody classified ads. In a weird form of vanity publishing, he paid fourpence a word to see his jokes in print. The one-liners, sprinkled through a column of 'Musicians Wanted' ads and fan club announcements, told their own story:

"HOT LIPS, missed you Friday, RED NOSE."
"RED NOSE, missed you Friday, HOT LIPS."
"ACCRINGTON welcomes HOT LIPS AND RED NOSE."
"Whistling Jock Lennon wishes to contact HOT NOSE."
"RED SCUNTHORPE wishes to jock HOT ACCRINGTON."

SEPTEMBER 14, 1961: *MERSEY BEAT* publishes 'Around And About'

Like his dissertation on The Beatles' history, this comic travelogue through Liverpool's beat clubs and other notable landmarks was written to order. It inaugurated what editor Bill Harry no doubt intended as a regular column, for which he gave Lennon the honorary title of 'Beatcomber' (after essayist J.B. Morton's *alter ego*, Beachcomber).

Despite references to the 'Casbin' and 'Jackarandy' clubs, Lennon's account was strictly a vehicle for another round of anarchic puns and non-sequiturs. Both the club-by-club guide and one particularly enigmatic sequence of sentences thereafter was omitted when the piece was reprinted in *In His Own Write* under the title 'Liddypool'.

The offending paragraph satirised the agony columns found in the popular press: "We've been engaged for 43 years and he still smokes. I am an unmurdered mother of 19 years, am I pensionable? My dog bites me when I bite it."

DECEMBER 14, 1961: *MERSEY BEAT* publishes more of Lennon's Classified Ads

With The Beatles performing either in Hamburg or on Merseyside almost every night – and most lunchtimes as well – Lennon had more profitable matters to hand than writing Beatcomber articles. But he still found time to visit Bill Harry's offices and waste a few more fourpences on cod classifieds – in this issue wishing an offbeat new year to The Beatles' Hamburg friend (and photographer), Jurgen Vollmer.

CHAPTER 2

January 1962 to March 1963

A s The Beatles' reputation grew, in Liverpool and Hamburg, they began to feel that they were outgrowing their surroundings. When record store owner Brian Epstein offered to become their manager in late 1961, he captured their imagination with his boasts of personal contacts within the major record companies, and the prospect of something more than local fame. Lennon was the group member with whom Epstein had most contact at this stage, underscoring his position as The Beatles' leader. Yet in creative terms, Lennon was in danger of being overshadowed by his younger but prodigiously talented songwriting partner.

1962: SONGWRITING 'Please Please Me'/'Ask Me Why'/'I Saw Her Standing There'

Paul McCartney continued to dominate The Beatles' songbook during 1962. 'I Saw Her Standing There' was basically his song, though he remembered Lennon altering "She was just 17/never been a beauty queen" to the rather less precise, and therefore more intriguing, "She was just 17/you know what I mean".

Aside from 'The One After 909' and 'Hello Little Girl', the only Lennon composition which The Beatles performed regularly during 1962 was 'Ask Me Why'. Like many of his pre-1964 originals, it boasted a rather uncomfortable melodic structure, hooked to a Latin rhythm no doubt inspired by the band's cheery rendition of The Coasters' single, 'Besame Mucho'. The lyrics were as contrived as ever, though it's easy to imagine that Lennon took some sly pleasure from singing "I can't conceive" to audiences of pubescent Cavern-goers.

As for 'Please Please Me', that was "My attempt at writing a Roy Orbison song". A year before The Beatles first supported, and then topped the bill over the Big O on a British tour, Lennon had been inspired by hits like 'In Dreams' and 'Only The Lonely' to write a song in the same dramatic vein. In its original arrangement, 'Please Please Me' had none of the zest of the eventual Beatles recording, though Lennon still had high hopes of its commercial appeal. Lyrically, the song went back to an even earlier influence, connected with Lennon's mother. One of the Bing Crosby numbers she had sung to her pre-school son had the memorable chorus line, "please lend your ears to my pleas". The wordplay struck a chord, as ever, and the double 'please' duly turned up in the Lennon composition as well.

Despite their regular songwriting sessions, and the inclusion of three original songs in their repertoire for their Decca auditions (see below), The Beatles clearly considered that their own compositions were likely to be of less interest to their Merseyside audiences than familiar cover versions. In the week that 'Love Me Do' was released, for example, the only Lennon/McCartney songs that The Beatles performed during a 15-song set in New Brighton were the two featured on their new single.

JANUARY 1, 1962: THE BEATLES' Decca audition: 'Like Dreamers Do'/'Money'/'Till There Was You'/'The Sheik Of Araby'/'To Know Her Is To Love Her'/'Take Good Care Of My Baby'/'Memphis'/'Sure To Fall'/'Hello Little Girl'/'Three Cool Cats'/'Crying, Waiting, Hoping'/'Love Of The Loved'/'September In The Rain'/'Besame Mucho'/'Searchin'

During late 1961, newly appointed Beatles manager Brian Epstein took a hand-held recorder into the Cavern Club in Liverpool, and taped a selection of songs as a demonstration of the group's abilities. The resulting tape was played to Liverpool record reviewer, and Decca Records sleeve-note writer, Tony Barrow. He declined to mention the recordings in print, later describing the sound quality of the tape as "abominable". But as a favour to Epstein, he put the manager in touch with his employer in London.

And so it was that on New Year's Day 1962, The Beatles found themselves at the Decca Records studios in West Hampstead, attempting to impress A&R assistant Mike Smith into giving them a record contract. Smith had already travelled north to watch the group perform in front of an audience at The Cavern Club, on December 13, 1961. But unbeknown to them, he had also arranged to audition a more local band, Brian Poole & The Tremeloes, at Decca that day. His boss, A&R man Dick Rowe, instructed Smith that he could sign one band or the other. On the basis of their auditions, and the fact that The Tremeloes would be easier to drag into the studio at short notice, Smith went with Poole's band – thus winning for the luckless Rowe the undeserved title of 'The Man Who Turned Down The Beatles', a tag that followed him to his grave. (Rowe was compensated to some extent the following year, when he signed The Rolling Stones to Decca – having been tipped off about their talent by none other than George Harrison.)

The important question is whether Rowe and Smith were right not to sign The Beatles. On the evidence of the legendary audition tape, the answer is probably yes. As on the 1960 rehearsal tape by The Quarry Men, John Lennon took a surprising back seat. George Harrison was the lead vocalist on 'Three Cool Cats', 'Crying, Waiting, Hoping', 'The Sheik Of Araby' and 'Take Good Care Of My Baby', while an appallingly over-dramatic Paul McCartney held the limelight on 'Love Of The Loved', 'September In The Rain', 'Besame Mucho', 'Searchin', 'Like Dreamers Do', 'Sure To Fall' and 'Till There Was You'.

That left Lennon with four opportunities to shine – one of which was the revamped 'Hello Little Girl'. Gone was the 'Maybe Baby' middle eight, and Holly-inspired guitar intro. In their place was a bridge that any professional tunesmith could have written, with all the lack of imagination that suggests. The whole song was taken at a much jauntier tempo than before. This had the dual effect of removing the Everly Brothers feel of the original arrangement, and substituting the first true stirrings of what became known as Merseybeat.

With no suitable pop material to hand – Brian Epstein having vetoed raunchier original material such as 'The One After 909' – Lennon was forced to rely on covers for the rest of his contributions. Strangely tired (or should that be hungover?) versions of The Teddy Bears' 'To Know Her Is To Love Her' and Chuck Berry's 'Memphis' gave no hint of Lennon's vocal potential. Only Barrett Strong's 'Money', built around two guitars playing the same riff in tandem, without any of the stop-start rhythms The Beatles gave the tune later, represented anything like Lennon in full voice, and even then his nervousness was apparent. If Decca had signed The Beatles in January 1962, might Lennon have been consigned to history as The Beatles' third-string vocalist? Certainly any producer listening to his mock-Peter

Sellers contributions to ensemble pieces like 'Three Cool Cats' might have reckoned that he had more of a future as a comedian than as a frontline singer.

FEBRUARY/JUNE 1962: BBC RECORDING SESSIONS

Between March 1962 and June 1965, The Beatles made regular recordings for the BBC Light Programme radio service. Complex agreements with the Musicians' Union over the number of records which could be broadcast each day – needle time, as it was known – meant that the BBC relied heavily on specially recorded or even live material to fill out their pop programmes. As a result, it was not uncommon for even the most major stars to report to a small studio at Broadcasting House so they could tape special inserts for shows such as *Saturday Club* and *Easy Beat*.

The Beatles were no exception, and their BBC recordings represent a goldmine for the band's archivists, that fuelled dozens of bootlegs before the official *Live At The BBC* set in 1994 stemmed the flow somewhat. Sadly, only documentary evidence remains of their February 12, 1962 audition in front of producer Peter Pilbeam. McCartney led the group through 'Like Dreamers Do' and 'Till There Was You' on this occasion, while Lennon took charge for 'Memphis' and 'Hello Little Girl'. Pilbeam gave Lennon's vocal abilities the thumbs-up in his official BBC report on the audition, but dismissed McCartney with a simple 'X' beside his name.

Despite this lukewarm reception, The Beatles were added to the BBC's approved list of talent. Almost all of their session appearances have survived on tape, though often only in lo-fi quality. Two shows in March and June 1962 require special mention, as they were the only BBC sessions to feature The Beatles with Pete Best, rather than Ringo Starr. Their *Teenager's Turn* appearance on March 3 (recorded live, but broadcast later that week) saw Lennon taking the lead vocal on 'Memphis' and The Marvelettes' 'Please Mr Postman', while McCartney was spotlighted on Roy Orbison's 'Dream Baby'. 'Postman', in particular, proved how little separated the unknown Beatles of early 1962 from their superstar incarnation of later years. Only a slightly weak grasp of dynamics betrayed their lack of big-time experience.

An appearance on the live show *Here We Go* on June 15 had George Harrison singing Joe Brown's hit 'A Picture Of You', McCartney reprising his Decca audition track 'Besame Mucho', and Lennon providing the national première of his own 'Ask Me Why'.

24 APRIL 1962: THE BEATLES recording 'Sweet Georgia Brown'/'Swanee River' with Tony Sheridan

The Beatles' second session with Tony Sheridan has long been the subject of conjecture and confusion. Most sources are agreed that the group provided instrumental support for Sheridan's version of the jazz-era standard, 'Sweet Georgia Brown' (arranged by McCartney, according to documentation from the time). More recent research confirmed that two backing tracks were taped on this date, for 'Sweet Georgia Brown' and 'Swanee River', ready for Sheridan to add his vocals on a separate occasion. Although 'Sweet Georgia Brown' was definitely released, the Beatle-backed 'Swanee River' apparently wasn't, although Sheridan did return to the studio later in 1962 to re-record the song with his own regular backing band, The Beat Brothers. He subsequently recorded an entirely different lead vocal track for 'Sweet Georgia Brown' in January 1964, which included new lyrics cashing in on The Beatles' success.

January 1964 marked the start of a blitzkrieg of Sheridan/Beatles releases around the world. Atlantic Records in New York licensed the rights to handle this material in the USA, and reckoned that the tapes needed some sonic punch before they could be released there. So top session players Cornell Dupree (guitar) and Bernard 'Pretty' Purdie (drums) were hired to overdub additional parts onto The Beatles' raw tracks. Purdie subsequently won much notoriety for his claims that Brian Epstein had used him to replace Ringo Starr's drumming on many of the group's biggest hits. These remarks were widely ridiculed, but there was at least a seed of truth at their root.

JUNE 6, 1962: THE BEATLES EMI audition 'Ask Me Why'/'P.S. I Love You'/'Love Me Do'/'Besame Mucho'

EMI's major labels, Columbia, Parlophone and HMV, had already turned down The Beatles when Brian Epstein secured them one last chance – a hearing from Parlophone A&R chief, George Martin. In fact, it was his assistant, Ron Richards, who took charge of the session; only when he and engineer Norman Smith realised that The Beatles might be worth further investigation was Martin dragged out of the EMI canteen.

The evergreen McCartney showcase 'Besame Mucho' aside, the band chose to demonstrate their own material. 'Ask Me Why' was once again Lennon's solo turn, while The Beatles also played the recent McCartney composition, 'P.S. I Love You'. 'Love Me Do' has traditionally been treated as a McCartney composition, not least by Lennon himself, but it appears that the original inspiration for this simplistic but undeniably memorable tune was actually Lennon's. He certainly took the lead vocal and delivered the punch of the title line at the end of every verse when the song first entered The Beatles' repertoire. But by June 1962, the song had also become a vehicle for his fast-improving harmonica playing, so Lennon was restricted to harmony vocals. Two weeks after this recording session, The Beatles met American hitmaker Bruce Channel of 'Hey Baby' fame. His harmonica player, Delbert McClinton, passed on several tips to Lennon, enabling him to make the instrument a Beatles trademark for the next two or three years. Sadly, though, there might have been no extended career to consider had the group retained Pete Best as their drummer. On the evidence of this first shot at 'Love Me Do', he clearly wasn't up to professional recording standards, as George Martin agreed.

Around the same time, The Beatles made two sets of recordings at the Cavern Club in Liverpool. An afternoon session (which Ringo Starr claims features his drumming) behind locked doors saw them tape reference versions of Lennon's 'The One After 909' – effectively unchanged since the 1960 rehearsal take – and McCartney's jaunty instrumental, 'Catswalk'.

A month or so later, an entire Beatles lunchtime session from the Cavern was also recorded; it is not certain whether this was at the behest of the group, or simply an enthusiastic fan. The tape featured just one Lennon/McCartney original, 'Ask Me Why', plus versions of covers familiar to us from other sets of Beatles recordings. These included 'Please Mr Postman', 'Words Of Love', 'Dizzy Miss Lizzy' and 'Matchbox', all with Lennon on lead vocals; 'I Wish I Could Shimmy Like My Sister Kate', 'Hippy Hippy Shake', 'Your Feet's Too Big', 'Till There Was You', and 'Dream Baby' (all with McCartney taking the lead); and 'Roll Over Beethoven', featuring George.

Less familiar additions to the group's repertoire included Tommy Roe's hit 'Sharing You', also sung by George, as were the old Elvis Presley country song, 'I Forgot To Remember To Forget' and The Coasters' 'Young Blood'. Paul sang James Ray's hit 'If You Gotta Make A Fool Of Somebody' and, almost inevitably, Bruce Channel's 'Hey Baby'.

AUGUST 22, 1962: THE BEATLES recording 'Some Other Guy' and 'Kansas City; Hey Hey Hey Hey' (Granada TV)

Though the clip wasn't aired until November 1963, Granada TV visited the Cavern on this date to take note of what was fast becoming a local Liverpudlian phenomenon. A major theme of the story was the fact that the city's most popular beat group were virtually unknown outside of the

Merseyside area. For their *Know The North* magazine programme, Granada's cameras captured one of the band's first lunchtime gigs with their new drummer, Ringo Starr, who had just replaced the hapless Pete Best. A hint of the protests that followed can be heard in Granada's film of Lennon performing Barrett Strong's 'Some Other Guy' – not only a favourite Beatles cover of the period, and more evidence of Lennon's natural empathy with American R&B, but also worth noting because the simple two-note piano intro of Strong's record cropped up almost eight years later as the start of the Plastic Ono Band's 'Instant Karma!'. "I'd like to make a record like 'Some Other Guy'," Lennon admitted in 1968. "I haven't done one that satisfies me as much as that satisfied me."

Granada never broadcast their film of 'Kansas City', but an acetate recording of the track does survive, on the same disc as a second performance of 'Some Other Guy', taped the same day. "We'll have to do that again," Lennon said sardonically at the end of that performance. Manager Brian Epstein apparently pressed up a small quantity of these acetates soon after the filming took place, for sale solely in his Liverpool music store, NEMS.

The Beatles finally made their television debut two months later, on October 17, 1962, when they performed 'Some Other Guy' and their new single, 'Love Me Do', live in front of the cameras for another Granada show, *People And Places*.

AUGUST 23, 1962: *MERSEY BEAT* publishes 'Small Sam'

Far removed from the dramas of The Beatles' line-up changes, and after a hiatus of almost a year, Lennon – alias 'Beatcomber' – returned to writing for *Mersey Beat*, rather than filling its editorial pages with his beat group exploits. 'Small Sam' was not included in any of Lennon's books, though in late 1964 he did request a copy of this issue of *Mersey Beat* from Bill Harry so that he could revise the piece for *A Spaniard In The Works*. He evidently decided that this extended joke wasn't worth reprinting, though its humour, based around Small Sam's possession of a club foot, would not have been out of place alongside the numerous cripples who littered the pages of both Lennon's early prose collections.

SEPTEMBER 4 and 11, 1962: THE BEATLES recording 'How Do You Do It'/'Love Me Do'/'P.S. I Love You'/'Please Please Me'

When Parlophone's producer George Martin sent The Beatles word of their first official EMI recording session, he enclosed a demo disc of a Mitch

Murray composition he felt they should record as their début single. Lennon and McCartney did as they'd been instructed, and rearranged Murray's song into at least a facsimile of their natural style. Back at EMI's Abbey Road studio, Lennon took the lead vocal on 'How Do You Do It', and turned in an appropriately lightweight performance on what was a catchy but insubstantial pop song. The track was eventually considered less suitable than 'Love Me Do' and 'P.S. I Love You', and was not released at the time – allowing The Beatles' Liverpool friends, Gerry & The Pacemakers, to inherit 'How Do You Do It' as their debut single (a UK No. 1 in 1963).

McCartney's voice was dominant on both sides of that record. But Lennon was definitely the focal point when The Beatles performed their single on Granada TV's *People And Places* on October 29 – located at a central microphone as if he were the lead singer, and holding no instrument other than his harmonica.

Legend has it that when The Beatles also had a stab at recording the Orbison-styled 'Please Please Me' during their second session, George Martin rejected their arrangement, and sent them away to prepare a more upbeat version. But the September 11 recording of 'Please Please Me' has no hint of an Orbison influence, suggesting that Martin's intervention either came a week earlier, or was a figment of collective imagination. When George Martin repeated the familiar story in a 1971 *Melody Maker* interview, Lennon fired back an open letter, in which he claimed: "I wrote 'Please Please Me' alone. It was recorded in the exact sequence in which I wrote it. Remember?"

Whatever the truth, this dry run at The Beatles' first No.1 single showed only minor differences from the finished record, notably the absence of Lennon's key harmonica introduction.

SEPTEMBER 6, 1962: *MERSEY BEAT* publishes 'On Safairy With Whide Hunter'

Literary parody was still Lennon's inspiration in this brief 'story', which according to the credits in *In His Own Write* was written "in conjugal with Paul" – though in *Mersey Beat* it appeared under the regular 'Beatcomber' byline. The McCartney involvement suggested that this was a fairly recent composition, a theory backed up by the opening lines, which were based on the lyrics to The Tokens' early 1962 hit, 'The Lion Sleeps Tonight' (also known as 'Wimoweh').

The piece was full of obvious puns: with characters like 'Elepoon Bill' and 'Jumble Jim', Bungalow Bill doesn't seem too far away. And the references to "rhinostrills and hippoposthumous" explained why literary critics thought they caught the inspiration of James Joyce in Lennon's work, and more pertinently demonstrated exactly what Lennon was borrowing from the language of Edward Lear and Lewis Carroll. The parody and the word-play were the sole purpose here; there was none of the social satire found in Lennon's slightly later work.

'On Safairy' was reprinted in *In His Own Write* in 1964. Just to prove that Lennon did more than simply reproduce his early writings verbatim, he added one explanatory sentence to the 'narrative', and also simplified some of the puns.

NOVEMBER 26, 1962: THE BEATLES recording 'Please Please Me'/'Ask Me Why'; auditioning 'The Tip Of My Tongue'

'Love Me Do' was duly issued as The Beatles' first single on October 5, 1962. Its mild chart success prompted a swift follow-up, and between September and November, Lennon and McCartney had spruced up the arrangement of 'Please Please Me' to the point where it was the obvious choice as their second single (issued on January 11, 1963).

The surge in confidence between this recording and the far more tenta-tive 'Love Me Do' was remarkable. Not only did Ringo Starr display some drum rolls unmatched on their other early recordings, but Lennon turned in a phenomenally relaxed and assured lead vocal. It was most noticeable in the "come on" passages leading up to the chorus, when the sexual nature of his invitation to indulge in some heavier petting than usual was made obvi-ous.

Little of that assurance carried over into Lennon's 'Ask Me Why', and even less into the Lennon/McCartney collaboration 'The Tip Of My Tongue', a true dog of a song which they later passed on to the luckless Tommy Quickly. The final verse included the mawkish lines: "Soon enough my time will come/And after all is said and done/I'll marry you and we will live as one". And the tune was no more memorable – which probably explained why The Beatles merely auditioned the song during the session and never committed it to tape.

DECEMBER 25 & 31, 1962: THE BEATLES live in Hamburg 'I Saw Her Standing There'/'Nothin' Shakin' '/'Twist And Shout'/'Falling In Love Again'/'Ask Me Why'/'Sheila'/'To Know Her Is To Love Her'/'Little Queenie'/ 'Red Sails In The Sunset'/'Reminiscing'/'Matchbox'/'I'm Talkin' 'Bout You'/'Long

**Tall Sally'/'I Wish I Could Shimmy Like My Sister Kate'/'Roll
Over Beethoven'/'Your Feet's Too Big'/'Hippy Hippy
Shake'/'I'm Gonna Sit Right Down And Cry'/'Sweet Little
Sixteen'/'Lend Me Your Comb'/'Mr Moonlight'/'I Remember
You'/'A Taste Of Honey'/'Everybody's Trying To Be My
Baby'/'Besame Mucho'/'Where Have You Been All My Life'/'Till
There Was You'/'Kansas City; Hey Hey Hey Hey'/'Red Hot'
(they also provide backing for German vocalists on 'Be-Bop-A-
Lula' and 'Hallelujah I Love Her So')**

Although 'Love Me Do' was already showing in the British charts, The
Beatles were under contract for one more residency at Hamburg's Star
Club, from December 18 to 31. On at least two nights during their engagement, the group were recorded on amateur equipment by Ted Taylor, the
leader of another Liverpool band with a Hamburg residency, Kingsize
Taylor & The Dominoes. The tapes passed into the hands of former Beatles
manager Allan Williams, who in turn offered them to Brian Epstein around
1964. Epstein took a brief listen to these noisy, muddy tapes and turned
them down. They then lay in the bottom of a cupboard for almost a decade,
until Williams rediscovered them, and began negotiating for an official
release.

Williams played the tapes to selected journalists in the early-to-mid
Seventies, building up a modest media buzz. After undergoing remixing and
cleaning up as far as late Seventies technology would allow, 26 songs were
issued on a German album, then later in Britain as a double, in the summer
of 1977. A further four recordings surfaced soon afterwards on the equivalent American release. Alternative versions of some songs have since
appeared on bootleg, together with Harrison's cover of Billy Lee Riley's
rockabilly classic, 'Red Hot'. A version of 'Hully Gully' included on an
American release of the tapes was not by The Beatles, however, but by
another British band, Cliff Bennett and The Rebel Rousers.

"In Liverpool, Hamburg and other dance halls . . . what we generated was
fantastic, when we played straight rock, and there was nobody to touch us
in Britain," Lennon recalled in 1970. "We always missed the club dates
because that's when we were playing music."

By the end of December 1962, The Beatles were outgrowing the
Hamburg beat clubs, and little of that excitement was captured on the Star
Club tapes. As a document, however, the recordings did suggest what The
Beatles must have been like before Brian Epstein smartened them up and
put them in suits. Lennon baited the drunken club audience throughout the

set, and the group showed their contempt for the occasion with appropri-ate lyrical changes, turning 'A Taste Of Honey' into 'A Waste Of Money', and 'Shimmy Shimmy' into 'Shitty Shitty'.

The band deigned to perform only two original songs for the clubgoers: 'I Saw Her Standing There' and 'Ask Me Why'. The rest of the tape charted their taste in covers, with Lennon in charge on 'To Know Her Is To Love Her', Chuck Berry's 'Little Queenie', 'I'm Talkin' 'Bout You' and 'Sweet Little Sixteen', 'I'm Gonna Sit Right Down And Cry' (as recorded by Elvis Presley on his 1956 début album), Dr. Feelgood's 'Mr Moonlight', Arthur Alexander's 'Where Have You Been All My Life', and a brief version of the Bert Berns song trademarked by The Isley Brothers, 'Twist And Shout'.

Ironically, the Hamburg recordings were not the only live documentation of The Beatles under consideration this month. On December 9, 1962, George Martin had visited the Cavern Club in Liverpool, to consider the possibility of taping the group's first album in front of a hometown audi-ence. He eventually decided that the conditions in the sweat-soaked cellar weren't a suitable location for EMI's expensive location recording equip-ment.

JANUARY 22, 1963: THE BEATLES recording 'Keep Your Hands Off My Baby'/'Some Other Guy' for the BBC

As we'll shortly see, The Beatles performed many more songs on radio in 1963 than they recorded for EMI; and one of them was Lennon's rendition of the Little Eva hit, 'Keep Your Hands Off My Baby'. Its title alone marked it out as a likely Lennon vehicle, though the song wasn't as vicious as its name suggested. It warrants mention here as one of the few non-originals that The Beatles played on tour early in 1963; and because constant rumour (and apparent confirmation in the pages of the British music press) sug-gested that the group recorded the song for the first album. It didn't show up in the EMI logs of the band's studio sessions, but a reviewer for *Beat Monthly* actually described the track when he first heard an acetate of *Please Please Me*, which hinted that there might have been some truth in the tale after all.

Late JANUARY 1963: THE BEATLES recording demo version of 'Misery'

Fancying themselves as tunesmiths for hire, Lennon and McCartney con-jured up 'Misery' on January 27, 1963, intending it for the young woman who was the billtopper on their current tour: Helen Shapiro. She liked what she heard, and so The Beatles stopped at a local studio later that week – possibly in Liverpool – to record a demo version for her manager to hear. At this stage, the lyrics were tailored for a female singer. But when Shapiro's manager rejected the song, they decided to offer it to Kenny Lynch instead, and duly rewrote the first verse. Even then, the lyrics weren't set in stone. The first line of Lynch's version went "You've been treating me bad", which was how it appeared on the sheet music; but when The Beatles subsequently performed the song themselves, they turned it into a chip-on-my-shoulder piece of romantic paranoia, in which "The world is treating *me* bad".

FEBRUARY 11, 1963: THE BEATLES recording 'I Saw Her Standing There'/'Misery'/'Anna'/'Chains'/'Boys'/'Baby It's You'/'Do You Want To Know A Secret'/'A Taste Of Honey'/'There's A Place'/'Hold Me Tight'/'Twist And Shout'

The single-day session which produced the bulk of The Beatles' *Please Please Me* album, plus an early rejected cut of McCartney's 'Hold Me Tight', has become the stuff of legend. The finished record had plenty of raw edges. Listen to the songs in the order in which they were recorded, and you could hear their voices fray, until the climactic first take of 'Twist And Shout' which would have assured Lennon of minor league immortality if he had never recorded another note. The Beatles took that song, like most white group R&B, at full volume. As early as February 1963, then, Lennon was translating his emotions into vocal noise, producing as frenzied a slice of pop music as anything cut outside Memphis. The fact that he was suffering a severe cold – one of a series of ailments that afflicted Lennon through The Beatles' perilously frantic schedule in 1963 – merely added raucousness to his voice.

Lennon's other covers that day had their moments, as well. The arrangement of Arthur Alexander's 'Anna' might have dragged, but not Lennon's vocal, which set the scene for his own efforts in a similar vein later in the year. Likewise The Shirelles' 'Baby It's You', where after some initial nervousness Lennon relaxed into the song, and produced another smooth vocal that threatened to bite if you came too close.

The important news here, though, was the sudden emergence of a batch of new Lennon/McCartney compositions. All three were primarily Lennon songs, which hadn't so far surfaced in their live shows. 'Do You Want To Know A Secret' said least of the three, though it was also the most commercial, as fellow Liverpudlian Billy J. Kramer proved later in the year.

Lennon thought little enough of the song, which was inspired by another Walt Disney film tune from *Fantasia* he remembered his mother singing, to give it to George to sing. "I thought it would be a good vehicle for him because it only had three notes, and he wasn't the best singer in the world," he explained shortly before his death.

Having passed through the hands of Helen Shapiro and Kenny Lynch, 'Misery' was still considered worthy of attention from The Beatles themselves. What was remarkable about their rendition was not the simplicity of the song structure, or its admission that even big Lennons could cry, but the sheer fact that a song about misery could sound so damn optimistic. In fact, like his 1974 version of Fats Domino's 'Ain't That A Shame', the whole piece had a swagger that suggested you shouldn't believe a single word.

'There's A Place' proved to be the landmark song, however. It had another unorthodox melodic opening, like 'Ask Me Why' – a hesitation before the action began. But it was the words that counted: Lennon's first real piece of introspection: "There's a place where I can go/when I feel low/when I feel blue/and it's my mind/and there's no time when I'm alone". (Uncannily, Brian Wilson of The Beach Boys tapped into exactly the same vein when he wrote 'In My Room' a few months later, although he hadn't heard The Beatles' record at that point.) Married to a joyous burst of harmonies, these simple lines escaped most people's attention; but this was Lennon's first admission that the external Beatle didn't tell the whole story. In times of trouble, he might escape inside – perhaps into the same pool of imagination that was already producing the stories, poems and conceits that would shortly be anthologised in *In His Own Write*.

MARCH 5, 1963: THE BEATLES recording 'From Me To You'/'Thank You Girl'/'The One After 909'

This was the era of true Lennon/McCartney collaboration, and 'From Me To You' was composed on February 28, between shows in York and Shrewsbury on their first national tour. The recording session was already booked, and both songs which eventually made up their third single betrayed signs of having been written to order. 'From Me To You' was perfectly commercial for the time, even a little simplistic – although not as banal as it might have been had the group persisted with their idea of opening the record with the kind of childish falsetto harmonies normally reserved for period Helen Shapiro singles. Its one-syllable lyrics could be adopted by any lovesick teenager as their own, and the song was early proof that The Beatles could be as calculating as any professional songsmiths. It was an art that came under increasing demand over the next 12 months, not so much on The Beatles' own records as on their gifts to fellow artists in the Brian Epstein management stable.

'Thank You Girl' was, as Lennon admitted in 1980, composed during the same quest for an A-side, and was briefly considered for priority over 'From Me To You', until common sense prevailed. Its ingredients were appealing enough – the rough Merseyside harmonies, the 'oh oh' hook, Lennon's raucous harmonica – but the entire performance never gelled. Not that the song was under any great threat in the race to become the next Beatles B-side. The band also attempted Lennon's 'The One After 909' during the same session, and in the effort to make it sound like R&B rather than the straight rock 'n' roll it patently was, they lost all the innocent enthusiasm which made their 1969 revival of the piece so attractive. The importance of the occasion also drove George Harrison into one of his least impressive guitar solos. Perhaps because he knew the song was slipping out of reach, Lennon was particularly irritable during the session. "What are you doing?", he snapped repeatedly at McCartney, only to be trumped when a later take broke down, and he was exposed as the culprit.

Another piece of faux rockabilly, 'What Goes On', was on the original agenda for the session. But the tired attempts at cracking 'The One After 909' persuaded George Martin to set the other song aside for the moment – and it immediately slipped out of the group's repertoire for nearly three years.

MARCH 16, 1963: THE BEATLES recording 'Too Much Monkey Business' and 'I'm Talkin' 'Bout You' for the BBC

As their record sales advanced, so the art of promotion became ever more important. During 1962, The Beatles' live shows had featured songs they felt like playing. Now material they had issued on record, or were about to, took pride of place. Partly that was down to a natural pride in their achievements; partly it was sheer business sense.

But The Beatles retained enough enthusiasm for the music to dip into their past repertoire for their BBC radio performances, and this live recording for the BBC's pop flagship, *Saturday Club*, saw Lennon unveiling fiery renditions of two Chuck Berry songs, 'Too Much Monkey Business' and 'I'm Talkin' 'Bout You'. The latter had already cropped up on the Hamburg tapes from the end of the previous year, but this remains the earliest extant Beatles take of 'Monkey Business' – unless you count the borrowed guitar intro that The Quarry Men superimposed onto Duane Eddy's 'Movin' And Groovin'' during their spring 1960 rehearsal session.

CHAPTER 3

May 1963 to March 1964

One chart-topping single was enough to make The Beatles famous amongst British teenagers; two in a row promised that their fame might last for a year or more. But none of the group was prepared for the speed and scope of their success over the next year. No British pop stars had ever enjoyed such international acclaim. There was little time for celebration, however. After a brief pause in late spring, The Beatles were catapulted into a devastatingly tight working schedule, against the backdrop of mounting external pressure. For someone as insecure as Lennon, the extremes of stardom and stress led him to question his own sense of himself, and his achievements.

MAY 1963: COMPOSING 'Bad To Me'

At the end of April, Lennon went on holiday to Spain with Beatles manager Brian Epstein – less than three weeks after the birth of his first son, Julian, in Liverpool. Almost as soon as the couple returned, Cavern DJ Bob Wooler (an early supporter of the group) insinuated to Lennon that he must have had an affair with his openly homosexual manager. Lennon promptly beat Wooler up, which rather begged the question. To his dying day, he continued to deny the rumours, although he left enough spaces in the story to suggest that there may have been a degree of sexual experimentation between the two men.

Whether the Lennon/Epstein flirtation was even consummated or not has little relevance to the other, less often reported fact about the holiday. Epstein used the break to persuade Lennon, and through him McCartney, that they should be writing more material for Epstein's other protégés – particularly Billy J. Kramer, who had already issued John and Paul's 'Do You Want To Know A Secret' as his début single, with McCartney's 'I'll Be On My Way' on the flipside. Epstein's interest was two-fold: The Beatles' talent might aid some of his lesser artists, and in the process Lennon and McCartney's reputations would benefit. Both expectations were happily and speedily fulfilled.

The majority of these giveaway songs were actually fashioned by McCartney – including 'A World Without Love', 'I Don't Want To See You Again' and 'Woman' for Peter and Gordon: 'One And One Is Two', originally offered to Kramer, who turned it down – "Billy J. is finished when he gets this song," Lennon muttered as he watched McCartney cut his original demo – and then gifted to the luckless Mike Shannon; and 'It's For You' for Cilla Black.

But it was Lennon who provided the initial example, composing 'Bad To Me' specifically for Billy J. Kramer during the Spanish vacation. Back in London, he recorded a double-tracked acoustic demo as a blueprint for producer George Martin to follow, leaving Kramer with a melodic, optimistic piece of romanticism that showed no signs of any emotional attachment at all. Around the same period, Lennon also completed 'I Call Your Name', a song which he'd begun at the end of the Fifties but never honed into shape. Kramer duly recorded it as the flipside of 'Bad To Me', before going on to record two further McCartney giveaways, 'I'll Keep You Satisfied' and 'From A Window', over the next year. Lennon also attended an October 14, 1963 session at which Kramer recorded 'I'm In Love' (also tackled by The Fourmost), and his voice can be heard amongst the studio chatter at the start of the performance (not released by EMI until 1991). Lennon and/or McCartney often attended the recording sessions for these songs, either to make suggestions about the arrangements, or simply to show support for their fellow Brian Epstein clients.

MAY/SEPTEMBER: THE BEATLES recording 'Money'/'You Really Got A Hold On Me'/'Too Much Monkey Business'/'Got To Find My Baby'/'A Shot Of Rhythm And Blues'/ 'Memphis'/'Some Other Guy'/'Hippy Hippy Shake'/ 'Sure To Fall'/'Young Blood'/'Till There Was You'/'Long Tall Sally'/'Everybody's Trying To Be My Baby'/'Roll Over

**Beethoven'/'Honey Don't'/'Side By Side'/'Pop Go The Beatles'/
'That's All Right (Mama)'/'Carol'/'Soldier Of Love'/
'Lend Me Your Comb'/'Clarabella'/'Sweet Little Sixteen'/
'Lonesome Tears In My Eyes'/'So How Come'/'Nothin'
Shakin''/'Matchbox'/'Please Mr Postman'/'I'm Gonna Sit Right
Down And Cry Over You'/'Crying, Waiting, Hoping'/'To Know
Her Is To Love Her'/'The Honeymoon Song'/'I Got A
Woman'/'Words Of Love'/'Glad All Over'/'I Just Don't
Understand'/'Devil In Her Heart'/'Slow Down'/'Ooh! My
Soul'/'Don't Ever Change'/'Lucille'**

Take a breath for a second. During the summer of 1963, The Beatles hosted their own weekly BBC radio show – a regular chance for the band to indulge in some of the songs which weren't featured in their live sets any more, and which they hadn't committed to vinyl so far. The *Pop Go The Beatles* series ran for 13 weeks from June to September, and The Beatles also contributed regularly to shows like *Side By Side* (for which they recorded a jolly version of the title tune with The Terry Young Six), *Saturday Club* and *Easy Beat*. The tunes listed above were the goodies – the tracks that wouldn't have been familiar to anyone who knew The Beatles solely through their records. Those aside, the band also cut numerous alternative versions of their hits, plus little-aired original material like 'I'll Be On My Way' and 'I'll Get You'. Most but not all of the gems from these radio sessions were compiled by George Martin on 1994's *Live At The BBC* set, alongside snatches of the band's most humorous dialogue with their DJ hosts.

The BBC renditions of their own songs generally kept strictly to the framework of the originals; they might just as well have played the records instead. To judge from the intensity of the performances, it was the covers that interested The Beatles the most, and the parade of rock and R&B songs they toyed with is an accurate summary of where each of The Beatles was at in 1963.

On his rare solo excursions, George Harrison voted for the rockabilly of Carl Perkins; Lennon reflected the same interest, loping through the country ballad 'Sure To Fall' in tandem with McCartney, and teaming up with his partner again on the Perkins hit 'Lend Me Your Comb'. And whereas McCartney settled for straight rock 'n' roll, in the shape of 'Lucille', 'Clarabella', 'Hippy Hippy Shake' and the rest, Lennon preferred something a little more subtle – which is how he came to deliver sly, knowing takes on semi-rock songs like Johnny Burnette's 'Lonesome Tears In My Eyes' and Presley's 'I'm Gonna Sit Right Down and Cry Over You'.

As ever, though, two strands of American music tantalised Lennon during these sessions. The first was Chuck Berry, represented here by sterling versions of 'Carol', 'Got To Find My Baby', 'Sweet Little Sixteen', 'Memphis' and 'Too Much Monkey Business' – all delivered with as much guts as the primitive BBC recording techniques would allow. The second? American rhythm and blues, then on the edge of transmuting into soul through the efforts of Sam Cooke and Solomon Burke. Arthur Alexander was a constant Lennon influence – witness 'Anna' on the *Please Please Me* album. From the same source came that widespread Merseybeat favourite, 'A Shot Of Rhythm And Blues', and – much more to the point – 'Soldier Of Love'.

Many aficionados rate 'Soldier' as one of The Beatles' finest moments in a recording studio, and it's hard to disagree. The band turned their usual trick when it came to a cover: they hardened the edges of the song, and tightened the arrangement with their foolproof vocal harmonies. But it was Lennon's calm assurance and utter conviction that turned a rather weak romantic metaphor – the doomed soldier on the emotional battlefield – into a piece of poetry. The irony of history ensured that Lennon's subsequent peace campaigns, and violent death, gave this once-only performance a poignant aftertaste that would not have been noticed at the time.

'Soldier Of Love' was the pinnacle of these sessions, but there were many other highlights – Lennon's wailing blues harp on 'Got To Find My Baby', for instance, or his tough rockabilly rendition of Ray Charles' 'I Got A Woman', arranged identically to Elvis Presley's 1956 version. And Lennon also threw in a titbit for future Beatles historians by delivering Carl Perkins' 'Honey Don't' with genuine rockabilly swagger. The song was subsequently tossed to Ringo Starr as his token contribution to the band's fourth album, *Beatles For Sale*.

JULY 1963: THE BEATLES recording 'She Loves You'/'I'll Get You'/'You Really Got A Hold On Me'/'Money'/'Devil In Her Heart'/'Till There Was You'/'Please Mr Postman'/'It Won't Be Long'/'Roll Over Beethoven'/'All My Loving' – plus Lennon composing 'I'm In Love', and Lennon & McCartney taping 'Rocking And Rolling' and an untitled instrumental

In an era when many artists regard writing a song and making a video as a hard year's work, it is difficult to comprehend the sheer physical and mental strain imposed on The Beatles in 1963 and 1964. They toured constantly throughout that period – mostly in Britain, at first, and then all over the world in 1964. They performed almost weekly on British radio; made a full-length feature film; recorded four albums and twice as many singles, mostly self-penned; appeared regularly on TV; gave scores of interviews to newspapers and magazines; posed for countless photo sessions; wrote songs for their friends and business colleagues; and dealt endlessly with the pleasures and perils of being the four most desirable young men on the planet, and the most recognised.

Small wonder, then, that for their second album the band decided to maintain the format of their first, mixing eight of their own compositions with six cover versions. First, though, there was the small matter of their fourth single. Those present at the session confirm that 'She Loves You' sounded most unpromising as an acoustic guitar duet between Lennon and McCartney; and the blatant attempt to widen the scope of their me-mine-you-us lyrics with the introduction of a third character was scarcely a masterstroke either. But ask anyone who lived through Beatlemania: 'She Loves You', another back-seat-of-the-coach collaboration between Lennon and McCartney, is still the song which evokes those hurricane days of 1963. Lennon's flipside, 'I'll Get You', had a rather coy 'Oh yeah' introduction behind the harmonica work which was in danger of becoming a Beatles cliché. But it featured a surprisingly flowing melody from a man who a few months earlier was still finding it hard to move from one section of a song to another. Here, the sheer liberation of the middle eight offered a stunning contrast to the stumblings of 'Ask Me Why' and 'Hello Little Girl'.

Back at the album, Lennon ran up another single-that-might-have-been in the shape of 'It Won't Be Long' – again built around a simple repetitive chorus, though not quite as simple or repetitive as 'She Loves You'. Otherwise, not forgetting to mention some remarkably precise rhythm guitar on McCartney's 'All My Loving', Lennon concentrated on his covers during these sessions.

'Please Mr Postman' and 'You Really Got A Hold On Me' were both borrowed from the Motown stable in Detroit – from The Marvelettes and The Miracles, respectively. Just as with 'Soldier Of Love' at the BBC, The Beatles added pace and precision to the naivety and charm of the originals, and anyone who's not an R&B purist would probably rather play their versions than the American originals. 'Money' came from the same source, but after two years of regular practice The Beatles had transformed the rather lame rendition on the Decca audition tape into a *tour de force*. The track was now built around pianos, not guitars, and the band added a series of stop-start breaks which revved up the excitement.

Lennon's most incisive moment on the track came on the final chorus, however. His vocal was raw and insistent, but then that was already expected. In what was probably a spur-of-the-moment vocal throwaway, though, he interrupted the repeated call "Money, that's what I want", with the desperate plea "I wanna be free". You have to hear it to feel the impact; for a second, Lennon laid himself bare, before covering up again with the request for something which he already knew couldn't buy him love, let alone freedom.

No such drama infected another Lennon composition dating from this time. In a final act of generosity, Lennon manufactured another potential hit single for The Fourmost, looking for a follow-up to their début (Lennon-composed) hit, 'Hello Little Girl'. And so emerged 'I'm In Love', a chirpy, entirely uncomplicated tale of teenage romance gone right. Questioned about the song shortly before his death, Lennon remembered nothing; and it's hard to blame him for the lapse.

Finally, a batch of tapes auctioned by Beatles driver Alf Bicknell in 1989 appear to date from around this time. They include an instrumental duet between Lennon (guitar) and McCartney (trumpet), around a set of jazz changes; plus a piece of musical pastiche that was presumably titled 'Rocking And Rolling'. The song, which sounded like the bizarre product of a chemical experiment involving Chuck Berry and The Goons, allowed the duo to satirise the 12-bar blues structure using very basic double-tracking techniques. They probably forgot it as soon as they finished it, but this tape marked the first step along the road to their more adventurous home recording experiments of the mid-Sixties.

Bicknell's tape collection also included off-cuts from The Beatles' 1963 studio sessions; and a recording of Lennon, George Harrison and Gerry Marsden (of Gerry & The Pacemakers fame) chanting the *23rd Psalm* and reciting extracts from *The Bible* in supposedly humorous style.

SEPTEMBER/OCTOBER 1963: THE BEATLES recording 'I Wanna Be Your Man'/'Little Child'/'All I've Got To Do'/'Not A Second Time'/'Don't Bother Me'/'Hold Me Tight'/'The Beatles' Christmas Record'/'I Want To Hold Your Hand'/'This Boy'

Three EMI recording sessions in the autumn of 1963 completed their second album, prepared the single with which they would conquer America, and produced a unique Christmas gift for all the members of their official fan club.

Of the songs awarded the 'Lennon/McCartney' credit, John wrote all or most of every one – with the exception of 'Hold Me Tight', the sole leftover from their February 1963 session for the *Please Please Me* album. 'Little Child' and 'I Wanna Be Your Man' were true collaborations; the latter had been offered to The Rolling Stones in an unfinished state, and the couple wrote the chorus in half an hour while the Stones waited expectantly. 'Little Child' bore signs of similar haste. Both of them said absolutely nothing, but survived on sheer enthusiasm. Lennon's rasping harmonica on 'Little Child' didn't harm matters, either.

'Not A Second Time' was an altogether more unusual piece of work. It was the first Lennon song which showed signs of having been written on piano, rather than guitar. Lennon was not as fluent on the keyboard as McCartney, but like Bob Dylan he evolved a style that fulfilled his own needs, rather than any technical criteria. From the start, the song had a slightly unsettling rhythm; and the lyrics matched it, with a hidden message that seemed to say: "You made me suffer, and I'm going to let you do it again".

'All I've Got To Do' and 'This Boy' added more confirmation of Lennon's infatuation with American soul music. 'This Boy' was styled like a Fifties doo-wop ballad – or at least like Smokey Robinson And The Miracles' adaptation of the same form. On record it sounded like a throwaway, but on stage Lennon turned its middle section into a catharsis, screaming out the elongated syllables of the words 'my' and 'cry' with anguished fervour. Ironically, in the original plan, the middle section was meant to be filled by a guitar solo; Lennon's lyrics were only written during the recording session itself.

'All I've Got To Do' was never performed in concert, but it was raised in the same school as 'This Boy', though Arthur Alexander, and his performances of songs such as 'You Better Move On', were the direct inspiration. Like a soul singer, Lennon stretched out the opening 'I' of the lyric over six notes, and then repeated the trick with frills in the next line. His shift into a higher octave in the final chorus was a real trademark of confidence – and also an outcry of passion in a song that ended with the hatches battened back down, and order restored. More than his colleagues, Lennon was learning that singing could convey an emotional message of its own, often at odds with the spirit of the words.

Such subtleties were soon proved irrelevant, of course, when 'I Want To Hold Your Hand' became The Beatles' biggest UK hit to date, and also their breakthrough record in the USA. In two ways, it marked a shift between one era and the next. It was the last Beatles A-side for two years that was an obvious Lennon/McCartney collaboration, at the same time as it transformed the role of The Beatles – and indeed Britain – in the world arena.

Finally, 'The Beatles Christmas Record' inaugurated an annual tradition. The Beatles gathered around the Abbey Road microphones with a suitably effusive script prepared by their press agent, Tony Barrow. The band delivered it with the spice of sarcasm ("This is John speaking here, with his voice") and added expletives, before George Martin edited it down into something more tasteful. In itself, it's as irrelevant to the story of Lennon's career as the version of 'Tie Your Kangaroo Down, Sport' which The Beatles recorded with Rolf Harris at the BBC a couple of months later. But his adulteration of the Christmas carol 'Good King Wenceslas', towards the end of the disc, gave Lennon's fans advance warning of what they could expect from his literary efforts in the New Year.

DECEMBER 10, 1963: READING 'The Neville Club'

Backstage at the Doncaster Gaumont, shortly before the night's second Beatles concert, Lennon was interviewed for Australian radio. This commonplace event is only worth noting because Lennon gave his listeners a preview of his first book, by reciting 'The Neville Club' against the distant backdrop of screams. Subsequent readings of his poetry and prose were usually taped in quieter surroundings.

c. JANUARY 1964: WRITING and recording home demos of 'If I Fell'/'Nobody I Know'

A taped message to The Beatles from a group of fans, recorded on New Year's Eve 1963, provided the raw material for Lennon to document the composing process of arguably his most ambitious song to date. More than twenty years later, the tape surfaced in a batch of material committed to auction in London by former Beatles driver Alf Bicknell. It captured a rudimentary but compelling performance from Lennon, his voice stretched to the limit by the uncharacteristic range of the melody. The essentials of the song were already in place, but what was especially intriguing about this tape was that it demonstrated how McCartney would subtly help to revise Lennon's ideas. In this original form, 'If I Fell' was heavily influenced by the melismatic style of Roy Orbison, while instead of the neat ending heard on the record, Lennon drifted into a virtual repeat of the girl-group style of 'Baby It's You'. Once McCartney had helped him remove the most derivative portions of the song, it was ready to be recorded during the group's next batch of sessions.

Also apparently taped around this time was a home demo of 'Nobody I

Know', again sung solo by Lennon, featuring the tune but very few of the words subsequently recorded by Peter & Gordon. This rather trite number was presumably rewritten by McCartney before being handed to the duo, allowing Lennon to shift all responsibility for the song onto his partner in later interviews.

JANUARY/MARCH 1964: THE BEATLES recording 'Komm Gib Mir Deine Hand'/'Sie Liebt Dich'/'Can't Buy Me Love'/'You Can't Do That'/'And I Love Her'/'I Should Have Known Better'/'Tell Me Why'/'If I Fell'/'I'm Happy Just To Dance With You'/'Long Tall Sally'/'I Call Your Name'

1964 was the most prolific year of John Lennon's songwriting career. McCartney had been consistently ahead in terms of quantity from the beginning, though by the second half of 1963 Lennon had begun to rival his output. The Beatles' third album, however, was dominated by Lennon, who also contributed the majority of the new songs for the fourth, also cut before the end of 1964.

What makes this outburst of creativity all the more remarkable is that it was shoehorned into two frantic songwriting binges – one at the start of the year, when The Beatles were on tour in France and then the United States, the other at the end of their world tour that summer. With the prospect of their first motion picture looming, The Beatles – and that meant Lennon and McCartney – were requested to come up with seven new songs. In fact, they wrote 13, which meant that the original idea for the *A Hard Day's Night* album -- that it should include not only the new material but also the older songs featured in the movie – had to be abandoned.

Of the songs on the eventual album, Lennon had the upper hand in the writing of ten. But none of them was ready when The Beatles entered EMI's Pathe Marconi Studios in Paris at the end of January, to record German language versions of 'I Want To Hold Your Hand' and 'She Loves You'. Cut during the same session was 'Can't Buy Me Love', a surprisingly bluesy McCartney solo effort earmarked as their next single

The band's February sessions began by continuing that shift in emphasis. They produced Lennon's 'You Can't Do That' – an unashamedly raw piece of mock-R&B, with John himself playing the fiery bunches of notes which passed for a guitar solo, and suggesting the four-to-the-bar cowbell accompaniment that, as he later acknowledged, came straight off a Wilson Pickett record. An earlier take, preserved on *Anthology 1*, proved that the arrangement was focused from the start of the session.

45

'I Should Have Known Better' was an exercise in craftsmanship, not inspiration, fashioned round a simple two-chord sequence on John's acoustic guitar. 'Tell Me Why' was aptly described by Lennon's 1980 account of its genesis: "They needed another upbeat song and I just knocked it off. It was like a black-New-York-girl-group song."

So that left 'If I Fell' as the session's real keeper. If McCartney had sung it, then no one would have doubted that he had written it – though if he had, he would no doubt have given himself a slightly less painful harmony part in the middle section. On the stereo mix, his voice cracked up completely as the tune reached its height. Lyrically, the song was every bit as ambiguous as later Lennon non-romances like 'Norwegian Wood'. It seemed straightforward enough at the start: Lennon had been hurt before, and wanted reassurance. But as the song progressed, the listener gradually realise that this tender song – for all the world, a ballad of weakness and need – was actually a quest for revenge. McCartney would never have dared to be so unromantic.

The remaining Lennon compositions from this batch of sessions were less weighty. Lennon himself dismissed 'I'm Happy Just To Dance With You' as a throwaway – "I couldn't have sung it," he announced later, in a sly dig at George Harrison, who could. And 'I Call Your Name' was The Quarry Men song updated. Lennon revealed a little about his current musical interests by forcing the band into an approximation of a Jamaican ska rhythm for the guitar solo, something noticeably absent on Billy J. Kramer's version cut the previous year.

FEBRUARY 27, 1964: *MERSEY BEAT* publishes 'The Tales Of Hermit Fred' and 'The Land Of Lunapots'

Barely three weeks before the publication of Lennon's first book, his old friend Bill Harry unearthed a couple of vintage Lennon poems from almost a decade earlier. The source? Apparently it was one of Lennon's school-teachers, who had kept them ever since confiscating them when Lennon was in his mid-teens. Either he was a painfully methodical man, or he had always realised that John was a genius.

Despite Harry's announcement that Lennon had given him permission to print other writings from the same source, this was his last appearance in the pages of *Mersey Beat*. Neither piece cropped up in *In His Own Write*, though Paul McCartney's introduction to that book did allude – inaccurately – to the final line of *Hermit Fred*: "As breathing is my very life to stop I do not dare". The literary origins of this piece of parody ranged from Gilbert and Sullivan's 'A Wandering Minstrel I' from *The Mikado* to

Wordsworth's 'The Leech Gatherer', though quite likely Lennon had neither in mind. But phrases like "I nit spaghetti apple pie" displayed the same manic wordplay as the "semolina pilchard" of 'I Am The Walrus' would in 1967.

'The Land Of Lunapots' was pure nonsense from start to finish – Lear, Carroll and Swift crossed with the native surrealism of Liverpool. But with one of those flights of the imagination that brooked no barriers, the teenage Lennon concluded his nonsense with a line that had a Yeatsian ring: "I who sail the earth in paper yachts".

MARCH 23, 1964: *IN HIS OWN WRITE* published in the UK

The first book by John Lennon – 'the writing Beatle' as he was helpfully credited on the American edition – was a publishing sensation. It topped the best-sellers' lists on both sides of the Atlantic, and the first editions of 50,000 copies in Britain and 90,000 in the United States were soon exhausted. Sales were boosted by a heavy schedule of media interviews, which included the chance for Lennon to read some of the contents on BBC Radio's *The Public Ear* on March 18.

The reviewers were equally enthusiastic – almost to a man. Although questions were asked in the Houses Of Parliament about the scandalous educational system in this country that could have produced such scant regard for standard English usage, most critics took the traditional Johnsonian line and were amazed to find a pop singer who could write. They were quick to place Lennon in a literary line that ran, eternally, from Lear and Carroll through James Joyce to James Thurber. The fact that Lennon pronounced that he had never read Joyce in his life did little to damage their confidence.

In retrospect, *In His Own Write* was scarcely a major work of literature. It was almost impossible to read at a sitting; hard enough, indeed, to take in more than a couple of its short pieces at a time. But it did sparkle with unrestricted imagination – a little short on form and discipline, maybe, but bursting with the enthusiasm of the recently liberated. Lennon himself was uncharacteristically modest about his brainchild; he figured that it might get reviewed alongside the week's new single releases, and could scarcely have imagined that he would turn up in the *Times Literary Supplement*. But he didn't allow his new-found critical credibility to go to his head.

On the evening of publication, Lennon appeared on BBC TV's *Tonight*, where he was interviewed by the critic and commentator Kenneth Allsop. During the course of a conversation in which Lennon mumbled some extracts from the book, Allsop wondered why none of John's fantasy and word–play had figured in his songs. Lennon had never considered the possibility; and though he shrugged off the query with his usual sarcasm, Allsop's remark sank deep.

It had not even been Lennon's idea to publish a book in the first place. He had shown his random scribblings to a friend – possibly Derek Taylor, then The Beatles' PR officer, and later the host of the expansive press division of the Apple empire – who in turn had passed them on to the publishers, Jonathan Cape. In the context of the times, Cape would probably have published Lennon spelling out the alphabet; the fact that the book had some literary standing was an unexpected bonus.

With a contract signed, Lennon set about compiling this first anthology. He asked Bill Harry for copies of the issues of *Mersey Beat* which had contained his early work, while the rest of the text appeared to have been written much more recently, most of it backstage during The Beatles' frantic criss-cross British tours in 1963. Little of the mix of elation and claustrophobia that touring produced actually surfaced in the book; but there were enough personal clues to allow even the most amateur psychologist an insight into the man at work.

Divided roughly a third apiece between prose, poetry and drawings, *In His Own Write* revealed an obsession with violent death – fuelled by the tragic loss of his mother, no doubt, plus the natural ghoulishness of the adolescent male. Family disharmony – another obvious reference to his own life – was another theme of the stories. Husbands murdered wives, or simply disintegrate under their smothering embrace, as in the tale 'Nicely Nicely Clive', which not only revealed a lot about a man himself just beginning a shotgun marriage, but also ended with a husband coming home from sea – just as his own father, the man Lennon dubbed "the ignoble Alf", had done 20 years earlier.

There were many rather negative references to 'jews' in the book's stories, not because Lennon was any more anti-semitic than the rest of the British population, but because 'jew' and 'jewy' were common grammar school insults for at least another decade. But it was possible to trace another general theme that had already been noted in Lennon's college days – his fascination with, and hatred of, cripples and spastics. Linked to the callous cruelty of 'Good Dog Nigel' and 'Randolf's Party' – in which a lonely soul was murdered by his friends on Christmas Day – this presented a picture of the author as sick, the kind of man who collected pictures of corpses and was likely to pass his time pulling the legs off stray animals. Emotionally, however, Lennon was still a teenager; and teenage boys (girls too, for all I know) are apt to be cruel and – in their fantasies at least – violent with it.

What was mildly charming about this aspect of the book was that Lennon seemed to have been quite unaware how revealing it was.

Stylistically, it varied little from the work he had already published. There was the same frantic word-play or invention of a new form of language, the same twisting of sense and sentiment. There were jokes that simply ended before the punch line ('The Wrestling Dog' and 'The Famous Five Through Woenow Abbey'); mild social and political satire ('You Might Well Arsk' and 'All Abord Speeching'); even, ironically enough, an outsider's view of a wild party where the participants were under the influence of such obscene narcotics as 'hernia', 'odeon' and 'hump' ('Neville Club').

A word of warning, though, to me as much as you. When attempting to analyse Lennon's prose, beware the example of Dr James Sauceda – an American professor whose book, *The Literary Lennon*, remains the only comprehensive study of Lennon's prose work. In it he devoted a section to the *In His Own Write* tale, 'The Famous Five Through Woenow Abbey', convinced that the Famous Five in question were, of course, The Beatles and Brian Epstein. As every British reader of a certain age could have told him, the Famous Five were a bunch of teenagers whose adventures were told in a series of fictional books by Enid Blyton – 'Enig Blyter', in Lennon's account, whom the innocent Sauceda assumed must be a travel agent.

These poems and stories should be taken in the spirit in which they were written, as the off-duty scribblings of an over-active brain. They were all restrictively short; Lennon obviously got bored very easily, and killed off his characters as soon as that happened. And the book's artwork was in the same vein – influenced by the shapeless figures found in James Thurber's work, but with an extra twist of Lennon applied, so that human faces were attached to unwieldy, joke-animal bodies, or else were distorted almost beyond humanity. The same hypnotic interest in cripples was repeated in Lennon's drawings – though there was more humour in the pictures, as in the illustration that accompanied 'Randolf's Party'. It showed Neanderthal men, some of them merely balloon heads attached to pieces of string, others boasting Cubist profiles with one eye hovering just outside their faces.

Two illustrations stood out, however. There was the humour of the one that accompanied 'The Famous Five', and which showed the Five (who were actually eight) standing "by the light of their faithful dog Cragesmure", who was brightly luminous. Another untitled sketch of a Lennon-like figure flying through the air evoked one of its artist's wish-fulfilment dreams. Through a haze of manic word-play and a twisting of the real into the surreal, dreams and nightmares made up most of *In His Own Write*. Gradually they would be transferred from Lennon's scribblings into his songs.

CHAPTER 4

April 1964 to September 1965

Little more than a year after they had abandoned the Liverpool club circuit, The Beatles had become global icons. Suddenly, every possible medium of reaching the public was opened up to them – films, television, radio and, in the case of John Lennon, books. There was a cynical commercialism behind the decision to exploit his talents for writing and drawing, but the more opportunities that Lennon was given, the more his creativity surged to fill them. The only problem now was that less than two years after making their first record, all four Beatles were beginning to feel as if their success had tied them to a treadmill. The trick was to sustain their fame without losing their souls.

MARCH/APRIL 1964: THE BEATLES filming *A Hard Day's Night*

Beatlemania was the working title of this project, which had been in preparation since the autumn of 1963. United Artists signed The Beatles to a one-movie contract, and set aside the smallest possible budget for what they saw as merely the latest in a long series of pop exploitation vehicles. There was no point in wasting expensive colour stock on a bunch of here-today, gone-tomorrow pop singers, especially as the original deal was signed before The Beatles' remarkable success in America. And so it was that the most phenomenal pop group of the century was launched onto the big screen with a black-and-white movie filmed more cheaply than any of the quick-buck Elvis Presley features.

Lennon and The Beatles were aware of the pitfalls of the genre. They had watched Presley's decline from *Love Me Tender* to *Fun In Acapulco*, and the generally lamentable series of British pop movies starring the likes of Cliff Richard, Billy Fury and Adam Faith stood as a grim warning of what to avoid. So, as Lennon told *Rolling Stone*'s Jann Wenner in December 1970, "We insisted on having a real writer to write it ... we didn't want to make a fuckin' shitty pop movie."

After a brief meeting, Alun Owen – creator of the TV drama *No Trams To Lime Street*, which had been among the first British television plays to deal with life outside London in a realistic manner – was chosen as scriptwriter, primarily because Lennon and McCartney, and no doubt the culture-conscious Brian Epstein, had seen his work. Lennon later described Owen as "a bit phoney ... a professional Liverpudlian", and slated his script as a caricature of The Beatles' public images. He lamented "the glibness of it, and the shittiness of the dialogue".

And caricature was undoubtedly what Owen produced, with Lennon stereotyped as the unflappable, ever-dominant witty Beatle, always ready with a smart line in put-down or sarcastic humour. Tight-lipped (though certainly not ashen-faced), the screen Lennon exuded menace, sexuality and power, against the cuddliness or sheer naiveté of his Beatle colleagues. It wasn't that Lennon was a great actor; merely that his public image was a classic creation, and one that the movie script did little to subvert. He added a few ad-libs to scenes like the opening footage in the railway carriage, but was mostly content to keep close to a script that rammed home the message the world had already heard: this was a Beatle with a savage bite.

Capturing Beatlemania had been Owen's brief, of course, and despite Lennon's later criticisms, *A Hard Day's Night* proved to be the first pop movie (well, maybe excepting *Expresso Bongo* and *The Girl Can't Help It*) to take pop itself as its theme. Owen's Beatles were simultaneously trapped by and revelling in their stardom, chased to the point of madness by hordes of desirable teenage girls whenever they ventured a nose outside their dressing rooms, yet without ever losing their good humour or matiness. And by combining documentary-style footage with a series of clever set-pieces, director Dick Lester was able to make you believe that what you were seeing was real life – the Beatles off-guard, the four mythical mop tops at work and at play.

Reality, of course, would have been a little harsher and more colourful; instead of Lester, The Beatles might have needed Kenneth Anger or Terry

Southern as their interpreter. *A Hard Day's Night* hinted at sexual tempta-tion, without raising the issue of groupies; but refreshments came no heav-ier than coffee, and sin no greater than failing to answer their fan mail.

Years later, Lennon remembered the filming rather differently: "I was on pills. That's drugs, bigger drugs than pot." Looking back at the movie, it's tempting to say you can see the signs in Lennon's unblinking stare, the speed of his vocal delivery; but then you could say the same for every early press conference or concert. After five years or more of pills on the road, speed had become normality, and an undrugged Lennon might have been rather less attractive to the eye.

In the end, *A Hard Day's Night* worked as entertainment, as the first step towards 'serious' rock films, and as the moving chronicle of a social phe-nomenon. Lennon admitted: "It was a good projection of one facade of us, which was on tour. It was of us in that situation together, in a hotel, having to perform before people. We were like that."

As I've already mentioned, the filming of *A Hard Day's Night* not only slotted in neatly between tours, cutting down on their potential relaxation time; it also necessitated Lennon and McCartney coming up with seven new songs to fill the holes in the script. With McCartney only producing ballads fit for giving away to their friends, the onus fell upon Lennon; not for the last time, he took The Beatles' weight on his own shoulders, and did-n't falter.

APRIL 16, 1964: THE BEATLES recording 'A Hard Day's Night'

If the movie had been called *Beatlemania*, there would probably have been no title song. As it was, Ringo let slip the "hard day's night" malapropism during a sleepy interview after a hard day's filming, and it was Lennon who emerged with a song of the same title the next day. At this stage, the com-petition for such honours was still friendly. McCartney not only didn't mind (he was getting half the writing royalties, after all), but took over the lead vocal for the middle eight when Lennon found his own melody line too tough to sing.

The song opened with a clanging 12-string guitar chord of George Harrison's invention; then in came Lennon's masterful lead vocal, forcing out lyrics that shifted suddenly from exhaustion to relief. The exhaustion was probably real, the relief supplied to satisfy Lennon's own inner longing as much as the expectations of his audience. For the rest of 1964, Lennon's songwriting gradually began to rival the weary satiation of the *Beatles For Sale* album cover.

APRIL 19, 27-28, 1964: THE BEATLES filming *Around The Beatles* TV special; pre-recording 'Twist And Shout'/'Love Me Do-Please Please Me-From Me To You-She Loves You-I Want To Hold Your Hand' (medley)/'I Wanna Be Your Man'/'Can't Buy Me Love'/'Roll Over Beethoven'/'Long Tall Sally'/'Boys'/'Shout'

British television producer Jack Good revolutionised the way in which pop music was presented on the small screen – first in Britain and then as the creator of America's most ambitious music show, *Shindig!* So he was a natural but still brave choice when the Beatles were offered the opportunity of their own hour-long TV special for the ITV commercial station, Rediffusion.

Before the filming began, the group gathered at IBC Studios on April 19, to pre-record the musical soundtrack for the show. In retrospect, it might have been preferable if they had played live in the special. Exactly a week later, they performed at the *NME* Pollwinners' Concert at Wembley and delivered one of the most thrilling performances of their entire career. Their set that day was broadcast on TV, and 'Long Tall Sally' in particular should be seen by anyone who believes that The Beatles were a lightweight live band.

There was certainly an air of chaotic liberation about the IBC sessions for *Around The Beatles*, as if the group relished being in the studio without having to worry about the results. Lennon took a low profile after leading them through 'Twist And Shout' and a strange medley of their early hits. Thereafter he was content to support the featured vocal performances of Harrison, McCartney and Starr, and then take his part in the four-man rendition of The Isley Brothers' 'Shout'.

The day after the *NME* concert, the group reported to Wembley Studios for a dress rehearsal of their special, and then the filming on April 28. Good's background was in classical theatre, and he couldn't resist placing The Beatles in a Shakespearean cockpit of a set, surrounded by male dancers, and hired hecklers, including singer Long John Baldry. Visually, the results were much more exciting than most orthodox TV shows of the era, with The Beatles surrounded and jostled from all sides.

That wasn't the limit of Good's Shakespearean vision. Several years later, he concocted a musical version of *Othello*, entitled *Catch My Soul*, and persuaded one of The Beatles' heroes, Jerry Lee Lewis, to take the leading role. He must have been inspired by the success of the comic sequence in which Lennon, McCartney, Harrison and Starr acted out a scene from *A Midsummer Night's Dream*, interrupting their lines to answer some timely

53

jibes from their audience. In the great tradition of pantomime dames, Lennon played the leading female role of Thisbe, which allowed him some highly camp flirtation with Paul 'Pyramus' McCartney.

JUNE 1/2, 1964: THE BEATLES recording 'Matchbox'/'Slow Down'/'I'll Cry Instead'/'I'll Be Back'/'Any Time At All'/'Things We Said Today'/'When I Get Home'

Two marathon sessions just before The Beatles set out on a world tour saw them complete the new recordings for the *A Hard Day's Night* album; finish their one-and-only original EP, *Long Tall Sally*; and send their drummer to hospital with tonsillitis.

There was no margin for error in these sessions, which made it all the more remarkable that they produced some of The Beatles' most professional recordings of 1964. But the haste at which proceedings were conducted probably explained why Lennon's 'I'll Cry Instead', for example, was taped in two separate sections and then edited together afterwards by George Martin while the band were absent.

'I'll Cry Instead' deserved attention for more profound reasons than that, however. It was the first of a string of 1964/65 Beatles songs that were obviously influenced by country music – or, to be more accurate, by rockabilly. Admittedly, neither 'I'll Cry Instead' nor the later 'I Don't Want To Spoil The Party' had the pace or bite of Carl Perkins or Elvis Presley at their peak. The influence was most apparent in Harrison's lead guitar playing, and in the rhythm work and chord changes evolved by Lennon.

'I'll Cry Instead', unlikely as it may seem, was also an unheralded slice of Lennon autobiography. The sheer admission of weakness was news in itself, but Lennon later saw the middle eight of the song – with its terror of being seen as weak, and desire to hide from the public gaze – as an honest personal statement. It was the corollary of Lennon's screen image, once again. Beatles couldn't be miserable, as that wasn't their role in life; least of all could the macho Lennon be seen to be lonely or misunderstood. The dawn of the self-pitying singer-songwriter was still some way hence; so Lennon could rest assured that his listeners would interpret his cry of emptiness as a metaphor for another teenage romance gone wrong.

Lennon's other three original songs were more interesting for their inspiration than their message. 'I'll Be Back', his self-conscious reworking of an unidentified Del Shannon song, was first attempted as a waltz and then reworked into straight 4/4 time. 'When I Get Home' was R&B-based, like

'You Can't Do That'; and 'Anytime At All' shared a similar influence, with, in Lennon's memorable description, the chords shifting from "C to A minor, C to A minor, with me shouting". All three were supreme examples of hackwork, exhibiting enough Beatles' trademarks to pass muster without ever threatening to be memorable. If they still *were*, after all that, it was down to Lennon's ever more commanding vocal presence, and the group's world-conquering self-confidence.

Since late 1963, when The Beatles discovered the art of double-tracking, Lennon had insisted on recording two parallel vocal lines for almost every song. He had begun to hate the sound of his own voice, so echo was also a necessity – a technique that assumed cavernous proportions in later years. From then on, it was a rarity to hear Lennon single-track his lead vocal, until he felt sufficiently sure of the truthfulness of his writing in the late Sixties to be heard naked. Double-tracking became a standard part of the mid-Sixties Beatles sound, giving them that air of class and ease which most of their beat group contemporaries lacked. But unconsciously or not, it was also – like the blunt wit and harsh demeanour – part of Lennon's defences against the outside world.

JUNE 3, 1964: THE BEATLES recording 'You'll Know What To Do'/'No Reply'/'It's For You'

Ringo Starr's unscheduled absence from the group on this occasion – he collapsed during a morning photo session and was immediately hospitalised until his tonsils could be removed – freed his bandmates to cut demos of their latest songs. While McCartney offered the stylish 'It's For You', intended from the start for Cilla Black, Harrison unveiled his second completed song to date, the almost unbearably trite 'You'll Know What To Do'.

Lennon's offering was also meant as a giveaway, this time to Epstein protégé Tommy Quickly. The three Beatles, with an unidentified drummer in place, romped through a tongue-in-cheek rendition of 'No Reply', which at this stage revealed none of the smoothness apparent when they returned to the song several months later. (Lennon subsequently attended the session at which Quickly recorded the song, and may have contributed percussion to that still-unreleased track.)

This songwriting playtime was preceded by a more serious task: a one-hour rehearsal with drummer Jimmy Nicol, who had been drafted in at short notice as a replacement for Ringo during the first leg of the world tour, scheduled to begin the next day.

55

AUGUST 11/14, 1964: THE BEATLES recording 'Baby's In Black'/'I'm A Loser'/'Mr Moonlight'/'Leave My Kitten Alone'

The most hectic year of John Lennon's life had already seen him record an album, two singles and an EP; make a full-length movie; tour France, America, Europe, Britain, Hong Kong and Australasia; and publish a book. Now, in the brief gap between the end of one tour and the beginning of a full-scale assault on the USA, The Beatles were asked to slot in another two days of recording sessions.

Somewhere between Surrey and Sydney, Lennon and McCartney had found time to begin work on their next album. Two of the songs recorded this month were covers, both starring Lennon; the others were originals. 'Baby's In Black' was one of the last of the true Lennon/McCartney collaborations. As if to highlight the point, the pair shared a microphone on stage whenever they performed this rather old-fashioned and overwritten melodrama, which could easily have been a leftover from The Quarry Men days exhumed to fill a gap in their schedule. Its sole musical novelty was its waltz tempo, which was enough of a throwback to pre-World War Two times to attract attention from pop critics in 1964.

'I'm A Loser' was something else again. It still had its elements of exaggeration, but they were mingled with psychodrama as Lennon used the acoustic guitar/harmonica sound of Bob Dylan to soften the harder edges of his songwriting. Looking back in 1980, Lennon made light of the lyrics: "Part of me suspects I'm a loser, and part of me thinks I'm God almighty." But beneath the cynicism was a grain of truth. Once again, the super-confident Beatle was admitting defeat. The words sounded a little false – "What have I done to deserve such a fate/I realise I have left it too late" was the very essence of adolescent self-pity – but the sentiments were real enough. Lennon couldn't leave the message that bare, however. As on 'Misery' the previous year, the flow of the music, the exhilaration of the chorus, and the sheer enthusiasm of Harrison's Carl Perkins guitar fills told against the sincerity of the song.

Lennon himself was the first to credit Dylan's influence on this song, and several more to come; but the inspiration was less obvious than onlookers might have imagined. By 1964 Dylan was moving away from political protest towards oblique comments on romance, and analysis of his own role as a singer and songwriter. Nothing Dylan wrote that year – except perhaps the overwrought 'Ballad In Plain D' from *Another Side Of Bob Dylan* – was as self-pitying as 'I'm A Loser'. For the moment, the Dylan influence went little further than a guitar, a harmonica and an attitude.

Beside the originals, Lennon used these sessions to record two covers. Dr Feelgood & The Interns' R&B tune, 'Mr Moonlight' boasted a throat-searing Lennon vocal undercut by some uncharacteristically leaden playing by his bandmates. In its finished state, it was as unconvincing a track as The Beatles ever recorded. And then there was Little Willie John's 'Leave My Kitten Alone', familiar to The Beatles through Johnny Preston's poppier cover version. When it first leaked out to collectors, 'Kitten' became an instant legend. It wasn't perfect, as the rhythm section teetered on the edge of chaos, but Lennon's vocal was peerless, as powerful a piece of white R&B/rock 'n' roll as Britain produced in the Sixties. Somehow, 'Mr Moonlight' made the *Beatles For Sale* album, and 'Kitten' was consigned to the vaults – where it officially remained until the release of *Anthology 1* in 1995. Ironically, plans for it to be issued as a nostalgic Beatles single early in 1981 were scuppered by Lennon's death.

SEPTEMBER 19, 1964: OXFAM print Lennon Christmas card

In the wake of the success of *In His Own Write*, Lennon received several requests for illustrations, both from charities and commercial organisations. Oxfam was the only recipient of Lennon's generosity, and a typically spherical robin adorned no less than half a million Christmas cards printed that autumn. Like most of Lennon's drawings, his Oxfam design must have taken all of five minutes to create.

SEPTEMBER/OCTOBER 1964: THE BEATLES recording 'Every Little Thing'/'I Don't Want To Spoil The Party'/'What You're Doing'/'No Reply'/'Eight Days A Week'/'She's A Woman'/'Kansas City; Hey Hey Hey Hey'/'I Feel Fine'/'Mr Moonlight'/'I'll Follow The Sun'/'Everybody's Trying To Be My Baby'/'Rock And Roll Music'/'Words Of Love'/'The Beatles 1964 Christmas Single'

The *Beatles For Sale* album marked the pinnacle of British beat – and the exhaustion of a formula. The cover artwork told its own story: the smiles were gone, replaced by deadpan glares at the camera. In format, the album followed *Please Please Me* and *With The Beatles*, barely outnumbering the cover versions with originals. The Beatles brought a new polish to these recordings; but when the polish thinned, as on 'Mr Moonlight' and 'Everybody's Trying To Be My Baby', the cracks were all too easy to see.

Five days of recording over three weeks saw the album completed, alongside the taping of the band's eighth British single. McCartney filled the B-side, with the playful and amateurish R&B romp, 'She's A Woman' but it was Lennon's assured 'I Feel Fine' which stole the honours. The song was impressive enough in itself, fashioned round a twisting, intricate and almost unplayable guitar riff inspired by Bobby Parker's R&B classic 'Watch Your Step'. (The same source fired the riffs at the heart of songs such as 'Ticket To Ride' and 'Day Tripper'.) The unmistakeable guitar hook first surfaced at an EMI session on October 6, when the group were supposed to be recording 'Eight Days A Week'. But it was overshadowed during the actual 'I Feel Fine' session on October 18 by an opening whine of feedback that baffled radio listeners in 1964. Lennon took great pride in this piece of sonic playfulness, claiming it as rock's first venture into deliberate distortion, and he was probably right. The session tapes prove that, far from being an accident, as EMI announced at the time, the feedback was always meant as the introduction to the song. It was Lennon who not only dragged the sound out of his protesting amplifier but also insisted on re-takes until the howl matched the noise in his head.

That same session saw Lennon and McCartney indulge their latent Buddy Holly fixation on a faithful, note-perfect recreation of 'Words Of Love'. Minutes earlier, Lennon had transformed Chuck Berry's 'Rock And Roll Music' from a novelty R&B tune into a savage rocker that lived up to the defining promise of its title. Like two of the other classic Beatles rockers, 'Twist And Shout' and 'Long Tall Sally', this was a first take. Perfection was still coming easily to Lennon and his companions in 1964.

Earlier in the sessions, Lennon had shown off the fruits of another hurried writing binge. 'Every Little Thing' was a clear collaboration, though Lennon later denied any such thing – but the verse, a simple tale of romance, bears his melodic hallmarks, just as the more orthodox chorus carries McCartney's. Likewise 'Eight Days A Week', which Lennon variously described as "lousy", "Paul's effort at getting a single" and "his initial effort, though I think we both worked on it". Internal evidence suggests they did. It was Lennon, after all, who sang the lead vocal throughout, which almost without exception was a clear sign of ownership. And although the song didn't signify much beyond the cute wordplay of the title, it said nothing with considerable charm.

Lennon's authorship of 'No Reply' and 'I Don't Want To Spoil The Party' was in less doubt. I've already fingered 'Party' as a piece of slowed-down rockabilly in the 'I'll Cry Instead' mould; Lennon apparently associated country music with sadness, which was no doubt the inspiration for the rather tired teen-angst lyric. Lennon's equally drained lead vocal deserved better. 'No Reply' was an altogether more convincing piece of songwriting, despite being one of Lennon's rare excursions into fake story-telling. The American song 'Silhouettes' provided the inspiration, as Lennon recalled: "I had that image of walking down the street and seeing her silhouetted in the window and not answering the phone, although I never called a girl on the phone in my life. Phones weren't part of the English child's life." But the subject was almost incidental alongside the power of the melody, and the effortless confidence of Lennon's vocals – and, to be fair, McCartney's harmony as well. The pair clearly loved singing 'No Reply', as was apparent from the two versions (from June and October) captured on *Anthology 1*. The same artistic confidence, if not always the innocent joy, warmed the whole album.

Back in front of a microphone with a script in their hands for their second Christmas message to their empire of fans, The Beatles sounded less stilted and more sarcastic than they had in 1963. Once again, George Martin was allotted the task of editing out the hesitations and deviations – leaving in Lennon's spirited rendition of an old music hall song about your father's shirt, but deleting his assault on the Louis Armstrong hit 'Hello Dolly', presumably to avoid any copyright wrangles.

NOVEMBER 20 & 29, 1964: APPEARING on *Not Only ... But Also*

The Beatles weren't the first Fab Four of the Sixties who managed to conquer Britain and then America. The four-man Cambridge University comedy troupe who masterminded the West End and Broadway revue hit *Beyond The Fringe* had introduced the world to a new brand of British humour well before The Beatles ever reached New York. Two of that team, Peter Cook and Dudley Moore, were rewarded with their own BBC TV show, *Not Only ... But Also*. Cook's acerbic, satirical humour had much in common with Lennon's, overcoming the vast gulf in their educational and social backgrounds. So the book-writing Beatle was a natural choice of guest for a pre-Christmas edition of the show.

Ironically, Cook and Lennon didn't perform together during the programme. In fact, Lennon was only featured in two scenes. In the first, he recited the autobiographical introduction to his book, 'About The Awful', and then shared a reading of 'All Abord Speeching' with Dudley Moore and his co-star from *A Hard Day's Night*, Norman Rossington. The same trio filmed a mock-silent movie clip, ironically reminiscent of Richard Lester's short, *The Running, Jumping, and Standing Still Film* to accompany another Lennon recital, 'Deaf Ted, Danoota (& Me)'. Meanwhile, the Lennon literary tribute concluded by Moore, Rossington and Lennon reading 'Good Dog Nigel' and 'The Wrestling Dog'.

FEBRUARY 15 TO 20, 1965: THE BEATLES recording 'Ticket To Ride'/'Another Girl'/'I Need You'/'Yes It is'/'The Night Before'/'You Like Me Too Much'/'You've Got To Hide Your Love Away'/'If You've Got Trouble'/'Tell Me What You See'/'You're Going To Lose That Girl'/'That Means A Lot'

In retrospect, it's almost impossible to appreciate the pace at which The Beatles were forced to work between 1963 and 1965. It's certainly not surprising that they cut back their schedule as soon as they had the power to do so. Less than four months after finishing *Beatles For Sale*, and having in the meantime notched up a lengthy British tour and a three-week stint in The Beatles' Christmas Show at the Hammersmith Odeon, they were required back in the studio with another set of original songs, ready for their second motion picture soundtrack.

At this point, no decision had been made about the title of the movie – though this same week producer Walter Shenson leaked details of the film's plot to the US press. In the same interviews, he also put forward his suggestion that it should be called *Eight Arms To Hold You* (weak word-play, presumably, on the international hit 'I Want To Hold Your Hand').

So there was no immediate need for Lennon or McCartney to compete for the honour of writing the movie's title song. What was taped during these sessions was no doubt written with the movie in mind, but without advance knowledge of the plot. It was hackwork, in other words, but it had the potential to be much more than that.

In retrospect, The Beatles' *Help!* album stands as their least inspired – more tired, even, than the bleary-eyed cover of *Beatles For Sale* suggested that album might be. As events later that year revealed, Lennon, McCartney and Harrison were on the verge of an artistic breakthrough; but there was little sign of it here.

Of these 11 songs, no fewer than two – 'I Need You' and 'You Like Me Too Much' – were Harrison compositions, his greatest contribution to a Beatles album to date. McCartney accounted for 'Another Girl', 'The Night Before', 'That Means A Lot', 'Tell Me What You See' and the original inspiration (such as there was) for 'If You've Got Trouble', a Ringo Starr showcase which was left unreleased for 30 years.

That left Lennon with four new compositions on offer: 'Ticket To Ride', 'Yes It Is', 'You're Going To Lose That Girl' and 'You've Got To Hide Your Love Away'. 'You're Going To Lose That Girl' was another in Lennon's tributes to New York girl-group pop, as the response vocals sounded as if they were taken straight off one of John's favourite Shirelles' singles. It was only

The Beatles' new-found production sheen, as on 'No Reply', that concealed the influence. Anyway, Lennon's adaptation of black pop styles was now regarded across the world as Beatlesque. Assumed to be perpetual trend-setters, the group were now treated as if they were the inventors of everything they touched.

Even so, it wasn't hard to trace the links between 'Yes It Is' and 'This Boy', and from there back to American vocal group harmony records by the likes of The Miracles or The Impressions. 'Yes It Is' was, at best, unpolished: even after multiple attempts in the studio, the band's vocal counterpoints were painfully off-key, and George Harrison's early use of a wah-wah pedal was more of a novelty than an innovation in this context. The least said about the Lennon guide vocal that was exposed on *Anthology 2*, meanwhile, the better for his reputation.

'Ticket To Ride' needs no such apology. Lennon later saw it as a proto-type for heavy metal, and certainly its mesh of rhythm guitars was as solid as anything recorded in England up to that point. He wrote the song around one of those R&B-styled riffs he borrowed from Ray Charles or Bobby Parker, which were a hallmark of the band's singles between 1964 and 1966. McCartney added some stinging lead guitar, and a sterling harmony vocal; Ringo began each verse with an expert drum roll; and Lennon himself obliged with another perfectly assured lead vocal, shaped with the dry, laconic, faintly weary air of control that had become his trademark. The result was as weighty as anything The Beatles had recorded to that date, and though 'The Night Before' might have been a more popular choice for radio play, the selection of 'Ticket To Ride' as a stop-gap single was an inspired move.

Finally, there was 'You've Got To Hide Your Love Away' – more acoustic guitar, more self-pity, but this time a recorder where Lennon's harmonica might once have been. The air of despondency was no doubt real enough. But Lennon translated it into a mythical lost romance, and so the lyrics have an air of fantasy that makes them, frankly, ludicrous when separated from the music, and the voice. The initial influence was Dylan, once again; but Lennon had yet to realise that sound and self-pity were not enough in themselves to masquerade as Dylanesque songwriting.

FEBRUARY to MAY 1965: THE BEATLES filming *Help!*

A Hard Day's Night having shattered box office records around the world, The Beatles were permitted the bonus of colour film for their second motion picture. They were also sent on location, first to the Bahamas –

where with the logic known only to the film industry they shot the final sequences of the film, and therefore had to avoid a suntan that would look unrealistic in the early reels. Then they travelled to Austria, with filming at Twickenham Studios tucked in along the way.

Director Dick Lester made the most of the increased budget; as Lennon noted in 1970, some of his comic-book parody sequences were a year or so ahead of the field. But although The Beatles were still nominally playing themselves, the caricatures of the first movie had become little more than cartoons in the second. Ringo Starr had stolen the critical plaudits in *A Hard Day's Night*, for the sequence in which he walked along a river bank kicking a stone. Ringo remembered little about it, as he was nursing a hangover on the day that scene was filmed; but the belief that he was the actor of the four not only won him a solo movie career in the late Sixties/early Seventies, but also made him the plot focus of *Help!*. Loosely, Ringo had a ring (surprisingly enough) which was sacred to the followers of the dreaded god Kaili, and ... well, you can imagine the rest.

As a 1965 comedy, *Help!* stood up well enough. But as a vehicle for The Beatles' meagre acting talents, or a documentary of their progress so far, it was laughable in quite another sense. Lennon described the film in retrospect as "bullshit", and rated The Beatles' roles as being "bit players in our own movie". It's hard to disagree: Ringo's position as sacrificial victim aside, The Beatles had nothing more to do in *Help!* than sound witty and look like Beatles, neither of which stretched their talents to excess.

So the same good humour which pervaded the first movie also hung over the second, though all but staunch Beatles fans were quick to note the decline in quality. Dick Lester made some attempt to place The Beatles' music in context, locating a couple of scenes at far-fetched Beatles' recording sessions (the group always made their records surrounded by Army tanks on Salisbury Plain, of course). But generally the music was as arbitrary and meaningless to the plot as in any other British pop film of the past. Ironically, when The Beatles met Elvis Presley a couple of months later, they berated him for the saccharine nature of his recent films. They were lucky that Elvis and the Colonel hadn't seen *Help!* first.

Backstage, Lennon found co-star Eleanor Bron to be a woman quite capable of matching and countering his own wit and intelligence; he may well have noted the feelings of inferiority and curiosity that this novel experience aroused. More importantly, The Beatles spent time smoking pot. "*Help!* was made on pot," Lennon explained later. "We turned on to pot and dropped drink, simple as that." And back in London, Lennon, Harrison and their respective wives were given their first taste of LSD, unawares. After that, their thinking processes were necessarily changed. *Help!* – the movie, not the song – was the last piece of work by the unselfconscious John Lennon. Pot, and then acid, unlooked a door into a room that he hadn't visited since his childhood. And everything he produced for the next three years stemmed from that trip, and what he saw there.

APRIL 13, 1965: THE BEATLES recording 'Help!'

Aside from an abortive second attempt to cut Paul's still unissued 'That Means A Lot' on March 30, this session was The Beatles' first since they had begun filming. *Eight Arms To Hold You* had been retitled *Help!*, and Lennon and McCartney went away – separately, of course – to write a theme song. As he had done the previous year, Lennon won the race, and so 'Help!' was hurriedly put on tape so that Dick Lester could assemble the film's opening credits. The track was also saved for the band's next single, to be issued (like the soundtrack album) alongside the worldwide release of the film.

'Help!' was commissioned to order, then, which makes it ironic that it was Lennon's most personal song to date. It was also his most naked statement of his lack of direction, his nagging feeling that life as a superstar Beatle might be fun but didn't have a future. On the surface, Lennon was every bit as keen to enjoy the pleasures of the road as the rest of the band: there are no tales of John demurely declining a teenage groupie in favour of a book of verse or a jug of wine. But Lennon the artist – his imagination slowly being unlocked by his use of drugs, and the increasing time which he spent locked away in his music room at home, just thinking or toying with his tape recorder – realised that this wasn't the whole deal. He wasn't going to turn it down, but he had more creative targets in mind.

It would be wrong to suggest that Lennon was alone in his voyage. Harrison was just as enthusiastic in his pursuit of the new and the unknown through drugs, hallucinogenic or otherwise; his mental adventures led him to mysticism, to the spiritual texts of the East. McCartney was far more careful with drugs, though eventually he was the Beatle who went public about their LSD use; but he had cultural ideals of his own. He was beginning to investigate the avant-garde theatre, to build up contacts with gallery owners and writers, actors and classical musicians. Marooned in the Surrey stockbroker belt with a wife and child to keep amused, Lennon was cut off from Harrison's spiritual quest and the bachelor McCartney's delvings into the British underground. So he turned inwards – both in a literal sense, away from his family, and artistically in search of an inner truth.

And in the *Help!* film theme, of all the unlikely places, he found it. In what Lennon came to recognise as his most honest style, the words of 'Help!' were quite straightforward: they said "Help!" without any dressing. Behind the song was the realisation that what once had been natural had become a pose, that behind the superficial glamour of success lay emptiness and confusion, that the older Lennon became, the less he understood. (Or, as Harrison put it in an adaptation of a spiritual text on 'The Inner Light' in 1968, "The farther one travels, the less one knows".)

"Instead of projecting myself into a situation, I would try to express what I felt about myself, as I'd done in my books," Lennon explained a few years later about the birth of his personal songwriting. "I think it was Dylan that helped me realise that: I had a professional songwriter's attitude towards songwriting. To express myself, I would write *Spaniard In The Works* or *In His Own Write*, the personal stories which were expressive of my personal emotions. I'd have a separate songwriting John Lennon who wrote songs for the meat market, and I didn't consider them to have any depth at all. Then I started not writing them objectively, but subjectively."

A decade later, Lennon described the song more succinctly: "I was fat and depressed, and I was crying out for help." But being a commercial songwriter with a hit record to make, Lennon allowed 'Help!' to become arranged as a rock'n'roll song. It's one of the fastest records that The Beatles cut in the mid-Sixties, and the beat effectively obscured the message. Anyway, no one was yet listening to Beatles singles for their autobiographical content, any more than they thought that Mick Jagger's contemporaneous cry of '(I Can't Get No) Satisfaction' had any basis in fact. That's why none of The Beatles' aides recalled him voicing the hidden message of the song at the time. Songwriters were supposed to write about love, in a way with which others could identify. Not even Lennon himself had realised that 'I'm A Loser', 'You've Got To Hide Your Love Away' and 'Help!' constituted anything more than three more steps towards another wall of gold discs.

MAY 10, 1965: THE BEATLES recording 'Dizzy Miss Lizzy'/'Bad Boy'

In a rare piece of complete self-indulgence, The Beatles recorded two of their final cover versions to fill up a forthcoming American LP. Used to seeing their work butchered by their US label, Capitol, they thought nothing of knocking off a couple of exuberant rockers for Stateside release. The outcry from British fans when it was announced that the tracks wouldn't be issued in the UK forced Parlophone to include 'Dizzy Miss Lizzy' on the

Help! LP and 'Bad Boy' as the sole titbit for long-term fans on the 1966 compilation album, *A Collection Of Beatles Oldies*.

The purpose may have been cynical, but Lennon no doubt relished two cracks at the work of one of his favourite fifties rock'n'rollers, Larry Williams. On 'Dizzy Miss Lizzy', the group accentuated the rhythm of the original record, and Lennon made up for some rather hollow instrumental work with a rasping lead vocal. The transformation of 'Bad Boy' was much more dramatic. Lennon clearly relished both the personal reference in the title, and the blatant Americanisms in the lyric. Despite another rather lack-lustre performance from the group's usually reliable rhythm section, the track remains one of the classic Beatles rockers, with a refreshing lack of side that none of their own attempts at the same formula could match.

It was a strange mental journey from a meaningless session at Abbey Road to the notorious stately home of Cliveden, where The Beatles were due to film another scene for *Help!*. There to document proceedings was another client of Brian Epstein's management stable, photographer Bob Whitaker. He'd been assigned the job of creating artistic shots of The Beatles, rather than the bland showbiz portraits proposed by most mid-Sixties photographers. Whitaker had a keen interest in surrealism, dada and pop art, which he used to place these ultimate icons of youth culture into unexpected and sometimes shocking visual situations. It was at Cliveden that he and Lennon discovered that they could communicate with each other on a level deeper than the normal Beatles chit-chat. Whitaker pro-vided Lennon with the kind of intellectual and artistic stimulation that Paul McCartney had been getting from London's avant-garde pioneers. This ensured that Lennon was ready to go along with Whitaker's more unortho-dox ideas – such as the so-called 'butcher' cover for the *Yesterday And Today* album that would stoke some controversy the following year.

JUNE 1965: THE BEATLES recording 'I've Just Seen A Face'/'I'm Down'/'Yesterday'/'It's Only Love'/'Act Naturally'

In three more days of sessions, after the end of filming and just before a European tour, The Beatles completed the *Help!* album. With both 'That Means A Lot' and 'If You've Got Trouble' having been rejected, the projected album was light on McCartney songs; but he filled the gap with ease, recording 'I've Just Seen A Face', 'I'm Down' and 'Yesterday' in the same remarkable session. Lennon chose not to compete, offering the folkie, vaguely Dylanesque 'It's Only Love' as his sole contribution at these record-ing dates. Judging by the way in which he talked about it later, dismissing it as "a lousy song . . . the lyrics were abysmal", this was hardly a labour of love, merely another day in the life of the trained songsmith.

JUNE 24, 1965: JONATHAN CAPE publish *A Spaniard In The Works*

Lennon book number one was written for fun; number two to fulfil a contract. The publishers obviously had no qualms about overstretching their author: his original deadline for the book was Christmas 1964, which he missed handsomely. The early months of 1965 saw him briefly considering a spoken-word album of readings from this book-in-progress, and from *In His Own Write*; plus, more humorously, a proposed book of erotica composed with Gerry Marsden of The Pacemakers. Brian Epstein would no doubt have blanched if that one had been published.

Instead, Lennon set himself to work to write *A Spaniard In The Works*, published to rather less critical applause than his first book, and proportionally fewer sales as well. "I wrote it with a bottle of Johnnie Walker," Lennon recalled in 1980. "Once it became, 'We want another book from you, Mr Lennon', I could only loosen up to it with a bottle of Johnnie Walker, and I thought, if it takes a bottle every night to get me to write . . . that's why I didn't write any more." Well, more or less, as we'll see later.

I'd love to know how many people actually read Lennon's books, rather than dipping into the stories, admiring the word-play, and moving on to less taxing fare. Parts of *Spaniard* were literally unreadable without a large bottle of Johnnie Walker, which probably figured. The mixed metaphors, shifts of (non)sense and provocative wit of the first book had mutated into something closer to gobbledegook in *Spaniard*, while the increased length of the prose offerings – which each seemed to represent an evening's writing, flat-out, ending only *in medias res* when the author lost interest – was not exactly conducive to reader participation.

But the book had its moments. For example, there was the wry political satire of 'Cassandle', a sarcastic parody of a popular British newspaper columnist; and the blatant cynicism of 'The General Erection' (obviously written in October 1964), in which the country's leading politicians were lampooned as 'Sir Alice Doubtless-Whom', 'Harassed Wilsod' and 'Joke Grimmace', and the whole pack aptly dismissed as 'the mentals of parliament'. The visuals which accompanied this piece showed, respectively, two blind men putting crosses on voting papers they couldn't see; two identical men (the bastions of left and right) in a pointless argument; and what was presumably Mrs Mary Wilson, the wife of the man who became Prime Minister at that election, naked and casting her vote down the lavatory.

In a similar vein, Lennon attacked the fake respectability of the church in 'I Believe, Boot ...' – where the reference to 'St. Alf' must have been an obscure shot at Lennon's wandering father – and threw in a cartoon in which a vicar couldn't help looking admiringly at the bare bodies of Adam and Eve. There were also some delightful visual puns to accompany the silly poem, 'The National Health Cow', and also on the "I am blind/I can see quite clearly" cartoon spread. Elsewhere, you could read what you liked into the fact that the character known as 'Snore-Wife' looked a little like John's wife Cynthia; or that 'Araminta Ditch' in the story of the same name was drawn as if she was an untamed, hirsute maneater. Trivia freaks could also note that the 'dwarves' in the 'Snore-Wife' story have three pairs of spectacles, just like John on the cover of *Walls And Bridges* in 1974.

But the rest didn't really bear too much attention. Poems like 'The Faulty Bagnose' and 'Bernice's Sheep' can have meant little to anyone apart from their author; while the lengthy title story and the Sherlock Holmes pastiche might have been funnier as straight parodies, without the interruption of endless wordplay. The fact that the Holmes piece ends with an anti-climax was either a cunning piece of narrative subversion, or else sheer exhaustion on the part of its author.

A Spaniard In The Works also had far fewer personal references than Lennon's first volume. Perhaps he realised how much he had given away in *In His Own Write*. Second time around, nothing seemed to have much relevance to anything, and Lennon was getting better at hiding his feelings, except when he wanted to show them off. Despite what he later said in interviews, there was far more of the real John Lennon in the mock-confessional songs of late 1964 and early 1965 than in the written-to-contract verbal slapstick of *Spaniard*. With the manuscript delivered, however, Lennon duly signed a contract for a third book – due to be completed by February 1966.

As with *In His Own Write*, Lennon made several media appearances to promote the book. On June 16, he read 'Fat Budgie' and 'National Health Cow' on BBC radio shows. Two days later, he treated viewers of BBC TV's *Tonight* show to 'General Erection' and 'Wumberlog'.

SUMMER 1965: DESIGNING 'The Magic Eye'

Lennon designed mosaics for two Beatle swimming-pools in the mid-Sixties. George Harrison's pool was decorated with a hugely enlarged reproduction of one of Lennon's cartoons from *In His Own Write*. For his own pool at his Kenwood home, however, Lennon drew 'The Magic Eye', a giant colourful eyeball of apparently mystical significance. His original design has not survived, but the 17,000 pieces of ceramic that made up the five-metre by two-metre mosaic were restored and exhibited in 2002. Reporters noted the influence of the Maharishi Mahesh Yogi's spiritual teachings on Lennon in the Sixties, but neglected to point out that the two men didn't meet until 1967, although John had embraced Eastern philosophies with 'Tomorrow Never Knows' the year before.

SEPTEMBER 9, 1965: PRODUCING The Silkie

In March 1965, Beatles manager Brian Epstein signed a group of university students from Yorkshire to his stable. The quartet were folksingers with a penchant for the work of Bob Dylan, an album of whose work they promptly issued at the end of the year. Initially Epstein approached Lennon and McCartney in the hope that they might donate a song for his new protégés. When it wasn't forthcoming, he bribed them into spending an afternoon in the recording studio producing The Silkie's version of John's Dylan-esque ballad, 'You've Got To Hide Your Love Away'.

In fact, it appears that John was nominally the producer of the session, with Paul (and George Harrison) physically down in the studio with the group, sharpening their arrangement and trying to dispel their nerves. The result was a slightly rough, atonal essay at the song, which lacked not only the blatant self-pity of Lennon's original version, but also its emotion. The novelty of the Beatle connection was still enough to ensure it became a minor hit in Britain, and a more substantial success in the States, where it also served as the title cut of the group's album.

CHAPTER 5

October 1965 to August 1966

On the surface, John Lennon was one of the most fortunate men on the planet in late 1965. Being a Beatle occupied much of his time and attention, although the group had chosen to relax their schedule after the mania of 1963 and 1964. In private, however, alone in his Surrey mansion, Lennon was becoming increasingly convinced that his fame was both essential to his well-being – and utterly meaningless. He sought salvation in endless gadgets and rich man's toys – and in the mind-opening, care-banishing haze of soft drugs. For the next year, Lennon treated his creativity like a chemical experiment, altering the dose and documenting the results with bemused fascination.

OCTOBER 12 to NOVEMBER 11, 1965: THE BEATLES recording 'Run For Your Life'/'Norwegian Wood (This Bird Has Flown)'/'Drive My Car'/'Day Tripper'/'If I Needed Someone'/'In My Life'/'We Can Work It Out'/'Nowhere Man'/'I'm Looking Through You'/'Michelle'/'What Goes On'/'12-Bar Original'/'Think For Yourself/'The Word'/'You Won't See Me'/'Girl'/'Wait'

Few months in recording history have ever been as productive. Once again, however, creativity was being squeezed out of The Beatles, not coaxed. Their timetable since the end of filming in June had seen them finish work on the *Help!* soundtrack, undertake a European tour, and then set out on a rather more extensive jaunt across the United States. A British tour was booked for December; there was the prospect of the third Beatles film, based on Richard Condon's western novel, *A Talent For Loving*, which was slated for early shooting in November, and all the while John had a February 1966 deadline for his next book to consider in the small hours.

Meanwhile, The Beatles' own aims had altered. They were no longer content to record an album at (as against on) speed, cranking out one near-perfect take after another. They had not yet discovered all the sonic potential of the studio, and the majority of these recordings featured the standard Beatles' line-up of guitars, bass, drums and an occasional keyboard. But in keeping with the songs they were writing, the group were intent upon perfection. February 1963 had seen them attempting eleven songs in a single day; now one or at most two was considered ample.

This more relaxed – in theory, at least – schedule allowed them a little tantalising time to think about what they were doing. And conscious thought was the ingredient that these songs possessed, which had not always been apparent in their predecessors. On occasion, the whirring of The Beatles' minds was all too apparent on *Rubber Soul*: for the first time, they once or twice erred on the side of pretension rather than simplicity. But most of the album has the stunning clarity of a group of performers who have chanced upon a higher level of self-expression, and have not had time enough to question its source.

Rubber Soul was certainly the first Beatles *album* – as against a mere collection of songs or, as on *Please Please Me* and *With The Beatles*, a rough representation of their stage shows. In 1965, only one other recording artist – the phenomenally prolific Bob Dylan – was using the long-playing record as anything more than an extended single. His first all-electric album, *Highway 61 Revisited*, had shattered the boundaries of what was feasible inside the popular song. 'Desolation Row' extended the linear possibilities; 'Just Like Tom Thumb's Blues', or 'Tombstone Blues', or 'Ballad Of A Thin Man', had demonstrated what could be done with the poetic vision of Allen Ginsberg, a dose of amphetamines and a willingness to speak (however obliquely) from the heart. And 'Like A Rolling Stone' translated all of that invention and daring into a hit single that threatened to become the national anthem of this generation of youth culture.

By comparison with what Dylan was creating in 1965, *Rubber Soul* was a comparatively modest effort, though none the less impressive for that. Lennon, McCartney and the blossoming Harrison did manage, for the moment, to resist the temptation to echo Dylan's wordplay and high-speed imagery: the combination of Lennon's acid wit and the scattershot verbiage of *A Spaniard In The Works* would have to wait for 'I Am The Walrus'.

But The Beatles' sixth album did shine with personal statements. Even on the previous album, Lennon and McCartney had been content to compose imaginary tales of romance about imaginary people called 'you' and 'me'. Now they were laying themselves bare for the world to see. McCartney had a fight with Jane Asher: you could find out how he felt by listening to 'I'm Looking Through You'. Harrison was discovering that his closest companions were not always equipped for the spiritual journeys he was making: he used 'Think For Yourself' to force the point home.

As ever, Lennon was at once the most honest, and the most evasive. The emotional force of his writing was unmistakable, however, and that's what helped lift 'In My Life', 'Norwegian Wood' and 'Girl' to their status as three of his most popular songs.

The *Rubber Soul* sessions began, however, with a much less weighty Lennon tune. Its author always dismissed 'Run For Your Life' as a petty trifle – "a throwaway song that I never thought much of". And as Lennon was the first to admit, it was enough of a throwaway to 'borrow' a line from 'Baby Let's Play House', the A-side of Elvis Presley's fourth single for Sun Records in 1955 (and a song performed by Lennon in summer 1957). That performance marked Presley's realisation of his own sexual potency as a rock'n'roll singer; when Elvis played house, he wasn't talking about cooking breakfast.

The line that Lennon borrowed – "I'd rather see you dead, little girl, than to be with another man" – became less a threat than a petulant sneer in an overt attempt to cut short 'his' woman's independence. As some of the more basic sections of *In His Own Write* had already revealed, Lennon gave most away when he wasn't concentrating. The lyrics to 'Run For Your Life' showed every sign of having been knocked off in five minutes: the verse that begins "Let this be a sermon" is as weak and anti-climactic as anything he ever wrote. But these hurried lines are the clearest indication we have in song of what the pre-feminist (or at least pre-Yoko) Lennon was like. Though he felt self-pity because no one understood him, it was clear that few women were ever offered the chance. As Lennon proudly announced in several Beatles interviews, "Women should be obscene and not heard." As the target for groupies the world over, Lennon regularly had his blindest prejudices confirmed. His comeuppance at the hands of A Strong Woman was several years away.

Or then perhaps not. Recorded on the same day as 'Run For Your Life' was an early version of 'This Bird Has Flown', which was retitled

'Norwegian Wood' on *Rubber Soul*. Begun while The Beatles were on a ski-ing holiday with George Martin earlier in the year, the song alluded to one of Lennon's more meaningful extra-marital liaisons. "I was very careful and paranoid because I didn't want my wife, Cynthia, to know that there really was something going on outside of the household," Lennon explained in 1980, "so I was trying to be sophisticated in writing about an affair." What made the song unusual was that Lennon wasn't in control of the tryst; he ended up in the bath, fucked and forgotten just as crudely as any of the teenagers that The Beatles had enticed into their beds on tour. For once, Lennon was aware of the irony: "I once had a girl/Or should I say/She once had me".

On autobiographical terms, then, 'Norwegian Wood' was a fascinating song. What made it a work of art, and Lennon's most satisfying composition to date, was the combination of words and music. Partly it was the way that John told the story by omitting the action; we could see the bath, the bed, the Norwegian wood, and those details helped us to imagine the rest. And for the first time, Lennon was able to use the folk guitar style of Bob Dylan to evoke something more than self-pity. Hinting at the strangeness of the experience, he allowed George Harrison to play a simple sitar line alongside his own acoustic guitar riff – one of the first occasions that the instrument had appeared on a rock record, and certainly the most influential.

The Beatles had two separate attempts at recording the song; it's the second that ended up on the record. The first (released in 1995 on *Anthology 2*) shared a similar arrangement, though Harrison's sitar was double-tracked throughout, and also echoed Lennon's vocal melody at the end of each line far more clearly than on the more familiar arrangement. The difference, though, was in the atmosphere. Version One had a slightly more ethereal feel – finger-cymbals and bells giving it more of the (imaginary) authentic flavour of the Orient. But Lennon's vocal was (emotionally, not technically) flat – 'dead' might be a more precise term. Version Two, the one that appeared on *Rubber Soul*, at least suggested that he had survived to learn from his experience. The original sounded like a slow moan of despair.

No such dramas surrounded the next song on the schedule, 'Drive My Car'. The impetus here was McCartney's, but it was Lennon who supplied the crucial metaphor, offering the blatantly sexual title line in place of Paul's much more juvenile "wear my ring". He also supplied some fine vocal har-monies – The Beatles' impeccable abilities as harmony singers are all too rarely mentioned – and helped to strip down the arrangement, influenced by Otis Redding's 'Respect' – to rock'n'roll basics.

Bobby Parker's 'Watch Your Step' guitar riff, which had already fuelled 'I

Feel Fine' and 'Ticket To Ride', re-emerged in another revamped form on 'Day Tripper', already selected as one half of the double A-sided single that was issued simultaneously with the LP. (Lennon reacted strongly when EMI, following Brian Epstein's advice, announced that 'Day Tripper' was actually the B-side of 'We Can Work It Out'. A few hours later, the two songs were back on equal footing.)

As on 'A Hard Day's Night', McCartney took much of the lead vocal spotlight, hitting notes that were beyond Lennon's more limited range. But as John made clear in his 1980 interview with David Sheff, the song was his – "including the lick, the guitar break and the whole bit. It's just a rock'n'roll song." The concept of the day tripper was all too familiar to British holiday-makers, but needed some explanation for American listeners, who in later years were quick to equate the trip with drug experimentation. More to the point, however, did John really write "She's a prick teaser" in his original lyric, as legend suggests? McCartney did his best with the line to make it seem he did, though the handwritten lyric sheet from which he was work-ing was more discreet. The finished record was raucous and yet not out of control – just like the best American R&B records that inspired it. Otis Redding made the song's origins perfectly clear with his later cover version, while Lennon even incorporated a mock 'Twist And Shout' build-up into the guitar break as a nod to his black mentors.

Two days later, after prolonged work on the three-part harmonies of Harrison's 'If I Needed Someone', The Beatles arrived at what proved to be the most durable song from these sessions – Lennon's 'In My Life'. In the wake of his murder in 1980, the song took on an almost unbearable poignancy, with Lennon's own admission of loss suddenly assuming a much wider significance. 'Imagine' aside, it is now arguably his most popular com-position.

In its original form, however, 'In My Life' was far less universal in its appeal. Back in mid-1964, you'll remember, interviewer Kenneth Allsop had suggested to Lennon that he should combine his literary imagination with his musical skill. A year later, under the influence of Bob Dylan and soft drugs, Lennon was ready to take the suggestion to heart. When it came to writing this song, as he recalled in 1980, "I had a complete set of lyrics after struggling with a journalistic version of a trip from home to down-town on a bus naming every sight."

Lennon's original manuscript for the song revealed, in fact, that the even-tual first verse – a simple elegy to the past – was intact from the start. What followed was not quite as precise: "Penny Lane is one I'm missing/Up Church Road to the Clock Tower/In the circle of the Abbey/I have seen some happy hours/Past the Tramsheds with no trams/On the five bus into town/Past the Dutch and St. Columbus/To the Dockers Umbrella that they pulled down." Brian Wilson of The Beach Boys might have been able to pull off the 'this-is-how-you-get-to-my-house' trick on 'Busy Doin' Nothing' three years later, but Lennon's day tripper's guide to suburban Liverpool could hardly have been turned into a public song, even if he could have made the verses scan. This early draft is really only valuable for the hint that it was Lennon, not McCartney, who first thought of translating the familiar location of Penny Lane into a song.

John knew from the start that this approach was a road to nowhere: "But then I laid back and these lyrics started coming to me about the places I remember." McCartney helped structure the middle eight, preventing the song from turning into an endless succession of identical verses; and one of Lennon's all-time classics was eventually delivered.

In its final state, what had been a dewy-eyed remembrance of the past became a tribute to the healing powers of romantic love. The mixed emotions of the past survived, but they were soothed by the presence of a lover. The key line was "These memories lose their meaning/When I think of love as something new". For the moment, something new was still a fantasy. When it became a reality, Lennon's break from the past was inevitable.

With one essay in understanding under their belts, The Beatles began work on another: 'We Can Work It Out'. The basic song here was McCartney's, a plea for tolerance and common sense, as long as the girl involved agreed with him: "try to see it my way". It was Lennon who emerged as the more conciliatory: "Life is very short, and there's no time for fussing and fighting".

The same combination of McCartney melody and Lennon lyricism helped complete another memorable Beatles recording, 'Michelle'. The concept was McCartney's from the start: another love song to a non-existent woman. It was Lennon who brought things back to basics, with a middle section that cut through the French lyrics and simply said "I love you". He later credited a Nina Simone song as his inspiration for the phrase.

Further collaborations resulted in the updating of 'What Goes On', a Lennon country rocker originally composed in the late Fifties, toyed with in 1963 as a possible contender for a single, and now revamped to give Ringo Starr his token vocal showcase on the album. The additional verses composed for this session included one memorable, meaningless couplet: "I met you in the morning/Waiting for the tides of time". Maybe that was what qualified Ringo for his composing credit on the song (some sources say he thought of the title), alongside Lennon and McCartney.

On the same day that they recorded 'What Goes On', The Beatles also attempted their first serious instrumental since 'Cry For A Shadow' in 1961. '12-Bar Original' was a four-man composition, firmly in the style of the British R&B boom; it was obviously the source of the long-held rumour that there was meant to be a *Rubber Soul* title track. The music matched that brand of inauthenticity perfectly: though George Harrison's experimental lead guitar work was fiery enough, it was the rhythm section, plodding along behind, which sabotaged any ideas that The Beatles might have had of rivalling John Mayall's band in the blueswailing stakes. Even when the track was released on the outtakes collection *Anthology 2*, it had to be chopped down to less than half its original length to make it bearable. Lennon's contribution to the piece was a Ray Charles-style rhythm guitar riff, which towards the end started to sound more like Carl Perkins and nothing like anyone's definition of soul.

Elsewhere on *Rubber Soul*, The Beatles showed clear signs of reflecting other recent developments in rock music. George Harrison's 'If I Needed Someone' was a clear nod to the folk-rock of The Byrds, and their intricate 12-string guitar patterns also seem to have inspired the instrumental work on Lennon's 'Nowhere Man', with some more traditional Beatles rockabilly thrown in during the guitar solo.

'Nowhere Man' was also powered by some gorgeous three–part harmonies; it flowed as smoothly as anything Lennon had written to date. On first hearing, though, its blend of social comment and finger-pointing sounded cynical, even callous – as if we were being invited to mock some outcast from the norms of hip society, without any of the affection that, say, Ray Davies would bring to a similar subject in 'Mr Pleasant'. Read the lyrics again, however, and it became obvious that Lennon had one specific target in mind as the 'Nowhere Man' – himself. In this context, the song looked ahead to 'I'm Only Sleeping' the following year, or even 15 years ahead to 'Watching The Wheels', in its portrayal of the author as a feckless dreamer, content to live in a fantasy world rather than worrying about the trials of everyday life. It was an indulgence that Lennon, in his Surrey mansion, found easier to make than most.

As October became November, and The Beatles demanded time for remakes of songs cut earlier in the *Rubber Soul* sessions, the pressures on them intensified. To their credit, they didn't fall back on their past remedy, by delving into their bag of R&B singles for some suitable American songs to cover; they simply went away and wrote some more. The final days of the session saw Paul emerge with 'You Won't See Me', George Martin dust down the *Help!* era tape box for McCartney's 'Wait', which was overdubbed to bring it up to date, and Lennon bring in two new songs for consideration, 'The Word' and 'Girl'.

Though it is Harrison who is usually pegged as The Beatles' resident mystic, it was Lennon who first put their spiritual discoveries into song; and being Lennon, he kept the ideas simple so that no one could miss the point. McCartney helped him finish the piece in the studio, but the framework was already intact, and 'The Word' was Love. The words, meanwhile, displayed a little breathlessness – "Everywhere I go I hear it said/In the good and the bad books that I have read" mightn't have survived a lyrical revision – and the musical setting for Lennon's lesson was simple three-chord R&B. But this time the message was more important than the medium: 'The Word' reflected The Beatles' discovery that smoking enough pot made everything much simpler. Lennon was always apt to reduce complicated issues into a slogan: here, for the first time, was the public announcement that all you needed was love.

What made 'Girl' so staggering a piece of work was the speed with which it was written – and the fact that none of that haste was betrayed in the song. 'Girl' had the lazy tempo and feel of a narcotic haze, but the woman in question was unsettling enough to shock Lennon out of his reverie. Looking back from another country, Lennon decided that the song showed him "writing about this dream girl again – the one that hadn't come yet. It was Yoko." That implied that the song was a simple statement of longing – or else that his relationship with Yoko was as difficult as the one in the song. This was no fairy-tale romance behind his wife's back; like 'Norwegian Wood', 'Girl' was a song of incomprehension, of bafflement that a woman could be stronger than himself. Only by idealising her as The Girl could Lennon relate to her, and try to ignore the stigma of her blatant superiority.

The final verse of the song, though, moved matters into a different dimension. 'Was she told when she was young that pain would lead to pleasure?' Lennon asked in an apparent sideswipe at Catholic teaching, 'Will she still believe it when he's dead?' And all the while Lennon undercut the seriousness of the song with his heavy breathing during the chorus, and the 'tit tit tit' backing chorale in the middle eight.

Both 'Norwegian Wood' and 'Girl' showed that Lennon was becoming aware – at last – of the complexity of human relationships. He was still seeing love as a powerplay: either the woman would run for her life, or leave him in the bath to contemplate his nature. But while McCartney continued to idealise love, even when it was going wrong, Lennon's increasingly realistic attitude – and the insight that gave him into the state of his own marriage – meant that for the next two years, he scarcely wrote about romantic relationships at all.

And if the standard refuge of marriage or sex wasn't working, then Lennon would have to look elsewhere for his salvation, or his key to the mystery. Here began a search that dominated Lennon's work for the rest of the decade: the quest for a system that would validate or excuse his feelings of confusion and longing; for a panacea that would take away the pain; and for a relationship that could take this complexity on board and channel it into creativity. The adventure was to lead him through drugs, primal therapy, meditation and religion, with each step of the way a response to the surprising changes that the next few years would bring to his private life. And in searching for a personal way out, Lennon – a born advertiser – couldn't help but try to steer the world in his own direction.

DECEMBER 1965: *McCALL'S* publishes 'The Toy Boy'

In the rush to complete *Rubber Soul*, and then begin a British tour, Lennon had scant opportunity to work on the third book of poems and prose which he had been contracted to produce for Jonathan Cape by February 1966. That deadline came and went with Lennon admitting that he had composed only one piece; and by the summer of that year, plans to complete the book were dropped.

The poem which Lennon did complete wasn't wasted, however: it was sold to the American magazine *McCall's* in the autumn of 1965, and duly appeared in their December 1965 issue, tucked midway through the magazine without any cover-line to attract potential readers. What marked this piece out from the verse in *In His Own Write* and *A Spaniard In The Works* was both its length, and its lack of the extremely dense wordplay which had become a Lennon trademark. The poem told the story of a boy and his toys, each of whom doubted the other's existence. The toys debated the question at night, the boy in the daytime. That was enough to have him certified insane by a psychiatrist.

On the surface, it was a typical piece of Lennon whimsy, with a cruel twist in the tale. But you didn't have to be more than an amateur psychologist to draw the links between the boy who saw visions and was thought to be mad, and the Beatle who admitted in later years that he had been blessed with surrealistic visions from an early age. Just as Lennon would lash out at his Aunt Mimi in his 1970 *Rolling Stone* interview, for destroying his poetry and drawings when he was a child, so he used the boy in this poem as a symbol of his own alienation. And he added a tongue-in-cheek poke at the pretensions of artists, himself included: "He was an artiste, so you see – He didn't like to chime for free!"

Why didn't Lennon finish his third book? There are many possible reasons. They include lack of time; simple boredom with having to create humorous stories for a public who didn't seem to be reading them, merely buying them; and, most probable of all, the fact that the shifting boundaries of rock songwriting now permitted Lennon to write more or less honestly about his feelings in his lyrics. Not only had Dylan introduced the dubious concept of 'poetry' into rock; Lennon had also found out how to connect himself overtly to his songwriting, without use of the subterfuge, mixed metaphors and Freudian imagery of his prose work.

At the same time, Lennon was experimenting more seriously with hallucinogenic drugs, which affected almost everything he wrote for the next 12 months. The unreal worlds he had conjured in his prose were now assuming everyday reality: what mattered was not to relive them on the page, but to make sense of what he had seen on his trips, to relate it back to the self he had left behind. And Lennon chose to use the stripped down form of songwriting to express these vague, shifting feelings, rather than the more fixed medium of prose. Coupled with The Beatles' musical adventures, his songwriting became a three-dimensional foray into the unknown, where the LSD visions of his private life could be recaptured in words and – more importantly – in sound.

MARCH 1966: RECORDING 'He Said He Said"

International fame had its undoubted advantages, and one of them was that The Beatles could buy whatever gadgetry and luxuries they wanted. Ringo Starr graduated towards film, and photography; during 1964 there was serious talk of a book of his portraits and tour snaps being published in the States, as a rival to *In His Own Write*. Lennon, McCartney and Harrison all bought cameras, too, but their major indulgence when it came to artistic home improvements was in the field of home recording.

By late 1965, all three Beatles had established well-equipped music rooms in their houses, where they began to tape home demos of their latest compositions as a basis for the rest of the band to work from. Lennon's studio in his Weybridge home was stocked with a bank of five tape recorders, allowing him as much freedom to multi-dub as most professional studios in Britain (although not, as yet, the freedom from ambient noise, such as the telephone and passing children and cats). Besides the expected guitars and

78

keyboards, John had also bought violins, saxophones, and a variety of percussive instruments.

Both he and McCartney were beginning to experiment with the concept of sound itself. McCartney's adventures in the British underground movement had already introduced him to the noise-as-music sonic playfulness of Cornelius Cardew and the avant-garde group AMM. He was also listening to the electronic compositions of Karl-Heinz Stockhausen, and delving into the more conceptual work of John Cage. In early spring 1966, he bought his own substantial home in London's St. John's Wood, and was soon inviting Lennon there to check out his latest musical discoveries.

McCartney was certainly several steps ahead of his songwriting partner in 1966 when it came to exploring new avenues of sound. He schooled Lennon in a variety of techniques and tricks: he demonstrated the potential of tape loops as a source of pure noise, and showed him how to record a piece of music and then run it backwards through one recorder while taping it on a second.

Stirred into action by his partner's enthusiasm, Lennon launched himself into this new medium. For the moment, though, he kept the results of his experiments away from the public ear. Only close friends and Beatles ever got to hear most of what he taped at home from the mid-Sixties onwards, until the advent of 'Johnandyoko' saw these ventures into the avant-garde being given a commercial release through the ever-benevolent Apple organisation.

More conventionally, Lennon began to use his tape recorders as a songwriting tool – something he continued to do right up until his death in 1980. He never learnt to notate music, and so rather than risk forgetting a tune or lyric in progress, he would tape entire songwriting sessions, recording over previous attempts with a wholesale disregard for posterity. Some of his earliest home recordings have survived, however, chief among them a batch of tapes which document the writing of one of his major contributions to the *Revolver* album.

'He Said He Said', as it was originally called, originated from an incident in August 1965, when The Beatles had taken advantage of a brief pause in their American tour to drop acid with some close friends at their house in the Hollywood hills. Alongside Byrds' David Crosby and Jim McGuinn, the guests at that select party included jobbing film actor Peter Fonda, son of Henry and brother of Jane, but not yet himself a counter-culture superstar, as he later became with the release of *Easy Rider* in 1969. Stumbling around the room in a hallucinogenic haze, Fonda kept accosting the literary Beatle and mumbling the disturbing words, "I know what it's like to be dead," into his ear. At the time, Lennon must have been less than gratified: a successful acid trip was a delicate highwire act between paradise and panic, and Fonda's stoned remarks could have tipped Lennon over the precipice. Maybe for that reason, the phrase stuck, and by the early months of 1966, Lennon was using it as the basis of a new song.

As the 20-minute collage of composing tapes reveals, the original version of the song involved Lennon repeating the same phrase over and over again, to acoustic guitar accompaniment: "He said, I know what it's like to be dead, he said". At this stage, the line was taken at a fast blues tempo, with Lennon picking Dylan-esquely in the background.

A couple of weeks later, Lennon had developed the song a little further. He'd slowed the tempo down, substituted a chopping rhythm guitar for the finger-picked original, and added some more lyrics, ad-libbing as he went along. Fortunately, gems such as "Who put all that crap in your head" and "It's making me feel that my trousers are torn" were taken no further. Also lost along the way was an entire section of the song, with ever-changing lyrics, but which began in a self-pitying tone: "When I was a little boy/I never had no toys". Gradually, Lennon realised that this approach would limit the song's relevance to his audience. As he went back over the skeleton of the tune, again and again, he experimented with a variety of different keys and tempos. At one point, he was using a slow, fingerpicking rhythm that threatened to drift into Paul McCartney's 1968 tune, 'Mother Nature's Son'. At another, he adopted a bleating voice for the final lines that didn't recur in his work until he was cutting his demos of 'Cold Turkey' in 1969. After a lengthy period of gestation, 'He Said, He Said' was finally ready to play to the other Beatles, though the song still had several more changes to undergo before it could be recorded by the group.

APRIL 6 TO 22, 1966: THE BEATLES recording 'Tomorrow Never Knows'/'Got To Get You Into My Life'/'Love You To'/'Paperback Writer'/'Rain'/'Doctor Robert'/'And Your Bird Can Sing'/'Taxman'

It's become something of a critical commonplace to date the fragmentation of a shared popular culture from the release of The Beatles' *Sgt. Pepper* album in June 1967. The artistry and imagination of that album, so the argument runs, divided musicians into those who wanted to take their experimentation a stage further, and delve deeper into self-expression; and those who were content to bask in the cosier surroundings of pre-acid commercial music. There were those who were broad enough to straddle both camps,

The Beatles among them, but the rock/pop divide gradually affected both the music and the way in which it was received, by public and media alike.

Given that 'Strawberry Fields Forever' was begun during the *Pepper* sessions, and represents better than anything on that album the gulf between traditional pop values and the new élite, the release of that track in February 1967 may be a more accurate benchmark of the Great Pop Divide. So *Revolver* could be regarded, alongside The Beach Boys' *Pet Sounds* (being recorded 6,000 miles away around the same time), as the pinnacle of the old pop. It showcased four musicians and their studio aides thinking on their feet to create sounds as wild as their imaginations. *Revolver* had its feet in The Beatles' past, but its head in the clouds of the future; and today it has a freshness, clarity and enthusiasm that little of The Beatles' other work can match.

Ironically, much of the songwriting on *Rubber Soul* was more 'mature', or whatever adjective you prefer, than its *Revolver* counterparts. Elements of the later album stood up more on attitude than on content. But there was an electric thrill to *Revolver*, a richness of sound and production, that is still the peak against which all subsequent pop music has to be judged. In the end, it's the work of a band of equals, each contributing their own individual talents, and sacrificing themselves for the sake of the whole. As such, it could only have been made while The Beatles were still a unit – while they were a touring band in other words, a situation which came to an end (much to their collective relief) in August 1966. Thereafter, there were still Beatles records, but they were the work of four artists constantly aware that they had a life outside of the monolith. *Revolver* was the last gasp of unity, and the finest testament to the strength of that brief collaboration.

Of the eight songs The Beatles cut during this fortnight, four were solo Lennon compositions, and another was written by Harrison with substantial assistance from Lennon. The latter was 'Taxman', essentially Harrison's song in concept and execution. Lennon's contributions were vital, however, including the final verse ("Now my advice for those who die/Declare the pennies on your eyes" – proof of a decent classical education!), the "Mister Wilson/Mister Heath" backing vocals, and also sharpening up Harrison's rhyming schemes in the middle section. Lennon later used Harrison's lack of acknowledgement of this assistance as a stick with which to beat his ex-colleague in the 1980 *Playboy* interview.

It was a Lennon composition, however, that kicked off the sessions on April 6 and 7. From the start, it was obvious to all concerned that this was a different group, with a different purpose, to the one which had cut *Rubber Soul* and the 'Day Tripper'/'We Can Work It Out' double A-side.

81

'Tomorrow Never Knows' (listed on the day's session sheet as 'Mark 1' and also known to Beatles insiders at the time as 'The Void') was so far removed from what had gone before, so obvious a step into new territory, that it is still staggering to remember that it was the first *Revolver* song to be recorded, before the far more basic 'Here, There And Everywhere' and 'Good Day Sunshine'. Lennon had doubtless prepared the song at home, though sadly the tapes of his work-in-progress don't seem to have survived: it would be fascinating to know how much of the concept of the recording was present on his original demo. By the time the song reached Abbey Road, it was already a step into the unknown, both for The Beatles and for popular music itself.

The first take of 'Mark 1', unveiled on *Anthology 2* in 1996, lacked the tape loops and charged intensity of the finished piece. But the surreal, lumbering rhythm and ghostly groan of treated organ and guitar acted as a stark message from the heart of the void. Even in this tentative form, it was a remarkable song. It proved that Lennon's venturing into the recesses of his own mind during his countless acid trips had come close to fragmenting his personality. It also offered evidence that he was delving into the spiritual literature of the East, with its non-Christian concept of one eternal soul that could survive all earthly life and death. He had clearly also investigated the druggy ramblings of Timothy Leary, acid guru and apologist *par excellence*, and an occasional Lennon cohort until his imprisonment in 1969.

The first line summed up the ideal preparation for a trip, "Turn off your mind, relax, and float downstream", and the rest of the lyric described the need to surrender to the unconscious so that you could grasp the oneness of being. "The game existence" had to be played "to the end of the beginning", and so we turned again on the great wheel of karma, amen. The central message was the same as on 'The Word', however: "Love is all and love is everyone". Turn on, tune in, and watch the problems of the world drift away, in other words. It was the perfect menu for a dreamer like John Lennon.

As Mark Lewisohn's research for *The Complete Beatles Recording Sessions* revealed, the making of 'Tomorrow Never Knows' involved two off-the-cuff inventions by the EMI studio staff: ADT (automatic double-tracking, which saved the singer from having to overdub a second identical vocal if he wanted to thicken up the sound of his voice – as Lennon always did); and the use of the Leslie speaker (the part of a Hammond organ which gave it that distinctive swirly sound, and which when applied to a vocal brought a thin, distant, disembodied feel which was perfectly suited to a song about the insubstantiality of physical being).

McCartney and Lennon also assembled a whole series of tape loops from their home studios, which were mixed into the track on the second day of proceedings. The overall effect was – and still is – breathtaking. Heralded by a sitar-like drone, the track burst into life with the corporeal presence of white noise, which only repeated listenings separated into Ringo's unsettling drum pattern (with its hints of Indian ragas), and the squeals of over-amped guitars. But it was the tape loops which gave the track its nightmarish quality – shut your eyes and you could hear flights of prehistoric birds swooping across the speakers, or ghostly string sections echoing in the sky. McCartney had been paying close attention to contemporary composer Luciano Berio's equally spectacular 'Thema', which explored similar sonic territory. The sound screeched and wailed, suggesting a desperate battle for the soul – while over the top, serene and surreal, lay Lennon's deadpan vocal, intoning the message of the collective subconscious.

It was a stunning performance, which could only have been placed at the end of the *Revolver* album; anywhere else, and it would have killed whatever followed. During the sessions, however, The Beatles moved straight on to record McCartney's soul number, 'Got To Get You Into My Life', and then Harrison's mock-raga, another essay in spirituality for the masses, 'Love You To'.

McCartney's 'Paperback Writer', already earmarked as the next single, returned the band to the here-and-now – with another skin-tight set of harmonies from Lennon, McCartney and Harrison to guide it home. The flipside of the single, though, harked back to the strange journey of 'Tomorrow Never Knows', in another acid-drenched attempt to remake the world in Lennon's own consciousness.

'Rain' remains a recording landmark for its use of backwards tapes over the final chords – an accidental discovery during a drug-induced haze at home, according to Lennon; George Martin's suggestion, in the producer's account. But the record was so much more than that. Once again, it attempted to evoke the other-worldliness of the LSD trip – the feeling that the physical world was insubstantial compared to the world of the mind. The lyrics said it straight – come rain or come shine, Lennon didn't care, as "it's just a state of mind". The music matched it, with droning guitars, Lennon's voice stretched wearily out over six or seven bars intoning the same syllable – an effect which was achieved by recording the song nearly 50 per cent faster than the finished record, and then slowing the tape down. And Ringo Starr's drumming, gradually assuming a life of its own on these revolutionary recordings, punctuated the dream with shotgun intensity.

83

'Doctor Robert' and 'And Your Bird Can Sing' were Lennon's other contributions to the first group of *Revolver* sessions – neither of them matching the artistic depth of 'Rain' or 'Tomorrow Never Knows', but both evidence of the fabulous lustre of the finished album. 'Doctor Robert' was a blatant drug song – it didn't matter whether there was a real 'Dr Robert', or whether Lennon was simply referring to himself as The Beatles' in-house drug courier. The message was simple: take these strange pills, and you'll feel a new man. Only the dry cynicism of Lennon's vocal suggested that the prescription might have any side effects.

'And Your Bird Can Sing' was a throwaway – John's lyrics couldn't decide whether he was being indifferent and superior (the verse) or warmly sympathetic (the middle eight). But the imagery was a definite step beyond the moon/June rhymes of his early work, sounding portentous without suggesting any too restrictive meanings.

What linked 'Doctor Robert' and 'And Your Bird Can Sing' was the sheer virtuosity of the playing. The simple twist-and-turn R&B riff of 'Doctor Robert' was powered by searing guitar-work, while 'And Your Bird Can Sing' was another blatant nod to the jingle–jangle of Byrds tracks such as 'Chimes Of Freedom'. The use of fuzz, echo and distortion gave the guitars a cutting edge that was a Harrison trademark from this record on. Equally incisive were Lennon's vocals: he had by now mastered the art of sounding devastatingly indifferent, overwhelmingly powerful, and slightly vulnerable, all at the same time, and seldom was his voice as gripping as it was throughout this album. Both songs buzzed with electricity, a quality they shared with the last of these April recordings, 'Taxman'.

As it turned out, this endearing version of 'And Your Bird Can Sing' was not released at the time; after a few days' break, it was one of the songs which The Beatles completed during their second batch of *Revolver* sessions. The hysterical giggling captured on the *Anthology 2* out-take suggests that Lennon and McCartney may have been too high on life or pot to concentrate on perfecting their final vocals.

APRIL 26 TO MAY 19, 1966: THE BEATLES 'And Your Bird Can Sing'/'I'm Only Sleeping'/'Eleanor Rigby'/'For No One'/'Taxman'/'Got To Get You Into My Life'

From *Revolver* onwards, The Beatles effectively abandoned the concept of cutting a single song in a single session. It was no longer satisfying for them to produce a recording in which the instruments and vocals were in tune and tempo. As long as there were fresh sounds to be added, or more remixing to be done, no track was ever quite finished. They were attempting to pin down on tape a fleeting mental image of a sound, or an atmosphere; and increasingly they began to try every conceivable instrument and studio gimmick in the hope of sliding ever closer to the unattainable fantasy.

That was why recordings like 'Taxman' and 'Got To Get You Into My Life' reappeared in this second batch of *Revolver* sessions, having been all but perfected earlier in the month. Likewise 'And Your Bird Can Sing', now converted to a smoother rhythm, with only the savage tone of George Harrison's lead guitar remaining from the original version. Gone, too, were the layers of harmonies that had adorned the first rendition of the track. They were replaced by a sparser vocal arrangement dominated by Lennon's laconic lead.

Lennon had already dominated the early *Revolver* sessions; now he was content to lay back and let McCartney and Harrison bear the strain – after recording the masterful 'I'm Only Sleeping', that is. Lennon wrote the song on his acoustic guitar, which was also the basis of the first pass at the song. In this unfinished state, 'I'm Only Sleeping' stood as a sly, stoned dream vision, a confession of laziness that was more autobiographical than most Beatles watchers realised. Partly the song was a simple plea to be left alone, to be allowed to dip out of the rat race and dream; the same basic need which inspired 'Watching The Wheels' in 1980, to which lines like "Everybody seems to think I'm lazy/I don't mind, I think they're crazy" clearly look ahead.

The not-so-hidden layer of the song, however, was drugs-based – pot, this time, rather than the more volcanic acid visions unveiled on 'Tomorrow Never Knows' and 'She Said She Said' (as it had now been retitled). On the first of those songs, Lennon had commanded his listeners to "float downstream"; here the movement was in the other direction, though the self-fulfilling nature of the journey was the same.

So the sleep, and the dream, and what Lennon saw along the way, were a little removed from the usual shifting senses that mankind experiences as they drift into somnolence. The challenge was to convey that aura of dislocation in sound, to create that shifting perception which was at the heart of the dream and the trip. The Beatles had discovered on 'Rain' the unsettling effects of speeding or slowing voices and instruments: so to heighten the gap between Lennon and reality, his vocal on 'I'm Only Sleeping' was speeded-up, while the backing track was slowed down, so that they seemed to be swimming in different dimensions.

Stage two of the exercise in submerging the listener into the dream came via George Harrison's backwards guitar – pieced together painstakingly over a six-hour session, and actually ending up in the mix in three different places, depending on whether you heard the final track in Britain, America or France. The effect was identical, however – placing the listener on that sliding path into sleep where you were not sure what is and what merely seems to be. Lennon was clearly unsure whether he had captured the effect he wanted, as *Anthology 2* includes the first take of a remake of 'I'm Only Sleeping' that was soon abandoned.

While Lennon was using the increased range of the studio to delve into his mind, McCartney's approach was far more technical, though no less inventive. 'For No One' was his song entirely, on which he used classical brass player Alan Civil to transform a delicate love song into a piece of baroque. 'Eleanor Rigby' was another track for which he is generally given credit, though Lennon later claimed to have written the second verse. The story element of the song was certainly McCartney's conception; Lennon's contribution was to edit the plot, help McCartney decide where the story was headed, and turn the events in the song into characterisation as much as action.

MAY 26 TO JUNE 8, 1966: THE BEATLES recording 'Yellow Submarine'/'I Want To Tell You'/'Good Day Sunshine'

'Yellow Submarine', custom-built as Ringo Starr's solitary lead vocal for the album, was that rarity of the period, a true Lennon/McCartney collaboration. The actual taping of the track brought out the spirit of play that had united The Beatles in the beginning. Lennon controlled the sound effects that were ultimately half of the record – the megaphone interjections, the blowing of bubbles, the ocean noises, the general air of mayhem that eventually became a familiar part of a Beatles studio outing.

It was McCartney who had concocted the childishly simple melody line. Lennon helped knock it into shape, and together with folk-rocker Donovan was there to polish off the outstanding lyrics. Charming though it was, however, it was too frivolous a piece of work for Lennon ever to take any great pride in it.

The other two songs taped in this fortnight, Harrison's 'I Want To Tell You' and McCartney's 'Good Day Sunshine', pushed Lennon into the role of high-class sideman – adding superb high harmonies to both numbers, and not even playing an instrument on McCartney's joyous love song.

MAY 27, 1966: FILMING scene for *Eat The Document*

By 1966, John Lennon was used to being the master of every situation. A year earlier, The Beatles had met their original rock'n'roll idol, Elvis Presley, and cut him down to size by sheer weight of numbers. Yet there was one member of the rock music community who still intimidated Lennon: Bob Dylan.

In May 1966, Dylan was careering through a speed-crazed world tour. Scarcely in touch with any kind of reality beyond the staggering music he was creating onstage every night with his band, The Hawks, he wandered through Britain that month like an alien from a highly advanced but ultra-paranoid planet, infecting everyone he encountered with a heady dose of his genius and madness.

Lennon and Dylan were supposed to be friends, as well as rivals, so it was inevitable that the Liverpudlian would eventually stumble in front of the cameras that were shooting a surreal documentary of Dylan's tour. The two men shared a limo ride from Lennon's Weybridge home, where the connection between them had proved tenuous at best, back to Dylan's Mayfair hotel. In the footage that is in circulation among collectors, Dylan was obviously suffering from an ill-judged intake of chemicals, and was threatening to vomit at any moment. Lennon dealt with the situation as he did with everything that threatened his equilibrium: sarcasm. Neither man would have wanted to see this scene again, let alone have approved it for public consumption – which is no doubt why it did not appear in Dylan's rarely screened *Eat The Document* movie.

JUNE 14 TO 21, 1966: THE BEATLES recording 'Here, There And Everywhere'/'She Said She Said'

With the sessions moving towards an enforced close, as The Beatles had to play the first night of another world tour on June 24, Lennon and McCartney came up with one last composition apiece to complete *Revolver*. Unlike 'Yellow Submarine', these were entirely solo efforts; Lennon loved McCartney's song, and would surely have claimed a piece of it for himself if he could; but he never did, even during his credit-greedy interview sessions with *Playboy* in 1980. Likewise, there was no question that 'She Said She Said' – now hurriedly finished off after Lennon had consulted his earlier demo – was a product of John's mind only.

Peter Fonda's paranoid rambling was still at the centre of the song, but by shifting the speaker from male to female Lennon placed this track into the same category of disturbing love song as 'Girl' or 'Norwegian Wood'. And in the final lines, Lennon shifted the paranoia from her to himself, as he repeated, "I know what it is to be sad/I know what it's like to be dead", over and over again.

Before then, he made an attempt to distance himself from the fear by evoking the past – not, as he would do on the *Plastic Ono Band* album to come, by registering his credentials as an orphan, abandoned twice over by his parents; but by the simple statement that "When I was a boy/Everything was right". The song shifted tempo in a liberating burst of optimism as Lennon sang these lines, only to be sucked back into the fog as the verse regained control. It was a brilliant piece of arranging, no doubt created instinctively, but none the less revealing for that. And The Beatles' musical setting for this tale of reality cutting through fantasy was equally well chosen, with Harrison's lead guitar, distorted through a Leslie speaker, leading the band through a twisting spiral arrangement.

c. JUNE 30, 1966: THE BEATLES painting in Japan

During their first and only visit to Japan, The Beatles received death threats from right-wing political activists who were furious that a pop group were being allowed to perform in the hallowed Budokan arena. Trapped in their Tokyo hotel rooms, the group filled the hours between shows by smoking cannabis and then painting a four-man abstract canvas, which was subsequently given to the local branch of The Beatles Fan Club. Each Beatle started at the corner of the canvas and worked towards the centre. While Harrison and Starr merely doodled like small children, McCartney's quarter of the painting was slightly fussy and self-conscious. Of the four, Lennon's contribution was the most confident and bold, without demonstrating any great threat to the New York abstract expressionists.

LATE 1966 ONWARDS: MAKING home movies and recordings

The Beatles bought a second set of executive toys in 1966 – movie cameras and home editing equipment. John was already using his tape decks to demo his new compositions, and to create frightening collages of sound, as a dry run for the bizarre tape loops of 'Tomorrow Never Knows'. A few months later, Paul McCartney would play him Morton Subotnick's pioneering synthesiser album, *Silver Apples Of The Sun*, which would open up expansive vistas of musical imagination for both men.

Meanwhile, with his 8mm Canon equipment, he could make pictures to match the sounds on his tape loops and in his head. What was surprising, though, was that Lennon chose not to indulge in the high-speed imagery of his songs – the lightning jump-cuts and juxtapositions that attracted most novices to film-making. Bruce Conner's *Cosmic Ray* and *Vivian* were two of the experimental films in vogue: they raced a succession of dazzling images across the eye, leaving no single shot on the mind, just the visual sensation of assault.

Lennon saw the Conner films, and wasn't impressed. They were too slight, too fast to have any meaning. He set out to create the opposite effect – lingering images from which there would be no escape. He worked with films that would last 10 minutes at normal speed, then projected them in slow motion. And his subjects – which could be anything from one of his family to an object in the room – were captured in lengthy, unbroken shots that showed little movement or pace. Editing on the camera, he was able to superimpose other images, using the same technique of multi-dubbing that he had perfected on his tape recorders. Then, when these languorous but unsettling combinations of pictures were ready, Lennon would put music to them. This might be Stravinsky's 'Rite Of Spring', the *musique concrete* of Stockhausen or his acolytes – or, eventually, when he had grasped the finer points of the process, his own dramatic soundscapes, culled from the darker reaches of his narcotic imagination.

Lennon didn't know it, but in New York a school of film-makers and artists were working along very similar principles. The Fluxus group shared his preoccupation with a single, extended shot – and his use of noise as a substitute for music. One of the most enthusiastic Fluxus film-makers was a naturalised Japanese-American: Yoko Ono.

CHAPTER 6

September 1966 to September 1967

None of The Beatles realised how significant the decision to quit touring would become. Overnight, it freed them from the daily responsibility of being public figures, and allowed them space to create as much – or as little – as they wanted. Lennon struggled to acclimatise himself to this more liberal regime, as if he was terrified to be given too much space in which to ponder his own existence. He tentatively began to explore this ambiguity in his music, little realising that while he was creating songs such as 'Strawberry Fields Forever' and 'Lucy In The Sky With Diamonds', he was already beginning to come under the sway of the most significant influence in his entire artistic life.

SEPTEMBER 6 TO NOVEMBER 7, 1966: FILMING *How I Won The War*; RECORDING 'It's Not Too Bad'

"That's it: I'm not a Beatle any more," announced George Harrison on August 29, 1966, on an LA-bound flight after The Beatles' final live concert at Candlestick Park, San Francisco. He was speaking with relief, not sadness; and though his was the most extreme reaction of the four, the hyper-accelerated treadmill of touring had long lost its appeal for all the Beatles.

Back in Britain, Harrison made plans to travel to India to learn the sitar with maestro Ravi Shankar; Paul McCartney began composing the film score to the movie *The Family Way*. And Lennon? His was the most obvious move away from The Beatles, as he accepted a solo acting role in a movie by Dick 'Beatles Films' Lester, shot almost entirely on location in Celle, West Germany in early September, and then Carboneras in Spain from September 19 to November 6.

How I Won The War was scripted by Charles Wood – shortly to become world-famous as the author of *The Graduate* – from a novel by Patrick Ryan. What attracted Lester, and Lennon, was its strong anti-war message. The plot concerned a beleaguered and abandoned bunch of British squaddies who were on a mission to build that most British of defences, a cricket pitch, behind German lines in the Second World War. It belonged to that same anarchic, *non sequitur* brand of British comedy as Spike Milligan (compare it to his 1969 film *The Bed-Sitting Room*, for instance). As the Goons – also Milligan's invention – were one of Lennon's great loves as a teenager, the script must have stood out alongside the four-lads-together synopses that were continually being submitted as a possible basis for the third Beatles film.

Making the film entailed not only a break away from The Beatles – enough in itself to provoke newspaper headlines about a possible fissure in the group – but also a change of image. The WW2 soldier required shorter hair than a Beatle, so Lennon submitted to the film crew's barber in front of a phalanx of photographers, and emerged with his most closely-cropped haircut since the late Fifties. He also used the opportunity to adopt the National Health 'granny specs' that later became a trademark; previously, only a handful of Beatles photos had caught Lennon wearing (horn-rimmed) spectacles, as he preferred to squint or wear contact lenses in public.

The dual process of being removed from the centre of The Beatles' hurricane, and physically transformed for his role, must have sent Lennon deep inside his own mind, searching for a key to the madness he had endured, and his own complicity in it; and wondering all the time whether he had a future outside of the performing flea circus. That doubt and introspection surfaced in a song which Lennon began at this time, 'Strawberry Fields Forever'.

Lennon had taken a portable tape recorder, offering only minimal sound quality, to Spain. Surprisingly, despite the amount of free time he had at his disposal, he seems only to have written the bare bones of one song – although it proved to be one of the most important that he would ever compose. Performing (suitably enough) on a Spanish acoustic guitar,

Lennon quickly laid down the basic structure for the 'Strawberry Fields Forever' verse – though at the moment the song went by the title of 'It's Not Too Bad', as he had not immediately made the connection with the Liverpool landmark from his childhood. Elements of the finished record were already recognisable, however: not just the melody, but striking phrases such as "no one I think is in my tree" and "you can't tune in".

He eventually taped six different versions of 'It's Not Too Bad' in Spain, slowly filling out the structure and content of the song. By the fourth pass, his imagination had leapt ahead to encompass the first mention of Strawberry Fields, and the key "nothing is real" rhyme. Next time through, he had another phrase to add to the chorus: for the moment, there was "nothing to get mad about", and only the final pay-off line to complete. Aware that he was tapping into something uniquely personal and endlessly strange, he resolved to continue the composing process when he returned to England.

Between the interminable delays while shots were set up and the sun arrived at the right place in the sky, Lennon also did a little filming – not as much as his later star billing in the movie might have suggested, but enough to make sure he was noticed. Charles Wood had made a few unfortunate concessions to Lennon's fame; references to his past as a musician made uneasy listening amidst the social comedy and stark satire of the wartime theme. And Lennon was not required to develop a character, or act outside his own experience: most of his speech was chopped into neat one-liners, delivered in the same sarcastic tone as his interjections in *Help!* or *A Hard Day's Night*. Other actors – notably Michael Crawford and Roy Kinnear – carried the weight of the plot, and furthered their growing reputations as comic performers. It was difficult to escape the feeling that Lennon was there for his name – and perhaps because director Dick Lester simply enjoyed his company when the cameras were turned off. The suspicion that Lennon was being exploited must have been confirmed in his own mind when the film company, United Artists, issued a soundtrack-single from this non-musical film. It was credited to Musketeer Gripweed (Lennon's film role) and the Third Troop, but contained just one tiny fragment of Lennon's on-screen dialogue to justify the fact.

How I Won The War eventually capsized beneath the weight of its own heavy-handed satire – but not before Lennon had, unwittingly, provided the film's most dramatic moment. As the troops were gradually wiped out trying to carry out their pointless mission, the wisecracks of Musketeer Gripweed served as an ironic comment that life continues while there's humour. When he was suddenly killed by a stray shell, the anti-war message of the film was thrown back into perspective. Seeing Lennon dying now has different connotations to those it had in 1967; then he was a symbol of youth, life and hope, and his fictional demise was as shocking an epitaph on the futility of war as any of Charles Wood's more obvious attempts at political commentary.

The film eventually opened to lukewarm reviews, and has only rarely been screened since. It did little to further Lennon's acting career; henceforward he only appeared in films alongside the other Beatles, or under his own direction. But by helping him to realise that he had an independent life away from the Beatle-faced hydra, *How I Won The War* was a pivotal event in Lennon's career. It confirmed the conclusion that George Harrison had already suggested: the tight-knit Beatles were no more. In their place were four individuals, whose efforts to make space for their own activities slowly pulled the group apart. The process began two days after Lennon's return from Carboneras to London, when he met Yoko Ono for the first time.

OCTOBER 27, 1966: PENGUIN publish *The Penguin John Lennon*

As an admission that his literary career was at an end, Lennon consented to the reprinting of his two earlier books as a single paperback, complete with all the original drawings – though their proportions in relation to the text were altered for this edition. At least three different cover designs were used for this book over the next four years. One showed Lennon dressed as Superman; another featured his face covered in several pairs of spectacles (compare, once again, the illustration for 'Snore Wife' and 'Several Dwarfs' in *A Spaniard In The Works*, and the cover of *Walls And Bridges*); and the last, introduced in 1969, used a distorted, pinched photo of Lennon the stern guru, hidden behind waves of hair and a flowing beard.

EARLY NOVEMBER 1966: RECORDING home demos of 'She's Walking Past My Door'/'You Know My Name' and 'Strawberry Fields Forever'

Lennon arrived back in London on November 7; the next Beatles recording session was already scheduled for a fortnight hence. While Lennon had been away, McCartney had been writing. The pattern for the next couple of years was set, as Lennon later explained: "Paul had a tendency to come along and say he'd written his ten songs, let's record now. And I'd say, well, give us a few days and I'll knock a few off."

According to Lennon, this happened with *Sgt. Pepper* and *Magical Mystery*

Tour. For the latter, he scarcely made the effort: for what eventually became *Pepper,* he set to work to finish the song that had been nagging him in Spain.

Begun at the same time, however, was a simple set of chord changes that evolved into one of The Beatles' most bizarre recordings. For the moment, 'You Know My Name (Look Up The Number)' was merely a few stabbing chords on the piano, with (on the surviving composing tape) Lennon feeling desperately for the changes and more often than not missing them, while he repeated the title again and again. This vignette was preceded by a formless song that might have been called 'She's Walking Past My Door', but kept threatening to burst into a verse from the as yet unwritten 'I Am The Walrus'.

Putting this aside, he spent some time translating the bare beginnings of 'Strawberry Fields Forever' into a potential Beatles song. Setting up the Studer recorders in his music room, he rolled the tape while he worked through the basic structure of the piece with his electric guitar. He established a chopping, insistent rhythm rather than the gentler picking of his early attempts, at the same time adding a little speed and urgency to his rendition. After the chordal strumming had been laid down, he overdubbed some raucous lead guitar, frequently stumbling into the wrong key. The result was an awful cacophony, far removed from the effect he was searching for. Yet he persevered, adding a double-tracked vocal to the mess, before realising that he'd hammered himself into a dead end.

So he began again, this time picking at his electric guitar rather than trying to thrash it into submission. He ran through eight takes, most of which collapsed because he couldn't master the guitar part. When he finally reached the end of the song, he added a mellotron to the tape and for the first time 'Strawberry Fields Forever' began to assume otherworldly proportions. These were only slightly dampened by the rather painful vocal overdubs he added next, before he stopped once again, fearful of destroying what he had created.

That was the tape that Lennon played to the other Beatles in the studio in late November, and which became the blueprint for one of the band's most complex and rewarding recordings. As Lennon recalled in 1980, 'Strawberry Fields Forever' was a conscious attempt to put one of his persistent childhood suspicions into words: "The second line goes, 'No one I think is in my tree'. Well, what I was trying to say in that line is, 'Nobody seems to be as hip as me, therefore I must be crazy or a genius'. It's that same problem I had when I was five: 'There is something wrong with me because I seem to see things other people don't see'. " Lennon went on to repeat the assertion he had made many times before: that he had seen surreal visions as a child, that he had been aware that he saw the world in a different way to those around him, and that the realisation that he didn't conform was at first frustrating, and then terrifying.

LSD had merely recreated that childhood state of awareness, with greater intensity than before. Once again, Lennon was seeing things that he couldn't place in words, and which no one else could see. 'Strawberry Fields Forever' was his attempt to bridge the gap between reality and acid dream, between what he saw under the influence of LSD and the concrete world. Lennon had already written several songs that expressed one point of view in the verse or chorus, another in the bridge. Now he changed his mind in every line – "It's getting hard to be someone but it all works out/It doesn't matter much to me" and "I think I know I mean a 'Yes' but it's all wrong/That is I think I disagree". With the way he thought and felt constantly shifting, all that remained to hold onto was the past – for which Strawberry Fields, a landmark site in his area of Liverpool, was a potent symbol, though no more than that.

So the chorus related back to Lennon's childhood, and invited us all to go along – though nothing there was real, and there was nothing to get hung about. It was the way in which Lennon constantly pierced his own bubble, floundering in his misunderstanding that made the lyric so disturbing, and so emotional. In this early form, with the eventual first verse still to be written, 'Strawberry Fields Forever' was part nightmare, wholly a dream, and as stunning a link between reality and fantasy as anything written by Shelley or Coleridge. But this was merely the skeleton: in the studio, The Beatles added the flesh, and gave it life.

NOVEMBER 24 TO DECEMBER 22, 1966: THE BEATLES
recording 'Strawberry Fields Forever'/'When I'm 64'/
'Everywhere It's Christmas'

Once The Beatles had recorded eleven songs in a day; now it took eleven sessions in the month up to Christmas 1966 to record two songs for their next project, plus one improvised mock-carol for their annual Christmas flexi-disc for Fan Club members.

Studio time was no problem; EMI had already learned from *Rubber Soul* and *Revolver* that The Beatles should be given a free hand to create whatever they wanted, at whatever speed felt most comfortable. The fact that the group were the company's cash cow did not go unnoticed either. From here onwards, there was no suggestion that the record company made any attempt to intrude upon the band's artistic decisions. (The same did not always apply to Lennon's later solo recordings.)

The Beatles were in such a heightened state of consciousness, through fair means or foul, however, that they found adding to an existing track easier than finishing one. After all, the next experiment might always be the one which transformed an interesting recording into a perfect one. The long, difficult process of taping 'Strawberry Fields Forever' was proof that this rather haphazard procedure was something more than self-indulgence.

When The Beatles regrouped for the first of their late 1966 sessions, they had no direct blueprint for what they were doing. The assumption was that they would record an album and that along the way a single would materialise in a puff of smoke, like a Pope from a Vatican conclave. But with no timetable to respect, and no initial concept for their album, the group were at liberty to take the sessions at their own speed.

So it was, then, that on November 24, 1966, The Beatles finished a six-hour session with less than three minutes of tape – the first take of 'Strawberry Fields'. Lennon had extended and rearranged the song he had played on his home demo. There were now three verses, the first of which was more didactic and definite than the other two, spelling out a message to himself and anyone else who cared to listen: "Living is easy with eyes closed/Misunderstanding all you see". This rebuttal of the dream world of 'I'm Only Sleeping' set up the later verses, with their self-probing analysis of Lennon's reaction to his uncertain future, and their honest account of his mixed emotions.

At home, Lennon had become one of the first people in Britain to install a mellotron – an instrument which acted as a rather cumbersome precursor to the synthesisers and samplers we know today. "It's all done by tapes," he explained at the time. "There are dozens of reels of tapes inside, and when you pull these knobs and press the keys they start playing."

Lennon probably got no closer to understanding the process than that, but he immediately began to use the mellotron for his home recordings. He also brought it into the studio for this first pass at 'Strawberry Fields', and it was the faintly unearthly sound of this instrument, like a dying concertina, that began the take, and underpinned the first verse. For the second, Lennon substituted a gentle electric guitar, combining both instruments for the chorus. His vocal was left high in the mix, an island of calm in an ocean of shifting currents and sounds; but for the third verse he was joined by a bank of luscious vocal harmonies, wavering under the melody line like a dissolve into a dream sequence. Back through the chorus again, and it was already time to fade on a meandering series of mellotron wheezes, heading slowly in no particular direction.

Lennon could have issued this recording as it stood, and 'Strawberry Fields Forever' would still have been one of The Beatles' most remarkable recordings. Instead, he thought about it over the weekend, and when The Beatles resumed recording four days later he was ready with a new arrangement.

Take one had been little more than a solo rendition; thereafter, Lennon designed the song round the band. The initial musical setting was still simple enough, however, with the pulsing mellotron that opened the finished record in place as early as Take Two, backed by exuberant drum fills that kicked through the haze, while George Harrison played a Byrdsian guitar jangle behind Lennon's deadpan, deadbeat vocal. Take one had a sense of wonder; this second arrangement was an emotional wasteland, with Lennon reciting the lyrics as if they were simply too tough to register.

Equally stunning in its way as the original version, the second 'Strawberry Fields' still didn't match Lennon's vision of the song. So after an interlude of just over a week, he and The Beatles prepared a third arrangement. The major difference was the tempo: this version was decidedly faster than its predecessors, requiring Ringo to dig deep into his resources for the drum fills that augmented the simple guitar and mellotron backing. Ringo came into his own on the fade-out, with a series of pulsating rolls around the kit that acted as an urgent call to arms – answered by the stabbing brass and flowing cellos that were overdubbed across the whole track a week later.

At the end of that latter session, Lennon overdubbed a suitably manic vocal – with an intensity quite missing from the previous rendition. Supported by the rushing brass and drums, it turned an elegiac piece of reflection into a crazed amphetamine rush of neurosis; the invitation to go to 'Strawberry Fields' suddenly felt more like a threat than a promise.

Lennon still wasn't satisfied, however; he liked both the claustrophobic atmosphere of the final take, and the spacy, melancholy tone of version number two. The solution, as all Beatles historians will know, was for producer George Martin to marry the first half of the slow version and the second half of the fast – speeding up the former and reducing the tempo of the latter to discover, quite by chance, that whereas they had been recorded a semitone apart, they were now in the same key. And so was born one of Lennon's – and The Beatles' – most compelling recordings: one which so astounded their fans when it was issued as a single that the record became their first since 'Love Me Do' not to top the British charts. Not for the last time, Lennon was moving too fast for his public.

No such worries attended the recording of 'When I'm 64', a McCartney song begun in the late Fifties, for which he had more recently written a new set of verses. Just as McCartney had supported Lennon on his song, so Lennon did likewise – without adding any notable creative input apart from the names Vera, Chuck and Dave.

NOVEMBER 27, 1966: FILMING scene for *Not Only ... But Also*

For his second appearance with comedians Peter Cook and Dudley Moore (see November 1964 for the first), Lennon took on the role of doorman Dan, greeting Cook outside a subterranean gentleman's toilet in Broadwick Street, Soho, London. One of the swinging nightspots in mid-sixties London was the Ad-Lib Club. In Cook's sketch, this became the Ad-Lav Club. Well, toilet humour was different back then. And so was Lennon, at least as far as the general public were concerned, because he wore his newly adopted granny specs as part of his characterisation for this brief role.

DECEMBER 29, 1966 TO JANUARY 20, 1967: THE BEATLES
recording 'Penny Lane'/'Carnival Of Light'/'A Day In The Life'

'Penny Lane' was McCartney's answer song to 'Strawberry Fields' – though in its lyrics it actually came closer to the original draft of 'In My Life', the guided tour of Lennon's Liverpool. McCartney's song achieved that object far more successfully; but by comparison with Lennon's ambiguous relation to the past, 'Penny Lane' was unashamedly nostalgic.

'Carnival of Light' was the name of a psychedelic event at the Roundhouse in London for which McCartney had promised a special Beatles contribution. Under his direction, the band spent one session assembling a barrage of noises, tape loops, screams and assorted madness, which Paul then mixed and gave to the event's organisers – since when it has never been aired in public again. Lennon went along with the idea wholeheartedly; his home tapes no doubt contained many similar ventures into noise as art. But it's worth noting that it was McCartney who not only conceived of the project and directed its completion, but who also had the avant-garde art world connections in the first place. By all accounts, Lennon – based in the plush stockbroker belt of Surrey – was jealous. The event no doubt fuelled his suspicions that there must be more to life after marriage than bringing up baby and hiding in his music room; and a certain Japanese artist was ready to take up the slack.

On the day that The Beatles finished recording 'Penny Lane', January 17,

1967, Lennon read in the *Daily Mail* a report about the discovery of several thousand holes in the streets of Blackburn, Lancashire. This minor scandal – food for a lively borough council meeting, no doubt – was one of the prime sources of inspiration for a song that The Beatles began recording two days later. 'A Day In The Life' – originally called 'In The Life Of' – was a wry piece of autobiography, which reflected Lennon's recent film role in Spain, the death in a horrific traffic accident of a friend, and then the news report from the *Daily Mail*. Placed together in apparently random succession, they provided a frightening vision of a world in which one sensory perception was just like another, and where strange happenings lurked around every corner. Emotionally, Lennon chose not to get involved: "And though the news was rather sad," he wrote, "well I just had to laugh". And the final surreal comment about the holes in the Albert Hall made a chilling link into that dubious invitation, "I'd love to turn you on" – a line actually provided by McCartney, who'd been searching for a song to put it in.

Thus arranged, 'A Day In The Life' was taped by Lennon on acoustic guitar, in another laconic, matter-of-fact vocal that expressed no sense of involvement in the bizarre workings of the world. (The air of removal from reality was heightened by his muttered introduction to the song: "sugar plum fairy, sugar plum fairy".) McCartney's simple piano supported the guitar, while Ringo turned in another epic display of drumming, using his fills as a comment on the proceedings. After the second verse, The Beatles left 24 bars spare, with aide Mal Evans counting them off in an increasingly echoed voice, while an alarm clock marked the end of the gap left for something to happen. For the moment, the middle section was left bare, filled by piano and drums, before Lennon resumed with the third verse, and another 24 bars ensued to bring the recording to a close. Satisfied with work so far, The Beatles took the best part of two weeks off, before regrouping at the beginning of February.

LATE JANUARY 1967: RECORDING home demo of 'Good Morning, Good Morning'

The Beatles' most complex album to date, *Revolver*, had been recorded over a period of two-and-a-half months, with occasional breaks included. Two months into the sessions for their next album, they had succeeded in taping just three complete songs, plus the skeleton of another. Already, in response to the need for a new Beatles single, the group had given EMI finished mixes of 'Penny Lane' and 'Strawberry Fields Forever' – which were then removed from consideration for the album.

99

That was ironic, as they were probably the two finest tracks to come out of these sessions – and also two of the only songs written before The Beatles began recording in late November 1966. The search was now on for new material, and while McCartney hit upon the tune that would become the eventual theme of the album, Lennon was ensconced at home in front of the TV. There he heard a banal commercial for Kelloggs' cornflakes, which used the phrase "Good morning, good morning" as its tag. Later that night, Lennon began writing a song – a piece which sounded at first like a trip into the mind of a bored businessman, before you realised that Lennon was once again singing about someone much closer to home.

"Nothing to do to save his life, call his wife in," Lennon's lyric began; clearly marriage and romance were not regular bed-partners in his scheme of things. The rest of the lyric reflected a search for meaning, for anything that would break him out of the rut; in the end, only "watching the skirts" brought him "in gear" and Lennon openly admitted his interest in a-woman-not-his-wife.

Lennon cut his basic demo on keyboards, combining a staccato piano part with the hazy tones of his mellotron, which initially produced a light orchestral feel reminiscent of 'Eleanor Rigby'. This primitive synthesiser came into its own in the middle section, giving the song a lazy, stoned feel perfectly complemented by his laidback, amused vocal. Though the Beatles' recording added decoration to the song, the essential ingredients were already intact.

FEBRUARY 1 TO APRIL 1, 1967: RECORDING home demos of 'Being For The Benefit Of Mr Kite'/'Lucy In The Sky With Diamonds;' THE BEATLES recording 'Sgt. Pepper's Lonely Hearts Club Band' (and 'Reprise')/'A Day In The Life'/'Good Morning, Good Morning'/'Fixing A Hole'/'It's Only A Northern Song'/ 'Being For The Benefit Of Mr Kite'/'Anything'/'Lovely Rita'/ 'Lucy In The Sky With Diamonds'/'Getting Better'/'Within You, Without You'/'She's Leaving Home'/'With A Little Help From My Friends'

Once established back in the studio on February 1, The Beatles continued recording solidly for two months, working almost every day, with only three separate gaps of four days apiece in which to take stock. In the process, they completed one of the most celebrated albums in music history – a record that has consistently been voted as the best album of all time, in both public and critics' polls, and that has often been used as a touchstone for subsequent developments in rock music.

Lennon, it has to be said, was never convinced by the *Pepper* myth. "It was a peak," he said in 1970, "but I don't care about the whole concept of *Pepper*. It might be better, but the music was better for me on the double album, because I'm being myself on it." Ten years later, he was more precise: "*Sgt. Pepper* is called the first concept album, but it doesn't go anywhere. All my contributions to the album have absolutely nothing to do with the idea of Sgt. Pepper and his band." The concept was McCartney's, at any rate, and Lennon never disputed it; and it was the idea of the concept, if that's not too vague, which got people excited, rather than the actual links between the songs.

And Lennon was accurate to admit that, 'A Day In The Life' aside, *Pepper* fell a long way short of being his finest hour with The Beatles. His work on *Revolver* and *Rubber Soul*, and then again on *The Beatles*, exposed much more of him and less of the professional songwriter; and during his solo career it was self-expression that became Lennon's constant yardstick for his own work.

What *Pepper* did have was imagination – a rich, playful experimentation with sound and lyric that opened the eyes of the audience and fellow musicians alike. *Pepper* was merely a reflection of the colour and excitement of the new psychedelic culture; but as the first record to catch that spirit of optimism – what was later dubbed the Summer Of Love – it came to look as if it had invented the era rather than celebrating it. Suffice to say, though, that the story of the cultural icon that is *Pepper* belongs in a book on McCartney. By the start of February 1967, Lennon was all too consciously creating new material out of desperation, and any raw materials he had to hand.

While in Kent to film the promotional clip for 'Strawberry Fields Forever' on January 31 – which together with the film for 'Penny Lane' accounted for the break in the *Pepper* sessions – Lennon had wandered into an antique shop and been taken by a poster for a 19th century circus. Intrigued by the names and skills of the acts on offer, he translated the circus bill into song, adding a few linking lines like the one that was reproduced as a pledge on the *Pepper* back cover: "A splendid time is guaranteed for all".

The new song was titled 'Being For The Benefit Of Mr Kite', and Lennon wanted, as George Martin remembered, "to smell the sawdust on the floor". To achieve this object, Lennon, McCartney and Martin prepared a series of tape loops from the workings of an old musical steam organ, threw them into the air, and stuck them back together, to produce the puffing, ungainly waddle of sound which supported the song. Above it all

101

droned Lennon's vocal, as distant, dead and certain as a century-old memory.

Similar ingenuity went into the recording of 'Good Morning, Good Morning' – based, as I've already said, on Lennon's home demo (as 'Mr Kite' had also been), but with the Sounds Incorporated brass section and a tearing McCartney lead guitar solo added in. The work-in-progress captured on *Anthology 2* illustrated the almost manic energy that The Beatles devoted to the recording, with Starr's drumming living out the amphetamine rush of meaningless daily existence. Then for the fade, Lennon requested a parade of animal noises – heard in succession so that each animal should be capable of eating its predecessor.

Meanwhile, The Beatles had also concocted a way to fill the Blackburn-style holes in 'A Day In The Life'. Paul McCartney played Lennon his own day-in-the-life-of-a-doper middle section, which Lennon agreed was a perfect foil for his own lyric; and after a couple of passes, the first of which McCartney ended with an unscripted "Oh shit", the section was recorded. A week later, on February 10, came one of the most famous recording sessions of all time – the orchestral overdubs for 'A Day In The Life'. The classical musicians performed in fancy dress garb and were encouraged to fill the song's two 24-bar holes with a sliding romp from the lowest note in each instrument's range to the highest. Dismissing the original idea of a massed hum to end the song, The Beatles eventually hit upon a four-part piano chord, overdubbed several times, which was allowed to fade naturally away to bring the musical element of the album to a close.

Other songs were McCartney's brainchildren – 'Fixing A Hole', for instance, which proved him to be Lennon's equal when it came to meaningful vagueness, the two versions of the 'Sgt. Pepper' theme, 'Lovely Rita', a mischievous ode to a traffic warden, 'She's Leaving Home' and 'Getting Better'. Each of the last two songs were a collaboration, however, at least up to a point. Lennon wrote and then sang the ironic counterpoints to the tale of an errant teenage girl in 'She's Leaving Home'. Taking the part of the parents rather than the child, they gave a rather one-dimensional song an unexpected depth and poignancy. Likewise 'Getting Better', with Lennon contributing the (autobiographical, so he later admitted) lines about "beating his woman" in the second verse, and answering McCartney's optimistic chorus with a grudging "couldn't get much worse".

George Harrison presented the *Pepper* sessions with 'Within You, Without You', on which he was the only Beatle to appear; and then 'Only A Northern Song', which was left unfinished for the time being. Ringo's major role at this time was recording a 22-minute drum track named

'Anything', for no apparent purpose whatsoever, in the session after The Beatles had recorded the 'A Day In The Life' piano chord.

Under pressure from McCartney's sudden burst of songwriting, Lennon did come up with one more new tune during these sessions. As he told the story, his young son Julian had come home from nursery school with a drawing. When asked what it was, he announced it was a classmate, Lucy, in the sky with diamonds. Like composers in all the best Hollywood musicals, Lennon felt a song coming on; and by the end of February he had taped a home demo of a slightly contrived exercise in psychedelia, named after his son's picture.

'Lucy In The Sky With Diamonds' is difficult to separate from the era which produced it. Lennon later expressed dissatisfaction with the way it was recorded, but that was somehow secondary to the message of the song. Except: the more you examined the words, the more you realised that there was no message, merely a string of unconnected fantasy images, a kind of adult fairy tale filled with "marmalade skies", "newspaper taxis" (McCartney's invention, as Lennon later admitted) and "tangerine trees". The words were there for their sound, and for the acid glow they evoked, rather than as literal images – which was probably why 'Lucy' dated less well than Lennon's other contributions to the album.

As every casual fan of The Beatles knows, the initials of 'Lucy In The Sky With Diamonds' were extracted by pundits to demonstrate that Lennon was eulogising the use of hallucinogenic drugs. In the same way, 'A Day In The Life' received little airplay because of McCartney's tag line, "I'd love to turn you on". To the end of his days, Lennon continued to deny the 'LSD' allegation. As with his vehement rebuttal of the rumours that he had a homosexual affair with Brian Epstein, it's difficult to imagine why Lennon kept the story up for so long when he had confessed to so much else. Denial in 1967 was one thing; this was still prior to The Beatles' public announcement that they had taken LSD. Thirteen years later, the story of Julian's painting would have been more newsworthy if he had confirmed it.

It took just two days to record 'Lucy In The Sky With Diamonds', lightning work in comparison with other *Pepper* cuts. Listening to the tune again in 1980, Lennon winced at the amateurishness of the production, which seemed to be as fragile as a fading dream. One of the reasons he agreed to help Elton John record the song in 1974 was that it offered him a chance to do the song justice after seven years. But from the opening notes through to the synthesised whistle that closes the song, 'Lucy' was as redolent of 1967 as anything The Beatles taped that year. (One bizarre artefact left in the Abbey Road tape vault, incidentally, was a version of the song prepared for the *Yellow Submarine* cartoon film, but eventually never used. It featured the completed Beatles track for the song, with the first verse performed by British comedian Dick Emery.)

That left 'With A Little Help From My Friends', a McCartney conception, finished in the studio with suggestions from anyone who was around. Lennon came up with the only lines in the song that suggested more than they said – "What do you see when you turn out the light?/I can't tell you but I know it's mine" – and chipped in some of the questions proposed by his and Paul's backing vocals. As the photographs taken during this session showed, The Beatles were using any instrument they could find in the Abbey Road studios. Having experimented with various harmonicas and keyboards, Lennon opted to play cowbell on this song.

On April 1, the band recorded the 'Sgt. Pepper' reprise, the last element in the jigsaw make-up of the album named after that song. After supervising the mono mixing, which was the version of the album that The Beatles still considered to be the most important, they left the more gimmicky stereo mix to George Martin and his engineers.

APRIL 20/21, 1967: THE BEATLES recording 'Only A Northern Song'/end piece for 'Sgt. Pepper'

The *Sgt. Pepper* album wasn't quite finished, however. After a further session of overdubs and re-recording on Harrison's 'Only A Northern Song' – presumably a last attempt to salvage it for *Pepper* – the band taped a selection of random dialogue to be inserted at the end of the album, which would play endlessly on manual gramophones until the needle was lifted bodily from the record. Lennon's final contribution to *Pepper* was even more bizarre. He it was who suggested that the engineers add a high-frequency whistle to the end of the LP's second side, too high for humans to hear, and therefore accessible only to passing dogs.

APRIL 25 TO MAY 3, 1967: THE BEATLES recording 'Magical Mystery Tour'

With *Pepper* finally complete, and set for release on June 1, The Beatles were free to begin work on another project. By his own later account, Lennon would rather have rested, or taken time to digest the copy of Yoko Ono's book *Grapefruit* that lay by his bedside. Aided by Lennon's jaded diffidence, McCartney had now become the effective leader of the group. He was the Beatle who had supervised the making of the *Pepper* cover; and he also came up with the idea that instead of making another big-budget feature film, The Beatles should write and direct a more experimental movie of their own.

Magical Mystery Tour was adopted as the title from the start; and for a while all four Beatles were intrigued by the project – not least because they hoped it would put an end to the constant media speculation about what the Beatles oft-postponed third film would constitute. But only McCartney was able to maintain his enthusiasm, and so it was no surprise that he arrived at the studio in late April with a projected title song for the film. Once upon a time, Lennon would have been competing for this honour; now he simply didn't care. His contribution to the proceedings was small; he added some backing vocals and rhythm guitar, but otherwise McCartney directed the sessions.

EARLY MAY 1967: DRAWING psychedelic sketches

John Lennon left the 14-Hour Technicolour Dream event in London's Alexandra Palace on April 29, 1967 in the company of John Dunbar – the man who had introduced him to Yoko Ono six months earlier. Lennon and Dunbar had been friends for around three years, since Dunbar was introduced into the pop milieu via his then girlfriend, Marianne Faithfull.

Some thirty years later, he revealed that the two men had then travelled to Ireland for several days, topping up their intake of LSD at regular intervals. He claimed to have recently discovered a sketchbook dating from that trip, in which Lennon had drawn several sketches featuring anguished, ghostly faces. He described at least one of them as being "Dantesque" in its depiction of mental and physical horror. Jennifer Dunbar Donn illustrated what she described as a Lennon "acid drawing" on the cover of her magazine *Square One* in 2003, and this illustration probably came from the John Dunbar collection.

More recently, a psychedelic painting by Lennon was sold in London from the collection of his late Sixties friend, Apple Electronics' boss Alexis 'Magic Alex' Mardas. Entitled 'Strong', it emanated from the opposite end of the psychological spectrum from the Dunbar drawings, with its vivid felt-pen patterns conjuring up the ultimate 'good trip'.

MAY 9 to JUNE 25, 1967: THE BEATLES recording untitled jams/'Baby You're A Rich Man'/'All Together Now'/'You Know My Name'/'It's All Too Much'/'All You Need Is Love'

A fortnight after deciding to make *Magical Mystery Tour*, The Beatles were obliged to sign another film contract: this time guaranteeing their participation in the making of a cartoon film based on their song, 'Yellow Submarine'. The deal meant that they had to provide at least four new songs for the film, which needed to be "relevant" to the as-yet-undetermined plot, plus unlimited use of their other recent recordings. The film company was no doubt hoping for four Beatles gems; in practice, every time The Beatles recorded something that was vaguely unsatisfactory (or written by George Harrison, which – as far as Lennon and McCartney were concerned – amounted to the same thing), it was filed away for the movie.

These sessions were also witness to The Beatles' last collective attempts at recording avant-garde instrumental material. Two full days were devoted to taping long, meandering and apparently aimless pieces of *musique concrete*. These were no doubt inspired by McCartney's investigations into contemporary music. But another influence was what Lennon had seen and heard at the 14-Hour Technicolour Dream event at London's Alexandra Palace on April 29 (where, coincidentally, one of the other performance artists was Yoko Ono). It's interesting to speculate, also, about the possible impact on The Beatles of the album *The Velvet Underground And Nico*, that manager Brian Epstein had been playing incessantly for weeks. (Apparently, Epstein was negotiating to take over The Velvet Underground's management at the time of his death.) Those who have heard the jam sessions stated, however, that The Beatles' journeys into the avant-garde lacked any rudimentary form, or even respect for the art of staying roughly in tune.

Luckily, several more illuminating recordings did emerge from these post-*Pepper* recording dates. They varied from the instantly catchy bubblegum of McCartney's 'All Together Now' to the full-blown acid rock of Harrison's 'It's All Too Much', which was enlivened by Lennon and McCartney's ridiculous backing vocals and trumpets. Note also Lennon's opening shout of "To your mother" (the ultimate insult in Latin countries) as the guitar feedback took control.

Several days of recording were given over to perfecting the bizarre backing track of 'You Know My Name (Look Up The Number)', a Lennon 'composition' for which he had already taped a home demo the previous autumn. Having written no words for the song beyond the title, Lennon decided to make the instrumental track a work of art in itself. From the heavy staccato piano and echoed drums of the opening section, the song moved in succession through a bossa nova rhythm, an ecstatic ska section, what sounded like a bulletin from a bird-warblers' convention, and then back into another Latin shuffle, before taking in a spirited saxophone solo by Rolling Stone Brian Jones. With the track complete, the song was placed to one side while Lennon and McCartney waited for lyrical inspiration to strike.

Lennon's only other new song at this point was recorded in a single day on May 11, as he led the rather erratic accompaniment on piano and clavioline (another recent invention which gave a keyboard the sound of a Turkish street market). The song was bathed in a swirl of dense, faintly eerie sound, with the clavioline adding the feel of a demented soprano sax across the surface. Deep in the mix were some half-hearted handclaps, a stoned mickey-take of the rhythmic clapping which had been a feature of the early Beatles' records.

What they were creating was 'Baby You're A Rich Man' – by legend a paean to the demoralised Brian Epstein, though there seems no truth to the cruel rumour that Lennon turned one of the song's final choruses into "Baby, you're a rich fag Jew". Despite the fact that on paper the lyrics read like a straightforward enquiry – "How does it feel to be one of the beautiful people?" – Lennon's icy vocals gave the song an ironic bite. Ultimately, though, 'Rich Man' worked better as a record than as a song, which was probably why it was relegated to the flipside of their next single.

That release turned out to be another Lennon solo composition – written on guitar, round a chord sequence which he revisited for 'Instant Karma!' in 1970, but which he played in the studio on harpsichord. 'All You Need Is Love' was, like 'A Hard Day's Night' and 'Help!' before it, written to order. The Beatles had been chosen to represent Britain in the first global television link-up, a lengthy and rather tedious programme called *Our World* that was transmitted on June 25. Their brief was to write a suitably simple song, which could be understood by viewers who didn't speak English; and then to appear to record the track live on the show. Lennon and McCartney each set to work; McCartney's effort, 'All Together Now', was set aside for the recently proposed *Yellow Submarine* cartoon film, as was Harrison's 'It's All Too Much'. But Lennon's song was considered perfect to satisfy the TV commission.

What Lennon concocted at short notice was little short of an anthem for the optimistic summer of 1967. 'All You Need Is Love' was a rather naive reaction to world affairs, as subsequent events demonstrated; but Lennon expanded the theme with a moralising lyric which preached that nothing was impossible if you would only try. The same spirit invested his work as late as *Double Fantasy* in 1980. The repetitive melody and gently punning lyrics interacted well enough, and over the fade, Lennon left a gap for improvisation – filled on the night by an off-the-cuff rendition of 'She Loves You', written when the concept of love was a little narrower.

The broadcast duly went out on time, showing The Beatles and heavy friends apparently making the record. In fact, only the lead vocal and guitar were not already on tape, though McCartney and Starr double-tracked their existing parts, and the orchestra brought in for the session also played over what they had already recorded. The arrangement actually owed more to George Martin than to The Beatles, as he added depth to one of The Beatles' simplest rhythm tracks of the period, and also thought up the idea of using a burst of the French National Anthem, 'La Marseillaise' to open the track. One delicacy lost in the overdubbing was the rare sound of Lennon playing the banjo – the instrument on which his mother had taught him to play rock 'n' roll songs over a decade earlier. The instrument formed part of a bafflingly bizarre basic track, which had featured the massed talents of Harrison on violin, McCartney on double bass, Starr's drums and Lennon adding harpsichord.

After the live recording was completed, Lennon took the opportunity to patch up a few lines of his vocal, before the track was mixed for release.

MAY 1967: RECORDING 'We Love You' with The Rolling Stones

Mick Jagger and Keith Richards had been among the backing vocalists on the TV broadcast of 'All You Need Is Love'. Lennon and McCartney had done the same when the Stones recorded their Summer of Love anthem, which later served the dual purpose of thanking fans for their support during the Stones' recent conflicts with the law. John and Paul added their distinctive falsetto harmonies to 'We Love You'. Three years later, John took the opportunity of telling Jann Wenner of *Rolling Stone* that the song was nothing more than an imitation of 'All You Need Is Love'.

AUGUST 22 TO NOVEMBER 2, 1967: THE BEATLES recording 'Your Mother Should Know'/'I Am The Walrus'/'The Fool On The Hill'/'Blue Jay Way'/'Flying'/'Hello Goodbye'; Lennon producing 'Shirley's Wild Accordion' by Shirley Evans; Lennon recording 'Jessie's Dream'

The sessions were long and disconnected, and The Beatles rarely worked for more than a day or two a week, but during the last few months of 1967 they did complete the musical half of the *Magical Mystery Tour* project. Along the way, outside events had intruded. At the end of August, their manager Brian Epstein was found dead at his London home. That same week, The Beatles had attended an introductory meeting about Transcendental Meditation, held by the Maharishi Mahesh Yogi; and while Epstein was dying in the capital, his boys were in Bangor, Wales, at an intensive TM induction course also run by the Maharishi. From here until their rather unhappy stay at the Maharishi's camp in Rishikesh, India, the following spring, TM played an increasingly important part in The Beatles' lives, supposedly encouraging them to abandon the use of narcotics and spend several hours each day concentrating on their own personalised mantras.

Little of that influence found its way into the band's music, any more than they ever referred to Epstein in song. But the dreamy mental state brought on by TM did haunt George Harrison's 'Blue Jay Way' and the group's instrumental 'Flying', which was cut down from a strange nine-minute-plus jam into a tighter but still mostly ethereal mood piece for the *Magical Mystery Tour* film.

McCartney's contributions to the soundtrack were characteristically lightweight, at least in tone. 'The Fool On The Hill' was one of his most striking ballads, and John added some colourful bass harmonica playing to the instrumental track for the song. His mellotron was at the heart of 'Flying', suggesting that this may have been the initial inspiration for the song. More interestingly, he was credited on an EMI session sheet for the first time as producer, during an October 12 session in which accordion player Shirley Evans taped 'Shirley's Wild Accordion' for the *MMT* soundtrack. This track was copyrighted as a Lennon/McCartney composition, and involved Evans double-tracking her accordion parts while Ringo Starr played drums and Paul McCartney added maracas and vocal encouragement. The ensemble discussed what an accordion would sound like played backwards; while John Lennon corrected Evans when she crept away from the arrangement that had been written out for her. But after a busy session comprising 15 takes of the instrumental, it seems not to have been used in the *Magical Mystery Tour* film. Lennon also supervised the mixing and editing of Harrison's 'Blue Jay Way' during this session.

There is also some doubt about the origin of another piece of *MMT* incidental music, 'Jessie's Dream'. Not recorded at EMI but concocted at one of the group's home studios, it was listed as a four-man Beatles composition. It accompanied the nightmare in which 'Jessie', a lady of rather weighty disposition, was overwhelmed by the swill shovelled onto her restaurant table by her ever-smiling waiter, John Lennon. The image was sufficiently disgusting to make it easy to ignore the musical accompaniment, but beneath the dialogue was what sounded like an early run at the avant-garde tape-play of the *Two Virgins* album – full of discordant pianos and echoed guitars, chopped into a loping, unearthly rhythmic pattern. On aural evidence, 'Jessie's Dream' was the world's first airing of one of

Lennon's experimental home recordings – created, it should be noted, several months before John first formally invited Yoko Ono to his home.

'Jessie's Dream' was taped in the middle of a batch of sessions for 'Hello Goodbye' – a McCartney song tailored as the group's next single, although its final section was also played over the credits of the film. It began a run of McCartney-composed Beatles singles that – with two exceptions – ran unbroken until the group split two-and-a-half years later. Lennon had enjoyed a similar series of A-sides from 1963 through to late 1965; then, as now, the identity of the author of The Beatles' hits was also a clue to who was controlling the group's overall direction.

The flipside of the single, and also Lennon's only major contribution to the film soundtrack, was altogether more substantial: 'I Am The Walrus'. When Lennon made the connection between writing for himself, as in his books, and writing for an imagined public, the results were usually closer to the personal content of *In His Own Write* than the surrealistic wordplay and nonsensical imagery. 'Walrus' represented a rare dip into that second stream, with its gushing flow of puns, innuendo and sheer invention – assembled, according to Lennon's long-time friend Pete Shotton, as a deliberate riposte to The Beatles' more pretentious critics, who were already scouring *Sgt. Pepper* for insight into the universe.

The initial inspiration was more prosaic, however: the recurrent two-tone whine of a police siren, passing a paranoic Lennon's Surrey home. That musical motif survived on the final recording, in the form of the riff that underpinned the basic instrumental track, and the repetitive melody line to which Lennon recited his stream-of-nonsense lyrics. And the policeman who lined up his troops in the final verse was another obvious nod to the song's origins.

Like the pastiche artist he could be, Lennon put together the rest from a variety of sources. The walrus itself came from Lewis Carroll's 'The Walrus And The Carpenter' (though Lennon later acknowledged that he'd misunderstood the poem and chosen the villain of the piece as his 'hero'); the Hare Krishna from the religious leanings of Beatle Harrison; the "I'm crying" chorus line, stretched out over several bars, from The Miracles' soul ballad, 'Ooh Baby Baby'; 'Lucy In The Sky' from his own son (and song); and the opening statement of common identity – "I am he as you are he ..." – from the Buddhist and Taoist scriptures into which he'd dipped during his acid-led search for spiritual enlightenment. But the construction was the product of a mind tuned to the message of the unconscious: the sound of the words was as significant as their meaning, or lack of it.

Lennon later rated 'I Am The Walrus' as his favourite Beatles song. It wasn't the most meaningful, merely the one that gave him the greatest plea-sure to record – just as McCartney looked back on the equally playful 'You Know My Name (Look Up The Number)' with particular relish. For a record that was awash with sound effects and bizarre asides, however, the backing track was remarkably simple – recorded with, for the time, a stan-dard line-up of Beatles instruments, guitars, drums and keyboards. Only after the lead vocal was added did the music begin to rival the lyrics. George Martin arranged an orchestral score for the song that included long, atonal slides up the scale, and plenty of gloomy, diminished chords; then a choir added the "oompah oompah" backing vocals and John's wry assertion that "everybody's got one".

Lennon's conscious mind only resumed control of the piece in the final mixing, when – in an obvious nod of the head to John Cage's similar experiments – he added in an extract of Shakespeare's *King Lear* that was being broadcast on the BBC Third Programme at the time. It could just as easily have been the cricket commentary, in which case Beatleologists would have had an entirely different set of theories to investigate.

In retrospect, 'Walrus' was a turning point in the Beatles' career – and Lennon's. Issued at the end of 1967, it was their last full-blown excursion into psychedelia. Subsequent Beatles visions were always tinged with senti-ment ('Rocky Raccoon') or cynicism ('Piggies'). In the new year, Lennon continued to experiment in sound; but increasingly he would indulge in the formless collages that he had already begun to assemble at home, rather than trying to capture that hallucinogenic chaos in words. And early in 1968 he found a willing partner in Yoko Ono – someone who could not only enjoy his experimentation, but who could give it intellectual justification.

SEPTEMBER 11 TO NOVEMBER 1967: FILMING *Magical Mystery Tour*

Conceived during a transatlantic plane trip in April 1967, *Magical Mystery Tour* was a McCartney brainchild. He wrote the rough shooting script, or at least the bare bones of one; he evolved the idea of The Beatles and friends travelling through the West Country on a bus; and he composed most of the soundtrack music. All four Beatles supervised the shooting and then the editing, particularly Paul and Ringo. Lennon's main contribution was to go along with the idea, and to map out a couple of scenes in the film, which McCartney offered him as a sop to his own domination of the project.

Lennon rarely discussed the film in later years; he talked more about the 'soundtrack' album concocted by Capitol Records in the States than he did

111

about his own first experience of movie direction. But this 50-minute TV film seems to have been a project that he allowed to happen, rather than controlled in any meaningful sense. True, he did improvise his own scenes in the film, but then so did everyone else, within the basic framework dictated by McCartney. Only a couple of scenes betray more than casual interest on Lennon's part, though he still managed to capture more screen time than Harrison, for example, whose glazed eyes and stoned expression suggested that he had prepared for the filming a little too excessively.

McCartney's initial enthusiasm for the project, which had led The Beatles to begin recording the title song back in April 1967, had dimmed over the summer. Only when he felt the band drifting apart after the death of Brian Epstein did he resurrect the idea, setting the unrealistic deadline of Christmas for a British TV première. A few days of filming in the West Country produced a batch of chaotic, disconnected vignettes, which had to be cobbled into some form of narrative logic in the editing studio. In the end, McCartney was forced to resume shooting to create visual settings for Harrison's 'Blue Jay Way' and his own 'The Fool On The Hill' – clips that, with their imagination and trickery, far outshone the original location footage.

As we've seen, Lennon became sufficiently involved in the movie to donate 'I Am The Walrus' to its soundtrack; produce Shirley Evans' elusive 'Wild Accordion'; and dig into his archive of home recordings for 'Jessie's Dream'. He also narrated the early stages of the story, and showed his gift for character in a number of brief cameo roles – like the ticket seller, and the evil Italian waiter in the dream sequence. With its anarchic distortion of everyday convention, that dream/nightmare scene, with Lennon attempting to drown the unfortunate Jessie in food, has the feel of some of Lennon's early prose pieces. In the same way, the film clip that accompanies 'I Am The Walrus', a vain but amusing attempt to match the surrealism of the song, was based on the wilder corners of Lennon's imagination.

Otherwise, it was difficult to see any guiding influence at work during some of the film's *longeurs* – the marathon race round a deserted airfield, Victor Spinetti's sergeant-major routine, the sing-song on the coach. What was also noticeable was the sheer incompetence of the camera work and editing – the work of people who were totally unfamiliar with the medium they were using, but who were sufficiently in thrall to their own mystique not to worry. Though the best of the film's humour looked forward to *Monty Python's Flying Circus*, far too much was self-indulgent, aimed at an audience of four and their close friends. Small wonder, then, that the movie attracted such a critical pasting; and that one of its four co-directors preferred to pretend that it had never actually happened.

CHAPTER 7

October 1967 to May 1968

Transcendental meditation appeared to be the stimulus and the belief system that Lennon had been searching for, ever since he became a Beatle. After his initial baptism into the teachings of the Maharishi Mahesh Yogi in August 1967, he became the group's most enthusiastic proselytiser of the guru's ideas. But it was another exotic influence that was beginning to dominate Lennon's thoughts. For the moment, he didn't know whether Yoko Ono appealed to his intellectual curiosity, his artistic drive, or his rampant sexuality. He certainly didn't realise that it would be possible for one person – a woman, no less – to tantalise and stimulate all three.

OCTOBER 11 TO NOVEMBER 14, 1967: LENNON sponsors Yoko Plus Me

On November 9, 1966, John Lennon attended the preview of an exhibition at the Indica Gallery in London, to which he'd been invited by his friend, gallery owner John Dunbar. The exhibition was the work of Yoko Ono, a Japanese performance artist who was now a leading member of the Fluxus group in New York. Equating performance art with the prospect of sex, Lennon was intrigued, then bewildered, as he found no hint of an orgy in progress, merely a set of minimalist sculptures: 'Hammer-A-Nail', a white board which invited the onlooker to do just that; an apple on a stand; most invitingly, a ladder which you climbed, to find a spyglass revealing the message: "Yes".

Lennon and Ono exchanged a few remarks, made mental notes of the other's existence, and then went on with their lives. Over the next few months, they met casually at other openings, while Yoko became a mini-celebrity as a result of the furore surrounding her *Film No. 4*, or as it was better known, *Bottoms*. The film was simply a collection of behinds, shot one after another from an identical position, complete with the bemused comments of the participants on the soundtrack. Earlier Ono films had been equally conceptual, concentrating on a single event or observation in the accepted style of the Fluxus group.

Yoko had also published a book of her 'instructions', comprising keys to her conceptual art, and suggestions for happenings or events or films. The book was called *Grapefruit*: Yoko had a copy delivered to Lennon during the *Sgt. Pepper* sessions. Both were present at the 14-Hour Technicolour Dream underground event, celebrating London's psychedelic culture at Alexandra Palace. Ono staged her controversial 'Cut Piece', in which she invited audience members to snip away an article of clothing from an attractive female, to which Lennon was a doubtless intrigued spectator. When the pair next met, Yoko happened to mention that she was looking for a sponsor for an exhibition at the Lisson Gallery. Lennon agreed to help out: and while the exhibition was being planned, found that he had also been chosen to participate in Yoko's *13 Days Do-It-Yourself Dance Festival*, in which selected people received conceptual instructions through the post, and chose whether or not to follow them.

On, significantly enough, Lennon's 27th birthday, Yoko Ono opened the exhibition of her work at the Lisson Gallery. Her media profile in Britain had already been heightened by the publicity surrounding *Film No. 4*; now her coy announcement in the event's programme that the exhibition had been financed by John Lennon guaranteed her further column inches. Despite its title, Yoko's show – also known as *Half-A-Wind* – had no direct input from Lennon: eager to avoid being linked too closely with the artist, he had made his financial contribution of £5,000 anonymously, and was perturbed when his name was, after all, mentioned in connection with the event. In fact, it appears that he didn't even visit the exhibition once it had opened.

He missed the opportunity to view a retrospective of Yoko's work to date. One floor was devoted to her 'Stone Piece' – featuring the artist, or so one was meant to presume, occupying a white bag in a stone-like posture. At this point, the concept of 'bagism' had yet to be invented, but the game was already in play. Another section of the exhibition featured a selection of equally familiar Ono pieces, including the 'Hammer-A-Nail' sculpture that had initially attracted Lennon's attention at the 1966 Indica Gallery show, and the apple on a stand. One new sculpture was on display: 'Windflute For John'.

The focus of the show was on the top floor of the gallery, however, where Yoko presented 'Half-A-Wind'. This featured apparently empty 'Air Bottles' bearing labels such as "half-a-dream" and "half-a-music", and also 'Half-A-Room', which comprised white items of household furniture neatly sawn down the middle, but otherwise arranged in conventional relation to each other. "Her work is always pure, honest and white," Lennon explained.

These were the concepts, or the conceits, that Yoko brought to her artwork with John. Their novelty intrigued him – and for a while he was content to treat her artistic world as an adventure playground. His sponsorship of this show meant that he had paid his entrance fee. On December 8, 1967, he received another glimpse into her unique world, when he attended her *Music Of The Mind* concert recital at London's Saville Theatre, until recently owned by Beatles manager Brian Epstein. Each close encounter with her mind heightened his curiosity – artistic and otherwise.

NOVEMBER 24/28-29, 1967: RECORDING tapes for *Scene Three Act One*, including 'Pedro The Fisherman' (alias 'Sailor Come Back To Me')/'Chi Chi's Café'/'Daddy's Little Sunshine Boy'/'Down In Cuba' (alias 'El Tango Terrible') and possibly 'Stranger In My Arms'; THE BEATLES recording 'Christmas Time Is Here Again'

On October 3, 1967, the newly-opened National Theatre in London announced to a bemused theatrical press that they would shortly be staging a dramatic adaptation of John Lennon's two books, *In His Own Write* and *A Spaniard In The Works*. A few weeks later, serious work began, with the play's title already fixed as *Scene Three Act One* (from an amusing playlet in the first book), and Lennon co-opted as one of three writers on the project.

As it transpired, Lennon's involvement with the finished play was fairly slight. But as early as November 1967 he did begin to prepare sound tapes and spoken-word recordings for use in its production. One session was devoted to the actors from the cast reading extracts from the script while classical music was inserted as a backdrop. Another saw Lennon supervising The Beatles as they recorded Christmas party noises, which consisted of mock-chatter and much clinking of glasses, with the ensemble breaking into 'Knees Up Mother Brown' at the close. Another tape was filled with 'Working Noises' – miscellaneous knocking and scraping sounds, with added tape echo. 'Electronic Noises' mingled with the rubbing of wine glasses with high pitched whistles; while for 'Celeste (Children's Hour)' George Martin played short spurts of BBC-style incidental music. Lennon directed proceedings throughout.

These sessions were almost certainly the occasion when a strange batch of Lennon home recordings, several of them made with the help of Ringo Starr, were transferred onto EMI master tapes. They mixed together musical compositions, mostly pastiches of light opera or music hall favourites, with madcap mellotron intrusions and comic interludes. The two Beatles crooned 'Daddy's Little Sunshine Boy' under the influence of some sweet medicine, while both 'Pedro The Fisherman' and 'Down In Cuba' found Lennon adopting a particularly playful Latino accent, as if he was auditioning as a minstrel in a seaside pizza joint. The most enjoyable item, 'Chi Chi's Café', opened with a jaunty Parisian jazz combo, before Starr announced: "Welcome to the Edgehill country club". The pair then made up vaudeville ditties over a cha-cha rhythm, before Lennon lapsed into his impression of an Irish folkie, 'Woody The Woodbine'. The Goons could hardly have done it better.

'Stranger In My Arms' may also have come from these sessions, though it was more complete and structured than its counterparts. Otherwise the recipe was similar: a drastically over-egged cabaret song, supported by mellow mellotron madness. Had Lennon completed an album of this stuff, it would not only have been infinitely more listenable than *Two Virgins* (and much less self-conscious), but it might also have been reclaimed during the early Nineties' Easy Listening revival as a definitive satire on the genre.

Lennon's second session for *Scene Three Act One* took place after The Beatles had recorded their 1967 Christmas Fan Club Record. Previous Christmas discs had either been spoken word messages or mock pantomimes: the 1967 effort followed the second course, but interrupted proceedings with an excerpt from a six-minute Beatles song, 'Christmas Time Is Here Again'. Credited to all four Beatles, the track had the air of a McCartney throwaway, with the same chorus repeated over and over again, like a rehearsal for 'Hey Jude' the following year. But Lennon and the others entered into the spirit of the occasion, chipping in weird sound effects and character voices as the performance gradually slid into mayhem.

c. JANUARY 1968: RECORDING home demos of 'She Can Talk To Me'/'Jai Guru Dev'/'Cry Baby Cry' plus untitled mellotron improvisations

It's probably not a coincidence that Lennon's whole-hearted adoption of meditation techniques should have coincided with a gentle rebirth of his musical creativity. Through much of 1967, he had struggled to compete with Paul McCartney's flood of new material. Now, with no album project on the immediate horizon, he began to assemble fragments that could be moulded into finished songs – and soon were.

One fragment consisted of nothing more than an Indian spiritual phrase, "jai guru dev", repeated over and over, with Lennon struggling to play the piano with one hand and the mellotron with the other. He attempted the same phrase as a jaunty music hall singalong. Elsewhere, he linked it into another work in progress, a mock nursery rhyme called 'Cry Baby Cry'. He had a variety of options at his disposal for that unfinished song: at one point he screamed out the chorus over a raucous electric guitar, as if he was trying to match McCartney's soon-to-be-recorded 'Helter Skelter'.

The same tentative home studio sessions also produced a chorus waiting for a song, entitled 'She Can Talk To Me'. He improvised some vague lyrics about marital distance, but soon discarded them, concentrating instead of conjuring up a riff to underpin his theme.

Two of these three fragments emerged fully grown in The Beatles' next batch of recordings.

FEBRUARY 3 TO 11, 1968: THE BEATLES recording 'Lady Madonna'/'Across The Universe'/'The Inner Light'/'Hey Bulldog'

Ever since the previous September, The Beatles had been trying to schedule a trip to the Maharishi Mahesh Yogi's meditation centre in Rishikesh, India – only to be forced to delay the visit because of their commitments to the *Magical Mystery Tour* project. A new departure date was set for February 15. Before then, The Beatles had to record a new single, to be issued in their absence, which they hoped would fulfil the expectations of their audience (and EMI) through to the end of the summer, when they might conceivably have had time to record a new album.

Just like the old days, Lennon and McCartney submitted rival songs for consideration. Paul's 'Lady Madonna' was started first, with Lennon supporting this pastiche of Fifties rock'n'roll on fuzz guitar and backing vocals. The following day, they began to record Lennon's 'Across The Universe' – stage one in a process that eventually became a saga.

Lennon regarded the song as a rare occasion where his lyrics stood up by themselves, as poetry, though he took little personal credit, claiming that the entire song had come to him one night as he lay in bed, seething over an argument with his wife, Cynthia. None of that conflict surfaced in the song:

its subject, instead, was the process of writing. Like much of the best romantic poetry, 'Across The Universe' celebrated the Muse – the creative process whereby words form in the mind and are transferred on to the page. Lennon merged the melody he'd pulled from his subconscious with the 'Jai Guru Dev' fragment he'd already composed.

What was striking was not the subject, but the power of the imagery, and the complete lack of the overblown lyricism that most writers would have brought to the subject. 'Across The Universe' could safely be given to those who doubted rock music's credentials as 'serious' art; yet because it emerged out of instinct, rather than conscious thought, it displayed none of the faults that attended most attempts to be 'serious' in the rock field. As Lennon recalled, "I didn't want to write it ... it wrote itself. It drove me out of bed ... It's like being possessed, like a psychic or a medium ... Letting it go is what the whole game is. You put your finger on it, it slips away, right?"

Sadly, little of that ease, of that yielding to the power of the art, survived into the recording process. It's difficult to imagine how commercial 'Across The Universe' might have been as a single; it was a Beatles record, so it would have sold, but it lacked the common touch of 'All You Need Is Love' or 'Hello Goodbye'. As The Beatles were supposed to be recording a single, maybe some of that doubt crept into their performance in the studio. Either way, what began as one of Lennon's most cherished songs ended up, in his words, as "a lousy track ... The Beatles didn't make a good record out of it. The guitars are out of tune and I'm singing out of tune because I'm psychologically destroyed and nobody's supporting me or helping me with it, and the song was never done properly." Lennon added that he felt McCartney was subconsciously trying to destroy his work at this period; though there's nothing to support that paranoia on the original session tapes.

The basic recording of 'Across The Universe' was done in a day, with George Harrison playing sitar and phasing applied to the guitar and percussion to support the Eastern mysticism of the lyric. Then two female fans were dragged in from the Abbey Road doorstep to sing high harmonies. In an inspired move, Harrison spent a couple of hours writing out and then performing little flurries of backwards guitar, which were inserted into the mix – transforming the song into a psychedelic haze – and then just as quickly removed. By the end of the session, and after some additional overdubs four days later, Lennon was unable to avoid the conclusion that 'Universe' could not be issued as a single.

So the song languished in the vaults for 18 months, until George Martin dug it out as The Beatles' contribution to a World Wildlife Fund charity

The public face of John Lennon in 1963: a harsh exterior masking sensitive psyche. *(LFI)*

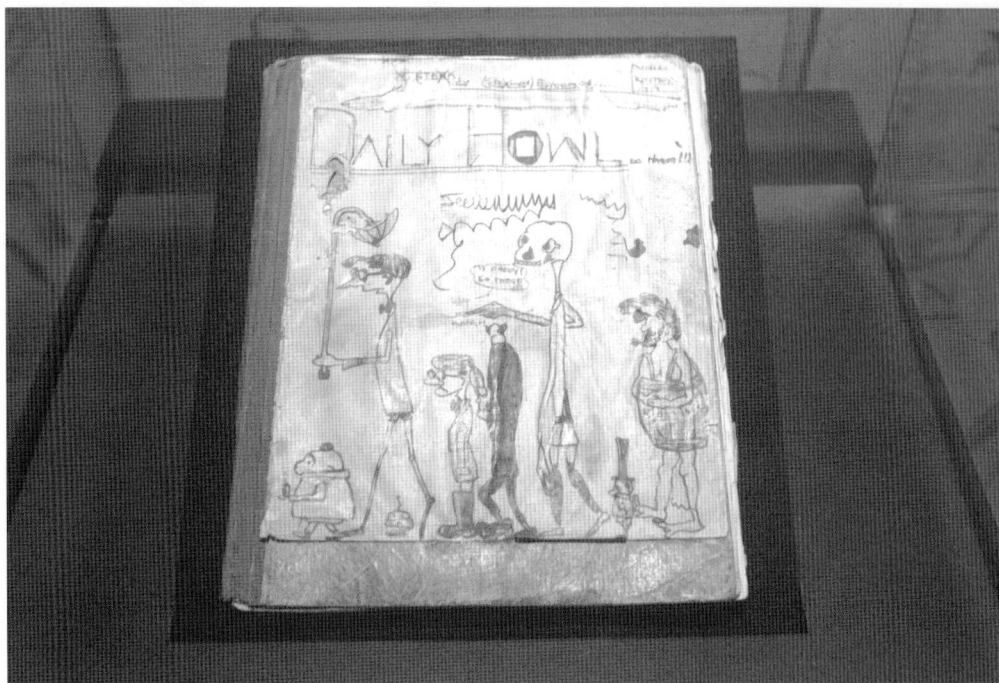

The Daily Howl, one of Lennon's teenage escape routes from the drudgery of school life. *(Masatoshi Okauchi/Rex Features)*

The Quarry Men perform at Walton Village Fete on July 6, 1957, on the day Lennon met Paul McCartney for the first time. *(LFI)*

The untamed Beatles on stage in 1960 in Hamburg, where Lennon always maintained that they gave their finest performances. Left to right: McCartney on piano, Pete Best on drums, Stuart Sutcliffe on bass, George Harrison on guitar and Lennon on guitar. *(K&K Ulf Kruger OHG/Redferns)*

The Beatles at a BBC session in 1963, a four-headed hydra that revolutionised the global pop industry. *(LFI)*

The Beatles meet up in the Star Steak House in London's Shaftesbury Avenue, October 1963. *(Getty Images)*

A partnership of equals, about to become a dictatorship of two: George Martin with the songwriting Beatles at Abbey Road.
(Terry O'Neill/Rex Features)

The Lennons (Mark 1): John and Cynthia en route to America, February 7 1964.
(Hulton-Deutsch Collection/Corbis)

The perfect encapsulation of the moptop myth: The Beatles in *A Hard Day's Night* – and Notting Hill, April 1964. *(Bettmann/Corbis)*

Lennon waiting for the wind to drop, or change, on Salisbury Plain during the filming of *Help!*, May 1965. *(Emilio Lari/Rex Features)*

Lennon filming *How I Won The War* in September 1966: the psychedelic madman, waiting to explode on an unsuspecting world. *(Mondial/Rex Features)*

Lennon, Brian Epstein and McCartney as The Beatles prepare to perform 'All You Need Is Love' for the world in June, 1967. *(David Magnus/Rex Features)*

Lennon's search for novelty briefly inspired him to experiment with unusual instruments, before discovering that his most novel ideas came from within himself. *(David Magnus/Rex Features)*

Lennon and Harrison pay court to the Maharishi Mahesh Yogi, August 1967. *(Cummings Archive/Redferns)*

A passenger on McCartney's *Magical Mystery Tour*,
late summer 1967.
(Hulton- Deutsch Collection/Corbis)

"I declare these balloons high": the Lennons
(Mark 2) open John's first art exhibition, July 1968.
(Bettman/Corbis)

While The Beatles recorded 'Hey Bulldog' in 1968, Yoko watched quizzically from the Abbey Road control room.
She would become Lennon's constant companion at subsequent Beatles sessions. *(Getty Images)*

A last show of unity on the Apple rooftop, January 1969. *(Getty Images)*

album, and overdubbed some bird sounds over the introduction. The following year, when Phil Spector was called in to assemble the *Let It Be* album, he also went back to the original 'Across The Universe', and produced an entirely different mix of the song. George Martin had speeded up the original Beatles' recording by about five per cent; Spector slowed it down by the same amount, and then added a heavenly choir and a full string orchestra to support the majesty of Lennon's lyrics. The author wasn't consulted, but voted his thanks by asking Spector to produce his next three albums.

We're getting ahead of ourselves, however. Back in February 1968, once The Beatles had decided to release 'Lady Madonna' and Harrison's 'The Inner Light' as their next single (and their first not to contain a Lennon composition), they made arrangements to film a special promotional clip, to be shown on TV while they were off in India. The original plan was to portray The Beatles at work on 'Lady Madonna', but rather than waste a day in the studio, they chose instead to record a new song, Lennon's 'Hey Bulldog', written to order for the *Yellow Submarine* soundtrack.

Watched by Yoko Ono, who wondered aloud why The Beatles always used such simple rhythms, the band built the song around a rewritten walking-blues riff, which once again harked back to the Fifties R&B songs of Ray Charles. Lennon's lyrics, which incorporated a rewrite of his home demo, 'She Can Talk To Me', walked a fine line between nonsense and inspired nonsense, and the gusto of the performance, and the sheer chaos of the fade-out, made this one of the warmest, most enjoyable Beatles recordings of the era. In a way, it was another landmark in their career, another milestone on the road to dissolution. Rarely in the future would they approach a session with such boyish enthusiasm. The disillusionment of the Rishikesh fiasco seemed to remove the last of the group's Four Musketeers spirit, that one-for-all camaraderie and mutual support which had seen them through every crisis from the sacking of Pete Best to the critical panning of *Magical Mystery Tour*.

FEBRUARY TO MAY 1968: WRITING 'I'm So Tired'/'Yer Blues'/'Child of Nature'/'Julia'/'Sexy Sadie'/'The Continuing Story Of Bungalow Bill'/'Dear Prudence'/'Revolution'/ 'Everybody's Got Something To Hide Except For Me And My Monkey'/'What's The New Mary Jane'/'Look At Me' in India; recording home demos of 'Julia'/'Sexy Sadie'/'Child of Nature'/'Everybody's Got Something To Hide Except For Me And My Monkey'/'Look At Me'/'Mean Mr Mustard'/'Polythene Pam'/'I Need A Fix'/'Glass Onion'

John Lennon spent three days short of two months in India early in 1968, most of that time at the Maharishi Mahesh Yogi's retreat in Rishikesh. The four Beatles had made the oft-postponed trip to seal their pact with Transcendental Meditation: in the land where the Maharishi had developed his theory, transcendence ought to have been easier to find than in London, where growing business commitments and personal anxieties were eating into their peace of mind.

John travelled to India with his wife, Cynthia; he admitted later that he had tried to find a way to take Yoko as well. As it turned out, two months' separation from Yoko seems to have kindled his interest, and within a month of his return, they had begun their affair.

Meanwhile, Lennon and the other Beatles threw themselves into the Maharishi's regime, each spending hours alone in their rooms, contemplating the infinite and repeating their individual mantras. It was a rare respite from the frenetic pace of life in the fast lane. Separated from the trappings of stardom, and from the hallucinogenic drugs that had become a regular method of escape over the last two years, Lennon was forced to look at himself, and his relationship with the rest of the world.

The Beatles had taken along acoustic guitars to India and they used their time of relaxation to write. By the time they had all returned in early April, McCartney announced that they had composed thirty songs in India and that the best of these would shortly be recorded for an album called *A Doll's House*, set for release by the end of the year. (That prospective title had to be abandoned when the rock band Family called their debut album *Music From A Doll's House*.)

Harrison was already using his music as a vehicle for his spiritual beliefs; his experiences in India merely strengthened his commitments. McCartney seems to have remained untouched by the experience; or at least he wasn't able, or ready, to translate his thoughts into song. He approached the leisure time as a professional tunesmith, cranking out a series of well-crafted, rounded songs that revealed little of his inner self.

Lennon did not find subterfuge as easy, however, or as satisfying; and the songs he wrote in India were necessarily a reflection of his own life. Seeing himself and the world with heightened clarity – induced as much by the absence of chemicals as by the Maharishi's teaching – he took the process of self-discovery he had begun with his prose writings and his songs on *Rubber Soul* a stage further.

What emerged were the same feelings of guilt about his marriage, loss over his shattered family life, confusion about his own direction, and hope for the future, which he had being trying to suppress – or twist into psychedelic visions – for the past three years. This time, however, the messages emerged without any metaphors. Lennon found himself, secure in a haven of inner peace, confronting his most virulent demons. Slowly these emerged in music and lyrics, in songs like 'Yer Blues' and 'I'm So Tired' – ironic offspring of a venture that had been intended to bring harmony and contentment.

At the same time, Lennon made a conscious attempt to persuade himself that the meditation process was working its magic. One of his new songs, rejected for release when John realised that it was patently insincere, offered an entirely optimistic portrait of the meditation experience, untroubled by the nagging pain of Lennon's real feelings. Set to a melody that was later used for 'Jealous Guy', 'Child Of Nature' offered an embarrassingly fulsome tribute to the Maharishi's teachings, with a title that harked back to the 19th Century Romantics' view of the natural boy uncorrupted by society. Lennon's proclamation that TM had returned him to such a state, however, was firmly punctured by the other songs that emerged during his stay in India – while the pomposity of his home demo, with dramatic (mellotron-created) mandolins and an affected lead vocal, added to the inauthentic air.

'Child Of Nature' was the work of a man writing what he felt he *should* be writing. The rest of his work from India was altogether more authentic, and more painful. 'I'm So Tired' was a blunt successor to the dreamy 'I'm Only Sleeping;' fashioned like an acoustic blues, with a self-pitying lyric to match, it burst into violent, electric life during the chorus, with its blatant appeal: "I'd give you everything I've got for a little peace of mind". Second time through, Lennon's voice rose uncontrollably as he cried out, "I'm going insane", nailing any idea that this was merely the suffering of the Romantic.

'Yer Blues' said it even straighter: "Feel so suicidal, even hate my rock 'n' roll", which was about as desperate as a rock star could get in 1968. The grim imagery of the verses, with their "black clouds" and "blue mists", were only slightly redeemed by the mocking reference to "Dylan's Mr Jones", the butt of Bob's 'Ballad Of A Thin Man'. Those were the most blatant of Lennon's self-examinations, the darkest visions unleashed by his solitude and inner searching.

From its imagery alone, 'I Need A Fix' (later incorporated as the middle section of 'Happiness Is A Warm Gun') suggested that Lennon might have become so desperate in India that he was willing to risk heroin addiction. But that joy was still several months ahead of him. The sexual nature of the fix in this fragment was made plain when he demoed the tune on his return. His tagline in the song made him one of the first people to come up

121

with that hackneyed joke: "Yoko Ono, oh no, Yoko, oh no, oh yes". He was clearly ready to say 'yes' to his Mother Superior.

Also written in India were two of his most affecting ballads, 'Julia' and 'Look At Me'. Lennon recorded a series of almost identical, double-tracked demos of 'Julia' when he returned to England. Like 'Look At Me', they demonstrated his new-found skill as a guitar-picker. The same simple acoustic riffs, taught to Lennon by fellow meditator, Donovan, could be heard behind several songs over the next couple of years, from 'Sun King' to Yoko's 'Remember Love'; the Indian spring obviously gave Lennon the chance to improve his musical skills as well as his songwriting.

'Julia' had a dual subject: his late mother, Julia Lennon, and the woman who was still only his artistic collaborator, and whose name translated into "ocean child" – Yoko Ono. If you didn't know his mother's name, 'Julia' would have sounded like a simple ballad of love; but Lennon never invented characters for his love songs, unlike McCartney's 'Martha My Dear' or 'Michelle', so he clearly had a real (Japanese) woman in mind.

'Look At Me' was more straightforward in its message: "Who am I supposed to be?" asked Lennon, in what was musically a continuation of 'Julia'. The question was obviously still relevant when John finally recorded the song in 1970, but as early as 1968 he could see the hint of a solution in his new relationship: "Nobody else can see/Just you and me".

Not all of Lennon's songs from India were quite as personal. Several of them continued the tradition of semi-nonsense lyrics begun the previous year. They were proof that for The Beatles, at least, he was still ready to act the part of hack tunesmith. In this guise, he churned out 'Mean Mr Mustard' (as yet unfinished) about a miser mentioned in a press story, and 'Polythene Pam' loosely inspired by an earlier attempt to inveigle him into an orgy with a bondage queen. Only slightly more serious, 'Everybody's Got Something To Hide Except Me And My Monkey' was a sturdy rocker built around a set of contradictions: at its most basic level, it said that the new Lennon didn't need any disguises, something of a manifesto for the years to come.

'What's The New Mary Jane' was altogether more mysterious, and lightweight. It was a stream of unconsciousness series of riddles, which may or may not have been meant to poke fun at one of Lennon's friends who was somewhat slow to sample the thrill of psychedelic drugs. (One Lennon insider from this period has confirmed to the author that the target was indeed Paul McCartney.) For once, the drug imagery – 'Mary Jane' for marijuana – was probably deliberate; but the message didn't go any deeper than that. Though he wasn't credited when the song was eventually released on

Anthology 3, some of the lyrics are believed to have been written by Apple Electronics guru, Alexis 'Magic Alex' Mardas.

'The Continuing Story Of Bungalow Bill' was equally mischievous. Lennon explained in 1980: "That was written about a guy in Maharishi's meditation camp who took a short break to go shoot a few poor tigers, and then came back to commune with God. There was a character called Jungle Jim and I combined him with Buffalo Bill. It's a sort of teenage social comment song and a bit of a joke." With its singalong chorus, it also worked well as a children's song – children being ideally placed to appreciate Lennon's cruel sense of humour.

Another, more pathetic fellow meditator inspired the beautiful 'Dear Prudence'. The woman in question was Mia Farrow's sister, who had meditated herself into her room and wouldn't come out. Lennon was chosen as the man to persuade her back into the real life, and wrote the song as a simple message that the world outside was beautiful, and so was she, so why wouldn't she come out to play? Its initial impetus aside, 'Dear Prudence' was as clear and convincing an advertisement for TM as Lennon ever created, with its childlike appreciation of the natural world, clarity of thought and open generosity – only slightly undercut on John's demo for the song by a spoken ending which turned poor Prudence into a candidate for the funny farm.

'Sexy Sadie' was Lennon's most memorable picture of the Maharishi episode, however. The Beatles began to feel that the Maharishi was showing far too earthy an interest in the women in their party; when Harrison, the band's biggest advocate of TM, started to believe the story, then Lennon was sure it must be true. As they made their plans to leave, teasing the baffled Maharishi with the fact that he couldn't read their thoughts, Lennon composed a vicious song of hatred – the cry of the abandoned follower (or the deserted child). "Maharishi", he wrote in the original draft, "you little twat/Who the fuck do you think you are?/Oh you cunt".

Back in Britain, Lennon mellowed a little, changed the title of the song to the more obscure 'Sexy Sadie' to avoid legal complications, and turned a gut reaction into a song. The finished result mixed sarcasm ("She's the latest and the greatest of them all") with aggression ("You'll get yours yet"), but couldn't dispel the aggrieved tone of the disappointed disciple. Lennon later admitted that he had seen the Maharishi as a kind of father-figure, a substitute for the ignoble Alf; and it was the child's burning resentment at being betrayed by someone who was supposed to protect him that was the song's underlying theme.

Lennon spent much of April recording home demos of several of these songs, generally doubling up his vocal and acoustic guitar parts, concentrating more on feel than accuracy or timing. The demos have a clarity sometimes missing on the final record – and a slightly trippy feel that suggested that John had lost no time in returning to the comforting arms of Mary Jane. There are slight differences between these demos and the finished records, but they are usually a matter of decoration rather than conception. The Beatles may have embellished the songs, but they didn't fundamentally change them.

During his home recording sessions, Lennon also composed and taped a double-tracked demo of an intriguing piece of self-mythology entitled 'Glass Onion'. Using familiar Beatles images and titles as the subject of wry humour, it began to hint at a growing distance between himself and the fabled Fab Four. Yet the mood was still playful, as Lennon even multi-tracked the outbursts of verbal gibberish that punctuated the song at this stage.

c. EARLY MAY 1968: LENNON/McCARTNEY produce Grapefruit

The Beatles' Apple company began life as a financial manoeuvre to lessen their tax obligations. The ideal of an artistic utopia came later. From the start, however, Lennon and McCartney wanted to play with their new toy. On December 11, 1967, they signed the members of a new pop group, named Grapefruit, to their Apple Publishing division – the first bricks in their intended empire. Lennon himself named the fledgling group, significantly drawing their title from Yoko's bedside book.

Taking their duties as publishers seriously, Lennon and McCartney also helped to supervise some of Grapefruit's recording sessions. Earlier reports that the pair produced the group's debut single, 'Dear Delilah', appear to be unfounded. But they were certainly present when Grapefruit recorded a song entitled 'Lullaby', which appeared on their debut album, *Around Grapefruit*. Because Lennon retained in his archives, an acetate of their work in progress, the track was copyrighted in the mid–Eighties by Yoko Ono, under the mistaken assumption that it was an unreleased song by her late husband. Lennon is also said by researcher Kristofer Engelhardt to have contributed the brass arrangement – or at least the idea for it – for the group's hit single cover of The Four Seasons' 'C'mon Marianne'.

c. MAY 18, 1968: THE BEATLES recording demos of 'Cry Baby Cry'/'Child Of Nature'/'The Continuing Story Of Bungalow Bill'/'I'm So Tired'/'Yer Blues'/'Everybody's Got Something To Hide Except For Me And My Monkey'/'What's The New Mary Jane'/'Revolution'/'While My Guitar Gently Weeps'/'Circles'/ 'Sour Milk Sea'/'Not Guilty'/'Piggies'/'Julia'/'Blackbird'/ 'Rocky Raccoon'/'Back In The USSR'/'Honey Pie'/'Mother Nature's Son'/'Ob-La-Di, Ob-La-Da'/'Junk'/'Dear Prudence'/ 'Sexy Sadie'

In mid-May, The Beatles regrouped to prepare for their own recording sessions, more than a year after they had completed work on their last official album, *Sgt. Pepper's Lonely Hearts Club Band*. Over a day or more of laidback sessions at George Harrison's home, Kinfauns, they taped demos of their new songs. For the first time since *A Hard Day's Night* in 1964, Lennon had accumulated more songs than Paul McCartney – testament to the mind-cleansing power of the Maharishi's techniques, regardless of Lennon's later misgivings.

The results exuded a high, stoned atmosphere that suggests the band were taking things very comfortably indeed. If they had been only a little more precise, then these demos might have made as satisfying an album as *The Beatles* eventually turned out to be. They have a communal feel entirely missing from the proper recording sessions, where (as has been noted many times in the past) each of the group effectively used the others as sidemen on their own compositions. At these demo sessions at George Harrison's house, they gave even their darkest new compositions a frivolity that came from co-operation and mutual understanding.

One of the most impressive of The Beatles' demos from this week was a new Lennon song, written just days before it was recorded. 'Revolution' was an instant, slightly confused response to the student uprisings on the streets of Europe, and the unrest around the globe about the USA's increasingly troubled involvement in the civil war in Vietnam.

'Revolution' saw Lennon as a gradualist, urging caution rather than full-blooded commitment to violent solutions. "But when you talk about destruction/Don't you know that you can count me out", ran one of the key lines, which caught Lennon midway between the need for a radical change in society, and the hippie ideal that everything could be achieved through love. The song was greeted by student radicals as a rather patronising piece of anti-realism: they felt that Lennon's repeated chorus line, "Don't you know it's gonna be alright", could only have come from

125

someone not personally affected by the problems which fuelled the student protests. In purely political terms, however, the lyrics made sense in quite another way: backing the line of the traditional Western Communist parties that revolution had to evolve rather than be imposed in a single direct action, as the ultra-left (the Trotskyists) were recommending. Whatever Lennon's true motives, The Beatles' first off-the-cuff recording of the song was wonderfully inappropriate, full of joyous harmonies that sounded like a celebration rather than a warning. Only later would Lennon find a more suitable setting for his lyrics, and begin to question his own ambiguous feelings about political violence.

Like 'Revolution', most of the Kinfauns demos were deliciously chaotic, with the double-tracking often completely out of phase – all of which added to the intoxicated atmosphere. 'What's The New Mary Jane', appropriately enough, sounded the most stoned of all, but the same heady air pervaded everything from 'Sexy Sadie' to 'Yer Blues', as if the most violent clouds could be blown away by a puff from the peace pipe.

One final discographical note: The Beatles' *Anthology 3* album listed Lennon's solo demos of 'I Need A Fix', 'Mean Mr Mustard' and 'Polythene Pam' as having been recorded during the sessions at Harrison's house. Internal evidence, however, suggests that they were actually taped at Lennon's home. Both Lennon and McCartney apparently brought reels of existing demos to the Kinfauns sessions, and Harrison appears to have collated both the group and solo tapes onto one set of reels, without distinguishing between the two. What is certain, though, is that Harrison was the source for the particular tapes aired on *Anthology 3*, while the Lennon estate doesn't seem to have John's original recordings of these songs in its own archive.

CHAPTER 8

May 1968 to December 1968

The events of May 1968 – the month, according to his old friend Pete Shotton, when John announced to the other Beatles that he thought he was Jesus Christ – overturned every aspect of Lennon's life. The public wasn't ready for one of the Fab Four to abandon his wife for a Japanese avant-garde artist. Neither were the other Beatles, especially when that involved welcoming this artistically self-confident woman into their collective sphere. Both privately and publicly, the world watched with amazement and horror as Lennon adopted his new girlfriend's ethos and working methods. The world's reaction soon haunted and corrupted the couple's romantic idyll.

MAY 19-20, 1968: RECORDING *Two Virgins* and out-take material, including 'Holding A Note'

Conveniently, both sets of spouses and children were out of the country. That left Beatle John Lennon free to invite avant-garde artist Yoko Ono to his Surrey home, ostensibly to play her his home recordings. Lennon made sure that his boyhood friend, Pete Shotton, was also in the house to lessen his own nerves. But when Shotton left the shy couple alone, they retired to Lennon's home studio upstairs. Lennon ran his tapes, Yoko recognised a kindred spirit, and the couple spent the night recording what was later issued as *Two Virgins*, before making love at dawn. By the time that Cynthia

Lennon returned from Greece, her place in her husband's life and home had been supplanted.

There's an Edenic, mythic quality to this episode that seems somehow typical of the John and Yoko story. But we have the recording as proof of their first night together, plus the fact that a couple of days later they made their first joint appearance in public, at the opening of the Apple-financed tailoring business in London's Kings Road. That same week, they attended Yoko's happening at the Arts Lab in Drury Lane, where she was exhibiting 'Objects To Be Taken Apart Or Added To'.

As we already know, Lennon had been creating his own tapes of noise and nonsense at home for some two years before Yoko entered his den. Her experiments with sound went back to the Fifties. It took a while for the two visions to coincide, however, and *Two Virgins* remains the least convincing of the partnership's forays into the avant-garde, more interesting as a personal document than in its own musical right.

Some copies of the finished *Two Virgins* album attempted to break the 30 minutes of sound into separate tracks, numbered from 1 to 10 for convenience. In fact, though, *Two Virgins* had no recognisable form at all. It merely extracted around 30 minutes from an audio vérité record of the night's work, a jumbled assemblage of voices, distorted musical instruments, sound effects tapes and the hum of the home studio. It's difficult to know how much of the album was recorded 'live', that is without any overdubs or editing, and how many of the more bizarre sound effects – explosions, bird song, Thirties music hall ditties (since identified as 'Together' and 'Hushabye, Hushabye') – were added afterwards. Comparing the instrumental sounds of the album to 'Jessie's Dream' in *Magical Mystery Tour*, though, you find many similarities – the same tone of treated, reverbed guitar, the same plinkety-plonk piano. It's likely, then, that Lennon merely set up several of his tapes and loops on various recorders, and then he and Yoko improvised over the top.

Those improvisations immediately distinguish the professional avant-gardist from the novice (though as the out-take bootlegged as 'Holding A Note' revealed, both performers were distracted by the thick scent of flirtation in the air). Yoko soon chimed in with her unique style of vocalising, letting out a ghostly wail that John answered with feedback guitar, then bursting into a full-blooded scream, which Lennon vainly attempted to match. While her contributions were as whole-hearted as any of her later recorded work, Lennon sounded ill at ease, tantalised by what he was doing but unable to turn off his irony. So, while Yoko wailed, John played nursery rhymes on the piano, or invented everyday conversations in an exaggerated Lancashire accent. "It's just me, Hilda, I'm home for tea", he announced at one point – to be answered by Yoko drifting as ever into the mock-philo-sophical, calling out "Tea's never ready".

Other highlights included John unable to find a tin-opener; the sound of collapsing buildings; and some genuinely fascinating moments when Yoko echoed the shifting sands of Lennon's guitar pedal with some heady bursts of vocal noise. But such moments were interrupted by periods of tedium, with only the whistle of the tape and the clunking of microphones to dis-turb the silence. It was this air of chaos that ensured *Two Virgins* was only ever going to be of minor artistic interest. But amidst the crashing barrage of noise and the half-hearted attempt at catharsis, it was possible to hear two cultures, two views of the world in collision – the ironic rock'n'roller, and the sure-footed performance artist. It was the audible effect she was having on him that gave these early ramblings their significance.

Whether the tape should ever have been released, however, is another matter. As Yoko said, "It was a bum album," though she was also referring to the cover photograph, shot in July, showing John and Yoko stark naked, in full front and back views. Lennon had originally intended for Yoko alone to appear on the sleeve, before realising that the album's theme – "we were two virgins conceptually" – required innocent nudity from them both.

EMI in the UK and Capitol in the States refused to distribute such a scurrilous package, even when it was discreetly wrapped in a brown paper bag in America with the description of Adam and Eve's nudity from Chapter II of *Genesis* printed on the back. As this was the intended first album release* on The Beatles' Apple Records label, the episode did not exactly bode well for the new company's artistic independence. At least the album had been released under their joint names, however: back in May, John had informed Yoko that EMI would only let him issue the record as a Yoko Ono album, or else under a pseudonym (Lennon suggested 'Doris & Peter'). Yoko admitted in her audio diary that if the couple couldn't use their own names, she would rather treat the record as a limited edition art-work, and hand out fifty signed copies to their friends. That would be a shame, she concluded, "because the message is going to be so beautiful that it could light up the world".

Eventually two independent labels, Track in the UK and Tetragrammaton in the US, did agree to distribute the record to shops. Even then, around 30,000 copies were seized by police in New Jersey early in 1969, because local obscenity laws had supposedly been breached.

---

* George Harrison's movie soundtrack *Wonderwall* took that honour from John & Yoko by four weeks in November 1968.

Lennon's closest colleague in The Beatles was also apparently unhappy at the couple's willingness to be pictured in the nude. Despite that, however, Paul McCartney was quoted on the album sleeve: "When two great Saints meet it is a humbling experience. The battles to prove he was a saint." Whether this grammatically obscure tribute was directed at the Lennons, of course, was a moot point. (See June 15, 1968 for a Lennon/Ono phrase that might have inspired McCartney's words.)

For John, sainthood didn't come into it. The album cover was a gesture of nakedness – "We felt like Adam and Eve," he commented later – and a way of showing the world that they had nothing to hide, that they were just like anyone else. Though the second half of this manifesto was soon forgotten, the attempt at complete openness haunted most of Lennon's public activities, and art, through to the end of 1970.

MID-MAY 1968: DRAWING 'The Special Derek Taylor Desk'; Apple letterhead drawings

At one of the most turbulent moments in his life, Lennon still found time to satirise his employee, and friend, Derek Taylor in an illustration included in The Beatles' *Anthology* book. The unfailingly elegant Taylor, newly recruited as Apple's press officer, was already famous in Beatle circles for his love of the finer things in life. Hence 'The Special Derek Taylor Desk (Prototype)', a typically primitive cartoon which displayed Taylor as a naked sausage man, sat motionless on a wheeled desk-and-chair contraption that kept him permanently within reach of his two most frequent tools at this time: telephones and alcohol.

Around this time, Lennon also doodled a dozen or so of his trademark cartoons on Apple notepaper during a rare quiet moment at The Beatles' new office. These artefacts ended up in the possession of his first wife, Cynthia, who sold them at auction twenty years later. Artistically, they displayed no progress since the days of *In His Own Write* or *A Spaniard In The Works*.

LATE MAY 1968: RECORDING 'The Maharishi Song'

'Sexy Sadie' wasn't Lennon's only musical response to the Maharishi. A few days after recording *Two Virgins*, he and Yoko taped this virulent little spoken blues over electric slide guitar backing. Yoko's role was to entice John through a searing attack on the supposed hypocrisy of the guru and his followers, fingering everyone from the Beatle wives and their infatuation for a leather-clad American actor to the Maharishi and the women who queued for a private consultation. "I wrote 600 songs about how I feel," Lennon noted in an aside. "I felt like dying, crying and committing suicide, but I felt creative." Mostly, though, 'The Maharishi Song' was a vicious assault – another cry from the heart of a man betrayed. Slipping in some snide accusations about the Maharishi's sex life, Lennon noted: "I thought, what the hell has this got to do with what that silly little man was talking about?". "He was a sex maniac", Yoko added gleefully. Not surprisingly, the song was never taken any further, as the sheer act of committing it to tape proved cathartic enough. But 'The Maharishi Song' confirms that Lennon had expected spiritual transport from the Rishikesh experience, and felt he had been sold short.

MAY 30 to JUNE 25, 1968: THE BEATLES recording 'Revolution 1'/'Don't Pass Me By'/'Revolution 9'; John recording sound effects and poetry

Despite the unprecedented pre-production for the album, in the shape of the demo sessions at George Harrison's house in late May, *The Beatles* – alias 'The White Album' – took almost five months to complete, with the band working regular five-day weeks in several London studios.

Despite its commercial potential, Lennon had decided to abandon the light-headed arrangement of 'Revolution' recorded a week or so earlier at Kinfauns, in favour of a slower, lazier version that accentuated the message of the song. In its original form, however, as Mark Lewisohn's researches in the EMI vaults revealed, 'Revolution 1' was some 10 minutes long. From what is audible on a circulating tape of a mixing session at Abbey Road, the unreleased section of the track was a cross between the fade-outs of 'Hey Bulldog' and 'What's The New Mary Jane'. Lennon unleashed a succession of Ono-esque screams and squawks, before the tempo increased, matched by a barrage of atonal noise. Finally, The Beatles gave way to a collage of operatic voices and electronic sound – not, perhaps inevitably, that far removed from what became 'Revolution 9'.

Sadly, the mixing tape only survives on a cassette that was evidently being used by Yoko as an audio diary. At times, this recording was intimate well past the point of curiosity. We didn't really need to know that Yoko preferred her lover to come inside her vagina rather than in her hand, for instance, or to hear her talking about her past promiscuity. But there was one devastating moment, when she considered the possibility that her new life with Lennon, "could be hell – like they would all hate me, or something".

131

Meanwhile, Lennon was leading The Beatles through an improvisation that could almost have come from The Grateful Dead, fuelled by his aggressive slide guitar playing, before the band slid gently back into a remake of 'Revolution', from which McCartney briefly careered into a reprise of 'Lady Madonna'.

None of this was captured on the ten-minute 'Revolution' that Lennon used as an avant-garde canvas. The first four minutes of that track, complete with rowdy electric rhythm guitar and some sleepy "shoo-be-doo-wah" backing vocals from Harrison and McCartney, was issued intact on the 'White Album'. Lennon overdubbed his lead vocal lying on the floor of the studio, and altered the lyrics slightly from one take to the next. First you could count John "out" when it came to violence, then it was "in". On the finished recording, he hedged his bets, slurring "out, in" as an indefinite comment on the use of violence as a political weapon.

Not satisfied with the song itself, Lennon then took the final six minutes of the original take, and used it as the bedrock for a remarkable sound collage, also titled 'Revolution' – though this time it was 'No. 9'. Just two weeks after the amateurish efforts of *Two Virgins*, Lennon and Ono were assembling an altogether more convincing portrait of chaos, the sound of society in tumult, of political demonstrations, explosions, gunfire, disintegration. Rambling in and out of the noise were the voices of John, Yoko and George Harrison, throwing in *non sequiturs* and ironic asides. To begin the tape, Lennon dug out an EMI test tape, with an engineer reciting 'Number nine' in a lugubrious voice. Then on June 20 and 21, the trio knitted the pieces together, using all three studios at Abbey Road to play the tape loops which were at the heart of the recording, and then taking another day's session to mix the results. Significantly, the piece was completed while one of its main critics, Paul McCartney, was on holiday in the United States.

'Revolution 9' was both the least popular of all The Beatles' recordings, and the most accessible of John's sound collages. By comparison, *Two Virgins* was indulgent and directed inwards, aimed at those who had made it rather than the rest of the world. 'Revolution 9' may have been a waste of valuable Beatles vinyl, or not; but at least it achieved its stated purpose, painting a violent revolution in sound. As such, it was a much more truthful record of the summer of 1968 than, say, The Rolling Stones' much-feted show of sympathy with the radical left, 'Street Fighting Man'.

On the same day that he began 'Revolution 9', Lennon taped a second set of noises and effects for the theatrical adaptation of his two books, originally staged late in 1967 as *Scene Three Act One*, and now ready for presentation at the Old Vic a fortnight hence under the more obvious title, *In His*

Own Write. (Adrienne Kennedy and Victor Spinetti's script was subsequently published in its own right as *The Lennon Play*, though John seems to have had no hand in the adaptation.)

Lennon's work on the play's incidental music seems to have involved raiding the EMI library of sound effects for suitable pieces of orchestral and Hammond organ music to accompany Lennon vignettes like 'Last Will And Testicle' and 'The Neville Club' and finding tapes of applause and party noises to be heard during other scenes in the play.

JUNE 2 to 9, 1968: FOUR THOUGHTS event at Arts Lab, London

Of all John and Yoko's artistic collaborations, this remains the most mysterious. Despite the fact that this exhibition was listed under both Lennon and Ono's names in underground magazines such as the *International Times*, it appears not to have been reported or reviewed in any publication. The event followed Yoko's solo *Water Show* the week before (May 28 to June 1), which was apparently abandoned because of lack of public interest. Instead, the Lennons hastily assembled a show of two dual pieces. One of the *Four Thoughts* was 'Build Around It', a Lennon instruction piece in which pieces of broken china and plastic were embedded in a wooden base, and the public were invited to add their own debris to the sculpture. It was twinned with Yoko's 'Danger Box'. Limited edition miniatures of this pairing were manufactured and given away to friends, in the form of a Perspex box bearing the inscriptions from the original art pieces.

Yoko's thoughts around this time were definitely dominated by sexual desire. One of her audio diaries has survived, taped in the control room at Abbey Road this month. While The Beatles listened back to some of George Harrison's demos from the Kinfauns sessions in May, Yoko confided her sexual fantasies, and insecurities, to her tape recorder. Back at her apartment later in the day, she masturbated to orgasm, while the tape was still running. Art took many forms for Lennon and Ono in the summer of 1968.

JUNE 15, 1968: ACORN EVENT at the National Sculpture Exhibition, Coventry

In late May, John and Yoko requested the opportunity to exhibit a work of art in the National Sculpture Exhibition, staged by Fabio Barraclough in the grounds of Coventry Cathedral. Rather than the tangled metal and plastic favoured by the leading artists of the day, the Lennons contributed a piece of 'living art': two acorns, to be planted, one facing East, the other West, symbols of the couple's union and a message of hope and spiritual growth for the future. The idea was Lennon's, though it was clearly influenced by Yoko. Lennon was catching on to the idea that a concept was as powerful as an *objet d'art*.

Barraclough was willing to indulge the pop star, but only so far; the Lennons could plant the acorns, but they wouldn't be mentioned in the catalogue. So John and Yoko prepared their own brochure, fronted by a photograph of the couple apparently growing out of the acorn pots, and with a simple text by John: "This is what happens when two clouds meet". To celebrate the meeting of their two cultures, the four-page leaflet (printed on 'English' paper) was wrapped inside a cover made of Japanese paper. Once again, the inspiration of Yoko's book *Grapefruit* was unmistakable.

At the Cathedral, the couple's extra-marital relationship meant that they were not allowed to plant their acorns in the main exhibition, which was on consecrated ground; nor, in the event, did the Canon allow the Lennons' catalogue to be distributed. But the acorns were finally laid to rest, beneath a plaque that read: "*Yoko* by John Lennon/*John* by Yoko Ono/Sometime in May 1968". Photographers duly captured the event, winning it far more publicity than the rest of the Sculpture Exhibition.

The aftermath was a clear indication of the rocky path that lay ahead, however. After a few days, the acorns were removed by an intruder: when the Lennons sent a replacement set, 24-hour security was called in to prevent a repetition. Acorns? Two clouds meet? The papers hinted that Lennon had gone crazy. Two decades or more later, it is likely that John and Yoko's living sculpture has been more productive than any of the metaphorical constructions or abstracts submitted by the other artists in the Exhibition.

JUNE 18, 1968: *IN HIS OWN WRITE* play staged

Beyond writing the original books on which this adaptation was based, and recording some background noise for the production, Lennon had no real involvement in this one-act play, or in its predecessor *Scene Three Act One*, staged in November 1967. But while he was in New York in May 1968, announcing the foundation of Apple Corps Ltd. to the world's press, Lennon let slip that he was writing a film script based around the same material. When the play proved unpopular, the film was abandoned; and no vestige of Lennon's script has surfaced since.

JUNE 26 to OCTOBER 13, 1968: THE BEATLES recording 'Everybody's Got Something To Hide Except For Me And My Monkey'/'Goodnight' 'What's The New Mary Jane'/'Ob-La-Di, Ob-La-Da'/'Revolution'/'Don't Pass Me By'/'Cry Baby Cry'/'Helter Skelter'/'Sexy Sadie'/'Hey Jude'/'Not Guilty'/'Yer Blues'/'Rocky Raccoon'/ 'While My Guitar Gently Weeps'/'Back In The USSR'/'Dear Prudence'/ 'Glass Onion'/'I Will'/ 'Birthday'/'Piggies'/'Happiness Is A Warm Gun'/'Honey Pie'/ 'The Continuing Story of Bungalow Bill'/'I'm So Tired'/ 'Julia'/'Los Paranoias' (NB: Other songs were recorded by various members of the Beatles during this period, but without any contributions from Lennon)

The remaining four months of sessions for the 'White Album' also produced the epochal single, 'Hey Jude'/'Revolution' – the flipside being an entirely new, much raunchier version of the song the band had already recorded once. Dominated by distorted fuzz guitars, in this 'Revolution' Lennon declared "count me out", despite the aural evidence that he was exhilarated by chaos and mayhem.

Like all the other Beatles, John wasn't present at every 'White Album' session; he missed the recording of several Harrison songs in early October, while Ringo Starr actually left the band for 10 days during the taping of 'Back In The USSR' and 'Dear Prudence'. Even when he was present, Lennon was often content to play sideman to McCartney – adding a nifty jazz guitar solo to 'Honey Pie', for example; bass on 'Rocky Raccoon'; organ on Harrison's 'While My Guitar Gently Weeps' in its original incarnation, and then joint lead guitar with Eric Clapton on the remake; and even saxophone on the frenzied 'Helter Skelter'. He also assembled tape loops of animal noises for Harrison's satirical 'Piggies', besides adding the lines about the pigs "clutching forks and knives/to eat their bacon".

The Beatles remains the band's richest treasury of songs, a pot-pourri of musical styles from country and western to music hall, rock'n'roll to sentimental ballads, each of them performed with more than a hint of satire. It lacked the formal unity of *Sgt. Pepper* and *Abbey Road*, or the air of community that had marked all The Beatles' albums up to *Revolver*. But it declared to the world that the group were capable of anything, and the performances ranged from ultra-tight, carefully arranged productions, to off-the-cuff ditties on the verge of imminent collapse.

Though Lennon was always a champion of the spontaneous, recording 'I'm So Tired' and 'Bungalow Bill' in a single session, his work was as diverse as anyone else's in the band. The new songs he contributed during the sessions varied between the lush children's song, 'Goodnight', and the self-mocking rocker, 'Glass Onion'. Even though Lennon had already worked out rough arrangements for his other songs during the demo sessions, that didn't mean that he wasn't open to embellishments. 'Dear Prudence' was soaked in three-part harmonies, some characteristically stabbing electric guitar (few albums in history have such an obscenely dirty guitar sound), and McCartney's finest drumming on record. 'Sexy Sadie' was hinged around a delicious McCartney piano part, over which Lennon delivered one of his most crushing, sardonic vocals. 'Bungalow Bill' was given a flowing Spanish guitar introduction, while everyone in the studio – including Yoko – joined in on the chorus, and Yoko was even presented with a whole line of her own.

From which you will also have gathered that Yoko was now a part of The Beatles' recording team, much to the disgust of the other band members. In the past, wives and girlfriends had known their place: now wherever John went, Yoko would follow. Beyond their affection for John's wife, Cynthia, the other Beatles found Yoko's presence a distraction. They resented her suggestions that they might vary their tempos, or (on 'Sexy Sadie') simply pull their socks up; and they were disgusted to find John more willing to listen to Yoko's comments than their own. For the first time, The Beatles began to feel uncomfortable about criticising each other's work: the outspokenness which had been their in-built defence mechanism against over-indulgence was put on hold.

On tape, Yoko's contribution was most obvious on 'Revolution 9', and on a song which was left off the final cut – 'What's The New Mary Jane'. John, Yoko, George and Mal Evans taped this late one night at Abbey Road, adding bizarre percussion to the basic instrumental line-up of piano and guitar, while Lennon chanted the off-the-wall lyrics over the top (in more ways than one). A three-minute mix of the song was prepared, and John and Yoko took the acetate home; but Paul vetoed its inclusion when he and John stayed up 24 hours assembling the final running order of the album.

Yoko had a less direct influence on Lennon's most brilliant song from these sessions – 'Happiness Is A Warm Gun'. The title came from an American gun magazine which George Martin showed to John; one of its features was headlined, "Happiness is a warm gun in your hand", which duly became the song's working title. Lennon used the phrase, and its sexual symbolism, as the basis for a piece of mock doo-wop, a throwback to the vocal groups of the Fifties, written around familiar C-Am-F-G chord changes. He then tied it together with two other song fragments. The first was another stream-of-nonsense lyric, partly constructed by Apple publicist Derek Taylor; the second was the already demoed 'I Need A Fix', stripped of its "Yoko, oh no" tagline. Alongside a printed set of lyrics, Lennon later divided the song into "dirty old man" (the nonsense images), "the junkie" (the "I need a fix" section) and "the gunman (satire of 50's R&R)".

Rather than being assembled in sections, however, the song was recorded whole – with the frequent changes of tempo requiring many retakes. It began with Lennon reverting once again to his favourite piece of guitar-picking, this time on electric rather than acoustic, interrupted by Harrison's blasts of fuzz guitar. Then came a bluesy linking section, the lyrics of which broke several taboos simultaneously; and finally the band fell playfully into the doo-wop segment, with John, Paul and George answering Lennon's raw vocal with a three-part harmony of "bang bang, shoot shoot". The lascivi-ousness of Lennon's vocal left no doubt that the guns and triggers in the lyrics were merely metaphors for an altogether more basic human occupa-tion.

Like much of John's work from the late Sixties, 'Happiness Is A Warm Gun' suggested much more than it stated. Likewise 'Glass Onion', Lennon's ironic tribute to the group he was slowly beginning to leave behind. Its lyrics referred to a sheaf of recent Beatles recordings, from 'Fixing A Hole' to 'The Fool On The Hill;' while the most quotable line revealed that 'The walrus was Paul'. It was a final gesture of respect and sympathy to the man who had until recently been his best friend, and to whom he would never be as close again. The aggression of Lennon's vocal concealed the fact that this was another of Lennon's production line jobs, spliced together like a dovetail joint. Not that he skimped on effort in the studio: *Anthology 3* con-tained a remarkable alternate mix that incorporated sound effects including smashing glass and an extract from BBC TV's commentary on the 1966 World Cup football final. That closing collage was replaced by an eerie string arrangement on the finished record.

'Cry Baby Cry' was constructed in the same manner, with a hook-line taken from a TV commercial (Lennon frequently watched TV while he was trying to write songs), and a story-line that read like a missing chapter from *Alice Through The Looking Glass*. Lennon thought so little of this acoustic folk song that when he was reminded of the song in 1980, he commented: "Not me. A piece of rubbish." But his prints were clearly on the gun. An outtake on *Anthology 3* hinted that the song could easily have been sidetracked into a piece of country-rock – or a swamp blues tune. Neither approach would have made it any more significant.

'Goodnight' was a precursor to 'Beautiful Boy' on *Double Fantasy* – a lullaby for a five-year-old son. First time around, it was meant for Julian Lennon, not Sean, and John gave it to Ringo to sing, backed by a full concert orchestra. Like McCartney's 'Honey Pie', 'Goodnight' sounded like a standard the first time you heard it: Bing Crosby could certainly have sung it back in the Thirties.

The last song recorded for *The Beatles* was 'Julia' – almost the first number Lennon had written for the project. Taped on October 13, it was an entirely solo performance, Lennon's only such contribution to a Beatles record. The arrangement was unaltered from the demos recorded back in April, so why did Lennon hold back the song for so long? Speculation is fruitless, but it's tempting to think that this might, after all, have been too personal a statement even for John Lennon. The publication of Hunter Davies' authorised Beatles biography during the recording sessions alerted the world to the fact that Julia was the name of Lennon's mother; maybe John felt he couldn't make his love song to her, and Yoko, public. And maybe the fact he was about to issue an album bearing a full-frontal naked picture of himself and his new lover changed his mind.

JULY 1, 1968: YOU ARE HERE exhibition opens

"John has these crazy ideas all the time," Yoko commented when this exhibition opened at the Robert Fraser Gallery in London's West End. "He just didn't use them. It was just a personal joke for himself. He has about 20 ideas in 20 minutes. So I say, 'Well, that idea is good, why don't you just do it?' and he had never thought of actually doing it, physically. The point is, when you do something, something happens, the concept is simple, but then you get all sorts of reactions and you've started something."

That was a very precise description of Yoko's influence on Lennon in 1968: translating fantasy into reality, and provoking a critical response. In the spirit of the Fluxus art movement she had joined a few years earlier, John's *You Are Here* exhibition was based around a single theme – expressed in a large white canvas hanging on a gallery wall, on which John had scrawled "You are here". The exhibition programme was equally bare, and direct. It consisted of four cards. On the first was a drawn circle, bearing the words "You are here". The second added "sometime in 1968" to the message. The third carried the artist's signature. And the fourth was a circular, grey-and-white photo of the two lovers, shyly clad in long black robes.

Lennon had assembled an array of charity collection boxes – once a common sight in British stores and streets, usually soliciting money for the blind or the care of animals. There were kids in wheelchairs, pandas, 'spastics' (close to Lennon's adolescent heart, that one) – a whole array of begging paraphernalia. It all made for a surreal complement to Lennon's own charity appeal, a hat placed on the ground, bearing a handwritten message: "For the artist. Thank you." There was just one painting in the show: an entirely black canvas, titled 'A Portrait Of Nothing'.

Like most conceptual art, the *You Are Here* piece was probably better imagined than staged; certainly the critics felt so, suggesting that Lennon was completely in thrall to his oriental artist friend, to whom the show was dedicated: "To Yoko from John, with love". Outside the exhibition on opening day, Lennon let loose 365 helium-filled balloons ("I declare these balloons high," he said), to each of which was attached a reply card (addressed to Lennon, c/o the Robert Fraser Gallery), asking for comments. "I got the idea for this exhibition from a childhood memory," Lennon explained. "I remembered how excited I was when I found a balloon in a field when I was little." As the cards slowly returned from around the Home Counties, John and Yoko began to feel the full force of public disapproval, sparked both by his abandonment of his wife, and his open dalliance with a Japanese woman.

The opening was filmed, at the Lennons' request – the first of their joint ventures into that medium. Snippets of the film have since been shown in various documentaries about the couple.

c. MID-AUGUST 1968: *FILM NO. 5 (SMILE)* filmed

Smile was the Lennons' first authentic collaboration on film, as the footage of the *You Are Here* opening was never released as a finished artefact. The subject of the film was simple enough: it documented the birth and life of a John Lennon smile, filmed on a high-speed camera in a few seconds' real time. When played back through a normal projector, it increased the length of the movie to just over 50 minutes.

As usual, the concept had come first. In the manner of her film scripts in *Grapefruit*, Yoko had wanted to capture every person in the world smiling. Gradually, she lowered her horizons, settling on the nearest subject at hand: John Lennon. He saw himself as a representative of the human race, and the film as a statement of optimism for the future: "A symbol of today smiling – that's what I am, whatever that means. I don't mind if people go to the film just to see *me* smiling because it's not that harmful. The idea of the film won't really be dug for another 50 or 100 years."

With its single sustained shot of Lennon's head, backed by a soundtrack made up of the natural sound of his garden – tweeting birds occasionally disturbed by passing airliners – *Smile* made for gentle reflective viewing. Despite its title, two smiles were actually observed, the only other action of note being Lennon blinking three times half-an-hour into the film, and then letting slip a brief glimpse of his tongue. The fascination was in tracing the minutest flickers of expression across his face, and the eventual satisfaction of seeing Lennon smile. "Bring your own instrument", was Yoko's manifesto for anyone who might watch the movie.

Credited as an Apple release, *Smile* was premiered at the Chicago Film Festival in December 1968; it remains the simplest of the Lennon/Ono films, but that simplicity was a blueprint for what was to follow.

CIRCA AUGUST/SEPTEMBER 1968: *TWO VIRGINS* filmed

Like *Smile*, *Two Virgins* was filmed at Lennon's Kenwood home in the summer of 1968, and first shown in public four months later in Chicago. This was the couple's first official film together, and Lennon's initial experiment in working with 16mm film, not the 8mm he had used for his home movies in the past. As we've seen, those Lennon solo movies had been the pictorial equivalent of his musical collages, but Yoko persuaded John to strip his work bare, and leave the central statement of each artwork – its concept – clear. It took John some time to incorporate Yoko's suggestion into his music; there were too many layers of tradition and expertise to cut through first. But in film, Lennon was happy to follow her lead, and retain the Fluxus characteristic that each piece of art should concentrate on one happening or observation.

Using sections of the as-yet-unreleased *Two Virgins* tapes as the soundtrack, John and Yoko produced a film that accentuated their similarities, and their innocence. They hired a film crew to shoot them both in turn against an identical background, centring on head-and-shoulders shots that could be juxtaposed and merged. When the two sets of film were edited together, John and Yoko dissolved into two faces of the same being, superimposed on beautiful shots of clouds. The result was a stunning evocation of uncomplicated love, which gave the couple an ethereal distance from the real world. Towards the end of the 21-minute film, the faces separated for the final time, the camera moved back, and the couple were seen in a lengthy, slow-motion embrace. Clad in white, the Two Virgins smiled beneficently at the camera throughout, secure in their mutual love. And as in *Smile*, the simplicity of the action merely heightened its sincerity.

AUGUST 24, 1968: APPEARING ON *Frost On Saturday*

Satirist and interviewer David Frost had been an *enfant terrible* of British television in the early Sixties, leading a wave of gentle humour that chimed with the mood of the country (or at least the younger half of it) in the same way that The Beatles did a few months later in 1963. By 1968, Frost was an establishment figure, an internationally renowned chat-show host, whose programme was chosen by the group as the venue for their first TV appearance in a year, performing 'Hey Jude' and 'Revolution'. That show was broadcast on September 8, but two weeks earlier Lennon had made his first TV interview appearance alongside Yoko.

A year earlier, Lennon and Harrison had used two Frost interviews to plug the benefits of meditation to a national audience. This time, John and Yoko introduced themelves to a potentially hostile world by introducing the concept of the interview as performance art. (To extend the metaphor, Lennon's 1970 *Rolling Stone* encounter was the interview as action painting.)

During the programme, the couple premiered an extract from their newly made *Smile* movie, and invited members of the sceptical audience to participate in Yoko's 'Hammer-A-Nail' concept piece. "There's no such thing as sculpture or art, it's just words," Lennon explained. "We're all art. Art is just a tag. Sculpture is anything you care to name. This is sculpture – us sitting here, this is a happening, we are here, this is art." The credits rolled with John leading an audience singalong to the forthcoming 'Hey Jude'. For the next three years, Lennon and Ono continued to use the TV interview circuit as a global gallery, an idea that reached its apotheosis with their 1969 bed-ins.

CIRCA OCTOBER 1968: RECORDING The Beatles' '1968 Christmas Record'; designing cover artwork

After four months of exhausting sessions for *The Beatles* album, the group could not muster the collective enthusiasm to regroup for their annual Christmas message to their fans. Instead, the four men recorded their contributions to the 1968 Fan Club record separately for the first time. DJ Kenny Everett was given the task of collating the individual offerings into some kind of coherent whole.

The Lennons' contribution comprised two spoken-word pieces, 'Jock And Yono' and 'Once Upon A Pool Table'. The latter was a bizarre collection of puns, metaphors and nonsense word-play, which sounded like a translation of one of the pieces in *A Spaniard In The Works* into another language. Biographically, 'Jock And Yono' was much more interesting, as it was a thinly disguised fairy tale (or nightmare) about John, Yoko, and their supposed friends in The Beatles' camp. As John recalled in 1970: "They all sat there with their wives, like a fucking jury, and judged us, and the only thing I did was write that piece about 'some of our beast friends' in my usual way, because I was never honest enough. I always had to write in that gobbledegook."

That line came from 'Jock And Yono': "They battled on against over-whelming oddities/Including some of their beast friends", and in retrospect it's remarkable that the first public criticism of the other Beatles' conduct towards Yoko should emerge on a Beatles record. Lennon still felt able to end on an optimistic note, however: "They lived hopefully ever after (and who could blame them)".

The Fan Club record was released in early December, inside a sleeve designed by Lennon and Ringo Starr, which featured a collage of Victorian and Edwardian faces from family portraits. The back cover carried a paint-ing by five-year-old Julian Lennon.

NOVEMBER 7, 1968: WRITING A Short Essay On Macrobiotics

The essay was actually a cartoon strip, written as a puff for a health food store in London, and originally published in the macrobiotic magazine *Harmony*, before being reprinted in an American magazine and then in the book *Lennon Remembers*. The strip caricatured John and Yoko's *Two Virgins* cover, and amusingly portrayed the transformation in the Lennons' shape as they adopted macrobiotic food at Greg's, and read *Harmony*. The strip ends with John and Yoko high in the sky, just like those two clouds meeting in the Acorn Piece back in June.

From this point onwards, Lennon accompanied almost every autograph or drawing with a quick caricature of himself and Yoko, made up of eyes, smiles and spectacles. After the birth of Sean Lennon in 1975, the caricature was extended to include the newest member of the family.

MID-NOVEMBER 1968: RECORDING 'No Bed For Beatle John'/'Baby's Heartbeat'/'Radio Play'/'Song For John' ('Let's Go On Flying'/'Listen The Snow Is Falling'/'Don't Worry Kyoko'/'Mulberry'/'Let's Go On Flying'

On October 18, 1968, the Lennons were busted in Ringo's Montagu Square flat for possession of cannabis resin. Though the resultant scandal fuelled the British public's growing dislike of the couple, the case at first seemed to have few long-term ramifications. But it eventually provided an excuse for the US government to carry out a vendetta by refusing to grant Lennon permanent visa status in the early Seventies. In the short term, the stress surrounding the arrest and the initial court hearing doubtless contributed to Yoko Ono's miscarriage on November 21, nearly three weeks after she had been admitted to Queen Charlotte's Hospital in London.

Even the loss of a six-month-old foetus, which was named John Ono Lennon II and buried secretly in a coffin, did not prevent the Lennons from continuing their artistic exploits. Lennon had remained by Yoko's bedside throughout her three-week stay in hospital, staying overnight in a sleeping bag by her bed when the ward ran out of spare beds. It was this event which, a week or so before the miscarriage, prompted the recording of 'No Bed For Beatle John'.

The track was in the style of a Gregorian chant, with Yoko and John reading stories from the British press about their activities, from the bed episode to the recent release, after long delays, of *Two Virgins*. On the same day, Lennon used his portable recording equipment to tape a few seconds of the unborn baby's heartbeat in Yoko's womb, which he later extended as a tape loop in his home studio until it lasted for more than five minutes.

Finally, John devoted more than 12 minutes of tape to the sound of a transistor radio switch being violently turned off and on, while he and Yoko made phone calls in the background. This was 'Radio Play', not a play for radio but *with* radio. Anyone who has listened to this track might feel that this was one piece of conceptual art more interesting in the planning than the execution. But such conventional niceties were now a thing of the past for John and Yoko. The Lennons were beginning to feel that, as they were artistic outcasts from society, their every movement and statement was worthy of documentation. "We're like a newspaper", John explained. Over the next three years, they would take this manifesto to extremes. For the moment, this chronicle of an unhappy period in the Lennons' lives was edited for release on the couple's second 'avant-garde' album, *Unfinished Music No. 2: Life With The Lions*. Its subtitle was not only a humorous nod to a BBC radio show (*Life With The Lyons*) Lennon had loved as a child, but also an ironic reference to the antagonistic media circus in which John and Yoko were now being forced to perform. Meanwhile John defined the concept of "Unfinished Music" as "a box we're giving you with a few chocolates in, and now you should make your own".

Omitted from the album, but recorded on the same day as 'No Bed For Beatle John', was Yoko's 'Song For John' – actually a medley of three of her compositions. She ad-libbed her way in distinctive style through a minute or so of 'Let's Go On Flying', continued with a brief snatch of 'Snow Is Falling All The Time' (later recorded by the Lennons under a different title), and concluded with two minutes of 'Don't Worry Kyoko' – the first known rendering of a song which she performed several times the following year. The last piece was separated from the rest of 'Song For John' when Ono prepared her back catalogue for CD release in the Nineties. This reissue programme also unveiled other recordings from these unhappy sessions, in the shape of 'Mulberry', on which Lennon played acoustic guitar while Yoko rolled her mouth around the song title, and an alternative version of 'Let's Go On Flying', included on the *Life With The Lions* CD under the title 'Song For John'.

Together with 'No Bed For Beatle John' and 'Radio Play', the original, full-length 'Song For John' medley was issued on a flexi-disc distributed with the Spring/Summer 1969 edition (No. 7) of *Aspen*, an American arts magazine. This issue of *Aspen* – subtitled *The British Box: Spring and Summer 1969* – actually took the form of a box, which also included a reproduction of a diary in which John had filled out endless variations of the traditional "woke up, went to bed" formula. Meanwhile, 'Baby's Heartbeat' and 'Two Minutes Silence' were offered to a London students' magazine (titled *Student Magazine*, no less) run by young entrepreneur Richard Branson, after Apple aide Derek Taylor had promised him some musical contributions for the Lennons for his launch issue. Understandably, Branson was a little disappointed by what he received, and launched a lawsuit against Taylor and the Lennons, which was eventually settled out of court.

EARLY DECEMBER 1968: WRITING and recording home demos of 'Everybody Had A Hard Year'/'A Case Of The Blues'/'Don't Let Me Down'/'Oh My Love'

No sooner had the Lennons lost a baby than they were dragged into court to plead guilty to a charge of drug possession. Lennon was now under assault from all sides, with hostile media attention increasing, Beatles fans apparently turning against him, and his efforts to have a child with his lover tragically stalled. It's no wonder that the songs Lennon wrote during this period were a cry of pain, and a last search for refuge against despair.

A short film, shot this month, showed a black-clad John (with Yoko) in the garden at Kenwood performing 'Everybody Had A Hard Year' on acoustic guitar; the clip was tagged on, post credits, to the Lennons' film, *Rape* (see next entry). There was also a home recording of the song, which ended up as Lennon's contribution to The Beatles' 'I've Got A Feeling'. In this initial form, it consisted of a long series of repeated verses written around John's acoustic guitar picking – a succession of universal statements sung in a dull, depressed voice that confirmed the personal relevance of the song's title.

'A Case Of The Blues' was an attempt at channelling the same emotions into positive creativity – and one of Lennon's final ventures into psychedelic imagery, with slightly surreal lines like "There'll be no coloured glasses wearing knock-kneed shoes". They were set to an insistent acoustic guitar rhythm that wasn't so far removed from his early attempts at 'Mean Mr Mustard'. Melodically, meanwhile, the song owed an unconscious debt to the mid-Sixties garage rock classic, 'I'm Not Your Stepping Stone' (best known in the version by the 'preFab Four', The Monkees).

'Don't Let Me Down' probably wasn't known as such in December 1968, as Lennon had yet to hit upon the title line and chorus. On his first composing tape for the song, he simply repeated the basic lines of the first verse over and over again, searching for the right chord changes. There were none of the rhythmic breaks of the final song, so – like 'Everyone Had A Hard Year' – it just flowed through the verse and back to the beginning again. Stage two of the writing process saw Lennon introducing the middle section for the first time, with the lines "I'm in love for the first time/Don't you know it drives me mad", before moving into another long, circular set of changes that was axed from the final version. The overall effect at this stage was more melodic than the record would be. Perhaps Lennon felt that the melody would get in the way of the message, which was a simple song of love for Yoko – as much wish-fulfilment as a statement of fact in the bleak final weeks of 1968.

But the most dramatic and direct expression of the Lennons' sadness came in the initial setting of a song that was completely rewritten two years later for the *Imagine* album. It was Yoko who wrote the original lyrics for 'Oh My Love'. Lennon then set them to music, and broke down the emotion into verse form. Such niceties were irrelevant, however, alongside the naked self-exposure of the words.

Though Lennon sang two of the three home demos recorded at this time, the song was written for Yoko's voice. One take even began with the line "John my love", the only part of the melody that remained unchanged for the next two years. "You had a very strong heartbeat", the couple sang to their miscarried child, "but that's gone now/Probably we'll forget about you but whoever you were, you were an angel". The rest of the lyric described the bonding process of mother and child, and offered the wish that the experience of loss would make Yoko a stronger woman. But the tone of Lennon's vocal undermined the hope.

DECEMBER 1968: FILMING *Film No. 6 – Rape*

Rape was the most professional, and successful, of all the Lennons' late Sixties ventures into the milieu of film – perhaps because it was a movie to which their major contribution was the concept, not the technique or execution. Just as John's songs from the end of 1968 were cries of rage and pain, so *Rape* also conveyed some of the misery, the cocoon of madness that surrounded the Lennons at this time. Its subject was persecution by the media – something of which they had recent experience. As a perverted mirror of their own tribulations, the couple sent cameraman Nic Knowland into the streets of London to locate an attractive young woman, who luckily for the film spoke no English. Knowland then pursued his prey across London, chasing her in a car as she tried to escape in a taxi, and eventually cornering her in a room from which she had no escape. That was the 'rape' of the title: not the sexual assault which it might suggest, but defilement by camera, the systematic breaking of a personality through constant invasion of privacy. The innocent subject's descent from amusement to suspicion, panic and then blind despair, mirrored the way in which the Lennons had seen their public personas change from clowns to buffoons to convenient targets.

There was a difference, of course; John and Yoko had chosen to play their games in public, and had invited media publicity by their choice of careers. Their complaint might have carried more weight had it come from people less willing to place themselves in the public eye. And the morality of the actual filming technique was also questionable. But *Rape* attracted positive reviews when it was premièred on Austrian TV in March 1969, and again after a screening in London that autumn. It also spawned a sequel, *Rape Part 2*.

The second *Rape* was a short – unlike the 77-minute duration of the original film. Shot necessarily with a hand-held camera, with the only dialogue in German, and with the last 45 minutes filmed in a darkened room, *Rape* was an endurance test for any audience. The relentless pursuit of the camera was broken only by the change of reels: the film forced the viewer into the role of voyeur. The audience was trapped inside the film – both metaphorically, as the 'rape' took place, and literally, by the sheer grinding pressure of the movie's technique.

Lennon was credited as one of the film's sound engineers, and also with music – which consisted of merely a few seconds of 'Radio Play' from *Life With The Lions* which accompanied the closing credits, and the acoustic 'Everybody Had A Hard Year' (see above entry).

DECEMBER 10/11, 1968: PERFORMING 'Yer Blues'/'Whole Lotta Yoko' at *The Rolling Stones' Rock 'n' Roll Circus*

The timing may have been accidental, but it testified to The Beatles' increasing fragmentation. Lennon chose to make his début as a solo performer in the same week when the group were supposed to begin rehearsals for their comeback live gigs at The Roundhouse in London. In the event, the Roundhouse gigs never happened, though the *Let It Be* film documented the rehearsals for a project that drifted from public performances to a TV show and finally the appearance on the Apple rooftop.

Meanwhile, Lennon found that performing without the other Beatles was easier and more liberating than he might have imagined. The occasion was the filming of The Rolling Stones' own TV film, which brought many of The Stones' favourite performers together in a circus tent. Lennon chose to perform with Yoko, of course, backed by Keith Richard from the Stones on bass, Mitch Mitchell from the Jimi Hendrix Experience on drums, and Eric Clapton on guitar. The impromptu group performed under the name of Winston Legthigh and The Dirty Mac. Tapes exist of their rehearsals on December 10, which include a playful duet between Lennon and Jagger on a fragment of 'Yer Blues', observed by five-year-old Julian Lennon. The following day, Lennon's band performed a searing version of the same song in front of the cameras, with a passion that lived up to the anguished potential of the song's lyrics – helped, once again, by recent days in the life.

The Dirty Mac then launched into a blues jam, sometimes known as 'Her Blues' but dubbed 'Whole Lotta Yoko' on the eventual commercial release on home-video, CD and finally DVD. Yoko's screams competed for space with a keening violin solo by guest musician, Ivry Gitlis, before the band roared to a halt. The success of The Dirty Mac's two-song performance must have encouraged Lennon to believe that there would be life after The Beatles.

The TV special wasn't aired at the time, supposedly because the Stones felt that they had been overshadowed by both Lennon and The Who. However, when it was finally unveiled in 1996, these misgivings proved to be entirely misplaced, and the subsequent DVD edition is a priceless artefact of the late 60s rock scene.

DECEMBER 18, 1968: JOHN AND YOKO perform at the Alchemical Wedding

'Perform' as in 'performance art' was the order of this day, as the Lennons' sole contribution to what was billed as the Christmas party of the British underground – in the august surroundings of the Royal Albert Hall, no less – was to cavort on stage encased in a white bag. The participants had been enlisted by underground scenemaker Jim Haynes, whom the Lennons had met during their summer activities at London's Arts Lab. Other participants at the event included beat chronicler Ken Kesey, several American members of the Hell's Angels motorcycle gang (who were currently making themselves at home at the Apple offices in Savile Row), devotees from London's Krishna Consciousness community, and a young woman whose unscheduled striptease prompted the Metropolitan Police to intervene.

Yoko had already adopted the bag disguise as her own way of dealing with sticky situations: film exists of her walking through the streets of London in a bag, being greeted warily by passers-by. Indeed, *Bagwear: How And When To Wear It* was the title of one of the pamphlets on offer in the infamous *Yoko Ono Sales List* printed in *Grapefruit*. From there, it was only a short step to Bagism, and then to naming John and Yoko's production company Bag Productions. Subsequent bag appearances will only be listed if they are accompanied by more tangible artistic performances.

CHAPTER 9

January 1969 to September 1969

The twin distractions of heroin addiction and Yoko Ono, not necessarily in that order, dragged Lennon's attention far away from The Beatles, much to the dismay of at least one other member of the group. But Lennon had larger concerns on his mind – not least the cause of world peace, to which he devoted himself throughout much of 1969. Such was the degree to which he allowed his campaign to take over his life that he became nothing less than a living artwork, with almost every personal need subjugated to the demands of his public persona. And all the time The Beatles receded further from the forefront of Lennon's mind.

JANUARY 2 to 31, 1969: THE BEATLES filming *Let It Be*; recording 'Going Up The Country'/'Dig A Pony'/'I've Got A Feeling'/'Don't Let Me Down'/'Rocker'/'Save The Last Dance For Me'/'She Came In Through The Bathroom Window'/'Get Back'/'Blues'/'Two Of Us'/'Teddy Boy'/'Maggie Mae'/'Dig It'/'Dig It 2'/'Bye Bye Love'/'Let It Be'/'For You Blue'/'Rip It Up'/'Shake Rattle And Roll'/'Kansas City'/'Miss Ann'/'Lawdy Miss Clawdy'/'Blue Suede Shoes'/'You Really Got A Hold On Me'/'Tracks Of My Tears'/'The Long And Winding Road'/

'Isn't It A Pity'/'Oh Darling'/'The Walk'/Billy Preston demos/'Love Me Do'/'The One After 909'/'I Want You'/ 'Not Fade Away'/'Mailman Bring Me No More Blues'/ 'Besame Mucho'/'God Save The Queen'/'Lady Madonna'/ LENNON writing and rehearsing (besides songs listed above) 'Suzy Parker'/'Shakin' In The Sixties'/'Child Of Nature'/ 'Sun King'/'Gimme Some Truth'/'Madman'/'Watching Rainbows'/'Negro In Reserve'

Out of the best of intentions, The Beatles crafted a month of misery and inertia. Having long since abandoned the idea of performing live shows, they decided to reward their fans by staging a concert for worldwide TV broadcast, and to film the rehearsals. Along the way, the project changed shape, and became a documentary of the band at work in the studio. After a month of painful and mostly fruitless work, The Beatles gave up, leaving assorted engineers and producers to pick up the pieces. Eventually, after 16 months of delays, Phil Spector assembled the *Let It Be* album, Michael Lindsay-Hogg the accompanying movie; and The Beatles called it quits.

The first fortnight of January 1969 was spent at Twickenham Film Studios, where The Beatles performed, bickered and chatted under the gaze of the harsh movie lights. No proper recordings were made during this period: all that exists (in profusion) are bootleg recordings made from the two camera Nagra sound reels while the movie was being edited. On January 22, The Beatles relocated to Apple, where they set about making a studio album – also watched by the cameras. The recordings listed above were all made during the Apple sessions. On January 30 they performed live on the Apple rooftop; a day later they repeated the exercise inside the studio.

The eventual *Let It Be* album was not exactly their most creative. Contributions from Lennon included a remixed version of 'Across The Universe' from early 1968; two humorous jams, 'Maggie Mae' and 'Dig It;' 'I've Got A Feeling', which married Paul's unfinished song of that name with his own 'Everyone Had A Hard Year', as taped at home the previous month; 'The One After 909', a late Fifties Quarry Men song unearthed on January 3 to ease the tension of working on new material; 'Two Of Us', a McCartney song to which Lennon added a line or two in a last show of creative unity; and 'Dig A Pony'.

John later dismissed this last song as "another piece of garbage," but he took it seriously enough at the time, a blend of nonsensical imagery ("I do a road hog ... I pick a moon dog") and encouraging philosophy, which repeated the underlying message of 'All You Need Is Love' (you can do whatever you want) with a dash of well-earned cynicism. Along with the skeleton of 'Don't Let Me Down', it was the only song that he had completed before the start of the sessions.

Given the harrowing events of recent weeks, Lennon's other new compositions aired this month were surprisingly lightweight. Two songs later destined for *Abbey Road* surfaced in early form, but at this stage 'Sun King' was merely an instrumental based around his trademark guitar-picking, and 'I Want You' was little more than a title and a riff.

Thankfully, Lennon had thought to finish off 'Don't Let Me Down', and the song remained his most poignant work from this month of intensive sessions. The basic structure of the verses remained from his December 1968 demo, but at the January 2 session McCartney helped Lennon to tighten up the middle eight with a touch of idealism ("It's a love that lasts forever/It's a love that has no past"). Lennon then inserted the chorus line both as a desperate plea for security, and an admission that dreams can easily be destroyed.

At the same time, Lennon began work on 'Gimme Some Truth', the title of which rapidly became a manifesto for his work over the next two years or more. The words had yet to come, as had all of the middle section beyond the phrase "money for rope" – and as the tapes made by the film crew prove, that entire sequence was composed by McCartney, not Lennon, though he was never credited for his contribution. But anger was what sparked the song into life – the fact that Lennon was sick and tired of being pushed around and treated as an object of contempt, both by the public and (as 'Jock And Yono' had already shown) by his fellow Beatles as well. It took two years before Lennon had sharpened his vision sufficiently to finish the song, and translate an incoherent rant into a searing attack on hypocrisy and double-dealing.

Two other songs premièred during the session showed promise, if no more than that. 'Madman' was essentially a one-verse idea – "There's a madman coming gonna do you no harm/wearing pink pajamas and he lives on a farm" – based around a catchy two-note riff that shared a rhythmic base with (once again) 'Mean Mr Mustard'. 'Watching Rainbows' was even more intriguing. It was powered by the same three-chord pattern that opened The Everly Brothers' 'Wake Up Little Susie', and ended up underneath Yoko's 'Don't Worry Kyoko'. (One version of 'Madman' also ran accidentally into an identical riff.) What's more, there was a song attached – a rather lethargic one, admittedly, that suggested an off-key version of Bob Dylan's 'The Mighty Quinn', but one that had a theme and a chorus line ("Instead of watching rainbows, I'm gonna make me some"). And with an ironic twist

151

of fate, it ended with Lennon calling out "you've gotta shoot me", before The Beatles (minus George Harrison) jammed off into the distance.

Most of the rest was chaos – half-finished ideas that were never knocked into shape, or off-the-cuff ramblings that were captured on film, and hence assumed an importance out of keeping with their ephemeral nature. Examples in circulation include John's 50-second dig at music publisher Dick James in 'Shakin' In The Sixties;' the faintly obscene rock 'n' roll song 'Suzy Parker' partly preserved in the *Let It Be* film ('when you get to Suzy Parker, everybody gets well done'); an improvised piece of nonsense that came to be known as 'Negro In Reserve'; two entirely different but equally pointless jams called 'Dig It', to which the phrase "Can you dig it?" is almost a complete lyric sheet; and endless variations on 'White Power' and 'Commonwealth', all of which were sparked by the initial set of lyrics for McCartney's 'Get Back', which were a parody of British racism long before they assumed their more familiar shape (which Lennon interpreted as a sub-liminal message to himself and Yoko).

Oh yes, Yoko. During pauses in the sessions, Yoko had her chance to jam with The Beatles, who did their best to look and sound enthusiastic about creating a barrage of feedback and assorted mayhem behind her piercing screams. Mostly, though, they ignored her, and she sat bored at Lennon's side or feet, reading, knitting or simply looking aloof.

Lennon, meanwhile, had rare moments of communal feeling: these were, after all, the men with whom he had conquered the world. But for every 'Two Of Us' rehearsal in the *Let It Be* film, with Lennon and McCartney playfully egging each other into Elvis Presley impressions, there are count-less moments like the agonisingly uninspired attempt to improve on 'Across The Universe', with Lennon ultimately giving up the ghost himself and leading the band into "a fast one" as an escape route. When McCartney noted on January 9, during another shot at 'Across The Universe,' that "there's an oriental influence that shouldn't really be there", it wasn't clear whether he was referring to the song or to the group's new Japanese mem-ber.

All The Beatles put more enthusiasm into their amateurish renditions of rock 'n' roll standards – and a few of their own. Lennon himself led the band into impromptu versions of 'She Said, She Said', 'You're Going To Lose That Girl', 'Help!' and 'Please Please Me', all unrecognisable as being the same musicians who had recorded the originals. He also pulled his colleagues into performing a remarkable array of cover versions – including 'Honey Hush', 'Hi-Heel Sneakers', 'C'mon Everybody', 'Good Rockin' Tonight', 'Fools Like Me', 'You Win Again', 'Tennessee', 'What Do You Wanna Make Those

Eyes At Me For?', 'Bad Boy', 'Sweet Little Sixteen', 'Around And Around', 'Almost Grown', 'School Day', 'Johnny B. Goode', 'Milk Cow Blues Boogie', 'Little Queenie', 'Blue Suede Shoes', 'Soldier Of Love', 'Rock And Roll Music', 'Sabre Dance', 'A Shot Of Rhythm And Blues', 'Devil In Her Heart', 'Don't Be Cruel', The Who's 'A Quick One While He's Away', 'New Orleans', 'Mailman Bring Me No More Blues', 'Move It' and 'Digging My Potatoes'. And those were simply Lennon's playthings during the sessions ...

Lennon later complained that the *Let It Be* film was "set up by Paul for Paul ... the people that cut it cut it as 'Paul is God', and we're just lying there. I knew there were some shots of Yoko and me, that had been just chopped out of the film for no other reason than the people were oriented towards Engelbert Humperdinck." That's an exaggeration, but it's symptomatic of Lennon's attitude to McCartney, to The Beatles, to the whole damned myth. In the event, his contribution to the project was slight because that was all he was prepared to offer.

Indeed, what's apparent from listening to the hundreds of hours of off-cuts is that Lennon's major impact on the January 1969 sessions was to drain the other Beatles of their pleasure and willpower. More likely than not, he was strung out on heroin for the entire month; he and Yoko certainly indulged in some childish banter about the joys of shooting up when actor Peter Sellers visited the studio on January 13. Three days before, George Harrison had quit the band – not, as it suited him to believe years later, because of the argument with Paul McCartney that was shown in the *Let It Be* film, but because he had become exhausted by Lennon's overt lack of interest in his work. Every morning during the first week at Twickenham, Harrison arrived with promising new material. And every morning, Lennon either mocked or ignored him. By lunchtime on the 10th, Harrison couldn't take any more. He told Lennon: "You can replace me. Put an ad in the *New Musical Express* and get a few people in. That's what Apple's for." When The Beatles carried on without him, Lennon (who coldheartedly suggested getting Eric Clapton in to replace his comrade) led the other two into an appalling version of (appropriately) The Who's 'A Quick One While He's Away' (fresh from Lennon hearing The Who perform it at the Rolling Stones' *Rock and Roll Circus* the previous month). "Take it, George," he called out to the absent guitarist when it was time to start riffing on an atonal, Yoko-led jam.

Harrison was eventually persuaded to return, and the sessions (which moved to the Apple basement studio on January 22) were salvaged when Harrison invited R&B organist Billy Preston to jam with the group, and

Lennon persuaded McCartney to let him stay for the rest of the project. By then, McCartney had long since given up on trying to force Lennon to compose something worthy of the group's reputation. "Haven't you written anything?" he gently scolded Lennon on January 8. "No," Lennon replied curtly, before adding: "I'm hoping for a little rock'n'roller". But it never arrived.

Worse still was Lennon's attitude when the group were trying to decide where to stage their live show. He allowed Yoko to speak on his behalf, though her entertaining conceptual ideas didn't exactly impress the other Beatles. When McCartney tried to force Lennon to talk, to offer at least some form of opinion, he was treated with disdain. "What do you think?" Paul asked at the end of a lengthy discussion on January 7. "Think about what?" Lennon sneered. And that was the way it stayed. No wonder that McCartney wrote 'Carry That Weight' soon after this month of sessions was finished: he'd been doing nothing else all month.

In retrospect it is clear that Lennon was reserving all his creative energy for his work with Yoko: for art-work, in other words, not what he considered hack-work. But in January 1969, art-work was in short supply. After this fiasco, The Beatles were doomed as anything other than a fictional legal partnership.

FEBRUARY 1969: WRITING 'A Is For Parrot' poem; CREATING Bag One lithographs

It was art critic (and future Lennon assistant) Anthony Fawcett who introduced John to the joys of lithography, short-cutting the laborious effort of drawing directly onto the plates and allowing him to create images on paper that could then be transferred onto litho blocks. John took away a supply of the requisite materials, and promised to return with a set of drawings that could be issued as a collected edition of his work. As a gesture of commitment to publisher Ed Newman of Curwen Press, he engraved a poem directly onto a plate this month, which would be used as a preface for the collection.

The result was an acrostic, of the kind used to teach small children their alphabet – albeit a subversive one, where "A is for Parrot which we can plainly see' and 'K is for intestines which hurt when we dance". It ended like any nursery rhyme should: "This is my story both humble and true/take it to pieces and mend it with glue".

The other lithographs were assembled during the course of the year, and were signed and collated in December 1969 (see entry that month for more details). The basic concept was simple and central to Lennon's view of the world in 1969: they would document his love, romantic and sexual, for the woman who would shortly become his wife.

FEBRUARY 22 AND APRIL 18, 1969: THE BEATLES recording 'I Want You (She's So Heavy)'

Less than a month after the collapse of the *Let It Be* sessions, The Beatles regrouped to attempt another album. The first song to be completed was one which they had rehearsed during their January sessions, and which shared the subject of the lithographs he was starting to create – Lennon's love for Yoko. Whereas his love songs had once been as opaque and cryptic as 'Girl' and 'Norwegian Wood', 'I Want You (She's So Heavy)' said it straight, with no metaphors or imagery to get in the way. The Beatles' performance was equally direct. It veered from a bluesy shuffle in the verses – melodically inspired by Mel Torme's unlikely clubland favourite, 'Comin' Home Baby' – to the multi-guitar powerhouse that closed the song, repeating the central riff over and over like an inescapable warning of doom. Just as the tension became unbearable, with synthesised white noise leaking out around the edges of the guitar chords, Lennon cut the tape in mid-note. Silence, as he was to discover on *Life With The Lions*, could sometimes speak just as loudly as noise.

MARCH 2, 1969: PERFORMING 'Cambridge 1969'

The scene? Lady Mitchell Hall, Cambridge. The occasion? A concert of experimental, left-field music, held as part of the Natural Musical Festival, curated by Anthony Barnett. The evening was a virtually seamless parade of avant-garde and free jazz performances, each one running into the next, in complete contrast with the package-tour environment that Lennon would have been familiar with from his gigs with The Beatles.

"This is a piece called 'Cambridge 1969'," announced Yoko Ono as the couple's unheralded segment began. From her lungs came an unearthly bellow that sounded like the rasp of twisted metal. Behind her, sitting cross-legged with his back to the audience, John Lennon wrenched his electric guitar around his amplifier, producing howls of feedback that acted as dissonance to Yoko's extended, atonal cries. Gradually her long, single notes gave way to cackles, screams and groans, all matched by Lennon's guitar. As the couple built towards a climax – Yoko screaming at precise intervals, Lennon forcing a wall of white noise from the amps – they were joined on stage by a percussionist and sax-player, who jingled and squealed ineffectually in support, and were then left exposed as the Lennons packed up their avant-garde credentials and went home.

Pure noise was nothing new for Yoko: at a concert at London's Royal Albert Hall a year earlier, she had performed with saxophonist Ornette Coleman – creating a mutated soundscape of passion typified by 'Aos', a rehearsal rendition of which was included on Yoko's first LP *Yoko Ono/Plastic Ono Band* (1970). For Lennon, though, Cambridge was a revelation. Aside from the Dirty Mac at the Stones' *Circus* and his silent appearance onstage at the Albert Hall in December, this was his first true experience as an avant-garde performer, not a Beatle, in contrast to the usual routine where Yoko was seen as the intruder on his territory. The Lennons were using noise as a statement of emotion, without sophistication or direction, admittedly, though the gist was easy to follow. Yoko's screaming had liberated Lennon's guitar work; this was a far cry from the tentative feedback of 'I Feel Fine' (though much closer to McCartney's 'Helter Skelter'). Next would come the freeing of his voice – and then his writing.

'Cambridge 1969' formed one side of the *Life With The Lions* album. The other was taken up by the recordings made at Queen Charlotte's Hospital the previous November – plus 'Two Minutes Silence', a self-explanatory concept blatantly stolen from Yoko's friend, John Cage. Except that theft wasn't a working concept in their avant-garde circles: Ono and Lennon preferred to think of their 'composition' as a homage to the pioneering creator of experimental music.

MARCH 12, 1969: MIXING 'Peace Song'

And that's the sum total of our knowledge: John and Yoko were at Abbey Road on this date, mixing a tape of an otherwise unidentified song that they'd recorded on Lennon's four-track equipment at home. 'Give Peace A Chance' had yet to be written, so this mysterious number was probably closer to the doggerel of 'Radio Peace' (see below) than a fully fledged Lennon classic. As the couple took the tape home at the end of the session, we shall probably never know for sure.

MARCH 25 to 31, 1969: FILMING *Honeymoon*; recording 'Amsterdam'/'Radio Peace'/'Jerusalem'/'Hava Nagilah'/'I Want You (She's So Heavy)'/'Don't Let Me Down -Those Were The Days'

Once both halves of the Lennon-Ono partnership secured divorces from their bewildered spouses, Cynthia Powell and Tony Cox respectively, the couple were free to marry. Their decision was doubtless spurred by the wedding of their chief Beatle rivals, Paul McCartney and Linda Eastman, in early March. McCartney's marriage sparked near hysteria amongst female Beatles fans, whose dreams of capturing the man dubbed by the media "the bachelor Beatle" had been crushed. No such scenes greeted the news of John and Yoko's liaison: this couple had long since appalled and aggravated all but their most broadminded followers.

All that remained was to find a country that would marry them immediately. Not willing to go through the several weeks of legal delays required in Britain, they flew to Paris on March 16. But once again, they were unable to arrange the instant ceremony they desired. So on March 20 they stopped briefly in the British territory of Gibraltar, where they were married in a short ceremony, signed the register and had the appropriate photos taken for transmission round the world. The colony's tourist shops still sell sets of these photos as a souvenir, more than 35 years later. The Lennons returned to Paris that afternoon, where a couple of days later they met painter Salvador Dali; and then on June 25 they began a bed-in for world peace in Room 902 of the Amsterdam Hilton Hotel.

So commenced 10 months of frenetic activity, promoting the concept of peace by whatever means were available. Setting their individual careers aside, the couple combined Lennon's international reputation and Yoko's conceptual sense to create a multi-media, barrier-free peace event, which saw them plastering the capital cities of the world with posters; releasing peace anthems; giving interviews to anyone who would listen, and many who wouldn't; sending acorns to world leaders; and arousing the fury (or at best amusement) of the establishment from London to Los Angeles. The decision not only threatened the continuation of The Beatles as anything other than an occasional distraction for John; it also marked a complete alteration in the couple's health and mental outlook since the dark days of January. Back then, they had huddled together during The Beatles' Twickenham sessions like two refugees under siege from the outside world; insiders talked starkly of their dependence on heroin. Now they were inviting the most intense form of scrutiny, with literally no place to hide. All their defences were down: they could be ridiculed, abused, admired or worshipped, but they could not be ignored. It was the birth of modern celebrity: a public relations masterpiece that any modern spin doctor would be proud of.

As reporters gathered outside the Lennons' room at the Hilton, convinced that they were about to witness the sexual consummation of the couple's marriage, John and Yoko prepared for seven days of incessant media attention, almost all of it filmed and recorded by the Lennons' ever-present assistants. The stage had moved from the couple's work to their lives: in effect, their lives were now becoming their art, and therefore needed to be preserved for posterity on film and tape. 1969 was the Lennons' most public year: and there was more media documentation of their activities during that time than exists for any other public figure, past or present. The complication was that John and Yoko soon began to regard themselves as works of art in their own right. Self-criticism was abandoned, as the couple rode headfirst into a monsoon of media mockery and public indifference.

About an hour of highlights from the Bed-In encounters were edited into a movie, entitled *Honeymoon* – shot with synched sound, and hand-held cameras. The Lennons did none of the photography, simply directing their crew to catch everything that happened on celluloid, and then sitting in on the final editing. As a documentary, it was slightly shambolic, but it caught the flavour of the moment. The same source produced one side of the couple's *Wedding Album*, a lavish package issued eight months after the event, in November 1969. Besides the record, which was almost incidental, the box set contained a photocopy of their marriage certificate, a photo of a slice of wedding cake, a Lennon cartoon strip about the event, even a book of press cuttings about their activities, most of which – an example of the couple's extreme generosity of spirit – were less than complimentary about Lennon and his Japanese bride.

'Amsterdam' was the title given to the 25 minutes of audio vérité recordings included on the *Wedding Album*. The suite began with Yoko's improvisation 'John John (Let's Hope For Peace)', sung acappella like a Japanese translation of a Roman mass; continued with a reasonably coherent (if naive) interview about their peace campaign, actually taped in London in early April, after their return from Amsterdam; and also featured John ordering tea and brown toast from room service, and meeting the press in bed. Several 'musical' interludes provided some aural novelty. There were a few brief seconds of John's 'Goodnight', performed solo; what sounded like the chord sequence for 'Because' featured behind one of Yoko's improvisations; and what could almost be a dry-run for the 'John Sinclair' riff used as the basis for Lennon to sing 'Goodbye Amsterdam'. Mostly, these fragments were an opportunity for Yoko to speak with her singing voice, as on 'Stay In Bed' ("grow your hair", Lennon added at the end), to the accompaniment of what could have been Bach's 'Air On A G String' on John's guitar.

Along the way, the Lennons also taped a hilariously inane ditty called 'Radio Peace;' impromptu versions of 'Hava Negilah' and 'Jerusalem;' and a few bars of 'I Want You (She's So Heavy)', as an illustration of what The

Beatles were doing currently. Funniest of all was Lennon's off-the-cuff medley during a radio interview of his own 'Don't Let Me Down' and Mary Hopkin's 1968 hit single 'Those Were The Days' – perhaps designed to subvert the expectations of any reporters who'd been expecting to meet a musical legend.

Throughout it all, cameras and tape recorders rolled, to maintain the illusion that all the Lennons' life was art. Hence the survival of such non-essential snippets as 'Hairpeace' (alias John playing a handful of guitar chords) and 'Bedpeace' (the film crew catching the couple as they woke up and ordered breakfast).

APRIL 14, 1969: THE BEATLES recording 'The Ballad Of John And Yoko'; subsequently filming *The Ballad Of John And Yoko*

The wedding, the Bed-In and the return to Blighty were documented in this song, written at the start of April, and recorded by a two-man Beatles line-up when Messrs Harrison and Starr were unable to make the session. That left Lennon to handle lead vocals, two lead guitar parts, acoustic guitar and percussive thumps; McCartney, meanwhile, chipped in on drums, bass, piano, maracas and backing vocals.

'The Ballad Of John And Yoko' was couched as a traditional blues, and handled as a piece of rockabilly, with Lennon spitting out the lyrics, and throwing in little stabs of electric lead. The production was sparse and loose – far removed from The Beatles' usual perfection – and there was little to distract attention from the words. The verses were devoted to a narrative account of the Lennons' recent activities, told with an ironic dig at the attitude of the British press; while the chorus boasted a self-conscious announcement of imminent martyrdom. Never mind the conceit of identifying himself with the martyred Messiah; even Lennon's use of the word 'Christ' as an interjection caused the record to be banned or bleeped in the American south. Lennon was certainly aware that controversy was likely. In a note to Apple plugger Tony Bramwell, he insisted: "No pre-publicity on 'Ballad Of John & Yoko', especially the Christ bit – so don't play it round too much or you'll frighten people – get it pressed first."

This piece of self-dramatisation – coupled with the Lennons' film clip for the song, which centred entirely on themselves with only fleeting reference to the rest of The Beatles – made the record something of an irrelevance to the group's catalogue. In retrospect, this was clearly Lennon's first solo release: only the 'Beatles' credit, and McCartney's vocal harmonies, stopped contemporary listeners from making the obvious association. For the moment, however, the world innocently assumed that there would always be a Beatles, even if the group now seemed to have sprouted an extra Japanese limb.

APRIL 20 to MAY 6, 1969: THE BEATLES recording 'Oh Darling'/'Octopus' Garden'/'Let It Be' (overdubs)/'You Know My Name (Look Up The Number)'/'Something'/'You Never Give Me Your Money'

While Lennon used The Beatles as his backing group, McCartney too transformed them into a vehicle for his own work. Though *Abbey Road*, taped over many months of infrequent sessions, proved to be one of The Beatles' slickest albums, it aroused little interest from Lennon. He clocked in when required, or more often than not, though he once again managed to avoid performing on too many of George Harrison's compositions. But he gave little of any lasting value away. His sole contribution to this batch of sessions, then, was finally recording the lead vocals (shared with McCartney) to 'You Know My Name', the jokey piece of rubber soul that had been hatched back in 1967. McCartney looked back on this as his favourite Beatles session, and it certainly sounded as if they were having fun. Lennon twisted his voice into an array of Peter Sellers-like characterisations, in response to McCartney's night-club crooning, while roadie Mal Evans shook gravel in a tray to make up for the absence of Ringo Starr. The relationship between Lennon and McCartney would never be so playful again.

APRIL 22 AND 27, 1969: RECORDING 'John And Yoko'

On April 21, the Lennons announced the formation of their company-within-a-company: Bag Productions Ltd, who henceforth handled John and Yoko's publicity, financing and co-ordination. A day later, in a ceremony on the Apple roof, Lennon changed his name by deed poll: from John Winston Lennon to John Ono Lennon. Yoko was also an Ono Lennon; together they now had nine 'O's in their names, and this was apparently a sign of great fortune. (John later discovered that he was legally unable to drop the Winston from his name; the tenth 'O' may have been less of a lucky charm.)

Flushed with optimism, the couple booked a session at Abbey Road for that evening, and recorded 'John And Yoko' – the track which, with 'Amsterdam', made up the musical portion of their *Wedding Album* package later in the year. Using a microphone shaped like a stethoscope, as used in the top teaching hospitals, the Lennons first recorded a few seconds of each other's heartbeats. These were superimposed on tape, and then made into a loop, which was repeated for 20 minutes or more while John and Yoko called out each other's names across the stereo divide. Their intonation ranged from the passionate to the disinterested, failing even to satisfy even that tiny minority who might have welcomed the Lennons' equivalent of Jane Birkin and Serge Gainsbourg's 'Je T'Aime (Moi Non Plus)'. This was fine as a statement of unity and love; but it lacked any objective interest, and its release to the public was an early sign of arrogance.

In the same way that the purity of Yoko's film *Bottoms* had been spoilt by the inclusion of semi-humorous voiceovers, so the beauty of the original statement – the two hearts pounding together to create a womb-like, mysterious pattern of sound – was subverted by the addition of the couple's voices. Having made the transition from 'Baby's Heartbeat' to their own, the experiment was repeated five days later, as the couple attempted to get a better take. Ultimately it was a collage of extracts from both recordings that appeared on *Wedding Album*.

Various Apple acetates are known to exist chronicling the Lennons' activities during this period, though their contents are not in circulation amongst collectors. Besides interviews and the 'John And Yoko' sessions, they include such potentially intriguing items as 'Bagism' and 'Music Now Ensemble'. On the basis of the recordings they did release in 1969, however, reality might be less exciting than speculation.

MAY 25 to JUNE 1, 1969: WRITING, rehearsing and recording 'Give Peace A Chance'; composing 'Come Together' (version one); recording 'KYA Peace Talk', plus impromptu renditions of 'Because'/'Happiness Is A Warm Gun'/'Oh Yoko-I Want You'/'Wake Up Little Suzie'/'Get It Together'; filming *Give Peace A Chance*, *The Way It Is* and *Bedpeace* (alias *Bed-In*)

Bed-In number two was supposed to be in New York, but Lennon's recent drugs conviction meant he wasn't granted an entrance visa – a harbinger of things to come. Having tried an expensive hotel in the Bahamas, the Lennons' party moved to Toronto, and then to Montreal, just across the border from the USA, and close enough to be monitored by countless US radio stations. By comparison, the Amsterdam event had been a dry run for this media explosion. For a week, the Lennons phoned radio stations across North America, and entertained a procession of journalists in person. During these encounters, John regularly picked up his guitar and reeled off an improvised ditty about peace, or a snippet from a recent song. Several of these were captured on tape or film, such as Lennon picking his way through the guitar accompaniment for soon-to-be-released 'Because', or using the framework of 'Happiness Is A Warm Gun' to tell Yoko that she was beautiful. Perhaps the most intriguing of these offerings was 'Get It Together', nearly a song-in-the-making, which used the 'Dear Prudence' guitar pattern as the backdrop for a series of contemporary Lennon slogans, from "give peace a chance" to "come together".

Besides the press, the Lennons were also visited by various figures from the North American counter-culture. Among them was Timothy Leary, guru of LSD, and prospective politician on a free drugs, free world ticket. Meeting one of the most enthusiastic followers of his acid-crazed manifesto, he commissioned Lennon to write him a campaign tune, entitled 'Come Together' – a project that appealed to the newly egalitarian Lennon. What resulted was a simple chant, in the style of 'Give Peace A Chance', which went: "Come together and join the party". That was it: not really enough to shake the castle walls, but it was still a Lennon original. Lennon promised to finish it off and record it, but along the way Leary was imprisoned for drugs offences himself. Lennon duly transformed 'Come Together' into another song, and the party anthem was forgotten. Leary briefly threatened Lennon with legal action, but soon discovered that his own court battles left him no time for such sidetracks.

The original 'Come Together' may have been interrupted before it could reach its climax. But no such problems afflicted the creation of 'Give Peace A Chance'. Lennon intended the song to become the anthem of the world-wide peace movement, to replace the more spiritual 'We Shall Overcome'. (It should be noted, however, that "we shall overcome" was a far more inspiring cry for the civil rights protestors in the USA who had adopted the latter song as the banner of their crusade.)

Lennon unveiled the basic chorus, with its simple message – "All we are saying is give peace a chance" – during an interview in Toronto on May 25, and during breaks in the Montreal Bed-In he made plans to record the chant in the couple's hotel room. He taped various rehearsal takes in the run-up to the session, and then on May 31 he ordered a four-track tape machine to be delivered to the hotel, alerted a cabal of friends and supporters, wrote out four makeshift 'verses' on large pieces of white card to be displayed around the room, and waited for the magic to begin.

Room 1742 of the Hotel Reine Elizabeth was eventually filled with around 50 people – among them a sound engineer in charge of the tape deck and, of course, a full camera crew, documenting the session for posterity. Several takes of the song ensued, with Lennon and comedian Tommy Smothers playing two basic chords on acoustic guitar, while DJ Roger Scott bashed a table to keep time. Lennon led the ensemble through the four verses, each beginning "Everybody's talking 'bout . . ." and proceeding with a litany of appropriate names or nouns, before the massed vocalists launched into repeated rounds of the chorus, while Lennon shouted out encouragement and asides. As a piece of instant art, it was – as Lennon's final comment had it – "beautiful". He took the tapes back to London at the start of June, overdubbed Ringo Starr's backbeat to replace the somewhat shaky percussion on the day, and also allegedly brought in a choir of session singers to stiffen up the equally erratic harmony vocals. Like the *Let It Be* project earlier in the year, then, 'Give Peace A Chance' wasn't quite as uncalculated as it seemed.

But it worked: it was a hit record around the world, was adopted as an anthem by anti-Vietnam protestors in Washington, and remains the most potent symbol of the Lennons' quest for peace. It also inaugurated a new concept: The Plastic Ono Band. On the picture sleeve for the single was a visualisation of this concept: a bank of hi-tech speakers, microphones and amplifiers, without a single human in sight. "The band is plastic", Lennon advised the sleeve designer alongside a cartoon sketch of what he wanted. "The small speakers are to give each member 'a voice'. It must be the LOUDEST band on earth."

Beyond a concept, however, his new group was meant to be anything but exclusive. "You are all The Plastic Ono Band" read the copy for the single's adverts, backed by a page from the London telephone directory with the names of friends and heroes inserted into the lists at random. Henceforward, The Plastic Ono Band would be anyone John cared to work with. And still the world, and The Beatles, thought that everything else would continue as before.

While Lennon was overdubbing 'Give Peace A Chance', Yoko was supervising the editing of the accompanying promotional film – which basically documented the hotel room recording session, capturing the delight on Timothy Leary's face as John sang his name. This clip formed a small part of a longer feature, chronicling the entire Bed-In. Extracts from the full-length *Bedpeace*, such as the infamous encounter with cartoonist Al Capp, turned up in the *Imagine: John Lennon* documentary nearly two decades later. The whole film was given a home video release in 1990, as *The Bed-In*, a glorious collage of hand-held camera footage that captured both the idealism and the insanity of the entire media event. The Lennons edited the footage in early 1970, adding Yoko's 'Who Has Seen The Wind' to the opening scenes, while filming themselves and their film crew for a zany end credits sequence. Meanwhile, Yoko's friend, avant-garde film-maker Jonas Mekas (seen having breakfast with John, Yoko and her daughter Kyoko), included clips of the bed event in his movie, *Diaries, Notes & Sketches*. But the Fluxus pioneer, noted for his use of high-speed film, was slow off the mark compared to the Canadian Broadcasting Corporation, who rushed their own documentary of the bed-in, *The Way It Is*, onto TV screens exactly a week after the Lennons had left for London.

SPRING/SUMMER 1969: RECORDING home demos of 'Woman Is The Nigger Of The World'/'I Love You My Love'

The March 1969 issue of the British women's magazine *Nova* featured an interview with Yoko, in which she proclaimed: "Woman is the nigger of the world". The editors were so startled and struck by her comment that it was pulled out on the cover of the magazine.

Lennon spoke on many occasions about the process of reverse sexism that he was forced to undergo during the early years of his relationship with Yoko. So it wasn't surprising that he should attempt to capture his nascent sense of feminist principles in a song, using Yoko's controversial phrase. In a home demo recorded a few weeks after the interview was published, he committed his first effort to tape, though without having settled on anything more than mumbled lyrics and a non-existent tune.

Around the same time, Lennon and Ono recorded the first of what they would later dub "heart plays" – a dialogue in music, no less, in which they would examine their relationship. 'I Love You My Love', otherwise known to collectors as 'I Want You' (though it bears no relation to The Beatles' song of the same name), began as one of Yoko's sing-song ballads, supported by Lennon's slide guitar. "Before you go back to your fickle self," she crooned, "we can have faith in each other." John responded: "You don't have to worry about my cynicism, I keep it in my pocket with my chewing gum." And as the track grew sillier and sexier, he made it clear that chewing gum was not the only thing he had in his pocket for Yoko. Soon she was extending the fantasy: "I dreamed I was inside your body, and that was something else, cos it made me feel so horny". If 'Oh My Love' a few months earlier had chronicled the dark side of their union, 'I Love You My Love' wiped the slate clean with a heady spray of impure romance.

EARLY JUNE 1969: RECORDING 'Remember Love'

Establishing a tradition that survived as long as John and Yoko's relationship, the flipside of The Plastic Ono Band's first single showcased Yoko Ono. To date, the public had only been treated to her more extreme vocal stylings: 'Remember Love', recorded at their home studio immediately after they returned from Canada, was by contrast a delicate ballad, with Yoko breathing her simple message of love into the microphone while John once again showed off his acoustic guitar picking, to a series of chords that came close to another of his recent compositions, 'Sun King'. Note that some sources state that this track was actually recorded during the Montreal Bed-In the previous week.

JUNE 17, 1969: *OH! CALCUTTA!* opens in New York

Critic and writer Kenneth Tynan was responsible for producing *Oh! Calcutta!* on the New York stage, and then thirteen months later in London. The play, a loose aggregation of sketches contributed by many hands, tore at the boundaries of sexual liberation and censorship, with its frank portrayal of roles, positions and language not seen and heard in public before.

Lennon was one of the notables whom Tynan approached for ideas. As John remembered in 1970, "He just said, 'I'm getting all these different people to write something erotic, will you do it?' So I came up with two lines, which was the masturbation scene. It was a great childhood thing, everybody's been masturbating and trying to think of something sexy, and somebody'd shout 'Winston Churchill' in the middle of it and break down. So I just wrote that down on a paper and told them to put whichever names in that suited the hero, and they did it." In the New York script, also published in book form, Tynan built a sketch around Lennon's idea, substituting The Lone Ranger in the role of fantasy-breaker.

In the show's program, Lennon contributed a brief autobiography: "Born October 9, 1940. Lived. Met Yoko 1966!" He was also credited on the play's cast album, though he was only featured on the record as an author, not a performer. Ironically, when Lennon finally saw the show, he hated it.

SUMMER 1969: WRITING 'Fuck You'

Susan Baker, member of the British performance and poetry act, The Barrow Poets, approached the Lennons in 1969, with a request for a poem that her troupe could use alongside their own. She was sent a linguistic sculpture consisting of the word 'fuck' written out in columns 104 times, around the central word 'you'.

"Dear Susan," Lennon wrote in an accompanying note, "here's the poem you wanted. You can publish it, but not make a record of it – for it turns into a song then, OK? Love John and Yoko."

165

JULY 1 to AUGUST 25, 1969: THE BEATLES recording 'Maxwell's Silver Hammer'/'Come Together'/'The End'/'Sun King'/'Mean Mr Mustard'/'Polythene Pam'/'She Came In Through The Bathroom Window'/'Because', plus impromptu versions of 'Be-Bop-A-Lula'/'Who Slapped John?'/'Ain't She Sweet'

This final set of four-man Beatles sessions saw the completion of *Abbey Road*, with most of the work concentrated on the 'medley' that took up the last third of the record. Lennon was suitably damning about the project: "*Abbey Road* was really unfinished songs all stuck together. Everybody praises the album so much, but none of the songs had anything to do with each other, no thread at all, only the fact that we stuck them together." And it's noticeable that for all its musical invention, and cohesiveness of sound, *Abbey Road* carries little of Lennon's best work. But as the album sessions began, Lennon was proudly trumpeting the prospect of the medley to the press, as if it had been his concept from the start. What stifled his enthusiasm at this point wasn't the idea of a medley, but the fact that as his attention was distracted by his activities with Yoko, he had precious little left to give to The Beatles. It was only in retrospect that he decided that the *Abbey Road* medley was contrived (as indeed it was) and therefore 'dishonest', at least by comparison with his own intensely personal solo work.

Most of his *Abbey Road* songs, in fact, were throwaways – vignettes, two minutes or less of hasty scene-painting with no personal content. And by 1969, if it wasn't personal, then for Lennon it didn't count. That took care of 'Polythene Pam' and 'Mean Mr Mustard', which had been polished into shape since their first outings in spring 1968, but still revealed little of Lennon's true preoccupations (though his Scouse accent on 'Polythene Pam' was wonderfully sarcastic). Likewise 'Sun King', which matched the acoustic guitar riff John had already used on 'Everybody Had A Hard Year' and 'Remember Love' to a set of luscious Beatle harmonies, as they crooned nonsense syllables in mock-Spanish. During a pause in the recording of this song, the group happily tumbled into a facetious medley of Gene Vincent classics, including a reprise of 'Ain't She Sweet', last heard in Hamburg fully eight years earlier. But unlike their conduct in January 1969, this was only a brief distraction from the business in hand.

'Because' produced another superb exhibition of harmonies, triple-tracked by John, Paul and George. John wrote the song after hearing Yoko play Beethoven's 'Moonlight Sonata' on the piano: he asked her to write out the chords backwards and play them, and the result was the guitar riff that underpins the song. For his words, Lennon dipped back into his bag of optimism left over from the summer of 1967, to produce a pantheistic vision of happiness and oneness with nature: "Because the world is round/It turns me on . . . Because the sky is blue/It makes me cry".

Lennon's only other contribution to *Abbey Road* was 'Come Together"; not the simplistic campaign chant he'd written for Timothy Leary, but a bluesy boogie based around a rhythm pattern he'd developed for an early version of McCartney's 'Helter Skelter' the previous year. The song kicked off from the opening lines of Chuck Berry's classic car-chase song, 'You Can't Catch Me' ("Here comes old flat-top/He comes grooving up slowly") into a set of free-association images inspired by his marriage to Yoko. The Berry influence was also apparent in the speed of the imagery, with each phrase passing too quickly to be understood at first hearing, the sound as important as the meaning. Yoko's inspiration could be heard in the verses ("He got Ono sideboard . . . he got Bag Production") and more blatantly in the chorus, a celebration of the couple's sexuality ("Come together, right now, over me").

Almost lost in the record's mix was Lennon's whispered injunction, "shoot me", between each verse – reminiscent of the ad-libs on 'Watching Rainbows' from earlier in the year. Maybe martyrdom still didn't seem that far away in the summer of 1969. Or maybe the 'shooting' had more to do with the Lennons' recreational habits a few months earlier. ("Shooting is exercise", Yoko had let slip during a pause in the January 1969 *Let It Be* sessions.)

Lennon missed several of the final *Abbey Road* sessions. During the first week of July, for instance, he and Yoko were on holiday in Scotland, where their car ran off the road and they wound up in hospital. The last time that all four Beatles gathered in the recording studio was August 20, when John remixed 'I Want You (She's So Heavy)', and helped out while the closing medley was assembled. A couple of sessions later, the album was complete; and within a week Lennon had told new Beatles manager Allen Klein that he was leaving the group.

AUGUST 1969: FILMING *Self Portrait*

Two Virgins had nothing on this. That controversial album cover had been a statement of innocence through nakedness: two 'born again virgins' rediscovering Eden through each other. *Self Portrait*, by contrast, took self-exposure to its ultimate extreme: 15 minutes of slow-motion footage of John's semi-erect penis, shot (like *Smile*) with high-speed film. The original plan was for the film to capture the process of erection, but Lennon found the presence of a film crew distracting, and Yoko's efforts to strike suitably erotic poses failed to elicit the right response. A copy of *Playboy* succeeded where his wife had not, and the film raced through the camera for a minute or two while Lennon attempted to concentrate on the nature of eroticism. "My prick, that's all you saw for a long time," Lennon explained later. "No movement, but it dribbled at the end. That was accidental." Fortunately, his claims that *Self Portrait* would be "the first audio-visual and smell film" weren't realised.

The motive for the film remained cloudy. Was Lennon attempting a further debunking of The Beatles' myth, after *Two Virgins* had proved that he was human, after all? Or was he influenced by the common notion that all underground film was inherently pornographic? Either way, the short picture failed to impress the avant-garde or the public, as its screenings were restricted to private cinema clubs. While their music and their peace campaigns were generously aimed at the world, rather than an élite, the Lennons had yet to make the same transition from experimental to populist in their film work.

EARLY SEPTEMBER 1969: WRITING and recording home demos of 'Cold Turkey' and *Wedding Album* promo message

During the bitter final months of 1968, the Lennons' use of LSD (sporadic) and marijuana (regular) decayed into heroin addiction. Although their use varied in frequency – they were apparently clean during the two Bed-Ins, for example – in the late summer of 1969 they decided to make the break, choosing to go 'cold turkey' (experience all the pangs of chemical withdrawal without medical supervision).

Now convinced that art was there to mirror his life, Lennon poured his experience into a song. It was titled 'Cold Turkey', a naked admission of its inspiration – at least to those familiar with narcotics terminology. In the event, the fact that there was some kind of drugs connection led the BBC and other radio stations to ban the finished record – unjust treatment for a song which, as Lennon insisted, was a warning against drug use rather than an encouragement to experiment. It was certainly difficult to imagine anyone hearing 'Cold Turkey' and being induced to try heroin for the first time as a result.

The chorus of the song carried its stark message: "Cold turkey has got me on the run". The verses, round a repetitive two-chord pattern, were equally basic, detailing the pain, terror and loneliness of withdrawal as the body craves for the drug and tries to torture the mind into giving way. The physical descriptions were scary enough, but Lennon's mental response to the pain was enlightening:"I wish I was a baby/I wish I was dead".That need to return to the womb, to the warmth and security of childhood, was sparked by the same feeling of betrayal that would later inspire 'Mother' and 'My Mummy's Dead'.A hint of the same desire can be found on 'John And Yoko', where the combined noise of the couple's heartbeats came close to the womb-sound therapy tapes occasionally prescribed to help troubled souls to sleep.

Marc Bolan, then leader of the acoustic duo Tyrannosaurus Rex, always claimed that Lennon had been trying to sound like him on 'Cold Turkey'. That sounded like arrogant blustering, typical of a man who thought he was bigger than The Beatles, until you heard Lennon's acoustic demos, where he bleated his way through the lyric like a mutant sheep, bleating out his pain over the final chords of the song (probably more in imitation of Yoko than Bolan). Ironically, this vocal effect was so extreme that it distracted from the emotional impact of the song.

Take One of his demo sequence was a simple acoustic guitar/vocal rendition; take two double-tracked the vocal, and added the song's addictive lead guitar line, which was duplicated by Eric Clapton on the record. A third take from these home recordings found Yoko helping proceedings along, adding her own cackles to Lennon's, and then screaming out "push me John" over the fade, in what was presumably a throwback to one of the darker moments of her own withdrawal.

Lennon took these demos to his colleagues in The Beatles, and proposed that they should record the song as a single. Knowing very well they would turn it down, he promptly made plans to issue the song himself, as The Plastic Ono Band's second single. He had previously announced his intention of issuing a lengthy instrumental called 'Rock Peace' as the P.O.B's next project, but the track never seems to have been recorded – if indeed such a piece was ever written. Various collectors have claimed to have discovered either the finished track, or a demo, or even a set of lyrics, but none of these has been remotely convincing to date. In fact, 'Rock Peace' may actually have been nothing more exciting than a rock arrangement of 'Give Peace A Chance', designed as karaoke for activists around the world.

Also around this period, Lennon and Ono recorded a radio trailer for the imminent release of their *Wedding Album* in October, chanting their promotional message in sing-song unison.

EARLY SEPTEMBER 1969: FILMING *Apotheosis*

In the first week of September 1969, three of John and Yoko's films – *Two Virgins, Smile and Honeymoon* – were given their British première at the

169

Edinburgh Film Festival. A week later, those three films, plus *Rape*, *Self Portrait* and the mysteriously undocumented *Folding* were shown at the newly opened ICA in London. "John and Yoko's evening of film events will end towards midnight," promised the couple's press release. "It will happen once. It will be what they want it to be." The audience were promised an appearance by The Plastic Ono Band: instead, the Lennons hired another couple to visit the cinema in a white bag, while infra-red cameras documented the audience's reaction.

When the ICA offered the couple further exposure in early November, they set to work to produce another batch of movies. The concept for *Apotheosis* came from Lennon, not Yoko; like *Self Portrait*, this was John working in a medium to which Yoko had introduced him, rather than merely supporting her efforts, as on *Smile* and *Two Virgins*. From the start, the idea of a helium balloon ascending into the sky was at the heart of John's idea. The ever-willing Nic Knowland agreed to go up in the balloon with a camera and a soundman. His brief was to capture John and Yoko in his lens as the balloon left the ground, then to offer a *cinéma vérité* portrayal, a balloon's-eye-view, of the ground and the sky as the entourage rose through the air.

Setting off from an airfield in Hampshire, Knowland and the balloon rose on schedule, with the camera tracking the Lennons as they slowly vanished from view, then offering a map-like view of the fields and runways below as the balloon reached towards the clouds. Then everything was pure white, until the balloon finally broke free into clear sky, and the sun sparkled into the corner of the shot. Knowland continued filming until the balloon was on the ground, but the arrival of the sun was used as the film's climax, a heady relief from the effectively blank screen of the cloud shots, which had occupied almost half of the film's 16 minutes.

Unlike their previous experiments, *Apotheosis* was shot in real time, with the noise of birds and the wind the only accompaniment. Its elemental simplicity gave it a stark, natural beauty; there was none of the authorial shaping that had marred the Lennons' earlier efforts. Indeed, Lennon had quite consciously chosen not to break the purity of the single continuous shot that made up the finished film. Knowland had been sent up in a helicopter to take pictures of a similar balloon in flight, which could have been cut into his original footage. But Lennon and Ono realised that the change of perspective would tarnish the concept, and the helicopter film was saved for use in *Apotheosis No. 2*.

CHAPTER 10

September 1969 to December 1970

From September 1969 onwards, John Lennon was only a 'Beatle' in legal terms. He had taken the decision to leave the group, although he agreed to toe the corporate line for a few months and keep his departure secret. Peace was still his crusade at this point, but increasingly his activities with Yoko came under strain from more pressing personal concerns. The shadow of heroin use continued to darken their lives, until they took the radical step of throwing themselves into an abrasive and confrontational form of psychotherapy. This overturned the Lennons' way of seeing the world, and liberated him – however briefly – to make the most naked music of his career.

SEPTEMBER 13, 1969: THE PLASTIC ONO BAND perform 'Blue Suede Shoes'/'Money'/'Dizzy Miss Lizzy'/'Yer Blues'/ 'Cold Turkey'/'Give Peace A Chance'/'Don't Worry Kyoko'/ 'John John (Let's Hope For Peace)' at the Toronto Rock 'n' Roll Revival Festival; performance filmed for *Sweet Toronto*

At the end of August 1969, Toronto promoters Brower and Walker announced that the city's Varsity Stadium would be hosting a rock festival starring The Doors, Alice Cooper and Chicago Transit Authority alongside a batch of Fifties heroes: Chuck Berry, Jerry Lee Lewis, Gene Vincent, Bo Diddley, Fats Domino and Little Richard. By the eve of the festival, however, it was obvious that the ticket sales were not going to cover their basic costs. In a desperate attempt to save the event, John Brower contacted John Lennon in London, and asked him to attend as compère. Lennon agreed, but only if he could perform as well. And so it was that a disbelieving Toronto public were told the news that the Plastic Ono Band would be making their first live appearance in their city, not previously known as one of the rock capitals of the world.

The next 24 hours brought a succession of conflicting messages from London, as the Lennons prevaricated over their plans – finally announcing from their bed, while the rest of their party were gathered at London Airport, that they had changed their minds. Guitarist Eric Clapton was sent back to twist their arms, and eventually the makeshift Plastic Ono Band were en route to Canada, rehearsing their set at the back of the aircraft on unamplified electric guitars.

Backstage at Varsity Stadium, the Lennons ordered cocaine, John threw up because of his nerves, and the tension mounted. The POB eventually took the stage in the early evening, introduced by MC Kim Fowley, and proceeded to deliver a 40-minute set divided into two distinct halves. Lennon began by powering his way through three of the rock classics he and The Beatles had played in clubs in Liverpool and Hamburg at the start of the decade, before delivering an anguished, if slightly shaky, version of 'Yer Blues', which Clapton had performed with Lennon at The Rolling Stones' *Rock 'n' Roll Circus* the previous December. For Clapton, drummer Alan White and bassist Klaus Voormann, however, 'Cold Turkey' was as new as it was to the audience, who heard the only public rendition of the song that ever kept close to the free-flowing rhythmic arrangement of John's original demos. Finally, John barked his way through a chaotic, mock-reggae 'Give Peace A Chance', before announcing: "Now Yoko's going to do her thing, all over you".

As indeed she did. As the band set off on the chord sequence that had already been the basis for John's 'Watching Rainbows' at the start of 1969, Yoko improvised a message to her daughter, Kyoko: 'Don't Worry Kyoko (Mummy's Only Looking For Her Hand In The Snow)'. ("Find a hand in the snow", read one of Yoko's 'Three Snow Pieces For Orchestra' in her book *Grapefruit*.) While the band careered onwards, Yoko wailed, cried and howled her obscure message of reassurance. Then, unaccompanied, she called out the words "Oh John, let's hope for peace" in agonisingly extended breaths, before Lennon and Clapton forced gales of piercing feedback from their guitars, and Alan White unleashed sympathetic fills and rolls across his drum kit. Finally, as Yoko broke into a long series of sharp screams, Lennon moved to shelter his wife from the crowd, placing his guitar against its amplifier. The other musicians followed suit, and as Yoko gave her last scream there was just the infernal hum of feedback cascading from the stage, roaring on and on until Beatles roadie Mal Evans turned off the equipment.

The audience, far from booing as reported in the British press, merely stood in silence, before emerging from their shock to call out for more. Backstage, Lennon announced that this was "1980s music", the wave of the future.

1969 was the year of the eternal document, so you won't be surprised to learn that the event was filmed and recorded. True to the Lennons' tradition of honesty and authenticity, Apple issued a live album of the event entitled *Live Peace In Toronto 1969*, clad in a beautiful sky blue cover broken only by a single white cloud. It could have been a film still from *Apotheosis*. The album came with a calendar for 1970 – or, as the Lennons styled it, Year One A.P. ('After Peace') – and captured the entire event from introduction to finale, omitting only Lennon's rather impatient gibe at the audience's lack of reaction after 'Cold Turkey'.

The event was meant to form the climax to the official movie of the festival, D.A. Pennebaker's *Sweet Toronto*. That wasn't completed until late 1970, by which time Allen Klein and John Lennon insisted the P.O.B'.s performance should be omitted from the film, which was duly issued as *Keep On Rockin'*. (Test screenings in mid-America had apparently discovered that the audience for vintage rock'n'roll didn't want to watch Yoko screaming for fifteen minutes.) Only in 1989 did the entire set appear on home video, revealing additional highlights of the proceedings – for example, Yoko entering a large white bag on stage during 'Blue Suede Shoes', and then having to be pulled out again after 'Dizzy Miss Lizzy' so that Lennon could retrieve his lyric sheet from her. The film soundtrack also revealed the extent to which Lennon had remixed the original tapes for the LP release. His most blatant manoeuvre was to remove or dampen most of Yoko's impromptu, intrusive squeals and yells, which had continued throughout John's set with the band.

SEPTEMBER 25 and 28, 1969: RECORDING 'Cold Turkey'

It took two separate sessions for Lennon and his Plastic Ono Band – Eric Clapton, Klaus Voormann and Ringo Starr – to capture the full intensity of his agonising heroin withdrawal in the studio. As if the lyrics were not harrowing enough, Lennon set about constructing a musical arrangement that would approximate the anguish that had sparked the song. He and Eric both played the lead guitar part mapped out on his demo, while the rhythm guitar heard in the Toronto arrangement a fortnight earlier was omitted – breaking the song into jagged fragments of pain behind Lennon's strangled vocals. The effect was like a message from hell, as if intense emotions had been squeezed into a narrow bottle and were about to break loose. The final two minutes of the record merely heightened the atmosphere, with Lennon groaning and screaming his way towards catharsis. The example of Yoko's full-blooded vocalising had obviously not been ignored.

The finished record (taped at the second session) had all the hallmarks of spontaneity, but it had actually taken 26 takes to perfect the track. A surviving acetate of an early take had Lennon bending and twisting some of his notes in the song's verses; but this approach was abandoned as too refined, too staged. The moment was too extreme to allow the distraction of vocal gymnastics. The only restriction was self-imposed, as Lennon's rudimentary production skills failed to deliver a rhythm track as weighty as the song or the performance. By the time he entered the studio to make his third solo single, this problem would have been solved.

OCTOBER 3, 1969: RECORDING 'Don't Worry Kyoko'

For the flipside of 'Cold Turkey', Lennon and his musicians (Clapton, Voormann and Starr once again) set about transforming Yoko's maternal cry, 'Don't Worry Kyoko', into the "fucking best rock 'n' roll record ever made", as Lennon put it a year later. Yoko began the song with an extended wail, while the guitars broke like a wave behind her, playing the same skin-tight riff over and over as she explored the possibilities of the human voice. Like 'Cold Turkey', this was communication beyond words: the Lennons were fast realising that lyricism was too indirect to convey their feelings.

LATE OCTOBER 1969: FILMING *Cold Turkey*

Like *Give Peace A Chance* and *The Ballad Of John And Yoko*, this was a promotional film, designed for use on TV pop shows as well as in art cinemas. John and Yoko gathered together off-cuts from the Montreal bed-in footage, plus a rough cut of their September gig in Toronto, and cut clips together with speeded-up film of traffic in New York to create a frenetic, exhausting collage that matched the intensity of the music, but made no attempt to run in sync with it. (This footage was shot by Yoko's friend, New York underground film-maker Jonas Mekas. Bizarrely, he actually intended it to accompany the somewhat less frantic 'Give Peace A Chance' single.) One motif looked to the future: in its rush from image to image, the film paused for a second on the words "Power To The Workers" typed on a sheet of paper.

c. EARLY NOVEMBER, 1969: RECORDING contributions to '1969 Beatles Christmas Single'

There was effectively no institution called The Beatles by late 1969 to create the usual flexidisc for their fan club, so it was left to their mutual friend, disc jockey Kenny Everett, to persuade each of the four to donate material. Christmas brought out something sentimental in the Lennons, who contributed more running time to the record than the other three Beatles combined. Not that there was much art involved. After some giggly conversation, taped while walking around the grounds of their Ascot home, during which Yoko opined, "It will be a quiet peaceful 1970, hopefully", John lurched into a parody of 'Good King Wenceslas', just as he had six years earlier when The Beatles were still 'the Fab Four'. Improvised Christmas ditties followed, with Lennon conjuring seasonal sounds out of his harmonium and Moog synthesiser. But the result was no more entertaining than the bulk of the *Two Virgins* album, which this nonsense strongly resembled.

NOVEMBER 26, 1969: RECORDING and remixing 'What's The News Mary Jane'; remixing 'You Know My Name (Look Up The Number)'

Since early October, the Lennons had suffered a second miscarriage; commissioned critic Tony Palmer to write a biography of John in a fortnight, and then lost enthusiasm after he'd finished it; issued their *Wedding Album*; and used the comparative failure of 'Cold Turkey' in the British charts as one of the excuses for returning John's MBE award to Buckingham Palace on November 25. As the Queen was considering her response, John and Yoko were at EMI remixing two vintage Beatles cuts, in preparation for issuing them as an immediate Plastic Ono Band single. Apple proudly announced that the single would appear within 10 days, and that it featured "some of the biggest names in the business".

'You Know My Name' was cut down from over six minutes to a touch over four, deleting the ska interlude along the way and tightening up the rest of this final Lennon/McCartney collaboration. "It was a bit camp", Lennon admitted. "I thought this would make a good Christmas record, because it's either a good laugh or you hate it." 'What's The New Mary Jane', effectively a Lennon/Ono project to begin with, was doubled in length as the couple added vocal wails, percussion noises and associated madness to the end of what was already one of John's least conservative songs. Two six-minute mixes were prepared, each sounding like a cross between a stoned nursery rhyme and a remake of 'Revolution 9'.

Lennon apparently didn't seek permission to use either track from his former bandmates. "I thought The Beatles wouldn't want it," he explained, "because they don't want another record out at the moment, so I could have it. But of course they did! I just wanted it out, I don't care what they call it, The Beatles or Tom & Jerry, just get the bloody music out!" Acetates of the Plastic Ono Band single were manufactured, but then the project was hastily abandoned, and 'You Know My Name' ended up several months later on the flipside of the final Beatles single, 'Let It Be'.

DECEMBER 4, 1969: RECORDING 'Item 1' and 'Item 2'

In late November, Lennon announced that the couple were about to record a fourth album of their so-called 'unfinished music', in the tradition of *Two Virgins*, *Life With The Lions* and *Wedding Album*. "One side is laughing," John threatened, "the other is whispering." To that end, he supervised two suitably chaotic recording sessions at EMI, with the assistance of aides and friends such as Mal Evans and Anthony Fawcett.

For 'Item 1', Lennon arranged the participants in a circle. They donned red clowns' noses and then – with what sounded like a little herbal stimulation – proceeded to laugh hysterically, while EMI's engineers dutifully captured the results on tape. Tracks of percussion and vocal chanting were added, before Lennon prepared a rough mix while Yoko passed sushi around to the performers. 'Item 2' required the assembled company to whisper into each other's ears – a process that inevitably led to a second outbreak of hysteria. Lennon intended to overdub this tape with studio sound effects, but the track was never completed – and neither was the album. Extracts from this session was filmed by the BBC for a *24 Hours* documentary on the Lennons.

DECEMBER 5 1969: FILMING *Apotheosis No. 2* and 'Fortunately/Unfortunately'

Another day, another balloon: this time it was dusk, rather than the early morning of the September *Apotheosis* shoot, and Nic Knowland shot evocative film of the Lennons lit by a flickering bonfire as his balloon left the ground in Lavenham, Suffolk. These shots, a primeval blend of darkness and flame, were combined with some of the leftover helicopter footage from *Apotheosis* to create a second essay in the genre. Meanwhile, the process of filming was documented for BBC TV's ongoing *24 Hours* documentary on the Lennons. The BBC's cameras were also on hand the following day, to capture John and Yoko playing a naive verbal game, 'Fortunately/Unfortunately'. Yoko considered this so amusing, or poignant, that an extract was subsequently used in Lennon's CD box set, *Anthology*.

DECEMBER 10, 1969: JOHN AND YOKO announce filming of *Hanratty*

World peace was not the Lennons' only concern at the end of 1969. They had been moved by the representations of the family of James Hanratty, who had been hanged in 1962 for a murder which both he and his family had always claimed he had never committed. Protests about the execution had continued throughout the decade, and the Lennons announced that their contribution to the campaign would be to make a film about the case, which would finally prove Hanratty's innocence. John and Yoko organised an event at Speakers' Corner in Hyde Park to launch their crusade, but then everything went quiet. It was generally assumed that the couple had lost interest in the case, but in the event a documentary film about the case, financed by John and Yoko, was given one belated screening at the Crypt, St. Martin's-in-the-Fields, Trafalgar Square. Aside from setting the project in motion, however, the Lennons seem to have had no involvement with the making of the film.*

DECEMBER 15, 1969: THE PLASTIC ONO BAND perform 'Cold Turkey'/'Don't Worry Kyoko' at the UNICEF benefit concert, the Lyceum, London; John and Yoko launch the 'War Is Over (If You Want It)' poster campaign

The Plastic Ono Band's only European concert – later events planned for Birmingham and Berlin were abandoned as the Lennons went into

---

* On 22 March 2001, James Hanratty's remains were exhumed so that a DNA sample could be taken for analysis. The results showed there was a 2.5 million to one chance that the samples came from someone other than Hanratty. In March 2001, DNA sample extracted from Hanratty's exhumed body was matched by forensic experts to two samples from the crime scene. On 10 May 2002, the Court of Criminal Appeal (Lord Chief Justice Woolf, Lord Justice Mantell and Mr Justice Leveson hearing the appeal) ruled that Hanratty's conviction was not unsound and that there were no grounds for a posthumous pardon.

seclusion during spring 1970 – saw them topping the bill at a benefit show for the United Nations' children's charity, UNICEF, in London. Transformed into the Plastic Ono Supergroup by the addition to their ranks of various heavy guests, including Delaney & Bonnie's entire band, Billy Preston, Keith Moon of The Who and George Harrison, they performed just two songs – 'Cold Turkey' and 'Don't Worry Kyoko'. 'Turkey' kept close to the blueprint, with the presence of a full horn section lending weight to the central riff. But 'Don't Worry Kyoko' was extended to over 20 minutes, which Lennon described a year later as "the most fantastic music I've ever heard . . . 20 years ahead of its time".

He had a point. The piece began with Yoko, emerging from her customary white bag, calling out "John, I love you", before claiming "Britain, you killed Hanratty, you murderers". Then the band set off – the guitarists taking the original three-chord riff as their base, the brass growling a countermelody behind. As the 15 musicians locked horns and blew, Yoko screamed and wailed, and the sound took on a life of its own, growing organically towards a climax as Yoko and the brass players supported each other on a tide of pure emotion. At its peak, the music finally gave way beneath the weight of its tension, collapsing into a free-form, apocalyptic section that only ended with everyone on stage pushing their instruments to their limits. As in Toronto, the audience was stunned into silence as the band left the stage.

Enraptured by the experience, the Lennons set plans in motion for the release of another live album. But their effective retirement from peace campaigning and the concert stage during 1970 meant that they didn't have enough material to fill a record. Only after they had appeared with Frank Zappa in summer 1971 did Lennon resurrect the idea, telling interviewers that an album entitled *Live Jam* would be released at budget price shortly. He revisited and edited the Lyceum tapes, calling in Nicky Hopkins to overdub Billy Preston's piano part, which had been lost in the mix. By this time, however, Lennon had other crusades on his mind, and the Lyceum performance eventually emerged in 1972 as one quarter of the *Some Time In New York City* double album.

On the same day as they appeared at the Lyceum, Lennon and Ono had paid for massive billboards to be erected in the world's major capital cities, bearing the simple, thought-provoking message: "War is over, if you want it. Happy Christmas from John and Yoko". Only in London were the posters vandalised.

DECEMBER 18 TO 20, 1969: SIGNING the 'Bag One' lithographs; recording 'Rap On Ronnie Hawkins' & 'Message To Japanese Fans'

Immediately after the Lyceum show, the Lennons had left for Canada to finalise plans for the giant Toronto Peace Festival – a multi-media event scheduled for July 1970, on an airfield near Toronto. The concept was grandiose: all the world's major rock stars (The Beatles, The Stones, Dylan, Elvis) would play together, a million people would attend, and the entire event would be staged for free. Meanwhile, John and Yoko would arrive on a hover-ship powered by air: it was that kind of festival. Lennon had apparently persuaded all The Beatles except Ringo to take part. But the proposal eventually collapsed in a welter of accusations on all sides, the Lennons being blamed for their naivety, and in turn declaring that their fellow organisers had betrayed the original concept of the festival.

The couple stayed at the home of rocker Ronnie Hawkins, for whom John recorded a brief message designed to promote his new album, while both Lennons taped another communication to their fans in Japan – Yoko speaking in her native tongue, while John added brief recitals of 'Give Peace A Chance' and guitar instrumentals of 'Dear Prudence' and 'Sun King'. In the context of his collected work, however, these performances are no more significant than the off-the-cuff rendition of a folk song, 'O Kristelighed', which the Lennons delivered when they moved on to Denmark a couple of weeks later.

While still in Canada, Lennon also took time to complete work on his *Bag One* lithographs – the result of the introduction to the art form brought about by Anthony Fawcett back in 1968. The drawings were converted from Lennon's small originals to poster size, organised into limited edition packages, and given to John so he could sign each lithograph. They were then placed inside special *Bag One* folders, and sold to art-minded (and rich) individuals around the world. It might have been more in keeping with Lennon's principles if they'd been issued as postcards instead.

Not that they would have got very far through the mail, as subsequent events demonstrated. The lithographs documented the Lennons' honeymoon – their sexual consummation, not the Amsterdam bed-in. Drawn in bold, simple lines, they depicted the couple making love, with the most graphic illustrations showing Lennon performing oral sex on his bride, in a pose that mixed tenderness, passion and supplication. The simpler and less cluttered the drawings, the more effective they were. On several illustrations, Lennon filled in the skeleton of the portraits with hurried strokes of his pencil, reducing the impact and stark beauty of his work.

When the lithographs were exhibited in London at the Arts Gallery in New Bond Street, the forces of law and order intervened, and several of the more erotic items were seized in the name of the Obscene Publications Act. The combination of John, Yoko and nudity had once again proved too hot for the establishment to handle.

In late 1969, Lennon had also contrived an entirely different visual arte-fact, a cartoon painting entitled 'Happy Fish'. It was created during a holi-day on a yacht moored off the Greek island of Hydra, and given to his companion on the boat, former Apple employee Alexis Mardas.

JANUARY 1970: TAPING John & Kyoko

The Lennons ended their year of frantic peace activity in Denmark. There they stayed with Yoko Ono's ex-husband Tony Cox and his new partner, Melinda, while they continued to plan the Toronto Peace Festival. Along the way, they became involved in lengthy discussions about the possibility of flying saucers that would run on air, which only needed a few thousand pounds of their money to get off the ground; and they had their hair sheared to crew-cut length, keeping their flowing locks in a bag ready to be auctioned for a deserving cause when they returned to England.

Their stay in Denmark brought the Lennons back into lengthy contact with Yoko and Tony's daughter, Kyoko. She was now a precocious seven-year-old, who clearly adored her new stepfather. John celebrated their rela-tionship (which seems to have been much easier for him to maintain than his ties with his natural son, Julian) by taping several hours of musical play-time. There is some evidence that he considered briefly the idea of issuing an album of this material, but that was never an option, even by *Unfinished Music* standards. Instead, he gave the tapes to Cox, who sold them to an American collector many years later.

Nothing of any great musical value was preserved on the tapes, unless you count Lennon serenading his stepdaughter with Frank Zappa & The Mothers Of Invention's mock-Fifties tune, 'Jelly Roll Gum Drop'. (Earlier, he had tried to persuade Apple band Trash to cover the same song.) John and Yoko joined in a singalong on 'Yellow Submarine', a perennial favourite among kids around the world; John serenaded his wife with the recently written 'Oh Yoko'; and he made up countless kiddie-flavoured ditties on the spot to amuse Kyoko. One of them was about Julian, who had become friends with Kyoko earlier in the year. Man and girl even performed some very basic acoustic guitar duets. Through it all, Lennon retained his temper and enthusiasm, but each tape ended with the grown-ups getting tired and the child wanting the fun to carry on, until way past her bedtime. 'Twas ever thus.

JANUARY 27/28, 1970: RECORDING 'Instant Karma! (We All Shine On)'/'Who Has Seen The Wind'

On the morning of January 27, 1970, John Lennon wrote 'Instant Karma!' around the same three-chord, three-blind-mice sequence as 'All You Need Is Love'. Anxious to record and release it immediately, he called a session for that night, and managed to assemble George Harrison, Klaus Voormann, Alan White and possibly Billy Preston at short notice. A request also went out to legendary producer Phil Spector, who was in London at the request of his (and three of The Beatles') manager, Allen Klein, to discuss his poss-ible involvement with The Beatles' ailing *Let It Be* project. As an audition, Lennon asked him to produce 'Instant Karma!', and was sufficiently struck by his contribution to sign him up as Apple's in-house A&R chief, and also the producer of his own records for the next two years.

Spector's hallmark was excess, forcing banks of musicians to play simple phrases and chord sequences in unison, till the sheer weight of sound assumed an emotional power that would have evaded a smaller band of instrumentalists. His sound was overpowering, the rage of a soul in torment – the opposite, in fact, of the clean, precise but ultimately rather brittle noise produced by George Martin and The Beatles, and equally well demon-strated by the pincer-thin rhythm section on the Lennon-produced 'Cold Turkey'.

Spector's skills went beyond bombastic, however, and within minutes of joining the session he had transformed another heavy guitar work-out into an exercise for piano, drums, vocal and not much else. He worked his magic instantly, forcing Lennon's foot down hard on the sustain pedal for the opening piano notes (nicked from Ritchie Barrett's 'Some Other Guy', a Beatles favourite from the Cavern days), and producing a drum sound that felt like bursts of artillery fire. Halfway through the first verse, he introduced handclaps, and for the chorus a crash cymbal that rang like an alarm bell. John's vocals were smothered in echo, while underneath, clanking pianos played chords, four to the bar, acting as percussion rather than instruments of melody.

Phil's final touch transformed a rabble of vocal chorus – consisting of Allen Klein and a collection of nightbirds from nearby Hatchett's club, rounded up by Billy Preston – into a choir, mixed so that their voices arched over Lennon's lead vocal. 'Instant Karma!' was Lennon's loudest and simplest record yet; and almost all the credit was Spector's.

What of the song, meanwhile? Well, it was open to interpretation. Across the bones of an old-fashioned R&B song, Lennon laid a democratic chorus ("We all shine on, like the moon and the stars and the sun") and a series of verses that debunked the notion that superstars were any more important than the rest of us, and suggested that immediate enlightenment wasn't always to be trusted. Was the message that you could do whatever you wanted? Or that easy solutions didn't always turn out so easy? Lennon wasn't saying. All he added in later years was that "the idea of instant karma was like the idea of instant coffee, presenting something in a new form".

The B-side, Yoko's 'Who Has Seen The Wind' was another private home recording (with overdubs). Like 'Remember Love', this showcased the child-like, innocent Yoko, not the titan wailing in the face of the storm. The song was a message of love, linked to Yoko's belief that we are all wind, all clouds in the sky, drifting in search of a meaning. A greater contrast to 'Karma' was hard to imagine.

EARLY FEBRUARY 1970: WRITES introduction to *Grapefruit*

The comparative success of this revamped edition of Yoko's anthology owed much to her marriage to a Beatle, of course, who duly obliged with a five-second sketch of the author, and a fulsome introduction: "Hi! My name is John Lennon. I'd like you to meet Yoko Ono." He added another blurb for a subsequent edition: "[This is] the best book I've ever burned".

Included in this updated edition were the full instructions for Yoko's *13 Days Do-It-Yourself Dance Festival* from 1967; and her *Sky Event For John Lennon* from the following spring. Various pieces also planted the seeds for Ono and Lennon song lyrics yet to be unveiled, but easy (in retrospect) to imagine...

FEBRUARY 11, 1970: PERFORMS 'Instant Karma!' on *Top Of The Pops*; home performances of 'Across The Great Water'/'Make Love Not War'

Five days after the single was issued, Lennon made a rare promotional appearance on British television, performing 'Instant Karma!' in two pre-recorded slots for BBC TV's *Top Of The Pops*, a first appearance by a Beatle on the show since 1966. In the first performance, Lennon sat at an electric piano and sang a fresh lead vocal over a backing tape, while Messrs White and Voormann, mimed appropriately. For this performance, Yoko sat blind-folded on a chair, a sanitary towel strapped to her forehead, holding up slo-gans like 'Smile', 'Peace' and 'Hope' while uttering wordless statements into a microphone. During the second performance, she was again blindfolded and seen knitting while Mal Evans banged a tambourine and pop journal-ist B.P Fallon clapped along, and Apple in-house hippie Richard diLello snapped photos. To further distinguish between the two clips, the Lennons are wearing denim in the first; black polo necks in the second.

Lennon sported an armband during the filming that proclaimed 'People for Peace'. Within a fortnight, however, the Lennons had pulled out of the Toronto Peace Festival, and their campaign for world peace was quietly retired. They had already laid down a clue as to their future intentions by appearing alongside black power activist Michael X on the London TV interview programme, *The Simon Dee Show*, on February 7.

Over the next four days, the Lennons' activities were documented on film by Yoko's former husband, film-maker Tony Cox, in an effort to smooth relations between the two parties, who were perennially in dispute over custody of Yoko's daughter. This footage – never screened in public, but sold privately in 2000 and since offered for sale again – captured the Lennons editing their *Bedpeace* documentary film, and John running through two songs on piano in his Apple office: Sam Cooke's 'Bring It On Home To Me', and his own work-in-progress, 'Across The Great Water' (which soon metamorphosed into 'Remember'). Then, on the day of the *Top Of The Pops* taping, Cox filmed Lennon performing the 'Great Water' song again, this time on guitar, alongside another new composition, 'Make Love Not War'. This wouldn't be the last occasion on which Cox would document an encounter with Lennon for posterity – or indeed the last appearance of this latter song.

MARCH 6, 1970: WRITES 'Have We All Forgotten What Vibes Are?'

Given the chance to comment on the collapse of the Toronto Peace Festival, Lennon sat down and hammered out this 2,500-word retort – published in *Rolling Stone* on April 16 – to the line which co-organiser John Brower had been selling the underground press (that the Lennons had betrayed the con-cept of the festival and were more interested in cash than conscience). Like his other letters to the press, 'Have We All Forgotten What Vibes Are?' burned with a righteous anger, detailing Brower's alleged campaign against Lennon's manager, Allen Klein, and the rationale behind John and Yoko's wish that Toronto should remain a free festival.

The couple's credo surfaced only at the end: "Someone said: 'Do we need a festival?' Yoko and I still think we need it – not just to show that we can gather peacefully and groove to rock bands, but to change the balance of energy power. Can you imagine what we could do together in the one spot – thinking, singing and praying for peace – one million souls apart from any TV link-ups, etc. to the rest of the planet. If we came together for one reason, we could make it together!"

This plea for unity, for power through collective action, was a clear signpost towards the Lennons' political radicalisation and belief in mass actions of revolt. For the moment, the end was still idealistic. But John was aware that the tide of the struggle was turning against him: "We need help. It is out of our control. All we have is our name. We are sorry for the confusion, it's bigger than both of us. We are doing our best for all our sakes – we still believe. Pray for us."

Within a week, the Lennons had agreed to enrol in Arthur Janov's primal therapy clinic in California, convinced that the mess inside their heads could only be cleaned out from within. Janov and his wife flew to England to carry out intensive preliminary work with John and Yoko, which forced them to cancel a planned headlining appearance at a Free Easter festival in London's Victoria Park on March 29. But Lennon did place a phone call to the festival site on the day, which was transmitted live to the audience.

APRIL 11 to JUNE 12, 1970: PRESENTING *Fluxfest* and *Lennon Tours*

Yoko had been a leading member of the Fluxus art movement in New York for many years. This festival represented her most public gesture of solidarity after her marriage to John. In the early months of 1970, the couple prepared three separate schedules for *Fluxfest*, a series of events, exhibitions and displays centred around the Canal Street 'store' of Joe Jones – a fellow Fluxus member, and the creator of the Tone Deaf Music Co, whose instruments supported Yoko on some film soundtrack recordings in 1971. The Lennons' involvement was purely conceptual, as they were either in Britain or in Los Angeles throughout the entire two-month enterprise.

The festival began on April 11 with a gathering clad in John and Yoko masks, who would be fed from a menu consisting entirely of grapefruit variations. The event launched an exhibition called 'Do-It-Yourself by John and Yoko', John's contributions to which included 'Two Eggs by John Lennon', which was exactly what it said (raw!). The following week, John contributed a variety of conceptual tokens tickets to "Tickets by John and

Yoko' and *Fluxtours.* Week three of *Fluxfest* saw the staging of 'Measure by John and Yoko', which involved gathering statistics about the weight and height of the visitors to the site.

The first week of May saw the unveiling of 'Blue Room by John and Yoko', a (white!) collage to which John's major contributions were 'Three Spoons by John Lennon' (consisting, naturally enough, of three spoons) and 'Needle by John Lennon'. 'Weight and Water by John and Yoko', staged between May 9 and 15, involved the flooding of the exhibition room, and the casual positioning of sponges, some dry, some wet. A film show, 'Capsule by John and Yoko' occupied week six; the seventh heralded 'Portrait Of John Lennon As A Young Cloud', an exhibit prepared by Yoko which consisted of a maze with eight identical drawers built into it, all of which were empty except for one which contained 'John's smile'.

'The Store by John and Yoko' brought back memories of the *You Are Here* show in 1968, with its collection of various vending machines from New York stores and stations. Finally, the Lennons suggested that the last week of the *Fluxfest* be given over to 'Exam by John and Yoko' a test to discover how well their public had understood their work.

The entire event was documented by photographer Peter Moore, 123 of whose black-and-white shots of this *Fluxfest* filled the ninth edition of the Fluxus group's occasional periodical, *Fluxus (V Tre).* In addition, John lent his name to the issuing of a limited run of ticket-sized lithographs, as exhibited during the festival. The full list of titles is unknown, but includes 'A Visit Through A Stage Door To Visit Gloria Swanson', 'Tour To Betty Rollins Legs Panorama', 'Future Trip To The Moon' and '15 Hour Walking Tour Around Manhattan Island NY'. Approximately three inches by one inch in size, these tickets made up a Fluxus event called *Lennon Tours.*

Although Ono continued to champion Fluxus for the next few years, Lennon's involvement with the group was mostly indirect – although that didn't prevent some of his 1970 work from being included in the 1972–73 touring exhibition, *Fluxshoe*, and more recently a retrospective tome entitled *Fluxus: A Conceptual Country*. It may not be a coincidence that the Lennons would unveil their own conceptual country, Nutopia, in 1973.

JUNE TO JULY 1970: RECORDING home demos of 'God'/'I Found Out'/'Love'/'Mother'/'My Mummy's Dead'/'Well Well Well'/ 'When A Boy Meets A Girl'

Though Lennon later dismissed Arthur Janov as little better than a charlatan, the months that he and Yoko spent undergoing the doctor's radical

Primal Scream therapy in Tittenhurst Park (March–April 1970) and then California (end of April–August 1970) altered the course of his life. Lennon had dipped into Janov's book, *The Primal Scream*, empathising with the personal accounts of patients who had discovered the roots of their neurosis in childhood pain, and through Janov's analysis and 'treatment' had freed themselves from decades of inhibition and guilt.

The principle was straightforward enough. Janov believed that the neurosis which modern Western man had accepted as his lot – the alienation from society, the difficulty in forging personal relationships, the constant anxiety of social existence – had been sparked by feelings of rejection and unhappiness in infancy or childhood. Janov's therapy attempted to peel away the layers of neurosis, slowly dragging the subject into his past, stripping bare the events which he had successfully hidden from himself and the world, and finally – by unleashing a primal scream of anguish and need for parental approval and love – reaching the initial moment of rejection. The scream, torn from the depths of the body and reducing the subject to the role of a helpless baby, would cleanse the mind, leaving it open to approach relationships and society in a more rational manner, and to face up to the reality of pain and the possibility of relief.

The aim, then, was catharsis: the violent achievement of inner peace through the unremitting confrontation of pain. To Lennon, the theory seemed sound enough: twice orphaned, to his mind abandoned as a child, he had little problem in identifying the source of his everyday hurt in the loss or absence of a parent. The pain that had driven him to explore himself and the infinite in meditation, in drugs, even in the contemplation of God, that had forced him to find refuge in personal violence or self-destructiveness: it was this pain that he hoped to destroy, through primal therapy.

For many weeks, Lennon took the tablets as prescribed – though drugs were one of the many staples which he was forced to abandon during the course of the therapy. He screamed helplessly like a child, raving on the floor of his room while Janov pulled him deeper and deeper into the darkest corners of his past, to confront the mother who had died, the father who had abandoned him. And in the morning he felt fragile but somehow cleansed, in touch with himself for the first time since he had left Liverpool, able to face up to his own identity rather than hiding behind the image that he and the media had conspired to invent in its place. And after months when he had scarcely written a song, Primal Therapy inspired an outpouring of new material – almost all of it directly linked to the experiences of the past few weeks. Taken together, the new songs effectively offered a précis of Janov's theories and of the complex liberation that they had induced in Lennon's life and mind.

The exact date and location of these recordings remains uncertain, but internal evidence suggests that they all dated from before the Lennons' enforced (by the US immigration authorities) return to England on August 1, 1970. Four songs were cut on electric-acoustic guitar, possibly in late June or early July; four more in late July on pure acoustic. 'God' was the only number tackled in both styles.

'I Found Out' offered a capsule history of how the summer had cleared his perspective, both of his music and of his life. Lennon cut a pair of sparse demos, backed only by his primeval, heavily-echoed electric guitar, which moaned like a voodoo behind his biting vocals. What began as a complaint against the "freaks on the phone", constantly calling him "brother" and wanting little slices of his soul, turned into an epic of self-discovery – railing against drugs, religion, sex, the great distractions on the quest for reality. And dropped into the verses were fragments of Janovism: "Now that I found out I know I can cry … No-one can harm you, feel your own pain."

With the confusions of the past stripped away, Lennon was reduced to bare essentials. He turned the nursery rhyme 'Three Blind Mice' into a chilling vignette called 'My Mummy's Dead'. Two passes were recorded, one of which was transferred straight onto the *Plastic Ono Band* album with only the mildest of studio trickery. The title told the story: "I can't explain, so much pain/I could never show it/My mummy's dead". Delivered in a voice that came from beyond despair, the song was honest to the point of being unbearably painful to hear.

The same primeval agony fuelled 'Mother'. The song told a simply story straight in three bleak verses: Lennon was emotionally crippled by being abandoned by his parents. With his heavily reverbed guitar creating the aura of a timeslip, he reeled off the raw facts of his betrayal. In a final verse that dripped in irony – fatherhood was never his strongest point – Lennon turned the message around, to tell his own children, physical and generational: "don't do what I have done".

'Love', another song first taped to electric guitar accompaniment, used the simplicity and uncluttered approach of the primal therapy songs to offer a stark, beautiful description of his relationship with Yoko. The lyric, set at this stage to a lightly amplified electric guitar, offered closed couplets that were simple and profound at the same time: "Love is real/Real is love/Love is feeling/Feeling Love".

Of the initial batch of post-therapy songs, only 'Well Well Well' lacked that directness of spirit. The chorus, which simply repeated the title, was an ironic comment on the verses, which offered snapshots of the Lennons at work in the sexual revolution, while one couplet deleted from the final lyric suggested John hadn't lost his sense of humour: "Because she's looking so much thinner/She looked so beautiful I could wee". Like all these summer '70 recordings, this was an entirely solo demo, accompanied by an ethnic blues guitar.

'God' began life on Dylanesque acoustic guitar, with one basic verse: "God is a concept by which we measure our pain". This was a bleak view of the spirit life, unlocked by Janov's therapy, and suggested that Lennon was now far removed from the optimist who had looked for spiritual guidance from the Maharishi or the Buddha. Repeating this verse twice at speed, Lennon then leapt into a litany of false idols, each one greeted with the declaration, "I don't believe in ...". With gods, gurus and pop stars attracting Lennon's denunciation, the litany ended with a denial of 'Beatles', before John announced: "I just believe in me, and that's reality". (On the finished record, he opened his horizons of belief far enough to include Yoko.)

At this stage, the song went no further, merely ploughing back into the verse and again through the litany. As the list proceeded, Lennon thrashed his guitar in anger, turning his disavowal of the past into a cathartic outburst of emotion. Not everything was so serious, however: Lennon opened one of his takes with a bizarre monologue, which sounded like a refugee from an early sixties Doo-Wop record, announcing "I had a message from above ..." ending with a quote from the Miracles' 'I've Been Good To You'.

One final song cut that summer didn't make the album, and was probably never finished. 'When A Boy Meets A Girl' was a rather desultory tale of love, filled with lyrical clichés – "If I'd lost you now, baby I'd be sorry" – that seemed closer to the teenage heartache songs of 1963 than the truth-seeking of 1970. Its main attraction was its descending minor chord sequence, played on acoustic guitar, which would nonetheless have been too pretty for the album to follow. It wouldn't have been out of place on *Rubber Soul* or *Double Fantasy*, however, and if Lennon had remembered it, he might well have exhumed and revised it for the latter record in 1980.

The Lennons had been out of the country for a week short of five months when they flew back to London on September 24. Two days later, they were ready to begin recording an album inspired by their experiences with Janov.

JULY 28, 1970: CREATING 'The Complete Yoko Ono Word Poem Game'

Half Fluxus concept piece, half Burroughsian cut-up, this playful jigsaw (intended, so the caption read, "for Yoko's with heads full of problems") comprised a colour photo of the artist, which John then snipped into 135 small pieces. On each of them he scrawled a word – anything from "julian" and "kyoko" to "grapefruit", not forgetting "toilet" and "shit" – or indeed "imagine". If he'd made the pieces magnetic, he could have patented one of the most popular novelty gifts of the Nineties.

SEPTEMBER 26 to OCTOBER 19, 1970: RECORDING 'Mother'/'Hold On'/'I Found Out'/'Working Class Hero'/'Isolation'/'Remember'/'Love'/'Well Well Well'/'Look At Me'/'God'/'That's All Right Mama'/'Glad All Over'/'Honey Don't/'I Was A Fool'/'Don't Be Cruel'/'Matchbox'/'Lost John'; YOKO ONO RECORDING 'Why'/'Why Not'/'Greenfield Morning I Pushed An Empty Baby Carriage All Over The City'/'Touch Me'/'Paper Shoes'/'Open Your Box'/'Something More Abstract'/'Between The Takes'

John Lennon/Plastic Ono Band remains Lennon's most radical musical statement. It stripped bare his deepest emotions, offering himself naked to the gaze of the world in a song cycle that bore testament to the piercing scrutiny of the Primal Scream technique. What Lennon uncovered beneath the trappings of stardom and adulthood were elemental needs, for security and comfort, and a meaning to existence: along the way, he examined the myth of fame, and the cult of working-class authenticity. All this and, with the help of Phil Spector, he made a remarkable-sounding rock record.

Despite only taking part in around three days of sessions, primarily to handle the mixing, Spector shared production credits with John and Yoko, who used the duration of the sessions to tape Yoko's first solo album (*Yoko Ono/Plastic Ono Band*) as well. Sparseness was the order of the day: both records were cut with a band consisting of Lennon, Starr and Voormann, with Spector and Billy Preston adding keyboard cameos on Lennon's LP.

Spector played piano on 'Love', essentially unchanged from the home demo, except that Lennon's whispered vocal gave the tune an almost unbearable poignancy, a hint that he was singing more from hope than expectation. The producer's contribution saved Lennon from having to perform the song on guitar. On earlier takes, one of which was featured on his posthumous *Anthology*, the complexity of the chord changes was clearly distracting him from his vocal performance.

Preston's showcase was on 'God', to which he brought a spiritual flavour that was an ironic comment on the philosophical materialism of the lyrics. Earlier attempts at the song, minus the piano, lacked the sense of structural separation which gave the finished track its sense of narrative progression. To the existing song, Lennon had added a coda around the theme, "The dream is over". The dream was the Sixties, The Beatles, religion – anything you'd used to escape from reality. To ram the point home, John concluded the saga of 'I Am The Walrus' and 'Glass Onion': "I was the walrus/But now I'm John". The underlying message was that you had to do it for yourselves; Lennon wasn't leading any generation into battle.

'Working Class Hero', ironic from its title downwards, crossed that credo with the theme of 'I Found Out' to produce a searing indictment of the way in which society used workers to build its wealth, and then fobbed them off with dull pleasures. "You're still fucking peasants as far as I can see," was Lennon's reassuring message to his fellow working-class, before sarcastically ending the song: "If you want to be a hero, then just follow me". Sadly, some critics took him seriously, and translated this bitter track, blatantly edited together from two different takes, as more of Lennon's self-glorification.

While 'Working Class Hero' was John's outward expression of his heightened world vision, 'Mother' performed the same function inside his head, without irony or any attempt at concealment. Spector's touch here was vital. He introduced the doomy, distorted church bells that kicked off the track and the album; persuaded Lennon to switch from guitar to keyboards; and turned a dry, echo-less mix into a sea of booming piano sustain and thudding drums, over which Lennon screamed out his desperate pleas for help: "Mama don't go/Daddy come home".

'Isolation' spread the web of loneliness to include Yoko, "Just a boy and a little girl/Trying to change the whole wide world". And in the middle eight, Lennon double-tracked his piano and vocal, making no attempt to keep his singing in sync, so that his despair echoed from one speaker to another. By comparison, the single-tracked take included on *Anthology* softened the blow, without offering any escape route from the inevitability of suffering.

'Remember' was extracted from an eight-minute piano work-out, though only after John had persuaded his rhythm section to calm down and play more slowly. It transferred the pain into anger – more bitterness, more betrayal, more belief that promises had not been fulfilled, that the mythical family happiness children are taught at school was never more than an illusion. The melodic framework of the song was built around a composition first captured on film earlier in the year, 'Across The Great Water'.

Only 'Hold On' offered any hope, and even then it was only the promise of survival, not rescue. "Hold on John," Lennon sang, before offering the same advice to Yoko, and the world. And as on 'Revolution', "it's gonna be alright". Though Lennon briefly toyed with attempting the song as a blues boogie, the final track was light as air, shimmering with reverb guitar, as if to highlight the shakiness of the man struggling to exist. Only the spoken reference to "Cookie" (a catchphrase from Andy Williams' popular TV variety show) lightened the load.

The eerie demos of 'Well Well Well' and 'I Found Out' were turned into full-blooded rock 'n' roll by the three-piece Plastic Ono Band, with Lennon's guitar slicing through the mix like a knife through skin. As ever, it was the clarity and depth of Spector's mix that counted: where Lennon might have ornamented the music, Spector helped it stand proud and clear, its message completely unhindered by prettiness or complication. Lennon's voice did the rest, acidic and sharp on 'I Found Out', self-lacerating on 'Well Well Well'. Like the long fade of 'Mother', the screaming vocal on 'Well Well Well' brought him close to the total release of a Primal Scream session. "We'd be in the middle of a track," Ringo Starr revealed in 2004, "and John would just start crying or screaming, which freaked us out at the beginning."

With the addition of 'Look At Me' and 'My Mummy's Dead', *John Lennon / Plastic Ono Band* emerged as a harrowing portrait of the artist in pain, delving deep into his psyche in search of relief, and throwing out shards of hurt in all directions. It remains the ultimate statement of personal expression, parodied and imitated but never equalled. Lennon's problem, however, at least from an artistic point of view, was where he went next. Having laid himself bare in front of the world, what else could be reveal? To the end of his days, Lennon rated this album as his most effective and powerful work – "Sgt. Lennon" – and so it was. But it was also an unrepeatable exercise. Lennon may not have been cleansed or reborn, but while the therapy did its work he was free of artifice and illusion. The flaw in Janov's theory was that after the therapy, the layers of neurosis and self-deceit began to gather again. Lennon never found the strength for a second confrontation.

Assuming that Yoko found her vocal exercises cathartic, then her neuroses never had time to grow. *Yoko Ono / Plastic Ono Band*, clad in a matching cover to John's album, was her response to her husband's soulbaring. Yoko didn't bother with words: if she was in pain, she just screamed, and on 'Why'

The Plastic Ono Band raged like titans behind her, Lennon striking sparks out of his guitar, Klaus Voormann and Ringo Starr laying down a tribal beat. As guitar and vocal sparred in bouts of near-hysteria, John and Yoko came close to creating the perfect soundtrack for Primal Therapy – uncontrolled emotion, squeezed onto the tape without any mediation. 'Touch Me' came close to the same amalgam of funk and fear, while 'Why Not' slowed the tempo for an unearthly exercise in spooking out demons. The rest – apart from 'Aos', recorded by Yoko with Ornette Coleman back in February 1968 – was Yoko's tape games, emulating a train on 'Paper Shoes', and reworking the theme of her 'City Piece' from *Grapefruit* ("Walk all over the city with an empty baby carriage") on 'Greenfield Morning'. Also taped was a raggedly funky stab at Yoko's 'Open Your Box', and a brief but electrifying jam later released as 'Between The Takes'. A brief audio-verite extract from the Lennon sessions was subsequently released on an Ono CD under the title of 'Something More Abstract', after Yoko's request to the band.

Along the way, Lennon, Voormann and Starr found time to exercise the same minimalist magic on a romp through Lonnie Donegan's skiffle hit 'Lost John' (later included on *Anthology*) and a medley of favourite rockabilly numbers, which was taped but never released. Carl Perkins' 'Honey Don't' saw Lennon spitting out the lyrics, and fusing the jagged edges of rock 'n' roll guitar with the free-form anarchy of Yoko's music. "I used to love that", he admitted at the end. He kept heading back to his roots during these sessions: the version of 'I Found Out' that made the album was faded just as he veered into another Perkins classic from the Sun era, 'Gone Gone Gone'. On Presley's 'Don't Be Cruel', Lennon predated The Cramps by a decade, turning himself into the creature from the swamp by slurring his vocals into one manic phrase. The obscure rocker 'I Was A Fool' continued the game, the entire song lost in a sea of echo. And returning to Perkins with 'Matchbox', he showed off his feelings for roots rockabilly, missing an occasional note in his solo, but making up for technical failures with bags of feel. In the autumn of 1970, everything Lennon played came out raw, sweating and real.

c. NOVEMBER/DECEMBER 1970: RECORDING home demos of 'Make Love Not War'/'I'm The Greatest'/'How?'/'Child Of Nature'/'Oh Yoko'/'Sally And Billy'/'Rock And Roll People'/ 'Help!'/'I'm Having A Baby By My Love'/'Somewhere In My Sky'/'People Get Ready'/'Can't Believe You Wanna Leave'/

'Mailman Bring Me No More Blues'/'I Promise'/'I'm Not As Strong As You Think'/'You Know How Hard It Is'/'Happy Girl'/'I'll Make You Happy', plus untitled instrumentals and Xmas message

Unable to write music notation, Lennon composed most of his songs from the late Sixties onwards on tape. Though he was apt to re-record over the original renditions of songs which he had since learned or taped in the studio, some of these composing tapes have survived. One such dates from the aftermath of the *Plastic Ono Band* sessions, with the exhausted Lennon feeling uncertainly round the piano for familiar chords that often seem to evade his grasp. Musically, this is not a Lennon landmark; but it does offer us an early glimpse of several songs that occupied his mind for the next five or six years.

Just as The Beatles had celebrated the release of *Sgt. Pepper* in June 1967 by aimlessly recording instrumental jams, so Lennon marked his *Plastic Ono Band* album by seeking out a new direction for his writing. The confessional mood of that record survived onto 'I Promise', the first of many apologetic odes to Yoko, which were still being written in Lennon's final days at the end of 1980. Yoko had been his only solace in the despair of the primal therapy songs; as such, she had to be respected and obeyed, and 'I Promise' came as close to self-abasement as anything in Lennon's career. It used the Fifties piano stylings of McCartney's 'Oh Darling' as its base, with a lyric that looked ahead to a more profound statement of regret, 'Jealous Guy'. For the chorus, however, Lennon harked back to another new song, 'Make Love Not War', with its hope that "love is the answer, and you know that it's true". Even he couldn't help but note his lack of inspiration: "I'm keeping the same middle eight for every song," he muttered.

'Make Love Not War' could have been an anthem to rival 'Give Peace A Chance' if Lennon had ever finished it. But he never moved beyond the simple repetition of the title, and the shift into the chorus; and the structure was first rejected, then recalled when Lennon turned the same melody into 'Mind Games'.

'I'm The Greatest' underwent a similar transformation. John eventually gave the song to Ringo, noting as an aside that if he'd sung the tune himself everyone would have complained at his arrogance. But he certainly began writing it for himself, to a loping, New Orleans-style piano accompaniment, with only a very basic set of lyrics, which displayed none of the iconoclasm or humour of the finished song. On this evidence, 'I'm The Greatest' could just as easily have turned into a confessional lament about his past

193

conduct. Either way, the piano motif at the heart of the song taxed his abilities to the limit. "Shit, balls, fuck," he groaned, as a second take crashed to a faltering halt.

The final version of 'Oh Yoko' in 1971 was a song of joy to his wife, so it is remarkable to hear this earlier pass at the tune, which was a slow lament, emotionless and insecure, taken at a similar pace to 'Mother'. The subject of the song warbled a distant harmony in support. Another of the *Imagine* songs debuted during this session was 'How'. He toyed with a couple of verses, and then was reminded of his Indian excursion of 1968, as he slipped into several fumbling attempts at 'Child Of Nature' – changing the location from Rishikesh to Marrakesh, perhaps under the influence of Crosby, Stills & Nash's hit single, 'Marrakesh Express'. Later he fell back into 'How' as he busked his way through The Impressions' spiritual call, 'People Get Ready'. After one take had broken down, Lennon went back to the top of the tune, and played as much as he'd written, over and over again, occasionally vocalising his pain in sound rather than words. In this form, the song structure was already intact, with a series of searching questions aimed at himself, emphasised by the definite pauses between lines. And the ghost of 'Mother' still walked, as Lennon improvised: "How can I go home when home is something I have never had?"

During his interview with Jann Wenner for *Rolling Stone*, Lennon expressed the desire to re-record 'Help!' at the slower tempo in which he'd originally written the song, rather than the hurried take preferred as The Beatles' single release.★ He devoted a minute or so during this composing tape to trying to perfect a new arrangement, but succeeded only in dragging the first verse through an agonisingly slow haul, and then giving up in disgust when he couldn't work out the piano chords for the chorus. The song could easily have withstood a sensitive transformation into a *Plastic Ono Band*-styled ballad, but not on this occasion. Yoko attempted to guide her husband with an off-mike suggestion that was greeted with a curt response: "I don't care how you want to sing it, dear, I'm singing it myself at the moment".

'Sally And Billy' was little more than a fragment, cast somewhere between the unrelenting piano chords of 'Remember' and the jaunty clanking of David Bowie's 'Oh You Pretty Things'. In McCartney's hands, it might have ended up as a successor to 'Maxwell's Silver Hammer '– or maybe a contender for the Eurovision Song Contest. Later that week, Lennon would tell Jann Wenner how he preferred writing first-person autobiography to third-

---

★ The idea went back further than that: "I've been doing a lot of 'Help!' recently," he admitted to the other Beatles at Twickenham film studios in January 1969.

person fiction. That's probably why 'Sally And Billy', an ill-focused narrative, was left to one side for five years or more.

'Rock And Roll People' was also destined to linger for several years on the verge of John's memory. It never became the definitive celebration of the music that Lennon had presumably intended it to be. But on this occasion it was easily the most positive item he had to offer, complete with its Fats Domino-style piano solo and a vocal that escaped the general air of depression. Inevitably, Lennon soon drifted into the kind of Fifties oldies he'd been attempting to match, though neither Little Richard's 'Can't Believe You Wanna Leave' or Buddy Holly's 'Mailman Bring Me No More Blues' exactly buzzed with rockabilly fervour. Lennon had more fun when he simply sat at the piano and improvised for several minutes, hitting random chord patterns that at various times threatened to mutate into 'Help!' or even 'Hey Jude'.

The only serious business at hand was recording John & Yoko's Christmas Message for 1970. Until they redeemed themselves in 1971, the festive season rarely brought the best out of the Lennons, and this year's singalong Xmas ditty was as embarrassing as anything they ever committed to tape. And worse was to follow. At various times during the recording, Yoko commandeered the piano to deliver trite ditties like 'Somewhere In My Sky' and the yet-to-be-fulfilled 'I'm Having A Baby By My Love'. She answered 'I Promise' with 'I'm Not As Strong As You Think', prompting John to busk his way through something that might have been called 'You Know How Hard It Is'. This may be the musical nadir of Lennon's career – a mock Motown R&B tune in which he complained about having to bring his wife breakfast in bed. She was then moved to croon the very twee 'Happy Girl', to which John replied with 'I'll Make You Happy' (a close musical cousin of Betty Everett's Sixties' soul smash, 'You're No Good'). Just as this heartplay threatened to reach new levels of bathos, Lennon strayed into a line from one of his earlier classics. "I keep going into 'Cold Turkey'," he explained to Yoko. "I never really used that chords in it, so I can use them again." Mercifully, perhaps, the tape ran out before he could recycle any more of his back catalogue.

DECEMBER 14 to 22, 1970: FILMING *Fly/Up Your Legs Forever*; recording 'Fly'

When the Lennons were offered an evening to exhibit their works at a film festival at the Elgin Theater in New York City at Christmas 1970, they not only gathered together prints of their previous work: they resolved to conceive, film, edit and produce two feature-length movies within a fortnight.

The schedule was duly met, though not without incident. Yoko invented the concept for *Up Your Legs Forever*, a 75-minute series of 'leg shots' in the tradition of her *Film No. 4 (Bottoms)* movie. This time the camera swung from the feet to the top of the thighs of the 367 denizens of the New York art scene who agreed to perform for the cameras. Each shot ended tantalisingly short of the subject's genitals, a wry joke at the public's expense. The film ended with John and Yoko exposing their naked buttocks, before John recited the credits. The rest of the soundtrack echoed the documentary style of *Bottoms*, capturing dialogue from before and during the filming – though the voices eventually gave way to John playing bottleneck guitar while Yoko improvised a blues song named after the movie. Lennon had little input to the project, beyond financing and supporting Yoko, and taking polaroid pictures of the more attractive auditionees.

Fly was also essentially a Yoko solo project, again with Lennon's wholehearted support. Like earlier avant-garde movies which had transformed the human body into a mysterious desert of hills and sweeping valleys, *Fly* used the naked female form of an actress, over which crawled a succession of suitably drugged flies. Ono's friend Jonas Mekas documented some of the audition process for the movie, with various young women stripping off and being introduced to flies, while Lennon reeled off acoustic blues guitar licks in the background.

The movie might have been a metaphor, or more likely a playful piece of experimentalism, but its production was blighted by the lack of co-operation shown by the flies, which repeatedly failed to follow Yoko's crystal-clear directions. No matter: the film was edited in time, and clearly pandered to the voyeuristic leanings of the average (male) movie-goer with its concentration on the actress' more private parts. Yoko obviously failed to realise that the true avant-garde would have chosen a less interesting subject: as it was, underground critics accused the Lennons of betraying their concept by pandering to the most basic desires of their audience.

Though he was credited as co-director and co-editor, Lennon's major contribution to *Fly* was to produce and play on Yoko's soundtrack. As she watched a rough cut of the 50-minute film, she improvised more than 20 minutes of vocal sounds, with Lennon offering a restrained, almost classical accompaniment on backwards electric guitar. Yoko synchronised her bleatings to the erratic movement of the flies, which lent the whole proceedings an undeniably comic air. Audience reaction in New York to the full-length *Fly* was so negative, however, that Ono cut the film to the same length as its musical accompaniment for subsequent screenings.

CHAPTER 11

January 1971 to August 1971

A s The Beatles' partnership was wound up in the High Court, so Lennon moved from self-discovery into an entirely new arena: radical left-wing politics. Although his campaigns initially focused on British issues, he soon began to consider a wider, internationalist perspective, which slowly and inevitably drew him away from London to the radical hub of the universe in 1971: New York. But there was one last project to complete in England, an album that would build on the revelations of *Plastic Ono Band*, but with a care for commercial concerns that had been one of the things he had mocked about The Beatles.

JANUARY 22 to EARLY FEBRUARY 1971: RECORDING 'Power To The People'

In theory Lennon should have spent all of January 1971 in Japan, which would have left him conveniently out of reach when his explosive *Rolling Stone* interview was published mid-month. Instead, he was called home by his lawyers, to deal with the unexpected turmoil of the court case that Paul McCartney had launched in London against his fellow ex-Beatles.

The couple arrived home on January 21, to discover that they could have fulfilled all their legal obligations by phone. So they were free to stage another lengthy interview, this time with political activists Tariq Ali and Robin Blackburn, acting on behalf of the Trotskyist newspaper *Red*

Mole. The pair had criticised the Lennons in print for their 'bourgeois' approach to the issue of world peace – their belief, expressed time and again during their 1969 bed-ins, that change could be achieved without revolution. Conscious of his own class origins, Lennon moved sharply to reflect the interests of his new friends. 1969 had been dominated by his work for peace; 1970 saw the personal take precedence over the fate of the world. In 1971, the pendulum swung back towards the masses, only this time John and Yoko were spouting the slogans of the left, not the peaceniks.

Lennon was always a populist, and though he willingly joined protest marches and signed petitions, he realised that music was his most effective means of protest. Hence the search for an immediate anthem of the left – and the writing of 'Power To The People'. The song's chorus, which merely repeated the title, left the means and ends unclear, and that meant it could be claimed by any group which wanted it. (Little more than a decade later, the middle-of-the-road Liberal Party in Britain staged their annual conference under a giant banner that proclaimed, "Power To The People".) The verses offered little in the way of analysis, beyond the need to get out on the streets in numbers – though the line which urged the politicos not to forget their women was both patronising *and* more feminist than most of the male ultra-left could manage in 1971.

Even in its demo form, 'Power To The People' sounded like a single. Phil Spector produced the finished record the following month, but only after Lennon's own attempts had proved inadequate. In the studio, the song took shape as an R&B lope like The Coasters' 'Searchin', with Lennon banging out piano triplets like Fats Domino during the verses, and Bobby Keyes honking away merrily on sax. Lennon then fleshed out the band with a chorus of female gospel singers, and attempted a final take. But the best he and the band could muster was a ragged, tired rhythm track, with Lennon straining desperately to find the notes as if he'd set the piece in the wrong key.

Lennon must have realised that this version couldn't be released. After toying with a reggae setting that was even more embarrassing, he abandoned the song until the following month.

EARLY FEBRUARY 1971: DESIGNING *Culture Carrier* stamp

On January 19, 1971, 200,000 members of the Union of Postal Workers across Britain went on an indefinite strike in a bid to secure a sizeable rise in pay. The stoppage eventually lasted for 47 days, causing much disruption to business, before the union and government officials reached a compromise – greeted as a sell-out by many of the UPW activists, but accepted by the majority of members.

To raise funds for the strikers' cause, art curator Anthony Mathews contacted some of the leading names on the British art scene, to join a crusade entitled *Culture*Carriers: Stamp*Out*Art*. Each of the participants, who included David Hockney, Ralph Steadman, Christo and Richard Hamilton, was requested to produce a design for a postage stamp that could be sold, either in bulk or as a limited edition artwork. The stamps would then be stuck onto special *Culture Carrier* envelopes.

In the event, the strike was settled before anything was ready to go on sale, and what began as agitprop soon turned into fine art, as almost all of the designs formed an exhibition that travelled around Europe. Only one of the commissions failed to turn into a finished artefact: John Lennon's. He sent Mathews a photocopied design for a stamp that would bear a picture of his own clenched fist. Just one set of proofs was printed up bearing Lennon's design, with the fist portrayed in solid black on red stamp paper. Given Lennon's activist commitment at this time, it was perhaps just as well that his work wasn't featured in the unashamedly elitist *Culture Carrier* exhibition.

FEBRUARY 11 to 16, 1971: RECORDING 'Power To The People'/'I Don't Want To Be A Soldier, Mama'/'It's So Hard'/'Well (Baby Please Don't Go)'/'I'm The Greatest'/ 'Open Your Box'/'O Wind (Body Is The Scar Of Your Mind)'

Just two months after the release of the *Plastic Ono Band* albums, Lennon launched into the sessions for a new record. Tellingly, he didn't rely on the unfocused material he'd demoed back in December. Equally significant was the choice of musicians, and stylistic approach.

Rightly convinced that his *Plastic Ono Band* LP was a breakthrough, both artistically and emotionally, Lennon decided to preserve the skeletal rock-'n'roll feel for his next batch of sessions at EMI. Klaus Voormann was on permanent call for solo Beatles projects by this time, and duly answered the call. But Ringo Starr was on holiday, having completed his acting role on Frank Zappa's *200 Motels* movie, so Lennon recruited drummer Jim Gordon – at a loose end following the recent collapse of Eric Clapton's band, Derek & The Dominos. Also on hand was Bobby Keyes, who'd played on 'Power To The People'. But one vital member of the *Plastic Ono Band* team was only briefly available. Phil Spector was in London this month, but was working with George Harrison on another Apple project, a projected album for his wife, Ronnie.★

Top of the agenda was completing a single. After the aborted shot at 'Power To The People' the previous month, Lennon tried again, stripping the arrangement back down to basics, so that the instrumental track sounded like an out-take from the *Plastic Ono Band* sessions, built around piano, bass and drums. The vocal was still strained, and the sax fills never quite took off, but over the lengthy fade Lennon burst into a series of howls that owed more to primal therapy than political revolution.

Enter Phil Spector, for the only time during these sessions. He took Lennon's basic track and reinvented it, adding cavernous echo to the vocal and sax, forcing Bobby Keyes back before the mike to blow his lungs out, and turning the gospel singers from a small group into a choir. And, as a master-stroke, he gathered everyone in the studio together and taped their marching feet, which he used as a backdrop to the opening chorus. It created the sound of a political rally in the recording studio; and with Lennon's heavily echoed lead sounding as if it could have been sung through a megaphone, the record hammered home the spirit of community and revolt that John had been searching for. He was later to disown the record, or at least its message, as mere sloganeering, naive and ill-thought; but he must still have loved the sound, which brought to life the amateurish enthusiasm of one of John's (and Spector's) favourite records, 'Quarter To Three' by Gary 'U.S.' Bonds.

For the flip, Lennon took aside his rhythm section and told them to play it funky. Over a devilishly tight riff, midway between James Brown and reggae, Yoko squealed out 'Open Your Box', an idiosyncratic call for freedom of speech and body that she'd first tried during the *Plastic Ono Band* sessions in October. Lennon produced the record, and this time without the need to carry the whole show, he gave Yoko's piece a sound to match the starkness of its conception. It was a stunning performance, as futuristic as anything in her entire catalogue, and still contemporary enough more than 30 years later to be sampled and remixed for cutting-edge dance records. Yoko also cut the spacier but equally intense 'O Wind (Body Is The Scar Of Your Mind)', supported by the chattering percussion of Gordon, Voormann and Keyes, punctuated by occasional squawks from Lennon's guitar.

'Open Your Box' demonstrated that Lennon didn't need Spector to roll

★ Lennon is believed to have made a brief contribution to Ronnie's recordings, as a backing vocalist on the Spector/Harrison composition, 'Tandoori Chicken', in the first week of February 1971.

the tapes, but the producer had made vital contributions to all his records since 'Instant Karma!' a year earlier. Without him, the sessions soon ran out of inspiration, not helped by the paucity of new material that Lennon had prepared. So only four other songs were attempted during these sessions, none of them suitable as a follow-up single to 'Power To The People', or – so it seemed – a helpful signpost towards an album worthy of Lennon's name.

Ironically, the most cohesive track from these sessions was a cover: 'Well (Baby Please Don't Go)', a Walter Ward song released by The Olympics as the flipside to their 1958 R&B hit, 'Western Movies'. Freed from the need to convey a message, Lennon turned in a tight, intense piece of R&B, fuelled by a chugging sax riff, some 'Cold Turkey'-style guitar, and *Plastic Ono Band* rhythm section. In between the repeated verses, he took control for a free-form guitar solo, its feel more important than the actual notes, before Bobby Keyes rekindled the spirit of The Coasters' records of the Fifties with a King Curtis-like sax break. 'Well' was presumably cut as a potential B-side, but it remained unissued until it was edited for inclusion on the Lennon *Anthology*.

The only song that Lennon retrieved from his composing tape two months earlier was 'I'm The Greatest'. After he'd passed it on to Ringo Starr in 1973, he claimed that he'd never considered issuing it himself. But there's no hint of distance or humour on the skeletal versions he cut during the February sessions, nor any sign that he was singing about anyone but himself. "Yoko told me I was great", he mumbled on one rough take, but it didn't sound as if he believed it.

The songs on *Plastic Ono Band* had burned with an intensity that matched the emotions Lennon was desperate to express. By contrast, the two completed songs from these sessions signified nothing more than a mood of vague, unfocused discontent. 'I Don't Want To Be A Soldier' was a long, doomy rage against military madness and societal expectations. In its original form, it sounded like a hybrid of 'Cold Turkey' and 'Well Well Well' – a raw funk riff churning beneath a muddy mesh of rhythm sound, before Lennon built up towards a catharsis that was only fulfilled when the sax solo came roaring in. The first take had Bobby Keyes breathing long exhales into his instrument, before he duelled with Lennon's guitar in the same way that he'd locked horns with Keith Richards and Mick Taylor on The Rolling Stones' 'Can't You Hear Me Knocking' a few months earlier. Second time through, the song vanished into the exhilaration of a swampy blues jam, edgy as hell, but rhythmically suspect. Lennon was already imagining this song as the album opener. "We'll start the beginning of it with footsteps running," he explained, "and end with a toilet flushing." He also intended to add the sound of roaring motorbike engines to the mix.

'It's So Hard' was an equally powerful performance. The lyrics of this conventional 12-bar blues took the burden of life-after-primal-therapy and stripped it down to the message of the title line, with Lennon growling out lines like, "you gotta be somebody/you gotta worry" like a native New Yorker. And like Buddy Holly on 'Peggy Sue', Lennon played a guitar part that acted as both rhythm and lead, while the band laid down a minimalist backing, Voormann in particular retrieving the exact sound he'd produced on *Plastic Ono Band* two months earlier. With Keyes absent for this track, however, there was a gaping hole in the mix – and in the entire project. Uncertain how to proceed, Lennon filed away these tapes, and began to assemble songs in an entirely different style.

MARCH 4, 1971: RE-RECORDING vocal for 'Open Your Box'

Hidden in the lyrics to 'Open Your Box' were Yoko's injunctions, "Open your trousers/Open your skirt/Open your legs". EMI felt this was obscene, so Yoko apparently re-cut the first two lines with less upsetting words, though the end result sounded identical. In fact, it's quite possible that the Lennons only changed the words conceptually, and that no one at EMI spotted that the first version of 'Open Your Box' was the same as the second.

LATE SPRING 1971: COMPLETING filming of *Erection*

Self Portrait had dealt with one kind of erection; this slyly titled movie – listed as being 'By John Lennon', though Yoko was credited as co-producer and director – focused on another. Though it was completed in 1971, its conception actually dated back to the previous summer. Aware that the London International Hotel was about to be built in north Kensington, John asked permission for photographer Iain Macmillan to take regular slide shots of the building site from an identical position. These were then photographed in sequence, as a piece of advanced time-lapse work, to document the erection of the hotel.

Time-lapse photography was scarcely a novelty in 1971; neither was the concentration on a single developing shot, which had long been a central theme in one strand of the avant-garde cinema. But of all John and Yoko's avowedly experimental movies, *Erection* was the most watchable, if only because it evoked every child's fascination with the workings of a construction site. In an obscure way, the accent on creation rather than destruction harked back to the Lennons' first meeting in 1966, and the 'yes' written on the ceiling that had attracted John when he had expected to be rebuffed.

Purely in visual terms, then, *Erection* had its satisfactions, notably when the shell of the building was suddenly filled out with the substance of the walls, and the physical presence of the construction altered the pattern of light and darkness which the viewer had grown used to from the beginning of the sequence.

The film ended with a nod of the camera to *Empire*, Andy Warhol's epic 1964 movie of the Empire State Building. Warhol's film depicted the building throughout an entire night: Lennon's ended with the lights in the hotel slowly being extinguished, until the screen was left in darkness. All that remained was for Yoko to record the soundtrack music, in June.

APRIL 1971: RECORDING home demos of 'Oh Yoko'/ 'God Save Us'/'Call My Name'

Having demoed 'Oh Yoko' on piano the previous December as a dirge, Lennon moved the song to guitar for this second attempt, and succeeded in bringing it slowly to life as a celebration of love and marriage. The number was as direct as any of John's compositions from this period, and as optimistic – a picture of happiness without a doubt in sight. This guitar rendition tailed off once Lennon had satisfied himself he had a viable format, and ended with him improvising a piece called 'I Want You Babe', which borrowed the famous "awopbopaloobopalopbamboom" hook from Little Richard's Fifties rocker, 'Tutti Frutti'. Yoko helped out on spontaneous backing vocals throughout the piece.

'Call My Name', completed on piano around the same time, then demoed on both electric and acoustic guitar, saw Lennon in the position of comforter, offering himself as a solution to anxieties and loneliness. "I'll ease your pain, girl", he promised, sounding as if he had a soul icon like Wilson Pickett in his sights. The tune of this fragment was identical to the *Mind Games* song 'Aisumasen (I'm Sorry)', which portrayed a very different picture of the Lennons' marital balancing act.

'God Save Us', meanwhile, was written to order, for a new political campaign. The editors of the British underground paper *Oz* were facing imprisonment for having distributed a copy of the magazine which contained material allegedly likely to corrupt minors. As a regular *Oz* subscriber, Lennon sprang to their defence. He made immediate plans to record a single to raise funds for their legal fees in the trial (due to open on June 23),

203

and hoped that his intervention in the affair would shift the current of opinion in their favour.

As ever when politics were at stake, Lennon kept the lyrics simple. He reeled off a series of threats from which God should do his best to save us, instructed his audience to "pick your nose and eat it too", and then anticipated the Sex Pistols by six years with his final line: "God save us from the Queen". Lennon then played this simple recording, cut on rhythmic acoustic guitar with backing by an anonymous conga player, for his pick-up Plastic Ono Band to hear and learn when they recorded it at his newly built home studio at Tittenhurst Park, Ascot.

MAY 22, 1971: RECORDING 'God Save Us'/'Do The Oz'

To avoid the public treating 'God Save Us' as his follow-up to 'Power To The People', Lennon arranged for underground musician/freak Magic Michael to handle vocals on the A-side of the single, which would be issued on Apple under the name of The Elastic Oz Band (featuring future *NME* scribe, then *Oz* contributor, Charles Shaar Murray among the acoustic guitars strumming along).

First, though, Lennon sang the lead vocals himself, holding onto his notes with a Yoko-like quaver, and encouraging the band to play it rough and raunchy. Bobby Keyes added a saxophone riff that wasn't a million miles away from the one that powered one of John's favourite Fifties' oldies, Larry Williams' 'Bony Moronie'. As a final aside, Lennon ended his list of demands by calling for freedom from defeat, deceit and de queen, which was hardly likely to satisfy anyone distressed by the anti-royalist tone of the original lyric, shouting out an impromptu tongue-in-cheek homage to "the Duke", John Wayne. Michael then listened to Lennon's vocal in the cans and tried to duplicate it. With Phil Spector on hand to add the appropriate echo, the track was complete – at least, until Lennon listened back to an acetate, and decided that Michael's vocal was unsuitable for release. In his place, session singer Bill Elliott (later part of George Harrison proteges Splinter) redubbed the vocal, and that was the version that was released. If fundraising was the motivation, however, Lennon would have been better advised to release his own version of the song, as The Elastic Oz Band's sole release failed to chart on either side of the Atlantic.

Lennon himself handled vocals on the B-side, a gritty mess of funk powered by grungy guitar, wailing sax and the equally tempestuous vocal sounds of Yoko Ono, who screamed her support as Lennon yelled out the title line over and over again.

MAY 24 to 28, 1971: RECORDING 'Imagine'/'Crippled Inside'/'Jealous Guy'/'Gimme Some Truth'/'Oh My Love'/ 'How Do You Sleep'/'How'/'Oh Yoko'/'San Francisco Bay Blues'/'Mind Train'/'Mind Holes'/'Midsummer New York'/ 'Mrs Lennon'/'The Path'; filming *Working Class Hero* (alias *Your Show*)

The Lennons had ended 1970 with a pair of albums that stripped away artifice and decoration, and took truth-telling as their credo. John exposed himself in words, Yoko in sound; and the music was as uncompromising as anything in rock. Second time around, one of the couple opted for a different approach. Lennon described the album he recorded during these sessions, *Imagine,* as "*Plastic Ono Band* with sugar coating" – a conscious attempt, then, to sweeten the bitter pill with melody and harmony.

It was the lightness of most of the arrangements, the comforting turns of the melodies, that helped make *Imagine* Lennon's most popular solo work. The anthemic qualities of the title track have disguised the slightness of some of the album's material, while the relevance of one of the most powerful tracks, 'How Do You Sleep?', passed as soon as Lennon's feud with its target, Paul McCartney, died down. The *Imagine* album is still easy on the ear, though, in a way which *Plastic Ono Band* could never be. Small wonder that McCartney was among those who felt it was his best work.

From the standpoint of the 21st century, what was most remarkable about the album was the fact that it was all but recorded in a week at the Lennons' home studio. John and Yoko then flew to the States for Phil Spector to supervise the overdubbing of strings and King Curtis's saxophone (see July 4-5, 1971); then they returned home to shoot the material for their *Imagine* feature film, and immediately began editing work. Along the way, they also knocked off a double album for Yoko.

But *Imagine* was not the product of the same burst of energy and need which created the *Plastic Ono Band* songs. Lennon admitted as the album was released that virtually nothing on the record had been written that year. Its earliest composition, the delicate balled 'Oh My Love', dated back to late 1968. Piano-based on the album, it was nonetheless firmly in the mould of Lennon's 1968/69 guitar picking songs, constructed around familiar ebb-and-flow melodic patterns and sharing the period's Manichean view of the world. Early takes of the song highlighted the delicate balance of the recording, with finger bells and a triangle supporting the fragile piano chords, while George Harrison conjured up some of his most elegant guitar picking.

'Gimme Some Truth' had been premièred, with compositional help from Paul McCartney, during the January 1969 Beatles' sessions. Since then, Lennon had heightened the song's biting invective, throwing in contemporary references to 'Tricky Dicky' Nixon, provided a memorable three-note guitar riff to hold it together, snarled a tough, sneering lead vocal, and finally forced George Harrison to sum up the whole song with a precise and cutting slide guitar solo. The song made such demands on Lennon's voice that he could only delivered two or three takes at a time. One magnificent effort, captured on the film, was greeted with a lukewarm response from Spector. "It's getting there," he said, prompting a disappointed Lennon to respond: "Oh, wasn't that it?" The next take *was* it, as Lennon howled out his message – "All I want is the truth" – until the band ran out of steam, and he pronounced: "This is the truth". But on the final record, the track faded before that line could be heard.

'Jealous Guy' was the other vintage song on the *Imagine* album. In this case, though, only the tune was familiar: Lennon had originally written it in India as 'Child Of Nature', in which form it was still being vaguely considered by The Beatles as late as January 1969. Its new words were another confession of guilt to Yoko – what *had* Lennon been up to in late 1970? – which opened, suitably enough, "I was dreaming of the past".

'Jealous Guy' had none of the mawkishness of 'I Promise', however: the lyrics were as sincere and honest as anything on Lennon's previous album, and they offered a disarming glimpse of the macho ex-Beatle discovering feminism through an examination of his own faults. Even before Spector added his New York strings, Lennon had duplicated their part with Nicky Hopkins' harmonium; 'Jealous Guy' was always meant to be lush. Also added in New York was Lennon's delicate whistle before the final verse, which added another layer of vulnerability to his admission of wrongdoing. He knew from the start that this song was commercial: "Here's a message to all Northern Songs shareholders," he quipped before one Ascot take. "Here's another half-million."

The shift in mood from 'Jealous Guy' to 'How Do You Sleep?' on the same record was the final proof of John's mercurial nature. 'Sleep' was a vicious assault on his ex-songwriting partner, which accused, judged and convicted him on counts of dishonesty, lack of talent, hypocrisy and – most heinous of all, it seemed – living with 'straights' (unlike the ultra avant-garde Lennons, of course). When the album came out, Lennon was unusually coy about the song – "I could have been writing about myself," he offered in his defence – but the lyrics pulled no punches. Allen Klein, who had his own good reasons for disliking McCartney, added the sly couplet that rhymed 'yesterday' with 'another day', but the rest was Lennon's entirely unbalanced swipe at an old, dear friend – which is how (on 'Dear Friend') McCartney chose to reply when he cut *his* next album at the end of 1971. Early takes of the song had lasted eight minutes or more, with Nicky Hopkins vamping away on electric piano in respond to Lennon's demand that he wanted him to sound like a Wurlitzer organ. The arrangment was still in flux at this point, shifting from a Claptonesque blues feel to a reprise of the 'Well Well Well' riff from John's last album, and even a brief excursion into reggae territory, before the band found the perfect tempo. Meanwhile, George Harrison threw in a delicious slide solo, apparently unperturbed by Lennon's address to their mutual ex-colleague, "How do you sleep, you cunt?" It was left to Spector to sharpen the blade in New York.

Spector performed similar magic on 'I Don't Want To Be A Soldier', taking the jagged February recording and adding a volcanic echo that made Lennon sound as if he was performing from beyond the grave. 'It's So Hard' was also retrieved from the earlier sessions, and both songs were sharpened and then smoothed by Spector, ready for sax overdubs a few weeks later.

Throughout the album sessions, Lennon recorded his initial guide vocals while the instrumental tracks were being taped, giving the music a live feel missing from most superstar sessions. Nowhere did that vibe survive in better shape than on 'Crippled Inside', a jaunty piece of rockabilly that gently took the rise out of Lennon's psychodramas on his previous album. There was also another supposed dig ("you can live a lie until you die") at the McCartneys, too. With honky-tonk piano and some startling dobro work (the latter from George Harrison, once he'd warmed up his fingers), 'Crippled Inside' was Lennon's most relaxed piece of music in years, an effective tribute to the country-blues rock 'n' roll which had inspired him in the Fifties. (Some sources list Blind Blake's 'Black Dog Blues' as the original inspiration for Lennon's song, but there are no apparent lyrical or musical similarities between the two.)

'Oh Yoko' caught much of the same spirit, with Spector's production giving an unexpected richness to what was essentially a small band recording. Spector also joined Lennon for the falsetto harmony vocals, having performed much the same function a few months earlier on George Harrison's 'My Sweet Lord'. The basic mix of the song was much longer than the final cut, lacking the first Dylanesque harmonica solo and the backing vocals, though Lennon's final play-in-a-day excursion round his harmonica was there from the opening take.

'How' was the *Imagine* song which came closest to the purity of the *Plastic Ono Band* album. Having set the mood on his December 1970 demo,

Lennon merely extended the song during the sessions, adding the delicious middle section (which harked back to the self-encouragement of 'Hold On') and letting the lyrics, with their series of unanswered questions, speak for themselves.

In terms of sound, 'How' was also a dry run for the 'Imagine' title track itself. On the first day of sessions at the Lennons' Tittenhurst Park Studios, John had taken the band aside and played brief piano renditions of the songs they were going to record. As participants Alan White and Nicky Hopkins both recalled, 'Imagine' stood out from the first, both for the power of its lyricism, and the haunting simplicity of its melody. "That's a nice one", Hopkins muttered as he heard Lennon's debut performance in the studio – in many ways the best ever rendition of the song, despite the fact that the composer was sufficiently embarrassed by what he was singing to ham up his vocal for the final chorus.

At this distance, it's hard to separate the song from the myth, which would have us believe that 'Imagine' is Lennon's finest song, his ultimate statement of hope for himself and the world. In fact, the words were far less straightforward than that: "Imagine no possessions/I wonder if you can", Lennon wrote, fully aware that he was not about to pass through the eye of a needle. The song's blatant denial of a Christian after-life, of any existence beyond today, was also at odds with any Utopian interpretation of the lyrics.

The song's lyrical structure – a series of ideas each calling for imagination – was directly based on Yoko's book *Grapefruit*, which is why in later years Lennon admitted that he should have given Yoko a co-credit on the song, as he did on 'Oh My Love'. In Yoko's art, the concept – the dream, if you like – was as important as the result. Lennon wanted results as well, but he followed Yoko in believing that dreaming of a desired event made the event itself more likely. The wider the dream, the more likely a change in the world: hence "I hope someday you'll join us/and the world will be as one".

What was interesting, in the light of 'Power To The People' and the promise of the radical sloganeering of the *Some Time In New York City* album, was the lack of a political programme in Lennon's imaginings. There was a large gap between "You say you want a revolution/you better get it on right away" and "Nothing to kill and die for . . . Imagine all the people/ Living life in peace". For the next year, the Lennons wandered between two manifestos – one which talked of violent action as the only way to secure change, another which preferred to lie back and dream.

There are countless alternate takes and mixes of 'Imagine' in existence, but all of them simply document the painstaking path to the finished arrangement, without shedding any fresh light on the song. Initially, Nicky Hopkins filled out the backing with a harmonium, and then attempted to double Lennon's keyboard part on electric piano, before John realised that this was a song which would benefit from extreme simplicity. Before the strings were added in New York, however, and Spector pumped up the piano echo, 'Imagine' sounded stark and strangely sinister, with the piano, bass and drums left dry on the tape, casting no shadow. Like 'How', this halfway mix would have fitted onto a soundalike successor to the *Plastic Ono Band* album; but to increase the audience for his message, Lennon chose to allow Spector his head, coating the basic tracks with a thin veneer of sweetness which bridged the gap between cult acceptance and mass commercial appeal.

The only out-take to have surfaced from the *Imagine* sessions was a much more spontaneous affair. While the engineers set up for a new song, Lennon broke into an impromptu rendition of Jesse Fuller's vintage 'San Francisco Bay Blues', complete with authentic acoustic blues picking on his 12-string. "Are you ready, you cunts?" he jokingly asked as he finished.

Maybe Lennon was in training for 'Mind Holes', one of several Yoko Ono tracks that were also taped during and immediately after the *Imagine* sessions. From the outset, it was obvious that Yoko had enough material for a double album: she and Lennon had already taped 'Fly', which would fill a side by itself and were about to record another side's worth of soundtrack material with the Joe Jones Tone Deaf Music Co's instruments. Yoko wasn't satisfied with this film music as an album in its own right, so Lennon and the *Imagine* band relaxed between takes of songs like 'Jealous Guy' and 'It's So Hard' by recording Yoko's compositions.

'Mind Holes' featured layers of Lennon's blues guitar picking, plus a little bottleneck for good measure, with Yoko bleating over the top. As ever, the means may have differed, but the Lennons' philosophy was the same: the simple, *Grapefruit*-style instructions of 'Mind Holes' – "Search for the holes in your feelings – memories – pain/Dream of the holes" – expressed in more basic terms the uncompromising vision of Lennon's *Plastic Ono Band* songs.

Slowly, however, Yoko was learning to marry her stark artistic notions with the rock technology inherited from her husband. 'Open Your Box' and 'Don't Worry Kyoko' were included on her *Fly* album as early examples; but the most powerful unison of East and West came on the chilling 'Mind Train', 16 minutes of eerie electric riffing which built up to an inferno of sound, while Yoko dispassionately chanted her lyrics of doom and pain: "I thought of killing that man … dub dub train passed through my mind …

33 windows shining through my mind". Presumably the 33 windows belonged to the 33 buildings that Yoko had once suggested you should watch being covered with snow in her 'Snow Piece For Solo' or 'Trio No. 2'.

Just as Yoko deserved credit for altering the way in which John saw the world, so in turn John twisted Yoko's music towards more traditional structures. The result of the latter process was 'Midsummer New York', with Yoko struggling to keep tempo with a simple rock 'n' roll 12-bar structure, which proved an effective basis for more tales of fear and loathing in the big city: "Midsummer New York/My heart shakes in terror". As on 'Mind Train', it was Lennon who took care of the guitar parts, with a freedom and vigour that he rarely displayed on his own records.

'Mrs Lennon' was chosen as the lead single from *Fly*, and its gentle, elegiac air must have surprised many who took the trouble to listen. (Big Star leader Alex Chilton certainly did: compare this song with his cult classic, 'Holocaust'.) The title of the song was ironic: Yoko hated being described as Mrs Lennon, Beatle wife, rather than as an artist in her own right. And the chilling series of surreal images that filled the song was certainly no straightforward declaration of love. Lennon's Bach-like piano accompaniment only added to the atmosphere of foreboding – shared by many of Yoko's songs, which seemed to look forward unconsciously to the dark days of December 1980.

Except for an occasional burst of Lennon's characteristic impatience, there was little darkness on display during the sessions. John and Yoko's sense of artistic importance ensured that there was a camera crew present throughout. They were working towards a project that was originally entitled *Your Show*, and then *Working Class Hero*. About 60 hours of film and sync sound were shot by Nic Knowland during the week's recording, intended for a full-length documentary film. Not even a rough cut was prepared from this footage, as the Lennons chose to pursue the conceptual *Imagine* movie instead. But the *Working Class Hero* film did provide the basis for much of *Imagine: John Lennon*, the 1988 biopic, and the subsequent DVD in 2000, *Gimme Some Truth: The Making Of John Lennon's 'Imagine' Album*.

JUNE 6, 1971: PERFORMING 'Well (Baby Please Don't Go)'/'Jamrag'/ 'Scumbag'/'Au' at Fillmore East

Having completed the initial stage of their album sessions, the Lennons flew straight to New York, where they met left-field rocker Frank Zappa, and were promptly invited to appear on stage with his band, the Mothers, at the

Fillmore East that night. Both Lennon and Zappa found that they had fallen for the other's media coverage: "I was expecting a grubby maniac with naked women all over the place," Lennon admitted afterwards. "He was expecting a couple of nude freaks." Audience expectations were not disappointed, however, as the Lennons and the Mothers produced one of the odder marriages in rock history.

The Lennons appeared as the evening's encore, John sporting an electric guitar, Yoko in her customary bag. Lennon announced "a song I used to do in the Cavern in Liverpool", and the band broke into The Olympics' 1958 B-side to 'Western Movies', a gritty blues titled 'Well (Baby Please Don't Go)'. The band played through the one-verse structure several times, altering the rhythm accompaniment on each pass; Lennon spat out the words, Yoko howled sympathetically, and Zappa lent on his wah–wah pedal between lines before letting rip for a fluid solo. After several minutes, though, the musicians began to lose direction. The Mothers' vocal team of Howard Kaylan and Mark Volman made themselves audible as Lennon crawled through the song's solitary verse one more time, and then again, before the entire exercise collapsed into cacophony, a bedlam of screaming and howling.

Yoko couldn't resist this opportunity to unleash her lung power, and for more than two minutes she and the Mothers competed at the microphone. Then Zappa led his band into one of their standard concert pieces, 'King Kong' from their *Uncle Meat* soundtrack. Yoko kept on wailing, before Lennon took advantage of a brief pause and coached the audience in lengthy repetition of the phrase "scumbag". Finally, after Zappa and the Mothers left the stage, Lennon remained to coax space-age feedback from his amp, while Yoko took centre-stage, in a 'Cambridge 1969'-style piece that the Lennons titled pretty much the way it sounded: 'Au'.

After the show, Zappa and the Lennons gave each other *carte blanche* to do what they wanted with the 16-track tapes. A heavily remixed and edited tape of the performance duly cropped up on the Lennons' *Some Time In New York City* album the following year. In place of liner notes, Lennon defaced the artwork of the Mothers' own *Fillmore East* album (some saw this as Lennon's sly way of repaying Zappa's memorable parody of the *Sgt. Pepper* cover on *We're Only In It For The Money*), which had been cut on the same night. The Mothers' pleasure at appearing on record with the Lennons, however, was no doubt tempered by the fact that John and Yoko took composer credit for all the band's improvised jamming, offering Zappa only co-credit for 'Scumbag'. Of 'King Kong' there was no mention: Zappa's memorable instrumental theme was now a Lennon/Ono composition entitled 'Jamrag'.

211

Zappa waited until 1992 to take his revenge, releasing his own edit of the performance on his *Playground Psychotics* compilation. Although 'Well' and 'Scumbag' retained their original titles, 'Jamrag' was divided into two cuts called 'Say Please' and 'Aaawk', while 'Au' was teasingly renamed 'A Small Eternity With Yoko Ono'. CD-R bootlegs remain the only source for the unedited tape, dubbed from a recently discovered film of most of the concert, shot by the Fillmore East's management.

JUNE 1971: RECORDING 'Airmale'/'Don't Count The Waves'/'You'/'Toilet Piece'/'Telephone Piece'

For the soundtrack of John's film *Erection*, Yoko made three recordings with the Joe Jones Tone Deaf Music Co, an offshoot of the Fluxus group which consisted of a collection of toy percussion instruments that played themselves. Their tumultuous rhythm, coupled with Yoko's vocal exhalations, provided an apt complement to the business of construction. 'Airmale' and 'You' were used in the film; 'Don't Count The Waves' was saved for Yoko's *Fly* album and the *Imagine* film. All three tracks were produced by John and Yoko, who also added more conventional rhythmic accompaniment from Klaus Voormann and Jim Keltner.

Two audio verite recordings from this period proved that the couple had not yet shed their playful vision of the artist's role. 'Toilet Piece' consisted of a flushing lavatory; 'Telephone Piece' (which also appeared over the credits of Yoko's documentary short, *Museum Of Modern (F)Art*, about her non-existent art exhibit in New York) was Yoko answering the phone. Only a few seconds long, these tracks simultaneously debunked the idea of art as an élitist occupation, and invited the world to look on the Lennons as clowns.

The British music press reported in June 1971 that Lennon had been invited to take part in the sessions for B.B. King's *In London* album. In the event, he was in New York while the sessions were being staged, leaving Ringo Starr as the only ex-Beatle to appear on the record.

JULY 4–5: RECORDING saxophone overdubs on 'It's So Hard'/'I Don't Want To Be A Soldier, Mama', and string overdubs on 'Imagine'/'Jealous Guy'/'It's So Hard'/'How Do You Sleep?'/'How'

Saxophone giant King Curtis had last seen John Lennon when his band supported The Beatles on their American tour in 1965. Six years later, he arrived late and exhausted from a late-night performance at the Newport

Jazz Festival. Once Lennon had remembered where they'd met, he remi-
nisced about those mid-Sixties tours to set Curtis at ease, and then left the
saxman to work his magic. Living up to his name, the King invented and
perfected the intro riff for 'It's So Hard' on his second pass, so Lennon
offered him a solo on the song as well. Then he was directed towards the
cavernous 'I Don't Want To Be A Soldier, Mama', on which Lennon
instructed him to enter in mid-song with the highest note he could reach,
and then stay there. In less than an hour, the overdubs were completed.
Sadly, King Curtis was murdered less than six weeks later, before his work
reached the public.

Meanwhile, Phil Spector was directing the work of the string players
that Lennon dubbed The Flux Fiddlers. Their contributions to songs such
as 'Imagine' and 'Jealous Guy' were orthodox, but Spector's genius surfaced
when he utilised them on 'How Do You Sleep?'. His arrangement under-
scored the vitriol of the lyrics with the most vicious string sound ever
caught on record, soaring over the guitar boogie riffs before screeching to
a halt at the end of each chorus like a knife across glass. After a couple of
days of mixing sessions, *Imagine* the album was complete. Now the
Lennons transferred their attention to the sister project: a movie of the
same name.

21–23 JULY and early SEPTEMBER 1971: FILMING *Imagine*

Imagine was the Lennons' most careful attempt at creating their art on film.
Their previous movies had been directed at the avant-garde community,
establishing their credentials, as it were. They certainly had little hope or
expectation of achieving the surprising commercial success of Yoko's *Film
No. 4 (Bottoms)*.

The *Imagine* movie was different. Here were John and Yoko creating a
visual counterpoint to their music – plus a vehicle which would promote
their own new records. Indeed, like *Cold Turkey* and *The Ballad Of John And
Yoko, Imagine* began simply enough as a promo film clip for John's album
title track, shortly to be issued as a single in the USA. From the start, as
Lennon revealed when the movie was completed, "The film was a back
drop to the sound. The interesting part was putting the picture to the sound,
not the other way around." Like modern long-form promo vehicles, which
offer a selection of promo clips linked by an elementary story-line, *Imagine*
sought to offer a pictorial accompaniment to the *Imagine* and *Fly* albums.
But at the same time, the Lennons refused to think in terms of lateral plot
development. As John explained, "*Imagine* was a discontinuum – a comedy,

213

not a tragedy. It's the epitome of nonsense. It was made in a very playful mood."

Hence the weird assembly of near-documentary footage, highlighted by the famous clip for the song 'Imagine', with Lennon sat alone at his white piano while Yoko opened the shutters separating the darkness of the room from the light of the sun; and pure surrealism, which reached its zenith with the Lennons playing chess with an all-white set, and then proceeding to eat the pieces. "With an all-white chess set," John explained, "you have to convince each other, you have to remember which horse is yours."

Convincing anyone apart from each other was something that the film failed to do, however. Though there were memorable moments – the Lennons boating across the lake in their vast grounds, or drawing their names in the Staten Island sand seconds before the tide swept their scribbling away – the film's determined lack of realism made it more a venture in self-indulgence than an insight into their creative thinking. "We were only playing ourselves on a surrealistic level," Yoko explained, but the 'playing' was never more than that. John recalled in 1972: "When we did *Imagine*, we felt great about it, and were saying, 'This is going to widen the field of film! This is it, this is the Seventies." ' Instead, the Lennons failed to find a distributor for the full 85-minute print, and only a cut-down, 55-minute film was screened publicly, omitting most of Yoko's musical segments. Among the footage lost along the way was Lennon choosing a Wendy House for the Tittenhurst Park garden; and a brief rendition of 'Make Love Not War', still no nearer to being completed almost a year after its initial creation. Yoko slightly re-edited this version of the film for the eventual home-video release in the mid-Eighties.

Ultimately, the *Imagine* film project – which used just 20 per cent of the footage shot during the filming in Ascot (July) and New York (September) – worked better in small extracts, as in the promo films for 'Imagine' and 'Mrs Lennon' circulated at the time, and the posthumous compilation clips for releases like 'Jealous Guy'.

JULY/AUGUST 1971: RECORDING *Grapefruit* readings; taping *Oz* solidarity message

A little over a year after the revised hardback edition of Yoko's book *Grapefruit* was published, a mass-market paperback version hit the streets. The Lennons devoted more time to publicising this event than they did for any of their records during this period, even staging a book signing at London's exclusive department store, Selfridge's, on July 15.

In addition, John and Yoko recorded around 30 minutes of readings from *Grapefruit*, designed to be made into a promotional record and played on radio stations in the States. Thankfully, these painfully embarrassing spoken word recordings, which featured both the Lennons doing their best to undermine the sense of Yoko's written words, were never issued to the media.*

As a final gesture of solidarity with the editors of *Oz* magazine, who were found guilty at the Old Bailey and sentenced on August 5, the Lennons also recorded a message of support meant to be included on a flexidisc inside the next issue. John flirted with the contempt laws by making plain his exasperation with the way that Judge Argyle had conducted the trial, before launching (with Yoko) into an *a cappella* rendition of that stiff-upper-lip anthem, 'Keep Right On To The End Of The Road'.

AUGUST 1971: CREATING Fluxus objects

During the summer of 1971, John lent his time to several Fluxus group projects. Among his creations, physical and conceptual, were 'Boiling Water In Tank Toilet' (part of the 'Flux-Toilet' concept), a 'Magnification Piece' in a cabinet, designed with artist George Maciunas; and a ten-foot-long wooden guitar titled 'Baby Grand Guitar For Yoko Ono'. This last piece was eventually hung outside the Hit Factory studio in New York.

Lennon also presented George Maciunas, who was colour-blind, with a paintbox containing fifteen tubes of coloured paint. It was accompanied by a card reading: 'Piece For George Maciunas Who Can't Distinguish Between These Colors'.

---

* These recordings may, as the previous edition of this book suggested, date from the hardback publication in 1970; either way, they didn't fulfil their purpose.

CHAPTER 12

September 1971 to April 1973

The Lennons hit New York with vast expectations of being able to channel their creativity and their radical zeal into projects that would threaten the American capitalist system, and halt the USA's imperialist venture into Vietnam. Reality was harder to shape than they realised, however, and gradually the strain of leading the revolution, fighting off government surveillance and maintaining any kind of marriage worthy of the name began to take their toll. Ironically, it was Lennon who flagged first. While his wife tapped into the emerging feminist movement for her energy, he found his creativity draining away. The contrast sent him spiralling into the deepest depression of his life – so far . . .

EARLY SEPTEMBER 1971: RECORDING home demos of 'JJ'/ 'Shoeshine'

Imagine and *Fly* were the Lennons' farewell to Britain. Having travelled to the States for final preparation of the two albums, they returned home to Tittenhurst Park to prepare another season of their films for the August 11 *Art Spectrum* at Alexandra Palace (where the *Top Of The Pops* film clip from January 1970 was shown as *Instant Karma*, alongside *Up Your Legs Forever* and a handful of other promo clips). On August 28, they appeared on the BBC TV programme *Parkinson*, discussing Bagism and their predilection for showing themselves in the nude; and six days later they were gone, arriving

216

in New York after a stopover in the Virgin Islands. John Lennon never set foot in Britain again.

The couple made their initial home at the St. Regis Hotel, where they quickly installed their home recording equipment and began to play host to a stream of visiting radicals and artists. Within days of taking up residence at the St. Regis, Lennon had written and recorded two new songs. The couple were both taking large quantities of methadone, as a replacement for heroin; once again, their personal lives were on the line. But John chose not to reflect this in his new music. Instead, 'JJ' was a third-person story-song, an acoustic guitar ditty set to the tune of what would become 'Angela' on their next album. In its initial form, though, the song showed little sign that Lennon had taken note of sexual politics, with its playful tale of a woman who "couldn't get laid at all". In the background, a Laurel & Hardy movie rolled on the omnipresent TV.

'Shoeshine' was an even simpler piece, set to a traditional acoustic guitar boogie. "Well I was sitting listening to some rock and roll/I said they don't play music like that no more", it began, before attempting to disprove the point by breaking into Gary Bonds' 'Quarter To Three'. Obviously unfinished, it was most interesting for its use of a couple of lines which turned up in the 1973 LP cut, 'Meat City', and a climax that was vaguely reminiscent of part of 1974's 'Old Dirt Road'.

During the October 1971 sessions for 'Happy Xmas (War Is Over)', British journalist Richard Williams heard Lennon performing a song about Chuck Berry and Bo Diddley, and then watched as he screwed up the words and threw them away. It is possible that Lennon revised the lyrics of 'Shoeshine' to include his Fifties idols without committing the song to tape. And it's intriguing that a year later, Lennon produced an Elephant's Memory's song about exactly the same rock heroes, 'Chuck And Bo'. But none of this helps to pin down the identity of the song that Williams heard.

SEPTEMBER 10, 1971: FILMING *Clock*; **recording 'Call My Name'/'Shazam'/'Honey Don't'/'Glad All Over'/'Lend Me Your Comb'/'New York City'/'Wake Up Little Suzie'/'Vacation Time'/'Peggy Sue'/'Not Fade Away'/'I Don't Wanna Be A Soldier, Mama'/'Greensleeves'/'Make Love, Not War'/'Baby I Don't Care'/'Heartbeat'/'Peggy Sue Got Married'/'Maybe Baby'/'Mailman Bring Me No More Blues'/'Rave On'**

Even with many hours of *Imagine* footage still to be edited, the Lennons carried on filming. *Clock* was shot in their St. Regis Hotel room: its visual

217

content marked the passage of an hour via a clock on the hotel wall. No doubt this was an oblique comment on the transitory nature of time. But what made this movie bearable was its soundtrack, which consisted of Yoko making phone calls in search of exhibits for her upcoming art show at the Everson Gallery, while John played solo acoustic versions of some of his favourite Fifties rock songs – mostly, as the list above reveals, by Buddy Holly and Carl Perkins. Lennon kept fairly close to the original models, and even remembered most of the words; but he took the opportunity to invest his vocals with a devilish quaver that was obviously inspired by the example of his wife. What was apparent throughout was the pure pleasure that Lennon derived from playing this material, whether he was vamping through an approximation of Duane Eddy's instrumental hit 'Shazam', or unleashing some commendable Perkins rockabilly licks on 'Lend Me Your Comb'. But reality was never far from hand: 'Wake Up Little Susie' was interrupted by a phone call, revealing that a persistent Beatles fan named Karen had managed to breach security and find her way onto the Lennons' floor of the St. Regis. John consoled himself the only way he knew how, delving deep into the past to crank out the riff from Johnny Burnette's 'Lonesome Tears In My Eyes' for a few seconds before launching into a procession of Holly tunes.

The most revealing minutes from the soundtrack documented Lennon's new material. Besides a reprise of the chorus of 'Make Love Not War', and several shots at 'Call My Name', the highlight was the first version of 'New York City', which evolved into a powerhouse rocker on the couple's next album. While the rockaboogie rhythm was already intact, this early take had completely different lyrics to the final version, though Lennon's slurred delivery suggested he was busking it rather than reeling off a fixed set of verses. The one link to the record was the chorus line – "Que Pasa New York".

EARLY OCTOBER 1971: RECORDING home demos of 'Happy Xmas (War Is Over)'/'Hi-Heel Sneakers'/'My Baby Left Me'/'The Walk'

"War is over (if you want it)" was the slogan that John and Yoko sent round the world in their late 1969 poster campaign for peace. The same phrase became the title of their 1971 Christmas event – a seasonal record, written at the same time as 'Attica State'. The original acoustic demo of 'Happy Xmas' boasted few words but the structure was in place, with John struggling manfully to hit the high notes in the middle section. Underpinning the song were guitar chords playing the riff that became the counter-melody, and carried the slogan that inspired the song.

Rather than pursuing any individual theme from the Lennons' campaigns, the lyrics acted as a catch-all request for universal harmony. Only the opening lines, with Lennon asking himself, "So this is Christmas/And what have you done?" took the song out of the mainstream.

The other tunes listed above were preserved via a familiar sequence of events. Someone turned a tape recorder on, Yoko went about her business, and John busked his way through some rock'n'roll standards. Nothing was revealed.

OCTOBER 9, 1971: THIS IS NOT HERE exhibition opens; begins to write 'Attica State'; RECORDS birthday party jam session: 'What'd I Say'/'Yellow Submarine'/'On Top Of Old Smokey'/'Goodnight Irene'/'Take This Hammer'/'He's Got The Whole World In His Hands'/'Tandoori Chicken'/'Attica State'/'Like A Rolling Stone'/'Twist And Shout'/'Louie Louie'/'La Bamba'/'Bring It On Home To Me'/'Yesterday'/'Power To The People'/'Maybe Baby'/'Peggy Sue'/'My Baby Left Me'/'Blue Suede Shoes'/'Crippled Inside'/'Give Peace A Chance'/'Uncle Albert–Admiral Halsey'/'My Sweet Lord'/'Imagine'/'Oh Yoko'

For 19 days in October 1971, the prestigious Everson Art Museum in Syracuse, upstate New York, played host to Yoko Ono's most comprehensive retrospective exhibition. The show had only been commissioned in the week that the couple left England, so with less than a month to prepare, Yoko invited John to participate as 'guest artist', and also solicited exhibits from her friends in the art and music communities.

The Lennons held a press conference on the eve of the opening, excerpts from which were later included on the LP series, *The History Of Syracuse Music*. Film clips of the event were also included on a documentary by Takahiko Iimura, named after the exhibition, screened on US television on May 11, 1972. It captured the moment when the Lennons joined several of their friends in performing Yoko's 'Piano Piece', slamming down their hands on the closed lid of an instrument. Meanwhile, the exhibition catalogue – in the form of a newspaper-shaped collage, prepared by Lennon and Peter Bendry – documented both husband and wife's contributions to the event. On the back cover of the catalogue, a sequence of photographs of John and Yoko were merged together to form a hybrid, asexual face. The same photos appeared on the label of the couple's 'Happy Xmas' single a few weeks later. For Fluxus collectors, an *Everson Catalogue Box*, prepared by Ono's friend George Macunias, featured not only the catalogue and a copy of her book *Grapefruit*, but something billed as 'Multiple Works By John And Yoko'.

Although *This Is Not Here* (a slogan which the Lennons had displayed on a sign in front of their Tittenhurst Park home in England) mostly consisted of Yoko's earlier work, there was some new material on show. *Clock* was screened continually in the foyer; inside, there was a room devoted to 'Water Pieces' (objects contributed by Yoko's friends), all of which were designed to be filled with water. John had made a small fish tank, inside which was a pink sponge, labelled 'Napoleon's Bladder'.

That night – Lennon's 31st birthday – the couple stayed up late to party, and scoff the cake that Yoko had ordered: decorated with a dedication "To John from Yoko and the whole world". Being John and Yoko, the event was recorded, capturing for posterity the dubious delights of a stellar assembly (including Phil Spector, Klaus Voormann, Jim Keltner, Neil Aspinall, Ringo and Maureen Starkey and a very over-excited Allen Ginsberg) performing drunken renditions of favourite rock oldies, folk songs like 'Goodnight Irene', more recent Lennon classics like 'Give Peace A Chance' and 'Imagine' (delivered in a painfully weedy voice by Spector when John refused to join in the fun) and even Paul McCartney's 'Yesterday'. Spector (who'd donned one of Yoko's *Fly* T-shirts for the occasion) took the role of producer on himself, over-ruling Lennon's song suggestions and leading a singalong version of his own 'Tandoori Chicken'. He also inspired a round-the-room rendition of the late Fifties Laurie London hit 'He's Got The Whole World In His Hands'. Yoko's solo verse marked an all-time musical low point. By comparison, Lennon delivered 'What'd I Say' and 'Crippled Inside' with some precision, at least compared to Ringo's memory-lapsed 'Yellow Submarine' and the chorale's tongue-in-cheek massacre of McCartney's current US hit single, 'Uncle Albert-Admiral Halsey'.

Earlier in the evening, before too much drink had been consumed, Lennon had begun to compose a new song. "It was conceived on my birthday," he explained a couple of months later, "we ad libbed it, then we finished it off." After Lennon had borrowed a chunk of the simplistic melody of 'Tandoori Chicken', the result was 'Attica State', a strident political protest about the September killings in a New York State jail. As a chant for demonstrations, the chorus had its moments; but as an example of radical songwriting, it showed that Lennon still had much to learn before he would rival more experienced social commentators like Phil Ochs. By declaring "Rockefeller pulled the trigger/That is what the people feel", John also showed an alarming tendency to equate 'the people' with himself – a perennial folly of political activists the world over.

After the birthday celebration, Lennon sent Ringo Starr a postcard thanking him for attending the party and the exhibition. More interesting than the message was the picture: Arnold Bocklin's 'Spring Evening 1879', a romantic woodland idyll. Lennon personalised it by adding Yoko's face to the naked body of the nymph, and his own to the devilish satyr, playing the pipes of Pan. He even replaced the artist's name on the postcard with his own. The exercise was carried off so professionally that it seems likely he had a whole run of these postcards printed up, making them an exclusive limited-edition Lennon artefact.

OCTOBER 14, 1971: BROADCASTING *Freetime*

Back in June, the Lennons had taken part in an experimental New York radio show which involved them playing with words and concepts, and generally stretching the patience of their audience. Four months later, they repeated the exercise on cable TV station, WNET. *Freetime* formed part of an evening of Ono-related broadcasts that also included extracts from *Fly* and *Up Your Legs Forever*.

During *Freetime*, an invited audience was allowed to fire questions at Lennon, Ono and their friend, film-maker Jonas Mekas. The catch in this exercise in Fluxus television was that every query would be answered deadpan with another question. (Yoko had first performed her very similar 'Question Piece' in Tokyo in 1962.) What ensued was occasionally humorous, but more often embarrassingly lame. A random extract: "Why do you answer every question with a question?" John's answer: "Why do we?". He enjoyed more success with the perennial "When is a door not a door?" joke, which was high culture compared to the rest of the proceedings. Such was the level of tedium that Lennon's special mention of George & Pattie (Harrison) and Allen & Betty (Klein) was an absolute highlight. A few fashion notes: during the programme, Lennon and Mekas taped sanitary towels to their foreheads, as Yoko had done the previous year in England on *Top Of The Pops* (Lennon would repeat this jape for real during a heavy night on the town with Harry Nilsson in 1974.) And Jonas Mekas also sported a hat with the inscription: "Fool".

Far more inviting was Yoko's conceptual exhibition, *The Museum Of Modern (F)Art*, advertised as taking place at New York's contemporary gallery from December 1 to 15. Anyone tempted to visit MOMA by the posters discovered that in the spirit of Yoko's phrase, "This is not here", they themselves were the exhibition. But outside the gallery, Yoko did display an empty glass container, which had supposedly been filled with flies. Participants were invited to track the flies' progress across the city.

Yoko filled a short film with the most amusing public responses, and it has been a popular item at Ono movie retrospectives ever since. Also worth noting is Yoko's catalogue, which acted as a sampler of her work over the previous decade. Meanwhile, the MOMA box office was forced to display a picture of Yoko's poster for the event, with the handwritten explanation: "This Is NOT Here".

OCTOBER 28 and 29, 1971: RECORDING 'Happy Xmas (War Is Over)'/'Listen, The Snow Is Falling'

In Phil Spector, Lennon had found an expert in making Christmas records: his *A Christmas Gift To You* album from 1963 remains the pinnacle of the genre. For the Lennons, he brought out his full coterie of effects, using sleigh-bells and celestes to capture the seasonal feel, and bringing in the children of the Harlem Community Choir to sing the final choruses. Yoko, meanwhile, took over the song's middle section when Spector realised that Lennon's voice couldn't stretch that far.

'Happy Xmas' was at once a surprisingly conventional Lennon record, and an altogether more thoughtful piece of work than the average seasonal offering. Yoko's flipside, written early in 1968 and premièred briefly on 'Song For John' at the end of that year, was equally memorable: out came the tapes of feet trudging through the snow to top and tail the song, while Lennon supported Yoko's fragile, gentle vocals with some melodic reverb guitar.

AUTUMN 1971: FILMING *Freedom* films

Invited to contribute work to the year-end Chicago Film Festival, John and Yoko each shot a 60-second illustration of *Freedom*. John scratched the word onto the film itself, leaving it to flicker on the screen for a minute and then die. Yoko was more ironic: to the accompaniment of two repeated notes from John's electronic keyboard, she shot a brief sequence of herself trying to remove her bra – and failing. Her footage neatly undermined its title, and the naive optimism of the Lennons' political associates.

NOVEMBER 12, 1971: RECORDING demos of 'Luck Of The Irish'/'Attica State'

Two months into their residence in New York, the Lennons had already found their feet in the city's radical community, as activists like Abbie Hoffman and Jerry Rubin latched on to the power of their media profile. 'Attica State' was an early result, with Lennon choosing to comment on events he knew little about. Having written the song in early October, he and Yoko cut home demos a month later. The first take broke down immediately, so they went back and wiped it, only for their second attempt to fail in the same place, as Lennon missed his cue for the chorus. The third pass was more successful, and revealed the original format for the piece – Lennon and Yoko alternating solo lines, and then singing in unison (or as close as Yoko could muster) in the chorus.

Premièred on the same day was a song about a political issue slightly closer to John's experience. Like most of the British left, Lennon had been quick to support the campaigns of the Irish Republican Army against what they saw as the colonialist British state. 'Luck Of The Irish' was John's general response to the problem; later 'Sunday Bloody Sunday' would chart his reactions to more specific events. The song was spurred by a protest march in London that the couple had led in August, and saw John sympathising with the oppressed Irish in their struggle against "a thousand years of torture and hunger" and "the British brigands". For all its melodic charm, the song was always an outsider's view, and its release angered many people in Britain. In its earliest version, it was self-consciously a folk song, written as if it had been passed down the generations. Gradually, the lyrics evolved, as John first whistled and then wrote words for Yoko to sing in the middle section, a parade of idealistic images of Irish beauty to set against the harshness of John's political lament.

This November 1971 demo tape, which ran for nearly twenty minutes, was actually part of a film about the Irish situation being assembled by John Reilly and financed by the Lennons' Joko Productions company. The project was originally announced as *The Luck Of The Irish*, a joint venture between Apple Films and Reilly's company, Global Village. In that guise, it was due to be released in spring 1972, but there were long delays, presumably caused by the Lennons' immigration problems that year. Reilly's film was eventually screened in 1973 at the Mercer Arts Center in New York, and given a more general release in 1975 under the title of *The Irish Tapes*. This version of the film was apparently completed without any of the Lennons' footage. His B&W video camera actually caught a rather unharmonious mood in the Lennons' apartment, with the first take being abandoned as John chided Yoko for not paying attention; but the second run, backed by solo acoustic guitar, was a blueprint for the full studio take the following spring.

NOVEMBER 16 and DECEMBER 16, 1971: PRODUCING Indian Mosk (sic) and Tibetan Chants

One of the most comprehensive works of Beatles scholarship in recent years, Kristofer Engelhardt's *Beatles Undercover*, revealed the existence of two unreleased tape boxes in the archive of the Record Plant East studio in New York, bearing John Lennon's name as producer. One was a two-song tape from November 1971, featuring 'Bodhnath (Gellupka) I' and 'Bodhnath Part II', credited to something or somebody called Indian Mosk. The second item, dated a month later, listed the artist as Tibetan Chants, and the contents as 'Tantric Lamas' Parts 1 & 2.

Lateral thinking and some basic research provides an explanation of these tapes, though not of their supposed connection with Lennon. Bodhnath is a major Buddhist stupa (sacred burial site) in Nepal; Gelupka (sic) is a Buddhist sect from the same country. So the Indian Mosk may actually be a mosque – or more accurately, as this is Buddhism we're talking about, a monastery – and both tapes may contain religious chants from the Himalayas (Tibet, Nepal and India all being much the same as far as rock stars and studio engineers are concerned). But none of that offers a clue as to why Lennon would have been recording these items for Apple at the height of his religious cynicism and political radicalism.

NOVEMBER 19, 1971: PERFORMING 'Wind Piece'

One of the glories of New York's art scene during the Sixties and Seventies was the annual Avant Garde Festival, curated by Charlotte Moorman. The 1971 event was staged in the unlikely surroundings of the 69th Regiment Infantry Armory, on Lexington Avenue and 25th Street. 20,000 New Yorkers apparently attended this festival of left-field film, music and art. Among the works on display were Yoko Ono's 'Human Maze' (described as a sixteen-foot plexiglass installation), and John Lennon performing his orchestral 'Wind Piece'. The latter was presumably a brief silent appearance, in keeping with Yoko's instruction piece of the same name, which read: "Make a way for the wind". The couple returned to Moorman's festival the following year, for another equally quiet performance.

LATE NOVEMBER/DECEMBER 1971: RECORDING home demos of 'New York City'/'Woman Is The Nigger Of The World'/'Free The People'/'John Sinclair'/'People'/'Call My Name'/'Man Is Half Of Woman'; YOKO ONO recording 'South Wind'/'Will You Touch Me'/'Dogtown'

Warming to his new stance as the balladeer of the barricades, Lennon leapt to document the changing US political map in song. John Sinclair was his first priority – a campaign anthem for the jailed White Panther and rock manager (of The MC5), serving time in Detroit for possession of a small amount of marijuana. The Lennons had already agreed to headline a benefit at Ann Arbor's Chrysler Arena on December 10: a fortnight or so earlier, John completed the song, a bluesy, steel-guitar stomp which – true to his new ideals – told the story of Sinclair's imprisonment in simple verses. He hammered home the chorus line by repeating 'gotta' some 15 times before finishing the line "set him free".

On the same day, Lennon made an early pass at another attempted anthem, 'Free The People' – the song that came to be known as 'Bring On The Lucie'. At this stage, it was simply a three-chord dobro riff, around which Lennon had strung the phrase "Free the people now". 'Give Peace A Chance' this was not.

A few days later, Lennon made his first serious attempt at setting 'New York City' on tape, at the Bank Street apartment in Greenwich Village that had been their home for the previous month. Since previewing the song in *Clock* in September, he had completed the first verse, a Chuck Berry-inspired rock 'n' roll diary of what happened when the Lennons hit New York. The second verse was still improvised, however, and its opening words shed some light on its conception, with Lennon opening up, "Well, I was shooting up speed".

As well as updating 'New York City', Lennon had also spent time rewriting 'JJ'. He loved the melody, but couldn't find a suitable lyric. The sexist description of 'JJ' wasn't it; nor, it transpired, was attempt number two, titled 'People'. Lyrically, this was a rather bland call for peace and understanding, using themes that wouldn't have sounded out of place from the lips of Barbra Streisand, and that would be rekindled on 'Only People' in 1973. After this brief acoustic outing, the song was again rejected. So too was the never-bootlegged 'Man Is Half Of Woman', believed to come from this period.

'Call My Name' dated back to the summer 1971 sessions that also produced the earliest version of 'God Save Us'. Second time around, Lennon set the tune on acoustic guitar, and completed the lyric, as an updated take on his 1963 composition, 'All I've Got To Do'. The message here was one of support, offering a shoulder to lean on: "I'll ease your pain, girl/All you got to do is call my name". But the song's personal politics didn't suit the upcoming album, and so 'Call My Name' was left to be gutted and reshaped into 'Aisumasen' for 1973's *Mind Games*.

225

The most important song to come from this demo session also had a lengthy gestation. More than two years after he'd first toyed with setting the phrase to music, the would-be feminist John Lennon finally made a song out of Yoko's claim that 'Woman Is The Nigger Of The World'. Cut first in their hotel room, then on more professional equipment in their New York apartment, 'Woman Is The Nigger Of The World' shaped up as a savage portrayal of man's inhumanity to woman, equating the plight of the female sex with that of American blacks. The song's finger-pointing lyrics sat uneasily in Lennon's mouth, but were evidence of the enormous impact Yoko had had on his thinking. All he needed now was to put his own ideals into practice.

Meanwhile, Yoko recorded at least three of her own songs at Bank Street around this time, with John on acoustic guitar accompaniment. 'Dogtown' was a dry run for the song she taped a year later on *Approximately Infinite Universe*. 'South Wind' was a 16-minute-long, free-form vocal improvisation; and 'Will You Touch Me' was a jazzy, almost vaudeville tune that looked forward to her work on subsequent albums, especially *Feeling The Space*.

DECEMBER 1971: PRODUCING 'I'm A Runaway'/ 'Everybody's Smoking Marijuana'/'F Is Not A Dirty Word'/ 'The Hippie From New York City'/'McDonald's Farm'/ 'The Ballad Of New York City – John Lennon And Yoko Ono'/'The Ballad Of Bob Dylan'/'The Chicago Conspiracy'/ 'The Hip Generation'/'I'm Gonna Start Another Riot'/ 'The Birth Control Blues'/'The Pope Smokes Dope' by David Peel

Yippie street singer David Peel was one of the first members of the New York underground that the Lennons met, and his madcap live performances immediately appealed to the free spirit in John. Peel accompanied the couple to their Ann Arbor benefit, and like Jerry Rubin was a constant part of the Lennons' entourage during the early weeks of 1972. Around that time, John and Yoko produced an album for Peel, and issued it on Apple in April – a successor to his two earlier efforts on Elektra.

In fact, producing Peel was scarcely a chore. He performed with, at most, three other musicians, calling in a choir of friends off the street for his choruses. At a time when Lennon himself was writing slogans rather than songs, Peel's populism was bound to raise his enthusiasm. In retrospect, only a couple of the tracks have outlived their contemporary relevance: 'The Pope Smokes Dope' and 'The Ballad Of New York City – John Lennon And Yoko Ono' both looked forward to the basic structures of the late Seventies new wave, marrying chanted lyrics to simple, uncluttered music. Lennon's voice was heard sporadically during the album.

DECEMBER 10, 1971: PERFORMING 'Attica State'/'Luck Of The Irish'/'Sisters O Sisters'/'John Sinclair' at John Sinclair benefit, a performance filmed for *Ten For Two*; recording 'Chords Of Fame' with Phil Ochs

15,000 people filled the Crysler Arena in Ann Arbor, Michigan, lured as much by the prospect of seeing the Lennons and Stevie Wonder as by the virtue of the cause for which this was a benefit – John Sinclair's appeal fund. The entire concert was filmed, at the Lennons' expense, on 16-mm, and a rough cut of the movie was shown to the couple under the title *Ten For Two* – taken from one of the key lines in Lennon's 'John Sinclair' song. But the movie was never released.

The Lennons took the stage in the early hours of the morning, by which time the audience had worked themselves into a frenzy of anticipation, expecting the reformation of The Beatles at the very least. Instead, they were given John, Yoko, guitarists Leslie Bacon and David Peel, and percussionist politico Jerry Rubin. The quintet had rehearsed just four songs, all of them new to the audience, some of them, to judge by the rather amusing film of the event, new to the band.

'Attica State' was symptomatic of the problem. Trying to fill an entire arena with acoustic guitars would have been trouble enough; singing the song when your wife is consistently half a beat out-of-step was nearly impossible. 'Luck Of The Irish' was slightly smoother, though only after Lennon's guitar-strap had broken, along with his temper. Then came Yoko's solo, on her new song, 'Sisters O Sisters', a feminist call for unity. Lennon tried to rescue the occasion with some idealism: "We came here to say that apathy isn't it," he told the audience, "and that we can still do something. So flower power didn't work. So what? We start again." And he did, easing the combo through a surprisingly tight rendition of 'John Sinclair'. With that, the mini-concert was over. The audience were apparently disappointed by its brevity, but it served its purpose: within three days, Sinclair was free.

Backstage, someone's tape recorder was running while another of the night's performers, protest singer Phil Ochs, ran through his bitter analysis of showbiz, 'Chords Of Fame', with Lennon accompanying him on dobro. Ochs also gave Lennon a quick lesson in the history of the American folk ballad, singling out Woody Guthrie's epic 'Tom Joad' as something that the ex-Beatle ought to check out.

DECEMBER 16, 1971: PERFORMING 'The Ballad Of New York City'/'John Sinclair'/'Luck Of The Irish'/'Sisters O Sisters'/'Attica State'/'A Hippie From New York City' on The David Frost Show

On a somewhat bad-tempered return to *The David Frost Show*, Lennon previewed four of the songs from his and Yoko's next album. Behind him was not the crack team of sessionmen that most superstars would have chosen, but the more ramshackle support of David Peel and his Lower East Side, featuring Jerry Rubin on percussion (sporting a *This Is Not Here* exhibition T-shirt). They opened and closed the show with Ono playing bongos and (on 'A Hippie') John thrashing a string bass, skiffle-style. When Lennon and Ono took centre stage, they scarcely made use of the band. On 'Luck Of The Irish', meanwhile, John was still rewriting the lyrics: for the moment, it was "the kids, the church and the IRA" who were to blame, "as the bastards ['bummers' for the TV broadcast] commit genocide". The church was let off the hook when the Lennons finally taped the song in the studio; the line certainly scanned better that way.

DECEMBER 17, 1971: PERFORMING 'Attica State'/'Sisters O Sisters'/'Imagine' at the Attica families benefit

A few days after Ann Arbor, the Lennons appeared with an acoustic band at a concert held in Harlem at the legendary Apollo Theatre, showcase of black music. They were there to raise funds for the dependants of those killed in the Attica State prison riots – the event which had sparked John to write a song in October. They repeated two of their selections from the Ann Arbor show, Yoko lagging behind the beat as ever, before John told the audience: "I lost my old band, or I left it. I'm putting an electric band together, but it's not ready yet, so I have to just busk it." There followed a stark, beautiful version of 'Imagine', backed only by acoustic guitar and percussion (the latter provided by Yippie activist Jerry Rubin). "Imagine no possessions – try it", Lennon sang, the sentiments uncluttered by any musical ornamentation.

JANUARY 1972: RECORDING home demos of 'Pill'/'He Got The Blues'

Throughout their frenetic relationship, John and Yoko had never been far removed from drugs. Only during the Janov-inspired cleansing of 1970 had illicit chemicals been forsaken entirely; but by the end of the year John was apparently using heroin again. After the avowedly acid-drenched visions of

228

1966/67, however, and the confessional 'Cold Turkey', little of his drug experiences showed up in his songs. An acoustic number called 'Pill' might seem to be the exception, but the reality was a little disappointing. It consisted of one repeated line, set to a chunky guitar riff: "You need a special pill to keep you on the line". John bent the last word round a sequence of tight melodic curves to make the piece more interesting, which he eventually used in 'Steel And Glass' three years later. Suggestions from some commentators that the song referred to his methadone treatment can't be confirmed or denied on the evidence of the song.

Likewise 'He Got The Blues', a thinly-veiled piece of self-pitying autobiography, that began, "Johnny was a poor boy . . . he did the best he can", and meandered nowhere in particular. 'Johnny' was himself, of course, and also the hero of Chuck Berry's 'Johnny B. Goode' but his adventures were never completed.

JANUARY 14 to 28, 1972: CO-HOSTING *The Mike Douglas Show*: performing 'Woman Is The Nigger Of The World'/'Luck Of The Irish'/ 'Imagine'/'Sakura'/'Johnny B. Goode'/'Memphis'/'Attica State'/'It's So Hard'/'Sisters O Sisters'/'Midsummer New York'

Afternoon talk shows were never the same after this exercise in cross-cultural fertilisation, which saw the Lennons co-hosting the extremely popular *Mike Douglas Show* with a man not known for his artistic or political radicalism. All three hosts were able to choose guests for the five shows: the Lennons selected a series of underground figures and politicos, plus John's hero, Chuck Berry; Mike Douglas answered with a more sedate mixture of entertainers and charity workers.

The encounters between Bobby Seale and Jerry Rubin on one hand, and Mike Douglas on the other, ranked among the classic moments of television comedy – Douglas visibly freaked by the reputation of his guests, Rubin and Seale unable to come to terms with selling their message to mass America. The Lennons bridged the gap, diluting some of the more radical statements, or making them more accessible to the audience, and also performing much of the material that they were about to record for *Some Time In New York City*.

This was the Lennons' first public performance with their new support crew, Elephant's Memory – a New York bar band who had contributed to the soundtrack of *Midnight Cowboy*. Jerry Rubin advised Lennon to check them out, and John loved their raunchy approach to rock 'n' roll, and their radical street feel. For the next eight months they became his constant back-

229

up, as he made another studio album, and planned his return to the road. "It was really nice just to have a solid group," he reflected. "It reminded me of the early days at The Cavern."

Their apprenticeship had to be brief. Musical highlights included Yoko missing her cue after the guitar solo on 'Midsummer New York' and apologising to the band; Yoko again performing a Japanese folk song, 'Sakura'; and Lennon and the Elephant's Memory band joining forces for a majestic version of 'Woman Is The Nigger Of The World'. Equally fearsome was the passion that Lennon and his band brought to his *Imagine* blues, 'It's So Hard'. What ought to have been a highlight, but wasn't, was the meeting between Lennon and Chuck Berry. The pair performed two of Chuck's classic hits, but spent most of 'Johnny B. Goode' each trying to sing harmony to the other's lead, while on 'Memphis' they were distracted by Yoko squalling along on the other side of the stage. Berry did not appear to be amused.

The surreal encounter between the Lennons and afternoon TV was broadcast between February 14 and 18 – by which time the couple had already begun work on their next studio album.

FEBRUARY 5, 1972: PERFORMING 'Luck Of The Irish' at Civil Rights demo

Outside the 44th Street offices of the British national airline, BOAC, the Lennons made their first protest about the events on the streets of Northern Ireland the previous weekend, when soldiers shot dead 13 civilians on what became known as 'Bloody Sunday'. John had already begun work on a song to mark his disgust; at this demo, however, he and Yoko performed 'Luck Of The Irish', before rushing back to their Bank Street apartment to dictate a press release for New York's news media – none of whom were in any great hurry to use it.

FEBRUARY 13 to MARCH 8, 1972: RECORDING 'Woman Is The Nigger Of The World'/'Sisters O Sisters'/'Attica State'/'John Sinclair'/'Born In A Prison'/'We're All Water'/'New York City'/'Sunday Bloody Sunday'/'Luck Of The Irish'/ 'Angela'/'Roll Over Beethoven'/'Honey Don't'/'Ain't That A Shame'/'My Babe'/'Not Fade Away'/'Send Me Some Lovin'/ untitled Yoko jam/'Whole Lotta Shakin' Goin' On'/'It'll Be Me'/'Honey Hush'/'Don't Be Cruel'/'Hound Dog'/'Caribbean'

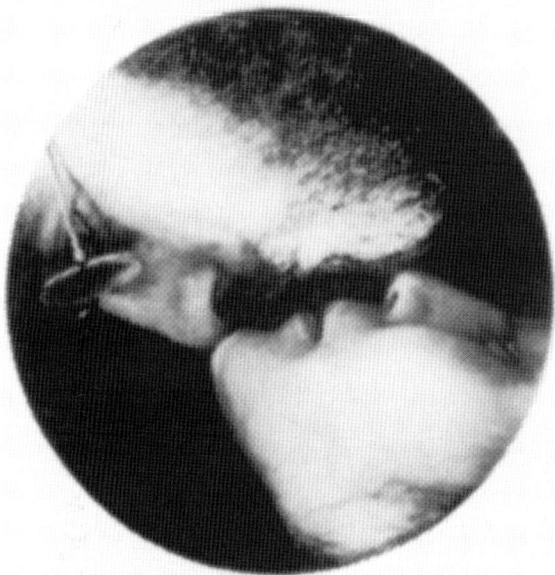

Bag Productions Inc.
Tittenhurst Park,
Ascot, Berkshire.
Ascot 23022

Bag Productions was the Lennons' declaration of independence from Apple and The Beatles. *(Rex Features)*

Bed Peace in Amsterdam: a public honeymoon in March 1969. *(Getty Images)*

Lennon recording his first solo single, 'Give Peace A Chance', in front of the world's media. *(Getty Images)*

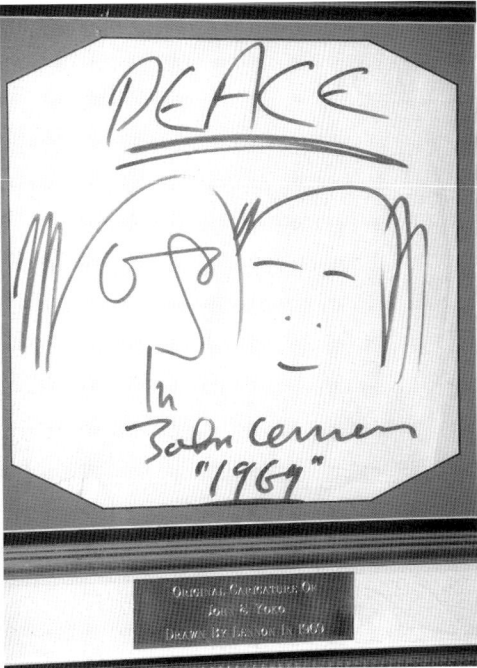

A typical Lennon caricature from 1969, transformed into a 1997 auction artefact. *(Nils Jorgensen/Rex Features)*

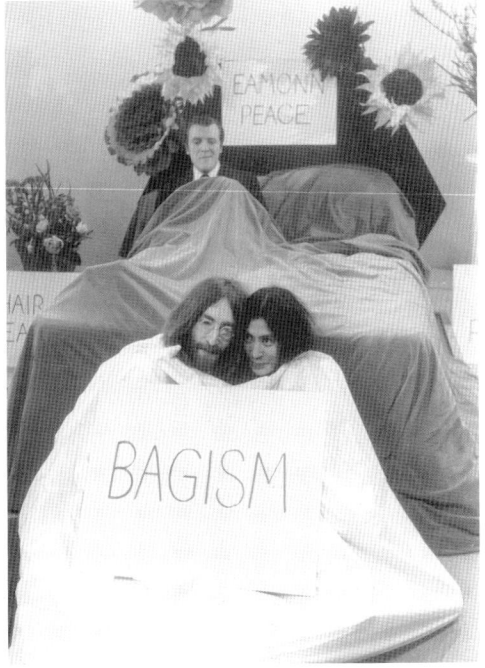

TV presenter Eamonn Andrews encounters Bagism in 1969. *(Getty Images)*

The Lennons' final UK live appearance, at London's Lyceum Ballroom in December 1969. *(Getty Images)*

War Is Over; and so too was the Toronto Peace Festival, abandoned soon after this December 1969 press conference. *(Bettmann/Corbis)*

January 1970: The opening of Lennon's Bag One exhibit in London. The Metropolitan Police were among the early visitors to this "obscene" display. *(Getty Images)*

Lennon at Abbey Road during one of The Beatles' final sessions, with Yoko never more than a few feet from his side. *(Tom Hanley/Redferns)*

One of the two *Top Of The Pops* performances Lennon filmed to promote his 'Instant Karma' single in February 1970. *(Chris Walter/WireImage)*

Radical chic personified: the Lennons take on the establishment in 1971. (Bettmann/Corbis)

July 1971: John and Yoko pose at Selfridges department store during their publicity campaign for her literary debut. (Hulton-Deutsch Collection/Corbis)

Chaos and creativity: the Lennons in their Tittenhurst Park mansion near Ascot. Note the extended version of their *Two Virgins* artwork sent to them by an admirer. (Tom Hanley/Redferns)

Lennon in the control room of the Ascot studio where he recorded the bulk of the *Imagine* album in 1971.
(Tom Hanley/Redferns)

Goodbye to all that: the Lennons at the English home
that they would soon leave forever.
(Tom Hanley/Redferns)

This Is Not Here: the Lennons fool with the exhibits
at Yoko's Syracuse art retrospective, October 1971.
(Bettmann/Corbis)

John and Yoko with Chuck Berry and Elephant's Memory on *The Mike Douglas Show* in February 1972. *(Jeff Albertson/Corbis)*

Lennon's last live performance, with Elton John at New York's Madison Square Garden in 1974. Backstage, the John and Yoko myth was about to be reborn. *(Stephen Morley/Rex Features)*

Lennon and Ono photographed during their visit to Japan, September 1978. *(LFI)*

A shortlived double fantasy on display in the New York streets where Lennon was killed in December 1980. *(LFI)*

For the third consecutive album, John called in Phil Spector to act as production co-ordinator – controlling the quality and mixing of the sound, rather than the entire session, as was his normal practice. Most of these songs and arrangements were set before the album was started: Spector's job was to take the political pills, and sugar them for American radio.

Spector's work aside, though, there was little hint of compromise on this package. It emerged eventually as a double set, with the December 1969 Lyceum and June 1971 Fillmore East recordings thrown together as an album entitled *Live Jam*. The set was presented as a newspaper in a sleeve and title parodying the *New York Times* ('Ono News That's Fit To Print'), an up-to-the-minute comment on the news of the day, seen through the eyes of a radical couple who had been moving in even more radical company. The artwork displayed such delights as a drawing of an oriental woman committing hari-kiri; and, in lighter mood, the heads of Richard Nixon and Mao Tse-Tung pasted on top of naked, dancing bodies. (The latter was censored in many American stores.) The lyrics, with their bold message of revolution and rebellion, occupied most of the front and back cover, however: this time, no one could ignore the Lennons' intentions, except by leaving the record in the stores, which is the way it turned out.

Some Time In New York City – its very title heightened the diary-like nature of the project – gathered together all of the Lennons' recent forays into politics. These included their protests about Attica State Prison and John Sinclair, the birth of John's feminism on 'Woman Is The Nigger Of The World', Yoko's call for women's solidarity, 'Sisters O Sisters', and John's sad tale about 'The Luck Of The Irish'. Two songs last heard in incomplete form were also present. 'New York City' was now a fully-fledged story-song, a series of snapshots of the Lennons in radical New York, alluding to their immigration problems; "if the man wants to shove us out/we gonna jump and shout", replying to the call of the city's harbour: "The Statue of Liberty said come!"

At the heart of the song was John's liberation at having escaped England, with its petty morality and racist attitude towards Yoko, and its refusal to see beyond the myth of The Beatles in approaching John's more recent work. New York City, a melting pot of races and ideas, had taken the Lennons to its heart: the song was Lennon's vote of thanks.

Elsewhere, 'JJ' had become 'People', and then in turn 'Angela'. This rapid shift of subject-matter rather diminished the emotional force of the song, a call of sympathy to Angela Davis, a Black Panther supporter on trial for kidnapping and murder. Though the message to Ms Davis was heartfelt enough, its lyrical content left a little to be desired; only speed-writing can have produced a couplet like, "They gave you coffee, they gave you tea/They gave you everything but the jailhouse key". But in Yoko's line, "There's a wind that never dies" (first included in her 1966 message, 'To The Wesleyan People'), the album found one of its rare links to the couple's work before they discovered politics.

Yoko also contributed 'Born In A Prison', a thoughtful ballad about the barriers that afflict, and make up, society. While Lennon had stripped away any metaphors or personal concerns from his new songs, Yoko was still approaching problems with poetry. On 'We're All Water', she simply rewrote her 1967 poem 'Water Talk', which had read: "You are water/I'm water/We're all water in different containers/That's why it's so easy to meet/Someday we'll evaporate together". Substitute "rivers" for "containers", and you effectively had the chorus of the song, to which Yoko added a series of amusing verses about the essential lack of difference between, for instance, Chairman Mao and Richard Nixon.

The album's most recent song was 'Sunday Bloody Sunday', a fiery rant about the Derry killings of late January, with Lennon acting as spokesman for the Irish people: "All you Anglo pigs and Scotties/Trying to colonise the North/You wave your bloody Union Jacks/But you know what they're worth". Sloganeering, no matter how sincere, rarely wins battles, however, and the Lennons gradually abandoned their support of the IRA in the wake of its terrorist attacks on civilian targets.

Much of the album was, it has to be said, simply crass; but it was saved by the sheer power and excitement of the music. The difference was partly Spector's production, which turned 'Sunday Bloody Sunday' into a swamp-rock inferno, 'The Luck Of The Irish' into a gentle, lush ballad and 'New York City' into a powerhouse rocker that The Rolling Stones would have killed for. And partly it was the sparks struck in the studio between Lennon, always a man for the spontaneous rather than the precise, and Elephant's Memory. In particular, Stan Bronstein's majestic sax playing on 'Woman Is The Nigger Of The World' was reminiscent of King Curtis's finest R&B performances. It topped off one of Lennon's most powerful and poignant vocal performances: proof of his sincerity to the cause of feminism.

Left to their own devices, though, Elephant's Memory wouldn't have recognised precision if it had offered them a record contract. The band's anarchic attitude to musical form was proved by a series of out-takes cut during the sessions – late-night romps through favourite Fifties rockers, which even enticed Phil Spector out from behind the production desk to shake a hand. "Phil, you're in the wrong room," Lennon sighed as a particularly chaotic jam around 'Not Fade Away' fell to pieces. Some Fats

Domino, Carl Perkins and Elvis Presley standards also bit the dust, with Elephant's Memory offering lively but completely uncoordinated support. And the band fell apart totally when Lennon launched into Sam Cooke's R&B tune, 'Send Me Some Lovin', clearly unable to work out the rudimentary chord changes.

Yoko made her presence felt on 'Don't Be Cruel' in inimitable fashion, spurring John to ask, "What are you doing there?" "Can you hear me?" Yoko replied innocently, to be greeted by the husbandly message: "You're louder than me, so shut up!" But that didn't stop her screaming her way through 'Hound Dog', while the band struggled to keep track of the song's three chords. Ironically, the most successful jamming came when they abandoned the 12-bar structure and followed Yoko in a funk screamfest that sounded like a distant cousin of 'Open Your Box'.

During the rock oldies, John broke briefly into Mitchell Torok's 'Caribbean', a Latino shuffle that prefigured Ringo's 'No No Song' by a couple of years. But such delights were the exception during these sessions, the pinnacle of the Lennons' brief career as political commentators and organisers.

FEBRUARY 28, 1972: PERFORMING 'Attica State' for *Aquarius*

In 1969, Lennon had commissioned writer and broadcaster Tony Palmer to write his full-length biography, and given him a two-week deadline. Somehow, Palmer met this impossible schedule, only for Lennon to decide that he didn't want to be immortalised in print after all.

Maybe Lennon felt guilty, or maybe he was just keen to sell his political messages wherever he could. Either way, when Palmer contacted him in early 1972 as the producer of LWT's London-based arts programme, *Aquarius*, Lennon agreed to take time out of the sessions for *Some Time In New York City*, and film a piece for the show.

He used the opportunity to announce that he planned to schedule a music/politics tour for later in 1972, to coincide and hopefully influence the US Presidential Election; and in the same breath he complained about America's immigration officials, who were trying to kick him out of the country. The connection between the two seems not to have occurred to him.

Accompanying himself on dobro, Lennon also performed as much of 'Attica State' as he could remember, before launching into a revamp of the speech about apathy that he'd given at the John Sinclair benefit two months earlier. People were thinking, he lamented, "that there's nothing to do and

233

it's all over". The solution was to "get out there and change their heads". The movement wasn't over, he concluded: this was "only the inception of the revolution".

EARLY APRIL 1972: SUNDANCE publishes 'It's Never Too Late To Start From The Start'

Late in 1971, Lennon was invited to take part in a charity auction to raise funds for the launching of *Sundance*, a radical journal concerned with the meeting between politics and art. Editor Craig Pyes subsequently asked him and Yoko to contribute to the magazine's first issue. In fact, the Lennons agreed to host a regular column in *Sundance*, headed – what else? – 'Imagine'.

Their initial column was written in the early weeks of 1972, and then included in the magazine's first issue in April. It had been written around the same time as Yoko had composed a piece for the *New York Times* on 'The Feminization Of Society:' the *Sundance* feature shared a similar tone, so it's safe to assume that it was Yoko who actually wrote it, with John merely submitting ideas. Like her evocative song, 'What A Bastard The World Is', the article pointed out the difference for the average working-woman between her gut acceptance of the principles of radical feminism, and the difficulty she had incorporating them into her own life. From a writer who usually favoured the conceptual rather than the specific, this was a rare show of insight and sympathy, which went far beyond John's slightly simplistic rhetoric in 'Woman Is The Nigger Of The World'.

John's major contribution to the *Sundance* spread was a series of pencil drawings, off-the-cuff sketches of women engaged in daily life who were being oppressed by men. The couple returned to the pages of *Sundance* two issues later.

SPRING 1972: COMPOSES limerick for *The Gay Liberation Book*

Sexual liberation being the message of the moment, John didn't hesitate when asked to contribute to an anthology of homosexual writings. His offering was a limerick: "Why make it so sad to be gay?/Doing your own thing is OK/Our bodies are our own/So leave us alone/Go play with yourself – today". There was even a drawing of a nude male perched carefree on a cloud to match.

APRIL/MAY 1972: PRODUCING 'Liberation Special'/'Baddest Of The Mean'/'Cryin' Blacksheep Blues'/'Chuck 'N' Bo'/'Gypsy Wolf'/'Madness'/'Life'/ 'Wind Ridge'/'Power Boogie'/'Local Plastic Ono Band' for Elephant's Memory

The New York rock 'n' roll of Elephant's Memory had made them an ideal back-up band for the equally earthy songs on *Some Time In New York City*. To return the favour, John and Yoko signed them up to Apple and produced an album for them, a heady mix of raunchy rock, R&B, and the street-ass feel which had attracted Lennon in the first place.

As ever in the production chair, Lennon simply recorded the sound the band made, doing nothing to embellish it beyond adding a little guitar to 'Power Boogie' and 'Cryin' Blacksheep Blues', percussion to 'Chuck 'N' Bo' and electric piano to 'Wind Ridge'. In addition, he and Yoko turned up in the vocal chorus on several songs, Yoko doing her best child-like singalong over the fade of 'Local Plastic Ono Band', while each half of the couple had a solo line on the stompin' 'Power Boogie', the album's strongest track. Much of the rest was standard bar-room fare: the Elephants boasted a superb sax player in Stan Bronstein, but no vocalist to match him, and for the most part they sounded like a down-market version of the J. Geils Band, or a less vicious MC5. By 1972 standards, though, the *Elephant's Memory* album was no slouch, and it did cement the band's image as, indeed, the Local Plastic Ono Band.

MAY 1972: EDITING *Ten For Two*

The movie of the John Sinclair benefit was never released, and the Lennons' completion of the film seemed more like a gesture of dismissal than a step towards making it public. After *Some Time In New York City*, in fact, the Lennons felt the heat of John's deportation case – fuelled on the surface by his drugs conviction in Britain back in 1968, but covertly inspired by the Republican Party's fear that Lennon might lead political demonstrations against their national convention. The rumour had been sparked by the posturing of some of their radical friends, who had already set Lennon up as their figurehead. What's certain, though, is that John was intending to take Elephant's Memory on the road, together with Jim Keltner and Phil Spector, employing David Peel as an advance party to drum up support in each new town. The tour was roughly scheduled for mid-summer, and would no doubt have been an amalgam of music, politics and play-politics, an underground cabaret for the anti-Vietnam movement. When the lawyers began making threatening noises, however, John and Yoko quietly drew back from the fray, and the Convention and the Republicans were left in relative peace.

MAY 5, 1972: PERFORMING 'Woman Is The Nigger Of The World'/'We're All Water' on *The Dick Cavett Show*

In retrospect, the major event on this evening talk-show appearance was Lennon's claim that he was under government surveillance as a result of his unresolved immigration case. At the time, that was dismissed as laughable paranoia, "The ravings of a clown," as Phil Ochs said in another context. The controversy in May 1972 was about the title of 'Woman Is The Nigger Of The World', and the offence it might or might not cause to the black community. Cavett was forced by the network to recite a mild disclaimer before the Lennons performed the song, though Yoko's full-blooded rendition of the mighty 'We're All Water' needed no such apologies. This show (aired on May 11) brought the Lennons' current sequence of TV appearances to a close; subsequent performances would be less controversial.

LATE JUNE 1972: PRODUCING David Peel's 'Amerika'

In the same month that *Some Time In New York City* was released, the Lennons briefly began work on a follow-up to David Peel's Apple album *The Pope Smokes Dope*, which had sold in its dozens rather than thousands since its release two months earlier. 'Amerika', featuring Yoko on backing vocals alongside The Lower East Side, proved to be only result of these sessions. Difficulties at home, with the US Immigration Service, and in England with the running of Apple, forced Lennon to abandon all thought of Apple projects outside those by himself and Yoko, and the Peel album was cancelled. 'Amerika' was finally released on Peel's *John Lennon For President* album in 1980, less than a month before his one-time producer was shot dead. By then, Peel had already become notorious for making the most of his Lennon connections, having renamed his group The Super Apple Band, and issued records such as *Bring Back The Beatles*.

SUMMER 1972 TO 1975: SONGWRITING sessions with Bruce Bierman; making home recordings

Just as this book was being completed, new evidence surfaced of a possible set of previously undocumented Lennon compositions. The story was as follows: after Lennon produced the album *The Pope Smokes Dope* for David Peel and The Lower East Side, he accidentally bumped into 17-year-old band member Bruce Bierman on several occasions in Manhattan. According to Bierman, Lennon interpreted this as a sign that the two men should get to know each other better, and they soon became close friends, staying in touch until Lennon's murder in 1980.

This relationship was not documented in any Lennon biography, but as Bierman told me, "There was no quicker way to end a friendship with John than advertising it to the outside world". Bierman claimed that he and Lennon bonded over similarities in their backgrounds, and met each other regularly during the mid-Seventies, either in Central Park or at places like Bierman's mother's apartment. As Bierman was also a musician, he said that they inevitably began to make music together, and gradually amassed a collection of co-written songs. These were created solely for their own entertainment, rather than with any thought of making a record.

As an example of how they came about, Bierman recalled watching an old black-and-white movie called *Million Dollar Baby* with John, in which actor Ronald Reagan supposedly 'composed' a song about Central Park. "John said, 'That's awful, we can do better than that'," Bierman remembered. "He asked me if I had a piano, and I said, 'No, but I knew where we could get access to one, at my old school, Vanderchild High School in the Bronx. So we snuck in there, where there were one or two grand pianos in an otherwise empty music room, and we wrote a song of our own. John began banging out chords on the piano, and we came up with the chorus line, 'Meet me in Central Park', because that's where we often used to meet."

Bierman said that he owns a number of reel-to-reel home recordings of himself and Lennon performing, among them a version of the song eventually released on Lennon's *Anthology* as 'Help Me To Help Myself'. He explained that the sound quality of these tapes made them unsuitable for release without heavy overdubbing, in the style of The Beatles' 'Free As A Bird'. He first announced the existence of this archive to *Billboard* magazine in the early Nineties, but only began to record his own versions of the songs in recent years. He intended to release a record, provisionally entitled *Message*, later in 2005; the story may indeed have broken to the international media by the time you read this.

At the time of going to press, Bierman's official website (www.brucebierman.com) listed the following songs as being Lennon/Bierman collaborations: 'Central Park', 'Message From Heaven', 'Great To Be Back', 'Surprise', 'There Has To Be Peace (On Earth)', 'Love In A Dream', 'What Do You Know', 'I'm Here For You', 'Hold All My Love',

'I KnowYou', 'Valentine', 'What Am I To Do', 'The Ballad Of John', 'Tonight's The Night', 'Don't Worry' and 'That Girl'. The site also featured downloads of Bierman's performances of several of these compositions, 'Central Park' and 'I'm Here For You' being the most intriguing. Bierman claimed that he had replicated the arrangements that he and Lennon had formulated for the songs in the Seventies: these included a mock-'Day Tripper' riff to power 'Great To Be Back', for instance. Interested parties are advised to check out the website, listen to the music, and make up their own minds about its authenticity. Meanwhile, Bierman said that he still hoped to be able to let the public hear the original Lennon recordings eventually, once possible legal problems had been sorted out. Stranger things have happened ...

AUGUST 1972: SUNDANCE publishes 'Some Time In New York City' column

The Lennons' second 'Imagine' column in *Sundance*, again primarily written by Yoko, was a defence of the new, political element in their work on *Some Time In New York City*. John's contribution was the introductory section, a brief explanation of their new album. "The songs we wrote and sang are subjects we and most people talk about," he claimed, "and it was done in the tradition of minstrels (singing reporters) who sang about their times and what was happening."

He insisted that "This is not a 'new phase' John and Yoko", a sarcastic reference to the boast in the sleeve-notes to the last Beatles album, *Let It Be*. "It does not necessarily mean that every record we make will be 'political'. To us, it is a direct descendant of Yoko's early peace events and *Grapefruit* (pre-John), and also John's 'satire' in *Spaniard In The Works* and onward. It isn't a trend but a thought, a song." Lennon ended his piece by claiming that the *Live Jam* album included in the *New York City* package was "free", ignoring the fact that the set cost a dollar more than any other record on the market in 1972.

Yoko later contributed to a third issue of *Sundance*, this time without any obvious help from John. Thereafter the magazine joined a proud tradition of radical journalism by folding within a year.

EARLY AUGUST 1972: FILMING performances of 'Woman Is The Nigger Of The World'/'Fools Like Me'/'Caribbean'/'Peggy Sue'/'Maybe Baby'/'Well (Baby Please Don't Go)'/'Rock Island Line'

TV investigative reporter Geraldo Rivera set the *One To One* concerts in motion, when in his usual flamboyant style he exposed the callous treatment of mentally retarded children at the Willowbrook Hospital in New York State. In late July, Rivera called on the Lennons in California and suggested they help him stage a benefit concert for the kids at the end of August. Despite the fact that they were hiding out on the West Coast in an attempt to kick another bout of methadone addiction, they agreed, and were willing to be filmed with Rivera in the initial announcement of the show.

Rivera also took a guided tour around San Francisco with the Lennons, tracked by a TV camera, even riding a cable car to Fisherman's Wharf while John playfully interviewed some of his fellow passengers. Lennon then agreed to film an impromptu music session in their hotel suite. Yoko held Rivera's microphone, while Lennon picked at his Gibson Les Paul and cruised through some erratic versions of his favourite oldies – everything from the old Jerry Lee Lewis flipside, 'Fools Like Me', to Mitchell Torok's 'Caribbean'. But the keeper from the session was 'Woman Is The Nigger Of The World', with Yoko adding harmonies to the chorus and throwing in sardonic parodies of male sexism between lines. This remains the only place where you can hear her telling John to "show us your tits, man". But the performance ended with Yoko screaming out, "pain, help us", as the horror of drug withdrawal cut through even the couple's most passionate political message.

AUGUST 18 to 29, 1972: REHEARSING with Elephant's Memory for 'One To One' concert; recordings made during rehearsals include 'Instant Karma'/'Give Peace A Chance'/'Cold Turkey'/'Hound Dog'/'Long Tall Sally'/'New York City'/'It's So Hard'/'Woman Is The Nigger Of The World'/'Well Well Well'/'Come Together'/'Honky Tonk'/'Mind Train'/'We're All Water'/'Move On Fast'/'Sisters O Sisters'/'Unchained Melody'/'Born In A Prison'/'Mother'/'Open Your Box'/'Roll Over Beethoven'/'Don't Worry Kyoko'/'Tequila'/various instrumentals and jams/various radio and TV spots; also recording solo performances of 'Well (Baby Please Don't Go)'/'Rock Island Line'/'Maybe Baby' for TV announcement of show

When tickets were already on sale, Lennon – as terrified of public performance as he had been in Toronto three years earlier – attempted to opt out of the show. Rivera pulled him around, and after Yoko's attempt to persuade Paul and Linda McCartney to join them for the performance had failed, the Lennons called in Elephant's Memory and began rehearsing for John's only full-scale concert performance after he left The Beatles.

To be precise, there were actually two performances, as the first sold out as soon as Rivera had screened his early August footage of John performing an acoustic medley of Fifties rockers. When the second show was fixed, another set of commercials were filmed and taped, some of them featuring the Lennons and the band chanting the news in unison, others with Rivera making his speech while John and the band kicked into 'New York City' behind him. "You ARE The Plastic Ono Band", Lennon reassured the members of Elephant's Memory when they didn't get a mention in one of the ads.

The Lennons hired out Butterfly Studios in New York, and then the Fillmore East concert hall, to get the feel of playing in public again. All their rehearsals were taped, but though a tantalising list of songs was attempted, few of the performances lived up to the fantasy. Yoko steered the band through a ferocious version of 'Mind Train', before trying to throw oil onto the fire, by announcing that on the night her songs "may go on and on". An exasperated Lennon explained that this wasn't the kind of concert where she could veer off at a tangent for hours: "they need an ending". This annoyed his wife, who responded: "It's my song and I want to do it more my way".

Meanwhile, John was petrified of losing his voice before the shows, so he mumbled his way through most of the rehearsals. He took the songs an octave lower than in concert, and only let himself go on a fiery, intense 'It's So Hard', and a raving assault on 'Long Tall Sally', every bit the equal of McCartney's performances of the same song. Ironically, that number didn't make the show, where the only non-Lennon/Ono composition heard was 'Hound Dog'. Only one Beatles number was considered, 'Come Together'. "It's something very simple," Lennon told Elephant's Memory keyboardist Adam Ippolito as he struggled to perfect the original keyboard lick, "otherwise Paul couldn't have played it."

The rehearsals also saw Lennon changing the word 'nigger' to 'nipple' in one of his recent songs – Freudian habits die hard – and investigating the possibilities of turning 'Give Peace A Chance' into a reggae singalong, something he'd tried rather less successfully at the 1969 Toronto show. Most of the surviving tapes, however, show the musicians practising intros and endings, unable for once to rely on the studio trickery of Phil Spector to fade them gracefully away.

AUGUST 30, 1972: PERFORMING (first show) 'New York City'/'It's So Hard'/'Move On Fast'/'Woman Is The Nigger Of The World'/'Sisters O Sisters'/'Well Well Well'/'Born In A Prison'/'Instant Karma!'/'Mother'/'We're All Water'/'Come Together'/'Imagine'/'Open Your Box'/'Cold Turkey'/'Don't Worry Kyoko'/'Hound Dog'/'Give Peace A Chance'; (second show) 'New York City'/'It's So Hard'/'Sisters O Sisters'/'Woman Is The Nigger Of The World'/'Move On Fast'/'Well Well Well'/ 'Instant Karma!'/'Mother'/'We're All Water'/'Born In A Prison'/ 'Come Together'/'Imagine'/'Open Your Box'/'Cold Turkey'/ 'Hound Dog'/'Give Peace A Chance'

At lunchtime on August 30, 1972, thousands of handicapped kids attended the One To One festival in Central Park. John and Yoko had already purchased $50,000 of tickets to allow the children to attend the afternoon show at Madison Square Garden, where – after performances from Sha Na Na, Roberta Flack and Stevie Wonder – the Lennons and Elephant's Memory played for a little over an hour. That evening, they played a second set, slightly altering their repertoire from the afternoon. Together, the two shows raised $180,000 on the night, plus another $350,000 for the sale of rights to the concert to ABC TV, who screened a cut-down version of the show, nominally produced by John and Yoko's Joko Films company, on December 14. But the live album of the show, which John and Yoko had hoped to have in the shops by Christmas, took some 14 years to materialise. It was stymied by a combination of exhaustion, conflict and political cowardice/wisdom on the part of the Lennons, who were afraid that any public act might inflame their precarious immigration position.

The shows themselves were a triumph. Even the hollow mix of the afternoon concert that Yoko primarily used for her 1986 video and LP releases, *John Lennon Live In New York*, couldn't hide the power and ease of the performance. The Lennons and Elephant's Memory caught fire together, stripping the *Some Time In New York City* songs down to basics, and destroying none of the stark strength of the Plastic Ono Band material with their extra instrumentation. Though the afternoon show was a little rusty in places – "Welcome to the rehearsal," Lennon quipped at one point – it still had a series of climaxes. There was another gritty run at 'It's So Hard', a no-nonsense, sleek 'Instant Karma!', a throat-searing 'Mother', with Lennon close to primalling on stage, and an equally intense 'Cold Turkey', as John screamed his way towards public catharsis. 'Mother', introduced as being "from one of those albums I made since I left The Rolling Stones", was dedicated to "99% of the parents, alive or half dead". After the show, Lennon was ecstatic: "It was just the same kind of feeling as when The Beatles used to really get into it," he crowed.

The evening show, chosen by ABC TV for their coverage, was even more striking. The sole Beatles' song, 'Come Together', was a gritty highlight, transformed into a churning cauldron of R&B licks. "Come together/right now/stop the war", Lennon cried in the choruses, showing he'd not yet sacrificed all his radicalism. For the first, but not the last, time Lennon widened the lyrics of 'Imagine', to conjure up "a brotherhood and sisterhood of man". Clearly his wife's feminist teaching was beginning to stick. A rowdy cover of 'Hound Dog' closed the show in rollicking style, with Lennon finding space to shout out, "Elvis, I love ya!" between lines. And the finale, featuring the musicians and guest Phil Spector wearing construction-style hard hats, was a drawn-out version of 'Give Peace A Chance', half funk and half reggae. It stretched for ten minutes or more, with the audience clanging the percussion instruments left in front of every seat, and Stevie Wonder scatting a series of answer lyrics to the endless choruses. Legend has it that the audience left the Garden as one, and continued chanting 'Give Peace A Chance' for an hour or so in the streets outside. As the TV coverage showed, it was that kind of show.

SEPTEMBER 6, 1972: PERFORMING 'Imagine'/'Now Or Never'/'Give Peace A Chance' at the Jerry Lewis Telethon

Just a week after the One To One shows, the Lennons and the Elephants were back on stage, performing on a charity telethon staged by comedian Jerry Lewis to raise money for the disabled. Radical critics protested that the Lennons were treating every charitable cause as one, and that the telethon was as much a part of the problem as a solution. John and Yoko believed in the cause, and saw the chance to repair their image in the eyes of the great American public. John again toasted the "brotherhood and sisterhood of man" on 'Imagine', before Yoko premièred 'Now Or Never' – not an Elvis Presley hit, this time, but a new composition which neatly summed up the Ono philosophy: "Dream you dream alone is only a dream/But dream we dream together is reality". Finally, Lennon led off another rowdy version of 'Give Peace A Chance' – "This is reggae, baby, like they do it in Jamaica" – and the Lennons' performance was over. They never appeared on stage together again.

Yoko Ono chose to include an extract from the telethon on the Lennon *Anthology* CD set. Inexplicably, she opted not for any of the songs they performed, but for Jerry Lewis's embarrassing stage banter after the Lennons had finished playing.

OCTOBER 28-30, 1972: APPEARING AT New York Avant-Garde Festival

After contributing 'Wind Piece' and 'Human Maze' to the 1971 festival of experimental art, the Lennons returned to Charlotte Moorman's ninth annual event, most of which was staged on a ship in the New York docks. The ship was also supposed to travel to locations in upstate New York, but logistical problems made that impossible.

In the event, some of the festival was obviously held on dry land, as photographs exist of the couple performing 'Silent Piece'. This comprised Lennon playing air guitar, while Yoko screamed silently into a microphone. Their appearance formed part of a memorial concert to the radical theatre and audio-visual artist Ken Dewey, who had been killed in a plane crash earlier in the year.

Lennon's appearance at this festival marked his last public link with the avant-garde in general, and the Fluxus movement in particular. Yoko continued to make regular contributions to Moorman's festival through the Seventies, the last documented occasion being in 1978. But aside from the Nutopia episode in April 1973, all of Lennon's interest in experimental art dissipated as his relationship with Yoko soured. When the couple were reunited in the mid-Seventies, they abandoned front-line artistic participation in favour of seclusion from the world (Lennon) and corporate business affairs (Yoko).

LATE OCTOBER to EARLY NOVEMBER 1972: PRODUCING and recording 'Yangyang'/'Death Of Samantha'/'I Want My Love To Rest Tonight'/'What Did I Do?'/'Have You Seen A Horizon Lately'/'Approximately Infinite Universe'/'Peter The Dealer'/'Song For John'/'Catman'/'What A Bastard The World Is'/'Waiting For The Sunrise'/'I Felt Like Smashing My Face In A Clear Glass Window'/'Winter Song'/'Kite Song'/'What A Mess'/'Shiranakatta'/'Air Talk'/'I Have A Woman Inside My Soul'/'Move On Fast'/'Now Or Never'/'Is Winter Here To Stay?'/'Looking Over From My Hotel Window'

Neither John Lennon nor Yoko Ono were noted for their willingness to take second place in any artistic endeavour, so their relationship was bound

243

to produce personal collisions as often as cultural ones. While John was the songwriter, Yoko the conceptual artist and film-maker, the marriage could survive: each partner could handle minor incursions into their own territory. When Yoko struck a seam of writing creativity that threatened Lennon's musical dominance, trouble lay ahead.

Since making *Some Time In New York City* in February 1972, Lennon had made no further records; he hadn't even completed any songs. By contrast, Yoko approached the sessions for her next solo album with enough material for two records, and songs to spare. What's more, this wasn't the avant-grade soundscape work of yore: Yoko had channelled her feminist beliefs into a set of riveting, intensely personal material, that both attacked male domination and displayed empathy with the insecurity which lay behind it. By any standards, *Approximately Infinite Universe* was a remarkable album.

In the studio, Lennon supported his wife as she recorded 'Catman', a playful rallying cry for a bunch of castrating feminists; 'What A Bastard The World Is', with its portrayal of liberation held back by the economic and emotional contract of marriage; and 'What A Mess', a hilarious satire on men's attempts to deny abortion rights to 'their' women. John acted as co-producer of the project, translating some of Yoko's more conceptual requests to the band (Elephant's Memory, on their last Lennon project), and pulling off some remarkable reverb guitar work on the scorching 'Move On Fast' and the blues jam, 'Is Winter Here To Stay?'. But this was Yoko's project, a brilliant marriage of the personal and the political, and as thought-provoking a sequence of songs as the feminist movement has ever produced. Lennon had nothing to offer in reply.

DECEMBER 1972: PERFORMING on *Flip Side*

At the end of a year when the Lennons had become a regular sideshow on American TV, Yoko plugged her forthcoming *Approximately Infinite Universe* album on WNEW TV, while Lennon stayed a virtual spectator by her side, lending only the briefest of musical support alongside Elephant's Memory as well as being interviewed about his wife's work. It was a miniature tableau of their relative artistic power as 1973 dawned.

MARCH 13, 1973: RECORDING 'I'm The Greatest'

At the end of 1972, the Lennons moved into an exclusive apartment in the Dakota Building on New York's Central Park West. Still waging war against

US immigration, and with Yoko also fighting a legal battle to win custody of her daughter, Kyoko, the couple were in little mood to perform. Yoko continued to write; John mooched around the house, and snapped at anyone who came too close.

Then in the spring of 1973, an invitation to California beckoned, in the shape of Ringo Starr, then beginning work on his third solo album. He had sent out a request to all three of his former Beatle colleagues for new material; Lennon had little in reserve, so he dug out his rehearsal tapes of 'I'm The Greatest' from February 1971, and began to tailor the lyrics towards Ringo, rather than himself. The experience was clearly liberating, both musically and psychologically, as the result was both the highlight of the *Ringo* album and the first public exhibition of Lennon's humour in years.

In the studio, Lennon set Ringo behind the drum-kit, George Harrison on guitar and Klaus Voormann on bass, while he played piano and tried to lay down a basic track and guide vocal. It took about 12 passes in all, most of them false starts, before Lennon was satisfied: after each one, he simply counted the band straight back in, as if frightened to lose the momentum of the moment. "I was the greatest show on earth," he slurred in his best Bronx accent, working laconically through his tongue-in-cheek history of The Beatles, complete with references to 'Billy Shears' from the *Pepper* album – later emphasised by producer Richard Perry, who threw in bursts of *Pepper*-style laughter.

None of Lennon's takes was that spectacular, or involved, but they served their purpose: they gave Perry a basic track to build on, and Ringo a sympathetic voice in the cans as he laid down his lead vocal. Ringo only made one change to John's lyrics, playing down his role by singing "I was *in* the greatest show on earth".

APRIL 1, 1973: CREATING a conceptual country

The couple began April with a press conference to announce the formation of Nutopia, in the rather unrealistic hope that the United Nations would recognise the existence of this conceptual country and grant the Lennons asylum as its diplomatic representatives. Lennon repeated the manifesto – supposedly issued from the Nutopian Embassy at One White Street, NYC – on the inner sleeve of his *Mind Games* album, which also contained Nutopia's (entirely silent) national anthem, but otherwise this event was never mentioned again. Meanwhile, the couple's relationship had reached crisis point. At the Nutopia press conference, the couple waved the pure white flag of their newly created homeland – "the white flag of surrender", they claimed, "a surrender to peace". Yoko later described her husband as "a man who surrendered to the world, life and finally to the Universe". But in April 1973 his surrender seemed more of an admission of defeat than a voluntary gesture.

CHAPTER 13

May 1973 to April 1975

"Strange days indeed", as Lennon sang later, were what awaited him after he stepped away from politics and, very soon, from his marriage to Yoko as well. What followed has entered the Lennon myth as 'the lost weekend', a period of exhilarating indulgence and crushing self-doubt, that produced some of the strongest work of his career, and nearly caused him to drown in self-pity. The turmoil ended with a return to the comforting arms of Yoko, the promise of a new son, and the hope that the Lennons might be able to regain the creative partnership that had proved to be so fruitful between 1969 and 1971.

MAY/JUNE/JULY 1973: RECORDING home demos of 'Intuition'/'How'/'God'/'I Know (I Know)'/'So Many'/ 'The Boat Song'/'Just Because'/'Steel And Glass'/'Rock And Roll People'/'Tight A$'/'Meat City'

The Lennons spent the first half of 1973 in virtual retreat from the world, appearing only at a couple of low-key political demonstrations in New York. Yoko continued writing the songs for her next album, *Feeling The Space*, and also built up a backlog of material that she would still be dipping into a decade later. And after a year of inactivity, John finally regained some contact with his muse. In late spring, he recorded his first home demos since January 1972, premièring two of the compositions he taped later in the year for *Mind Games*, plus another that would be recorded during the same sessions, but then left unissued for a further thirteen years.

As ever, Lennon's songs were a vivid insight into his state of mind. He no longer burned with the certainties of 1970 or 1972; his life was dominated by the day-to-day struggle of maintaining a relationship in a stifling atmosphere, cut off from the world. John and Yoko's romance was turning sour; and not for the first time, John pleaded guilty in song. 'I Know (I Know)', built around a more restrained version of the kind of guitar riff that had once powered mid-Sixties' Beatles singles, was a rather laboured ballad, which had to strain for its melodic effect. But its lyrics were unashamedly autobiographical, portraying a man forced to come to terms with his own inadequacies, "only learning, to tell the trees from wood". "Today, I love you more than yesterday", he sang hopefully in the chorus, a slice of the wish-fulfilment that Yoko had always recommended as a remedy for disaster. But the melancholy spirit of the music and the abject submissiveness of the tone, made the optimism sound misplaced.

John cut a series of near-identical acoustic demos of 'I Know (I Know)', already virtual blueprints for the finished record, and then spent even longer overdubbing a second layer of vocals. Next, on the same tape, he threw himself into the more arduous business of composing. He began with a line or three from the Elvis Presley rockabilly tune, 'Just Because', and busked through directionless chord sequences for several minutes. Eventually he found his way out of the woods and into the new landscape of 'Steel And Glass'. The melody line was there, and a couple of lines of lyric, but it was a long way from becoming the vicious diatribe found on the following year's *Walls And Bridges*. And then the doodling resumed, with Lennon repeating the same two-line, two-chord fragment over and over, crooning "so many stars, so many suns", without ever discovering an exit line or purpose. The tape continued with Lennon losing concentration and launching into a series of novelty songs – a doo-wop tune with the line, "I threw my underwear into the snow," a variation on 'On Top Of Old Smokey', and finally a sea shanty, before the reel finally ran to a close.

'Intuition' was thankfully more focused. At this point, Lennon had written the verses and the tune for the chorus of this jaunty piano tune, but no hook-line. It marked the opposite end of the spiral of optimism to 'I Know (I Know)', with John having "confirmed an old suspicion/it's good to be alive". Again, though, there was a hint that he was saying it was true to make it true. One demo of the song found Lennon playfully dragging the middle section of 'How' (1971) and the final verse of 'God' into the same piano rhythm, like some lounge bar crooner.

Two murky electric guitar demos for 'Meat City' also illustrated the way in which Lennon would cannibalise his own ideas. Elements of the song were pulled from his 1971 composition, 'Shoeshine', crossed with a little of 'Pill' from around the same period. Yet at this stage, the song – which sounded as if it could have developed into a Muddy Waters blues boogie – also contained the distinctive riff that would eventually surface at the end of another tune that was in the air at this point, 'Steel And Glass'.

'Rock And Roll People' was auditioned like a Bo Diddley work tape, all chunky electric rhythm with knee-slaps for percussion. The boogie tune had playful lyrics to match, a run of nonsense images that could have been borrowed from the pages of *In His Own Write*. On the composing tape, it was followed by an early pass at the very similar 'Tight A$' – though at this point the latter was introduced by the distinctive guitar lick that would later underpin 'Beef Jerky' on *Walls And Bridges*. Lennon made vague plans to record all these songs later in the summer, and started to wade through his earlier composing tapes in the hope of finding something else worth finishing off.

JUNE 3, 1973: PERFORMING at the International Feminist Conference

Yoko Ono had been a feminist pioneer, both as an artist and a wife, since the dawn of the Seventies. So she was a natural participant in the first International Feminist Conference, staged at Harvard University, in Cambridge, Massachusetts. While Lennon was easily persuaded by interviewers to drift away from the subject at hand – telling one reporter that he was finding that songwriting was "getting to be work, it's ruining the music" – Yoko never let her attention waver. She treated the other delegates to a brief musical performance, delivering an intense rendition of her new song, 'Coffin Car', over Lennon's guitar accompaniment. As the *Feeling The Space* CD documented, she introduced the song by recalling how supposed friends had encouraged her to smother her own artistic identity beneath her husband's when they first met. Lennon, now a pale creative shadow of his wife, must have grimaced at the irony of the situation.

JUNE to JULY 1973: YOKO ONO RECORDING 'She Hits Back'/'Woman Power'/'Men Men Men'/'Left Turn's The Right Turn'/'It's Been Very Hard'/'Potbelly Rocker'/'Mildred Mildred'

Less than eight months after completing *Approximately Infinite Universe*, Yoko had amassed enough new songs to begin recording another album. The initial sessions saw Lennon adding guitar to her feminist anthems, 'She Hits Back' and 'Woman Power', while on the sly shuffle 'Men Men Men', he heard his wife recite: "J–O–H–N–N–Y, God's little gift to a woman", knowing full well she was taking the piss. He even made a cameo appearance at the end of the song, as the archetypal henpecked husband responding to his wife's call. All three songs appeared on Yoko's *Feeling The Space* LP, while several out-takes from these sessions – including the all too pointed 'Potbelly Rocker' – later surfaced on the *Onobox* set. Lennon also accompanied his wife as she demoed 'Mildred Mildred', another wry dissection of gender politics.

AUGUST 1973: RECORDING 'Mind Games'/'Tight A$'/'Aisumasen'/'One Day At A Time'/'Bring On The Lucie'/'Intuition'/'Out The Blue'/'Only People'/'I Know (I Know)'/'You Are Here'/'Meat City'/'Rock And Roll People'; possibly singing on Crowbar's 'Rocky Mountain Tragedy'

The start of the sessions for *Mind Games* was preceded by a fortnight of hectic pre-production work, in which Lennon wrote several songs from scratch, and pulled three more together from left-over fragments. It is rumoured that John and Yoko both dropped into a session by the Canadian band Crowbar that was being produced by Jack Douglas at the Record Plant East studio in New York, and added background vocals to one of their songs, though this cannot be confirmed.

But what is certain is that John then went into the same studio, cut his new songs and completed the final mixes, all in around two weeks – a period that also marked the beginning of his relationship with his PA, May Pang, and of his 18-month separation from Yoko. She had apparently suggested that John begin an affair with May; then, just as suddenly, he was living with May, Yoko having kicked him out. Act one of 'The Ballad Of John And Yoko' was over.

The circumstances might have dragged Lennon's demons to the surface; but he chose to keep them hidden, acting instead like the professional tunesmith he had always tried to avoid becoming, churning out John Lennon songs to meet a contract. Ironically, in view of their marital circumstances, Lennon's choice of musicians was guided by his wife: "I used the same group Yoko used on her album. I heard her finished product and said, 'Hey, they're good', so I used the same ones exactly." Even so, *Mind Games* was the least inspired of his song collections, the overwhelming mood one of ennui. The title of the album said it all: Lennon was playing at being an artist, where in the past his life and his art had been virtually interchangeable. With the two distanced by his lack of emotional involvement, the music lost its personality. What remained was high-class hackwork, just the kind of fakery with which he and McCartney had filled Beatles albums like *Help!* when they had been under other kinds of pressure.

Nothing on *Mind Games* was more reminiscent of The Beatles' more formulaic moments than 'Intuition'. It was immediately appealing, and might have worked as a single, but beneath its playful charm there was little but good intentions and the power of positive thinking.

The 'Mind Games' title track itself was one of the album's more convincing musical moments, based as it was around a hook that dated back to the start of the decade. Lennon had long since abandoned his idea of turning the 'Make Love Not War' riff into another 'Give Peace A Chance', but the tune and a fragment of the original lyrics survived onto the 1973 cut, with John busking the 1970 chorus over the fade-out. He based the new words on a book called *Mind Games* by Robert Masters and Jean Houston. Like Janov's *The Primal Scream*, this was a guide to mental fulfilment, but through gentle consciousness-raising rather than violent therapy. Lennon effectively précised the book, but though he coaxed a remarkable performance from his band, and made his ascending guitar riff sound like an orchestra, lines like "Millions of mind guerrillas/Putting their soul power to the karmic wheel" meant that 'Mind Games' never transcended its literary origins. And as an early take of the song revealed, Lennon was willing to try out any vaguely spiritual cliché that would fit, with couplets such as "Love is a flower/The flower grows within", "Love is the answer/Miracles are slow" and "Yes is surrender/The messages are whole" nearly making it past quality control.

'Aisumasen (I'm Sorry)' also built on the past – on his unfinished demo for 'Call My Name' from 1971. Once a message of support to a lover, the song was rewritten as another confession of guilt, tied to an admission that 'All that I know is just what you tell me'. It's not difficult to imagine Lennon watching his marriage slip away, desperately owning up in song to the faults that he couldn't admit in real life. Painfully slow and long, the track dragged, just the way that his relationship with Yoko had done all year.

The two lushest songs on the album, both couched in the kind of string and vocal arrangements more associated with McCartney than Lennon, were 'One Day At A Time' and 'You Are Here'. Both were unashamed paeans of love for Yoko, which draw much of their pathos from the knowledge that she had broken off their relationship by the time the record appeared in the shops. 'One Day At A Time' offered an embarrassingly sac-

charine picture of the couple's life, but 'You Are Here' was genuinely moving, as warm and poetic a love song as Lennon had ever written.

'Out The Blue' rephrased the question a different way. Before Lennon
applied sweetening at the remix stage, the song sounded like a *Plastic Ono
Band* out-take – a heartfelt confession of debt to Yoko, performed with total
lack of embellishment, and with two lengthy piano solos to break the tension. Where 'You Are Here' painted the relationship in mellow tones, 'Out
The Blue' gave it the importance of life and death: "All my life's been a long
slow knife", Lennon gasped, before announcing proudly: "Anyway, I survived, long enough to make you my wife".

The other five songs were divided between political chants and no-nonsense rockers. Into the latter category fell 'Rock And Roll People', which
the band attempted many times on August 1 and 4 at the start of the album
sessions. The song regularly slipped into a boogie jam before Lennon shouted
out, "How do we get out of here?", and forced the best take to a halt with
a series of jagged chords on his rhythm guitar. 'Tight A$' was just as much
fun, a slick rockabilly confection with throwaway lyrics and an immaculate
Lennon vocal. The final take was chopped by almost a minute before it made
the album, with a couple of guitar solos vanishing along the way.

On 'Meat City' Lennon constructed a wall of guitar noise over which he
recited an obscure tale of snake doctors, mountains and rock 'n' roll. And
here's another clue for you all: if you played the tune backwards and the
mysterious voice between verses could be heard to say: "Fuck a pig". (Try
the same trick on the mix issued as a single, and it said: "Check the album".)

The album could take any number of rockers like this; they were a welcome antidote to the general air of gloom. Where it faltered was in trying
to return to the political passion of 'Power To The People' without the commitment to back it up. The chorus of 'Bring On The Lucie' had surfaced a
couple of years earlier as a straight piece of activism entitled 'Free The
People'. Lennon lacked the production skills to translate the finished song
into an anthem, as Phil Spector could have done, and the new verses raced
from incoherence to melodrama. But the savagery of the imagery suggested
that Lennon relished the sight of Nixon and his cronies being caught with
their hands on the smoking gun.

'Only People' best summed up Lennon's malaise, however. It was based
on one of Yoko's credos: "Only people can change the world". But Lennon
couldn't find the words to suit such a simplistic sentiment, and somehow
"We don't want no pig brother scene" didn't seem to be the slogan to bring
a generation together. From the political equivalent of a bull in a china shop
to self-parody in 18 months: that was the journey that *Mind Games* charted.

The discovery of a collection of alternate takes and early mixes from the sessions allowed us a belated chance to reassess the record, however. Before Lennon sweetened the tracks and flattened the overall sound picture in his final clumsy mix, *Mind Games* carried more *joi de vivre* than the finished album suggested. In the hands of an experienced pop producer – say, to pick a name at random, Paul McCartney – it could have been moulded into something as appealing as Wings' *Band On The Run* album, albeit with weightier ingredients. As it was, *Mind Games* was a slightly laboured affair, which cast a cloud over Lennon's career for the next two years.

SEPTEMBER 30, 1973: REVIEW of *The Goon Show Scripts* published in *The New York Times*.

Spike Milligan's radio scripts for the BBC Light Programme series *The Goon Show* invented a new kind of comedy – anarchic, witty, subverting values and narrative expectations. John Lennon lapped up the radio shows in the Fifties, recognising Milligan as a kindred spirit, and so he leapt at the opportunity to review the Goons' collected scripts for the *New York Times*.

In its way, John's 700-word review was every bit as anarchic as the book – ignoring the conventions whereby one described and analysed the text, and concentrating instead on explaining what the Goons had meant to him. "Their humour was the only proof that the WORLD was insane," Lennon recalled, describing it as "a conspiracy against reality". And he remembered his own efforts in the same vein, in *The Daily Howl*.

Much of the review was devoted to the difficulty of writing the review: "I'm supposed to write 800 words but I can't count. I could go on all day about the Goons ... but it doesn't seem to be about THE BOOK! I keep thinking how much easier it would be to review it for a British paper. What the hell! I've never REVIEWED anything in my life before. Now I know why critics are 'nasty'." *The New York Times* added their own parody at the foot of the review. In place of the usual academic credentials, they described its author thus: "John Lennon, the now and former Beatle, studied capitalization in the Liverpool school system". "It was a bit like doing a school essay", was Lennon's final verdict on the assignment.

c. OCTOBER 1973: RECORDING home demos of 'Here We Go Again'/'Nobody Loves You When You're Down And Out'

'Here We Go Again' was a lost Lennon classic, which has never received the attention it deserved. Though the eventual composing credit was split between Lennon and Phil Spector when the song was included on *Menlove Avenue* in 1986, John appears to have written the basic song entirely by himself. His demo, taped at home shortly before the Spector rock'n'roll sessions began, hinted strongly at what was to come, using augmented chords to map out the claustrophobic string build-up on the record. The lyrics were vague but telling, full of images of tiredness and betrayal – "All I wanted was a thank you, ma'am ... everyone's an also-ran".

With 'Steel And Glass' already fermenting in his brain since the *Mind Games* sessions, Lennon began to compose another of the songs destined for his next project, *Walls And Bridges*. In its original acoustic form, 'Nobody Loves You When You're Down And Out' certainly captured a space midway between self-pity and desolation, but there was nothing about the chord changes to distinguish this from any bedsit balladeer down on his luck. There were even hints that Lennon had been studying Hoagy Carmichael's veteran standard, 'You Belong To Me', before he penned this melody. Before the following summer, Lennon was able to fine-tune the progression and intensify the emotional impact of the song, which was more or less complete lyrically from the start.

OCTOBER 17 to DECEMBER 14, 1973: RECORDING 'Be My Baby'/'Here We Go Again'/'Sweet Little Sixteen'/'You Can't Catch Me'/'Just Because'/'Angel Baby'/'To Know Her Is To Love Her'/'My Baby Left Me'/'Bony Moronie', plus numerous other backing tracks; writing 'Mucho Mungo' with Phil Spector

"It was such a mess that I can hardly remember what happened. I was away from Yoko and I wanted to come back. When I was drunk, I would just ramble on or scream abuse at her or beg her to come back. I don't know what I was saying or doing half the time."

The infamous lost weekend: just another chapter in the John and Yoko myth. John and Yoko did separate in the late summer of 1973, and remained apart until the end of 1974. Lennon did get drunk in Hollywood and New York; his 'Oldies But Goldies' sessions with Phil Spector supposedly in command did collapse in chaos; and John did make a fool of himself often and in public.

But the same lost weekend did eventually bear fruit. 1974 saw him complete two albums, *Rock'n'Roll* and *Walls And Bridges*; produce an album for Harry Nilsson; and collaborate on hit singles for Ringo Starr and Elton John. Compare that output with 1973 (*Mind Games* and 'I'm The Greatest') or 1975 ('Fame' and 'Across The Universe' with David Bowie) and the weekend doesn't seem so lost after all.

The initial weeks of separation did have their moments of mayhem, though, fuelled by the slightly erratic behaviour of the man in whom Lennon was tempted to trust his new project: Phil Spector. The sessions collapsed after two months of heavy drinking and very slow progress. By then, Lennon and Spector had battled like kids on the floor of the studio, been thrown out of one recording complex (A&M in Hollywood) after Spector let off a pistol, attracted every musical drunk in town, and taped at least nine rather anarchic slices of rock 'n' roll. Lennon only considered four of them worthy of release when he approached the tapes in a more sober spirit the following year.

Tired of carrying the responsibility as creator, performer and producer, and aware that *Mind Games* was several notches short of his best work, Lennon equated the liberation of the bachelor life with the freedom of the singer who has a producer to fall back on. In the past, Lennon had always employed Spector, feeding him only enough rope to allow him to work to John's instructions. On the oldies project, Spector could do what he liked; John would do what he was told.

Lennon reckoned that the album would also solve another problem: his ongoing dispute with publisher Morris Levy, over his alleged plagiarism of Chuck Berry's tune 'You Can't Catch Me' on The Beatles' 'Come Together' back in 1969. To avoid a lengthy court case which he might well lose, and which would be embarrassing whatever the verdict, Lennon promised Levy that he would record at least three songs owned by the publisher on his next record. 'You Can't Catch Me' was perhaps inevitably the first of the oldies to be scheduled for the Spector sessions.

Oldies were in the air that autumn. David Bowie had just cut *Pin Ups*; Bryan Ferry was planning *These Foolish Things*. And Spector had just signed a deal to form his own record company, for the first time since he dissolved Philles Records in 1967. True to the nostalgic mood of the times, Warner/Spector's first releases were a mixture of reissues of his best Sixties productions, by the likes of The Ronettes and The Crystals, and remakes of Sixties tunes featuring Cher and Harry Nilsson.

Cher's magnificent version of The Ronettes' 'Baby I Love You' set the pattern. The vibrant girl group tune from 1963 was slowed to funereal pace, with a couple of dozen session-men playing the simplest parts in unison, and Cher left all the room in the world to emote over the top. Spector loved it, as did Lennon; and so Phil set about arranging another Ronettes' smash, 'Be My Baby', and his own début single with The Teddy Bears, 'To Know Her Is To Love Her', in the same way.

Spector also cut the pace of rockers like 'Sweet Little Sixteen', 'Bony Moronie', 'You Can't Catch Me' and 'My Baby Left Me' by half; and rearranged Rosie And The Originals' naive teen ballad, 'Angel Baby', into an extravaganza for brass and drums.

Spector's methods were painstaking, even painful for the musicians, who were forced to wait while the producer added layer upon layer to the mountainous ensemble sound before the tapes even began rolling. When Phil was finally ready to cut the vocals, deep into the night, Lennon would have drunk a bottle or more of whisky. Swaying in the vocal booth, John could hear this cavernous, awesome, emotionally overpowering noise in his headphones, crashing like a tide across the booze and the exhaustion, breaking down all the inhibition that his responsibility as a producer and a musician usually demanded. Like Janov's primal therapy, Spector's vast soundscapes liberated John's voice. What emerged was without ego or pretension. Some of it was brilliant, breath-taking, like 'You Can't Catch Me'; the rest the ravings of the drunken fool Lennon might have been in Liverpool if The Beatles had never made it to London. The frazzled dialogue interludes featured on *Anthology* captured the atmosphere of the sessions perfectly.

Looking back in 1980, Lennon dismissed the Spector tracks out-of-hand: his memories of late 1973 weren't pleasant. But as the *Menlove Avenue* album in 1986 revealed, the sessions had their moments. 'My Baby Left Me' was transformed from rockabilly to party piece, with Lennon's dry rasp echoed by an amateurish choir of revellers. 'Angel Baby' found John fighting for life amidst a cacophony of instruments, but still invoking the innocent spirit and emotion of the original record. Likewise 'To Know Her Is To Love Her', with Lennon's vocal pure emotion, almost regardless of the words he was singing.

Finer still was 'Here We Go Again' – a song Lennon had demoed in acoustic form before the sessions, and then given to Spector to arrange. Without revealing the details, 'Here We Go Again' sounded like a stand against the storm ahead, defiant but doomed. Spector's arrangement conveyed all that and more, and Lennon's vocal ranged from the laconic defeat of the verses to the screaming passion of the final chorus. But the track wasn't a single, and it didn't fit the oldies concept, so it stayed in the can, alongside the original Spector/Lennon co-write of 'Mucho Mungo'.

Some nights, though, the results weren't quite as coherent. The session when they recorded Lloyd Price's 'Just Because', Lennon could scarcely stand, let alone sing, by the time Spector had prepared the track. He tried, anyway, despite being distracted by the backing vocalists, who reportedly included Carly Simon: "I want to suck your nipples baby," he leered across the opening chords, before falling through the song hopelessly drunk, teetering on the verge of collapse. And across the fade, in the space left for him to compose some pithy monologue, Lennon let a little reality in: "I need some excuse for doing this," he slurred, "I need some relief from my obligations. A little cocaine will set me on my feet." And from there he scatted through a psychotic version of 'Yes Sir That's My Baby' before the music came mercifully to a close and he could be carried home to bed.

The rest wasn't that dramatic, though John must have winced when he heard the endless repeated choruses and one-note organ riff on 'Sweet Little Sixteen'. 'Be My Baby' had almost nothing wrong with it, however, with Lennon sighing orgasmically as the music built to a crescendo, and then letting himself go in a series of sensuous cries over the fade. On moments like that, the cathartic purpose of the Spector sessions was fulfilled. Ironically, that track wasn't included on the *Rock'n'Roll* album. Ironically again, the best moments on that record actually came from these troubled sessions.

The Record Plant sessions ended on December 14, after which Spector became mysteriously inaccessible – and so did the tapes. For the moment, Lennon had no choice but to abandon his oldies project until Spector returned to the world. Yoko has subsequently claimed that the project collapsed because she wasn't there to act as a buffer between the two men – and she may indeed be right.

c. EARLY 1974: CREATING Andy Warhol collage

In 1990, a London auction house sold a collage created by Lennon during 1974. Lennon had cut out numerous photos of Andy Warhol from *Interview* magazine, and pasted them on top of the heads of a photo of a troupe of girls who were riding motorcyles – in the nude, of course. Lennon continued to create similar collages for several years.

c. 3/74: PRODUCING 'Too Many Cooks' for Mick Jagger

In 2003, the British press got themselves very excited about the 'discovery' of a vintage blues recording by Mick Jagger, produced by John Lennon. Well, the personnel were correct, but the song had been circulating on bootlegs for more than 25 years. It was not even a blues tune, but a cover of the 100 Proof (Aged In Soul) single issued by Holland, Dozier & Holland's pop/soul label Hot Wax back in 1969. Jagger confirmed that the track had been cut during the regular Sunday afternoon get-togethers at the Record Plant West around this time, booked in the name of super-session drummer Jim Keltner. Doubtless many other potential gems were cut during these sessions, but the one confirmed piece of Lennon involvement was producing this vibrant piece of R&B, which would have been a guaranteed hit single had not record company politics prevented its release – then and now.

LATE MARCH 1974: RECORDING 'Little Bitty Pretty One'/'Something You Got'/'Lucille'/'Sleepwalk'/'Stand By Me'/'Cupid'/'Chain Gang'/'Take This Hammer'/'Midnight Special' with Paul McCartney and Stevie Wonder

If Charles Dickens had survived to the end of the 20th century, he'd not only have been nearly 200 years old but would also have been given the inspiration for a second volume of his classic *Great Expectations*. For a decade after The Beatles split up, fans salivated over the prospect of a reunion between Lennon and McCartney in the recording studio. Even after Lennon's death, the revelation in May Pang's book, *Loving John*, that the pair had shared a jam session in 1974 prompted much speculation. Pang recalled that they had sung the old skiffle/folk standard 'Midnight Special' together, and recounted that there had been magic in the air.

Then, in 1992, a bootleg entitled *A Toot And A Snore* was released, and all the fantasies burned to ashes. The CD was aptly titled: not only was cocaine the stimulant of choice at the session (you could hear Lennon offering Stevie Wonder "a toot, a snort – it's going round"), but a snore was the only sensible response to an audio document so lacking in drama and merit.

With a line-up comprising Lennon on piano, McCartney on drums, Wonder on electronic keyboards, Jesse Ed Davis on guitar, Bobby Keyes on sax and Harry Nilsson on whiskey-soured vocals, some degree of electricity might have been expected. Instead, the only time sparks flew was when Lennon complained to the hapless engineer at the Record Plant West in Los Angeles: "We had a beautiful mix in the ears about half an hour ago ... I can't hear a fucking thing ... just put it back the way it was" – on and on, ungracious, bored and over-agitated.

Along the way, there were snatches of music, the kind of late-night, disconnected jam sessions that musicians all over the world perform to avoid doing any real work. "I've done 'Ain't That A Shame' at twenty studios in these sessions," Lennon announced, thinking back through the long haul of rock'n'roll traumas with Phil Spector. To avoid yet another rendition, he fell into Curtis Lee's 'Little Bitty Pretty One' (originally produced by Spector;

strange how the brain makes these connections sometimes), before begging, "If somebody has a song that we all know, then take over".

So Stevie Wonder tried to steer the band into Chris Kenner's New Orleans oldie, 'Something You Got', and McCartney was up for the ride, but instead Lennon twisted the song into Little Richard's 'Lucille', which his old friend used to sing when they shared a band together. "It is a little better if we know the song," Lennon consoled himself, as he attempted to find the melody of Santo & Johnny's instrumental hit, 'Sleepwalk'. Eventually, he suggested 'Stand By Me', which he'd sung with McCartney in January 1969, and would soon record for real. "If anybody gets bored with me, take over," he asked again, before lambasting the engineer for several minutes. Briefly, he acknowledged his former partner's presence – "McCartney's doing the harmony on the drums" – but he was more interested in moaning about the sound. Finally, the song got underway, with McCartney offering some trite vocal support, and Lennon rasping like a man out of time. Then Harry Nilsson stumbled into microphone range, which did absolutely nothing for the quality of the music.

Stevie Wonder made one last attempt to rescue the session, with a tuneful rendition of Sam Cooke's 'Cupid', but clearly no one else knew the chords. So he compromised on 'Chain Gang', with McCartney and Nilsson behind him, and Lennon presumably slumped over his piano. McCartney headed back to the skiffle era with 'Take This Hammer' – and then the tape ran out, history slumped to a halt, and the musical collaboration of Lennon and McCartney was finally at an end. To paraphrase what John wrote on his *Rock'n'Roll* album: you shouldn'ta been there.

APRIL/MAY 1974: RECORDING 'Mucho Mungo' demos; producing 'Many Rivers To Cross'/'Subterranean Homesick Blues'/'Don't Forget Me'/'All My Life'/'Old Forgotten Soldier'/'Save The Last Dance For Me'/'Mucho Mungo; Mt. Elba'/'Loop De Loop'/'Black Sails'/'Rock Around The Clock'/ 'Down By The Sea'/ 'The Flying Saucer Song' for Harry Nilsson

After the collapse of the Spector sessions at the end of 1973, and Spector's subsequent disappearance after two serious car smashes in early 1974, John spent several months simply hanging out in Hollywood. His daily routine included drinking with Harry Nilsson, Ringo Starr and Keith Moon, getting thrown out of night-clubs, making the front page of the LA papers, and trying to fashion a relationship with May Pang while he was still phoning Yoko every day to find out if he could come home.

Towards the end of a whisky bottle, he agreed to produce Harry Nilsson's next album; and so in April, they set up at the Record Plant West and began work on *Pussy Cats*. Nilsson had written just four songs for the project, so Lennon offered him one of his own, a lightweight ballad called 'Mucho Mungo' which he'd started during the *Rock 'n' Roll* sessions, with Phil Spector adding a middle section to the basic chorus. Lennon cut three home demos of the tune, and was then ready to teach it to Nilsson; but Harry didn't like Spector's additions (which remain unheard to this day), and suggested instead that they segue John's tune into the folk song 'Mt. Elba'. Along the way, one verse from the pair's first acoustic run-through was dropped, for obvious reasons: "Sailing on the Good Ship Lollipop/Open up a drug store, nice kind of shop."

Like the Spector sessions, these dates were peopled by a cast of dozens, with every party animal in town demanding the chance to bang a tambourine. And with John arranging most of the oldies that they picked to fill the album up, much of the finished record had the same air of mayhem as the *Rock'n'Roll* tracks. Lennon gave Bob Dylan's 'Subterranean Homesick Blues' a frantic, claustrophobic R&B arrangement, with saxophones honking metallic riffs while a school of drummers pounded out a tattoo. (As a sign of the chaos which informed the entire project, John had to cut together the final take from a dozen or so incoherent efforts.) And Bill Haley's 'Rock Around The Clock' was equally bizarre, ending with the entire band playing in double tempo over the fade. The Spector influence pervaded the album, in fact: why else would John have chosen to slow The Drifters' 'Save The Last Dance For Me' to a painful snail's pace, or turn Jimmy Cliff's spiritual 'Many Rivers To Cross' into a funeral dirge that ended with a Primal Scream? But even at its most laboured, *Pussy Cats* had something – a spark of magic, a breath of life, which evaded most superstar collaborations. Or maybe it was simply the booze: as Derek Taylor said in his liner notes, "Most of what Harry and John said and did was bloody funny and sometimes terrifying. They have been living a vampire timetable recently...They are madmen in tandem." And the record sounds like it.

While the songs that Lennon arranged all shared that extreme quality, *Pussy Cats* also included some gorgeous, devastatingly emotional, ballads that were arranged by Nilsson himself. Lennon proved his production skills by capturing all the majestic defiance of 'Black Sails', for example. Two altogether lighter pieces from these sessions, 'The Flying Saucer Song' and 'Down By The Sea', were left off the final record, but released nearly thirty years later. Amusing though they were, they would have betrayed the dark madness of *Pussy Cats* if they'd surfaced in 1974.

This wasn't quite the last musical collaboration between Lennon and Nilsson. "We wrote a song together called 'You Are Here'," Nilsson revealed shortly before his death. "It's something we started to write but never really finished. I never hard the final product but we used to send tapes back and forth to each other." None of these tapes has ever been aired in public, sadly.

Finally, Lennon used a brief moment of respite during these sessions to tape a demo of a new song he'd written for Ringo Starr. 'Goodnight Vienna', a piece of hack-work from the same mould as 'Rock And Roll People', was based around a Liverpudlian catchphrase basically meaning 'I'm getting outta here', and was little more than an invitation to boogie. Several takes were recorded, one of which inexorably slipped into 'Many Rivers To Cross'. "I'm under the influence of drugs," Nilsson slurred as the track ended, and he probably wasn't the only one.

MAY to JUNE 1974: RECORDING home demos of 'Surprise Surprise'/'Whatever Gets You Through The Night'/'So Long'/'Move Over Ms L'/'What You Got'/'Going Down On Love'/'Steel And Glass'

Taking responsibility for the production of Nilsson's album had shocked Lennon out of his spiral of drinking and drugs. In the early summer of 1974, Ringo Starr invited John to write him some material for his own forthcoming solo album; at the same time, John began assembling songs for his own next project – his first for six years not to be conceived with Yoko.

A blend of rock traditionalism and scattershot imagery produced 'Move Over Ms L' – a title which took a sardonic swipe at the woman who had once referred to herself in song as Mrs Lennon. He cut a quick home demo while May Pang made a phone call, rehearsing boogie riffs on electric guitar and then breaking into falsetto for the chorus. He made a second, more serious pass at the song later in the month, whispering the nonsensical verses over acoustic guitar as if he was trying not to wake May up, and throwing in a quick impression of Yoko for good measure.

'Whatever Gets You Through The Night' was written around the same time – with Lennon documenting the process on tape, beginning with a title-line he'd heard on a TV show about alcoholism. Having found the right rhythm, he experimented with new inversions of the basic chords, and made up some tentative lyrics – "It's whatever turns you on" being one verse that escaped the final version. And at one point, he realised he'd heard the tune somewhere before, and ran it neatly into the opening lines of 'Jealous Guy'. Returning to the song later, he gradually assembled the lyrics for the verses, as a TV sports show blared in the background. Finally, he decided to finger-pick the rhythm rather than play straight chords, and worked out the skeleton of a middle section as well.

'Surprise Surprise' was an altogether meatier song – an unashamed paean of love to May Pang, the "bird of paradise" who had rescued him from the misery of his separation from Yoko. The song began life as an acoustic ballad – Lennon admitted that The Diamonds' Fifties doo-wop hit 'Little Darlin'' was an early influence – with some 'Julia'-style chording where the middle section would finally appear. Later home demos accentuated the bluesiness of the song, and suggested that new love might be something of a mixed blessing, as the performances had some of the quiet desperation of the *Plastic Ono Band* album. And gradually the middle section evolved, as John hit upon the key line: "I thought I could never be surprised".

'What You Got' was, at this stage, a Carl Perkins-influenced rockabilly tune, with only the chorus familiar from the final record. The message was basic enough: 'You don't know what you got until you lose it' and on the acoustic demo John simply busked words to fill the spaces before and after the chorus, grabbing the first line of Little Richard's 'Rip It Up' for the start of the middle section. The whole thing was like an exercise in Americana by numbers, as Lennon drawled out nonsense lines like "Your shaggy dog bin mothertrucking bad to me". At this point, the tune could have been headed towards country blues, Lynyrd Skynyrd's southern rock, or some strange territory in between.

'So Long' was equally unfinished, though its melody line was distinct – and clearly based on the tune that John had sketched out for the string arrangement on Nilsson's 'Many Rivers To Cross'. By the time he cut his second acoustic demo, John was putting together some lyrical ideas – a mixture of dream imagery and romantic discovery, the lure of the past and the deceptive nature of reality. There were spaces left for a guitar breakdown and a chorus that wasn't yet written. Bizarrely, at this point the melody line was closer to McCartney territory than anything recognisably his own. After a couple more weeks, the tune was edited and refined, and ready to be recorded as 'No. 9 Dream'.

On acoustic guitar, with few of the chord changes in place, 'Going Down On Love' was a contender for the dullest song ever recorded. Second time around, Lennon still sounded as depressed as hell, and now the melody was drifting somewhere between 'Everybody Had A Hard Year' and 'Don't Let Me Down', two numbers dragged out of the misery of late 1968. Only when Lennon switched the song to piano did it begin to take shape and lose its enervating atmosphere, especially when he briefly toyed with rocking it up, Little Richard style. But 'Going Down On Love' was a positive delight compared to the piano demo that Lennon prepared for 'Steel And Glass'. Marooned on a solitary chord, he droned out the acerbic lyrics like a man who had forgotten how to live. Both songs required a massive blood transfusion before he reached the studio.

JULY 13, 1974: REHEARSING 'Steel And Glass'/'Going Down On Love'/'Move Over Ms L'/'Surprise Surprise'/'Beef Jerky'/'Scared'/'Old Dirt Road'/'Bless You'/'Whatever Gets You Thru The Night'/'Nobody Loves You (When You're Down And Out)'

For around 10 days, John hosted pre-production sessions for his new album at Sunset Studios and Record Plant East, New York – rehearsing with the band from scratch, so that they would grow into the arrangements, rather than approaching them cold on the first day of full sessions. Some of these rehearsals appeared in edited form on the 1986 collection, *Menlove Avenue*. Together with the unissued cuts, they illustrate how much work John had put into his new songs since the end of June, completing all the numbers he'd demoed that month, composing several more, and digging up a second collaboration with Nilsson from the *Pussy Cats* sessions in 'Old Dirt Road'. John also wrote a new set of lyrics for a song called 'Jubilation' by his engineer Roy Cicala during these rehearsals (see January 1975 for more details).

What was remarkable about these tapes was not the material, though that was impressive enough. It was the subdued way in which the songs were performed, with the small group arrangements and slightly melancholy feel giving 'Bless You', 'Scared' and 'Nobody Loves You When You're Down And Out' a poignancy not always captured on the final recordings.

JULY/AUGUST 1974: RECORDING 'Going Down On Love'/'Whatever Gets You Through The Night'/'Old Dirt Road'/'What You Got'/'Bless You'/'Scared'/ 'No. 9 Dream'/'Surprise Surprise'/'Steel And Glass'/'Beef Jerky'/'Nobody Loves You When You're Down And Out'/'Ya Ya'/'Move Over Ms L'/ 'Ain't She Sweet'

From the vantage point of 1980, Lennon described *Walls And Bridges* as "the work of a semi-sick craftsman", by comparison with the supposedly inspirational way in which the *Double Fantasy* songs were created. In fact, most of *Double Fantasy* had been the labour of years, not hours: it was *Walls And Bridges* that was the work of inspiration. What it wasn't, of course, was a John and Yoko collaboration, so it didn't fit the Ballad myth. The fact that its best songs were as powerful as anything on *Double Fantasy*, or *Imagine*, for that matter, was subtly forgotten.

The *Walls And Bridges* material was certainly as graphic and revealing as anything Lennon had written in the past. There has rarely been a more mature song of romantic regret than 'Bless You', John's sober message to whoever was holding Yoko in his arms in John's absence. 'Surprise Surprise' reflected the sheer physical joy of his new relationship with May Pang; while 'Scared' and 'Nobody Loves You When You're Down And Out' were the view from the bottom of the bottle, but written from determination rather than despair.

The album had its throwaways, of course: 'Whatever Gets You Through The Night' began as a novelty, and ended as a number one hit single, thanks to the vocal duet with the era's hottest superstar, Elton John. "We sounded like Patience & Prudence," Lennon admitted afterwards, referring to a pre-teen novelty act from the Fifties. "People thought we'd speeded the track up, but we didn't." It took a while to perfect the arrangement, as it started out like a piece of funk rather than pop, but the result was as commercial as anything Lennon had ever recorded, with or without The Beatles.

'What You Got' was transformed into urban R&B, with a feel that echoed the great American records of the early Sixties, like 'Watch Your Step' and 'Money'.★ 'Old Dirt Road', the Nilsson collaboration, was a lazy piece of daydreaming out of the 'I'm Only Sleeping' school, with imagery that was as off-the-wall as anything from Lennon's two books. And 'Beef Jerky', built around guitar licks from the 1973 demo for 'Tight A$', plus elements from 'No. 9 Dream' and Cliff Richard's 1958 rocker 'Move It', was something no one could have predicted from this source − a righteous R&B instrumental, buoyed by churning horn riffs and some jagged lead guitar. 'Move Over Ms L' would have fitted into the same pile, if Lennon hadn't rejected the *Walls And Bridges* take of the song when the band couldn't catch the simple Jerry Lee Lewis-style rock'n'roll feel it required. So the honour of completing the album went to a minute of painful piano/drums jamming with John's 11-year-old son Julian on Lee Dorsey's 'Ya Ya'. It was included on the record as a sop to publisher Morris Levy, who was still pursuing John for royalties on 'Come Together', which Lennon had been foolish enough to admit had been based on Chuck Berry's 'You Can't Catch Me'.

★ John admitted in a 1974 radio interview that the riff was a variation of the O'Jays' current hit, 'For The Love Of Money'.

The rest of the material from the sessions (apart from a 30-second music hall romp through 'Ain't She Sweet') was more substantial. 'Going Down On Love' never quite worked as a piece of slow funk, but its subtle charm belied the desperation of its lyrics: "Somebody please, please help me/I think I'm drowning in a sea of hatred". On *Plastic Ono Band*, in 1970, it could easily have turned into a second cousin of 'Well Well Well'. 'Scared' said it even straighter, an unabashed admission that John couldn't survive without Yoko, though he was still trying to overcome the hatred and jealousy, "the green-eyed goddamn straight from your heart". The music burned in support, while Lennon emphasised the lonesome whistle of his song by starting the track with a library tape of a howling wolf at midnight.

'Nobody Loves You When You're Down And Out' was, like 'What You Got', structured around a familiar blues lyric. Lennon supposedly wrote the song for Frank Sinatra, but it sounded more like another gasp from the heart, and the production gave his vocal the rasp of a loser in his final decline. "I'll scratch your back and you knife mine," Lennon sang, aware that his drunken antics earlier in the year had crippled his public image. Surrender might have been an easy option, a slow descent into hell; these songs showed that Lennon preferred to fight his way out.

But it was the album's three songs of love that offered an insight into Lennon's real state of mind. 'Surprise Surprise', with another tight, twisting guitar riff like the ones he'd once provided for The Beatles, was a lyrical celebration of love and sex, and an admission that maybe there was life after separation after all. "She makes me sweat and forget who I am", Lennon sang about his new lover, in a naked declaration of passion he hadn't made in his music since 'Happiness Is A Warm Gun'.

The beautiful fantasy of 'No. 9 Dream' was also inspired by May, who could be heard calling John's name in the chorus. Caught in a haze of love and sleep, Lennon was lost for words, unable to articulate his feelings, not even sure what they were; like 'I'm Only Sleeping', though, the song augured no threat of a nightmare. The invented language John used for the chorus only served to heighten the idyllic flavour of the dream.

Alongside these songs of passion and security, though, Lennon was writing 'Bless You' – a slow, delicate ballad that was part farewell, part promise. Yoko was with someone else – session guitarist David Spinozza, as it turned out – but John still cared enough to wish her well. And the middle eight showed that hope of a reunion hadn't died: "Some people think it's over/now that we've spread our wings/but we know better darling/the hollow ring is only last year's echo". Love songs are always a form of imaginary letter, and John mightn't have been able to express this wish to Yoko in person; but the fact that the hope was still alive placed the joy of his songs for May in sharp perspective. May can't have failed to notice the fact.

'Steel And Glass' completed the emotional journey. An obvious successor to 'How Do You Sleep?', right down to the cutting string arrangement, it took a hefty sideswipe at former Beatles manager Allen Klein, though John was always too coy to say so. As ever, Lennon expressed betrayal by a father figure in vicious terms: 'Steel And Glass' stood alongside 'The Maharishi Song' as a character assassination, with John sneering lines like "You leave your smell like an alley cat". From the adult attitudes of 'Bless You' to this heady vitriol was a long trip across the tightrope of Lennon's emotions.

Autobiographical evidence aside, *Walls And Bridges* worked simply as a collection of pop songs – more sophisticated than *Mind Games*, and produced with infinitely more verve and imagination. In fact, Lennon never made a richer solo record, nor one which demonstrated such a wide mastery of styles. *Walls And Bridges* mightn't have been his strongest album, or his most durable; but it did represent his last entire album of new songs, and also the last time – almost – that his music would reflect the contemporary world around him. It hinted at a new maturity of sound to come, taking in elements of the black music mainstream just as The Beatles had done a decade earlier. In an imaginary future, Lennon might have followed his new buddy David Bowie into some hybrid of cutting-edge funk and rock. But things didn't quite work out that way.

AUGUST 26-27, 1974: RECORDING 'Only You'/'Goodnight Vienna' with Ringo Starr; recording 'Lucy In The Sky With Diamonds' with Elton John

Immediately after completing *Walls And Bridges*, John and May Pang jetted to California, where they recorded two tracks for Ringo Starr's *Goodnight Vienna* album, before moving on to Caribou Ranch, Colorado to repay Elton John's favour in singing on two of Lennon's new tracks.

As with 'I'm The Greatest' the previous year, Lennon controlled Ringo's sessions, cutting a rough lead vocal for Ringo to copy. John's version of 'Goodnight Vienna' was wilder than Ringo's, but still simple enough for the drummer to track; while on 'Only You' it was John who suggested covering the old Platters hit, and who not only laid down the rhythmic acoustic guitar accompaniment but also demoed the lead vocal.

That chore over, Lennon joined Elton John in covering 'Lucy In The Sky With Diamonds', singing harmony vocals and adding some guitar. He is also said to have suggested that Elton give the middle section a reggae arrangement. During these sessions, Elton tackled Lennon's *Mind Games* composition, 'One Day At A Time', with John supposedly playing guitar and adding vocals, though his contribution is impossible to hear.

OCTOBER 19-20, 1974: recording rehearsal takes of 'That'll Be The Day'/'Do You Wanna Dance'/'Stand By Me'/'Bring It On Home To Me'/'Peggy Sue'/'Rip It Up'/'Ready Teddy'/'Thirty Days'/'Slippin' And Slidin' '/'Ya Ya'/'Rumble'/'Ain't That A Shame'/'Send Me Some Lovin' '/'Be-Bop-A-Lula'/'C'mon Everybody'

Listening to the Spector *Rock 'n' Roll* tapes, which had been returned to him that summer, Lennon realised that it would be virtually impossible to mould them into an album – unless, as with the Beatles five years earlier, he was trying to kiss goodbye to a stage of his career. And perhaps he was, in retrospect. But he was still a pro, and so he pulled together the same basic group of musicians with whom he'd cut *Walls And Bridges*, spent two days rehearsing at the upstate New York home of Morris Levy, and then another five knocking off enough tracks to fill an album.

The rehearsals were, as ever, captured on tape. They were, at best, rough and ready, as the band felt their way towards the tight looseness that Fifties rock music requires. Lennon also tried out some songs that didn't make the final cut – a ragged 'That'll Be The Day', with John growling his way through Buddy Holly's lyrics; a reggae-ish lope round Chuck Berry's 'Thirty Days'; and a Chicago blues-inspired rendition of 'C'mon Everybody'. A spirited gallop through a jam around the riff of Link Wray's instrumental, 'Rumble', even led the band into a brief extract from Led Zeppelin's song (via Willie Dixon), 'Whole Lotta Love'. The only intriguing facet of these performances that wasn't carried over to the actual recording sessions was the New Orleans-style percussion of 'Ain't That A Shame' and 'Slippin' And Slidin'', which was knocked aside in the studio by the sheer energy of the band.

OCTOBER 21 to 25, 1974: RECORDING 'Be-Bop-A-Lula'/ 'Stand By Me'/'Rip It Up'/'Ready Teddy'/'Ain't That A Shame'/ 'Do You Wanna Dance'/'Slippin' And Slidin' '/'Peggy Sue'/'Bring It On Home To Me'/'Send Me Some Lovin' '/'Ya Ya'/'Move Over Ms L'; overdubbing new lead vocals on 'Just Because'

The *Rock'n'Roll* sessions themselves were more coherent than the rehearsals had been, though alternate takes of 'Bring It On Home To Me' and 'Peggy

267

Sue' suggested that the results could have been edgier than the rather slap-dash record allowed. With spontaneity the manifesto of the hour, the music was always likely to be erratic; and these recordings divided between rockers that capture the essence of the music and reshape it, and tired imitations of the original arrangements. 'Slippin' And Slidin' ' and 'Ain't That A Shame' – the latter with a wonderfully sardonic lead vocal – survived best, especially after the horn section had been overdubbed; while 'Be-Bop-A-Lula' and a Caribbean-flavoured 'Do You Wanna Dance' never came close to taking flight. Of the rest, an emotional reading of 'Stand By Me' was the stand-out, with John's acoustic playing obviously influenced by his near-identical work on Ringo's 'Only You'. Lennon chose to edit together his versions of 'Rip It Up' and 'Ready Teddy'. Yoko retrieved the full-length take of the latter for *Anthology*: its rampant enthusiasm made it one of that set's genuine highlights.

Finally, John picked out the cream of the Spector crop, and set about remixing and editing them. He chopped ninety seconds out of 'Sweet Little Sixteen', for instance, and moved around various elements of 'You Can't Catch Me'. His most significant move was substituting an entirely new lead line on 'Just Because', in place of the original drunken sprawl. Where he had once lusted over the backing singers, John added a disarming intro: "Ah, remember this? I must have been 13 when this came out? Or was it 14? Or was it 22? I could have been 12, actually." (Lennon admitted later that 'Just Because' had been Spector's suggestion, as he'd never heard the Lloyd Price song before.) And over the fade, John gave away his repair work with his reference to Record Plant East (in New York), rather than West (Los Angeles); and effectively waved farewell to his recording career. "Everybody here says hi," he concluded: "Goodbye!" As the take continued, he began to thank his friends by name, among them Paul, George and Ringo, though their namechecks were snipped out before the record reached the shops.

That wasn't quite as straightforward as it should have been. Remember the 'Ya Ya' jam that closed *Walls And Bridges*? That had been a vain attempt to satisfy the man who now owned Chuck Berry's publishing, Morris Levy. In a further attempt to win him round and avoid a court case, Lennon gave Levy a work-tape of his *Rock'n'Roll* album, so that Levy could issue it on his TV-advertised, mail-order label, Adam VIII. Quite how John expected EMI, Apple and Capitol to react isn't clear: they were collectively furious, however, and rushed through plans for their own competing release. Lennon went along with these as well, and in the resultant court case testified that Levy had broken his word by issuing the record – which surely begged the question of why John had given him the tapes in the first place.

None of this would have mattered to anyone who wasn't a lawyer if the two albums hadn't been subtly different. Levy called his *Roots: John Lennon Sings The Great Rock & Roll Hits*, a title that was accurate enough, though its 1968 cover photo scarcely began to fit the bill. It contained two more cuts than the Apple set, in 'Be My Baby' and 'Angel Baby'; an unedited take of 'You Can't Catch Me'; and marginally longer fades on a couple of tracks. All of which lent credence to the idea that giving Levy the tapes had been a passing whim: when John *really* wanted to release the record, he actually paid some attention to the results.

Meanwhile, the October 1974 sessions also finally produced a coherent take of 'Move Over Ms L', John's farewell message to Yoko – which ironically only appeared as the flipside of the 'Stand By Me' single in spring 1975, by which time John and Yoko had been reunited. The track rocked harder than anything on *Rock'n'Roll* itself, an irony that can't have been lost on Lennon.

NOVEMBER 28, 1974: REHEARSING 'I Saw Her Standing There;' performing 'Whatever Gets You Through The Night'/ 'Lucy In The Sky With Diamonds'/'I Saw Her Standing There'

The deal was this: if 'Whatever Gets You Through The Night' made number one, then John had to join Elton John on stage to perform it. Lennon readily agreed, never imagining that his low commercial stock would allow him a solo chart-topper. Remarkably, the single made it all the way in the States, and so on November 28, 1974, a very nervous John Lennon joined Elton's band at Madison Square Garden in New York for his final live concert appearance.

Earlier that day, the musicians had rehearsed their party piece, a raucous take of The Beatles' 'I Saw Her Standing There' having survived on tape. Lennon knew where it was inevitably going to end up, introducing the track as "Bootleg number five thousand and sixty-nine".

For the evening's encore attraction, they kicked off with Lennon's hit, moved into Elton's latest chart entry, which just happened to be John's 'Lucy In The Sky', and then completed their segment with 'I Saw Her Standing There', written, as Lennon announced, "by an old estranged fiancé of mine called Paul". The crowd went berserk: Lennon chewed gum and tried to look unmoved. From the audience, Yoko apparently saw only the loneliness of "her man". Backstage the couple met, and according to their myth-making 1980 interviews, the seeds of their reconciliation were sown there and then. It was two months, however, before Lennon returned to the Dakota for good.

JANUARY 1975: RECORDING 'Fame'/'Across The Universe' with David Bowie

David Bowie met Lennon for the first time in 1974, at a time when both men were sublimating their personal problems beneath chemical excess. Bowie duly invited Lennon to his next set of recording sessions, but he had already completed *Young Americans*, his first exercise in what he called "plastic soul", when John finally said yes. Bowie's slightly dubious plan was to record Lennon's 'Across The Universe' as a mock-dirge. As Lennon had always hated The Beatles' version, he was willing to go along with anything, though the results were no more exciting than the concept.

More significantly, Lennon and guitarist Carlos Alomar began jamming, and the result was 'Fame' – Bowie's first US number one single. Built around a James Brown riff, the track featured Lennon calling out the title at regular intervals, while Bowie used tape vari-speed to transform his voice from a Yoko-like squeal to a bassy rumble in the space of a couple of bars. Like the Elton John and Ringo collaborations, 'Fame' suggested that Lennon might profitably have worked more often with his musical peers; but all of that came to a halt when he went back to Yoko.

JANUARY 13 & 22, 1975: PRODUCING sessions by Lori Burton and Dog Soldier

Roy Cicala acted as first engineer on several of Lennon's mid-Seventies album projects. According to Kristofer Engelhardt's book, *Beatles Undercover*, Cicala asked Lennon to help him produce several sessions at Record Plant East in New York. Lennon was pulled between old and new love, and was maybe anxious to avoid having to spend too much time around his girlfriend, May Pang, at this point, when he was on the verge of going back to Yoko. Whatever the reason, he seems to have agreed.

Engelhardt documented at least two sessions, the first of which featured Cicala's wife, singer Lori Burton. Roy and John apparently produced her disco arrangement of the Nat Cole hit 'Answer Me, My Love', plus a delicious Philly soul version of The Rolling Stones' 'Let's Spend The Night Together' (on which Burton duetted with Patrick Jude), the former Toni Fisher/Del Shannon hit, 'The Big Hurt' (an old Lennon favourite) – and 'Incantation'. This was Lennon's lyrical rewrite of Cicala's 'Jubilation', full of the same kind of stream-of-consciousness lyrics as other recent Lennon throwaways, such as 'Rock And Roll People' and 'Move Over Ms L'. Burton was backed by Jude's band, who had once been known as Community Apple, and were now in the process of changing identity from BOMF (Band Of Mother Fuckers) to Dog Soldier.

Nine days later, if Engelhardt's research is correct, Lennon and Cicala handled another Record Plant session, this time starring Dog Soldier without Lori Burton. The band cut a feisty version of 'Incantation', which grooved like Sly & The Family Stone in their heyday, plus a Lennon rearrangement of The Beatles' 'You Can't Do That' and two other songs, 'April Rainbow' and 'Every Day Living'. Cicala and Jude agree that Lennon was keen to sign the band to Apple, but The Beatles' record label was quietly shedding its roster of everyone except the Fab Four by early 1975.

In the event, all of this material remained in the can until the publication of Engelhardt's book, which came with a three-track CD featuring 'Let's Spend The Night Together', 'Answer Me, My Love' and Dog Soldier's version of 'Incantation'. Very enjoyable they were too, though none of the tracks bore any obvious Lennon trademarks.

c. JANUARY 1975: WRITING and recording home demo of 'Tennessee;' writing 'Popcorn'

According to his girlfriend May Pang, the last song that John was writing before he returned home to the Dakota apartment was an ode to playwright Tennessee Williams. It began with the line "Tennessee, oh Tennessee, what you mean to me", so this was obviously not a random tribute. In fact, it seemed to have been sparked by a reading of Williams' *A Streetcar Named Desire*, a reference to which turned up in a later take of the song. At this stage, the piece had little effective structure; but John set down a rough piano take nonetheless, as a basis for future work. Pang says he had also composed a light, commercial tune called 'Popcorn'; but he doesn't seem to have committed this effort to tape. The fact that he was writing songs at all, however, showed that he hadn't yet decided to step away from his career.

February 1, 1975, was apparently the day on which the Lennons were officially reconciled – an event that scuppered the long awaited studio reunion between Lennon and Paul McCartney. Lennon had been invited to take part in the New Orleans sessions for Wings' latest album, and was ready to go, but as he explained shortly afterwards, "My personal life sort of interfered with that. I was just too busy being happy." Soon afterwards, Yoko became pregnant, and any thought of another album – or a collaboration with McCartney on *Venus And Mars* – was abandoned.

MARCH 1975: RECORDING 'Stand By Me'/'Slippin' And Slidin' '/'Lady Marmalade'

To accompany a filmed interview he'd held with Bob Harris, host of the BBC's TV rock show, *The Old Grey Whistle Test*, John agreed to shoot promo clips for two tracks from his newly-released *Rock 'n' Roll* album. Returning to the Record Plant East in New York, he had his band mime to the appropriate backing tracks, while he taped new lead vocals over the top, throwing in a quick transatlantic 'hello' to his son Julian along the way. At around the same time – possibly even the same afternoon – John was filmed busking his way through a chorus of the Labelle hit 'Lady Marmalade' on his upright piano at the Dakota, during a discussion about disco with a French interviewer.

APRIL 18, 1975: PERFORMING 'Slippin' And Slidin''/'Stand By Me'/'Imagine' for *Salute To Sir Lew Grade* TV show

This was a bizarre way for Lennon to end his performing career. In front of an audience of celebrities and socialites, few of whom seemed to have the slightest interest in his appearance, he sang two of his *Rock'n'Roll* tracks, plus the perennial 'Imagine'. The episode was aimed at ending another prolonged legal dispute, this time with the impresario Sir Lew Grade, who effectively owned the Lennon/McCartney songwriting credits through his control of ATV Music. As a slight hint of rebellion, Lennon was accompanied by the band Dog Soldier (renamed 'Etc'. for the occasion, as in 'John Lennon Etc'.) who wore face masks on the back of their heads, so that no one was quite sure which way they were facing. This was presumably an oblique comment on Sir Lew's two-faced way of doing business. In the event, they were there strictly for show, as they mimed to the backing tracks from the *Rock'n'Roll* LP for the first two numbers, and were then drowned out by the house orchestra during 'Imagine'.

Lennon was resplendent in a red jumpsuit and shoulder-length hair, looking as if he thought he was somewhere else entirely. But he kept his head amidst the plush surroundings, changing one verse of 'Imagine' to "Nothing to kill or die for/No immigration too", and answering his own rhetorical statement, "You may say I'm a dreamer" by shouting "He's a dreamer" off-mike. He hadn't forgotten his principles, though, as it was still a "brotherhood and sisterhood of man" that he was trying to imagine. He dedicated that final song to Grade, and to "my other friend, Yoko".

At the end of his brief set, marooned amidst a succession of night-club acts, Lennon bowed with a flourish, and walked slowly off stage – unaware that with that gesture his public life was effectively over.

CHAPTER 14

Early 1976 to Late 1979

A nd in the end . . . there was five years of public silence from Lennon, before a miraculously inspired rebirth, and the cruellest of tragedies to cut the story short. Yet the rebirth was a PR campaign, and the reality was that Lennon spent most of his last five years fighting off dread and boredom, questioning his reason for living, and trying to convince himself that he really didn't care if he ever functioned as a creative artist again. When he finally allowed himself to resurface in public, he appeared to have lost none of his energy or drive. If his skills were rusty after such a long lay-off, there was always the hope that intensive activity might help him regain his former status. But fate had other ideas.

EARLY 1976: RECORDING 'Mucho Mungo'/'Cookin' ' demos

October 1975 was a month for the Lennons to remember. John celebrated his 35th birthday, and the couple's son, Sean, was born the same day, thanks to the medical marvels of planned induction. His compilation album *Shaved Fish* was issued around the same time, collecting together his American A-sides and tossing in a fragment of the One To One 'Give Peace A Chance' for collectors. Meanwhile his prolonged immigration battle was effectively won, with the announcement that the US government had dropped their efforts to have him deported.

1976 would mark the completion of his nine-year recording contract with EMI. There had been periodic rumours about a reformation of The Beatles during the mid-Seventies, and now even Lennon was no longer denying them (though Harrison was). Unwilling to begin a new project for EMI/Capitol, Lennon chose to bide his time. By the time the contract actually expired on January 26, John had already decided not to respond to any of the multi-million dollar offers he had received from the world's leading record companies. For the first time since 1961, he was not under contract; he didn't owe anybody anything. So he resolved to devote his time to raising his new son.

Quite how involved he was in that process varied from one account to the next. Lennon recalled in 1980 that he had spent five years as a 'house-husband', rearing Sean while Yoko took care of business downstairs at the Dakota, bamboozling lawyers and selling cows for hundreds of thousands of dollars apiece. Other commentators, led by Albert Goldman in *The Lives Of John Lennon*, insisted that Lennon divided his time between drink and drugs; that he was an emotional and physical wreck for much of his final five years; that his relationship with Yoko was a virtual sham, on the verge of disintegration; and that the entire 'house-husband' episode was little more than a fairy tale.

Whom you believe is up to you: maybe some of the evidence that follows will tip the balance one way or the other. What's certain is that by early 1976, Lennon had not quite lost the will to create. His only commitment was to Ringo Starr: for the third album running, Ringo had asked his buddy for a new song, and Lennon obliged with the throwaway 'Cookin' (In The Kitchen Of Love)', which he demoed at home on the piano. He hadn't quite perfected the chord changes, but the song was already intact – complete with an extra tag-line in the chorus, "We're gonna have a party (bring your own stuff)". For the ending, John went back to his roots, to the same break-down Elvis Presley had used on 'I Got A Woman' on his 1956 début album. The whole concoction was every bit as trivial as 'Rock And Roll People', but without the same painful sense of having been squeezed out against his will.

Around the same time, John chose to tape another acoustic demo of a song he'd already cut with Harry Nilsson eighteen months earlier. 'Mucho Mungo' was a fantasy escape from reality, and a love song for May, so it made a surprising choice for recording at the Dakota with Sean crying in the background. Either way, this version hardly differed from the acoustic takes John had cut before the *Pussy Cats* sessions in the spring of 1974. But it did contain one extra melodic section, which may (or may not) be the elusive contribution that Phil Spector had made to the original version of the song back in 1973.

UNSPECIFIED SESSIONS FROM 1976 TO 1980: RECORDING 'Rock Island Line'/'John Henry'/'Sea Ditties'/unnamed blues instrumentals/'I'm A Man'/'Brown-Eyed Handsome Man'/'Twas A Night Like Ethel Merman'/'Beyond The Sea'/'Blue Moon'/ 'Falling In Love Again'/'Corrine Corrina'/'News Of The Day From Reuters'/'I Ain't Got Time'/'She'll Be Coming Round The Mountain When She Comes'

"I didn't even touch a guitar for five years," John claimed during his late 1980 comeback. These undated tapes, and many more besides, proved him wrong. In a sense, their exact origins don't matter, though they probably dated from early in his 'retirement'. They exhibited the same semi-serious attitude towards his musical roots as his work with The Beatles in 1969, or his jamming during the *Double Fantasy* sessions. The Fifties was Lennon's era, so it was no surprise to hear him busking his way through songs he had played with The Quarry Men, like 'Rock Island Line' (with John chugging away happily on electric guitar, and forgetting the list of cargo the driver had on his train) and 'John Henry', a traditional blues. In fact, the simplicity of the blues structure pervaded most of these tapes, with John concentrating more on the feel of the music than Clapton-style purism and scholarship.

The performances ranged from a light ramble through 'I Ain't Got Time' on acoustic guitar, to a Elmore James-inspired take on 'Corrine Corrina' and a tongue-in-cheek rendition of Bo Diddley's 'I'm A Man', complete with self-effacing lyrics ("I can't get it up at all").

Equally revealing was a fiery take of Chuck Berry's 1956 single 'Brown-Eyed Handsome Man', taken initially as a blues rather than a rocker, but with John redoubling the tempo for the final choruses just like Jerry Lee Lewis would have done. Along the way, he dropped in and out of Paul McCartney's 'Get Back', obviously forgetting he'd once seen the song as a none-too-subtle message of contempt for Yoko.

Not all the recordings from the late Seventies were rock-orientated. One archive tape contained John singing a bizarre piano medley of English music hall favourites, from 'My Old Man's A Dustman' and 'I Do Like To Be Beside The Seaside' to George Formby's 'Chinese Laundry Blues' and 'Leanin' On A Lamp Post' — the whole piece set within a sea shanty, and accompanied by the 'over the points' rhythm from the BBC's Fifties TV rock show, *Six-Five Special*. That programme could also have found a home, circa 1958, for Lennon's skiffle interpretation of the folk standard, 'She'll Be Coming Round The Mountain'.

Another medley found John in continental mood, busking his way through a cod French monologue before delivering 'Beyond The Sea' and 'Blue Moon' in a Gallic accent, and 'Young Love' like a native Cockney. On another occasion he delivered 'Falling In Love Again' (a Paul McCartney showcase early in The Beatles' career) with an impression of Marlene Dietrich. Equally bizarre was 'Twas A Night Like Ethel Merman', which sounded like one of his *In His Own Write* poems set to Scottish music. And in a parodic vein, John also recorded what he thought was a piss-take of Bob Dylan, reciting the 'News Of The Day From Reuters'. As Dylan impressions go, however, Lennon's was a dog, and so was his performance.

APRIL 1976: RECORDING 'Cookin' (In The Kitchen Of Love)' with Ringo Starr.

In late April 1976, John fulfilled his last professional obligation – helping Ringo Starr record 'Cookin' (In The Kitchen Of Love)' for his *Rotogravure* album, in Los Angeles. Third time around, Ringo's all-star formula was wearing thin: so was the quality of the material, Lennon's included. At the session, where John played keyboards and presumably once again laid down a guide vocal for Ringo to follow, everyone did their best to create a party mood; but 'Cookin' ' was so slight that it merely emphasised the hollowness of the song. The Lennon/Starr relationship didn't suffer, however. Ringo cut two disco-flavoured albums in the late Seventies, but when he returned to rock in 1980, Lennon was only too happy to offer him some new material. You get the feeling that whenever Ringo asked, Lennon would have come up with something.

SPRING/SUMMER 1976: WRITING *Skywriting By Word Of Mouth*; recording readings from the book

With no recording contract, no obligations to any outside party, Lennon was free to create, or not, as he chose. Fifteen years of consistent pressure had taken their toll, however, and he felt uneasy sitting around the Dakota watching the nanny change Sean's nappies. "When I stopped music and started this house-husband business," he told *Playboy* interviewer David Sheff in 1980, "I got frantic in one period that I was supposed to be creating things, so I sat down and wrote about 200 pages of mad stuff – *In His Own Write*-ish. It's there in a box, but it isn't right. Some of it's funny, but it's not right enough."

Lennon's close companion Elliot Mintz recalled that besides this manuscript, titled *Skywriting By Word Of Mouth*, which Lennon showed him in the autumn of 1976, John had also composed a play, and a couple of dozen songs. We'll get to the songs later; the play, meanwhile, has never been unveiled in public.

But *Skywriting By Word Of Mouth* duly appeared in 1986, in a volume of Lennon's writings compiled by Yoko. It was revealed as a curiously unsatisfying mixture of parody and confession, part frantic word-play, part social satire, part the same kind of ingenious character invention which Lennon would demonstrate on the taped playlets he sent to Mintz later in the Seventies. It was described in some quarters as a novel, but it lacked any kind of unity, formal or informal; if it had a fictional ancestor, it was the cluttered, almost opaque work of Thomas Pynchon, whose novels were often inhabited by equally unusual creations engaged in equally random pursuits.

But Pynchon's books were linked by narrative development, and by moral purpose, no matter how bizarre. The structure of *Skywriting*, by comparison, was determined by Lennon's patience. Just as he had done in the mid-Sixties, Lennon wrote out of inspiration, but abandoned the task whenever the initial flow seized up – usually after a thousand words or so, three or four pages of the printed book. As there was no plot to carry, there was also no plot to interrupt; so John could stop wherever he wished, without altering the fundamental impact of his chapter.

Taken sentence by sentence, *Skywriting* was a remarkable achievement: few other comic writers could match the sheer wit and imagination that invested Lennon's word-play, which – unlike his earlier work – was usually funny and more often than not pertinent as well. But the book was almost impossible to read at a sitting – simply because it wasn't a book but a collection of unconnected phrases that were just as striking in limbo as in context.

More interesting at this distance were the occasional references to John's own life. This included not just the sly chapter heading, 'Lucy In The Scarf With Diabetics', and the fact that one of the 'stories' had Lennon's alter ego, Dr Winston O'Boogie, as its hero, but also the references to historical events that broke into the fiction, as if Lennon was using this work as a mixture of placebo and diary. In the piece 'Nobel Peace Prize Awarded To Killer Whale', for instance, a fantasy about a masturbating biologist was interrupted by reminiscences. Lennon recalled "fucking my girlfriend on a gravestone" in Liverpool, and then the Maharishi's camp in Rishikesh, where "He made us live in separate huts from our wives ... Can't say it was too much of a strain".

Elsewhere, Lennon looked back to 'Across The Universe', and then gently satirised the way it was composed, with a tumbling, dazzling exhibition of verbal dexterity. Here's a sample sentence: "Words are flowing out like endless rainbow mixed grilling baron von oil field marshall tucker band wagonner rear end zone what you reap van winkle of an eyelid of grass blowers convention centre forward march hair raising the flag of truce is stronger than friction of a second helping". Not all of *Skywriting* was that rich, but there was the essence of the book in a single sentence – puns cascading from one cliché to the next, free-falling just as the lyric to one of Lennon's most poetic songs had done nearly a decade earlier. This was infinitely more creative than 'Cookin' ' or 'Mucho Mungo'; but it didn't lead anywhere, which is no doubt why John abandoned it.

Before he did so, however, he committed a series of readings from his manuscript to tape. The results were stolen from the Dakota shortly after his death, and have apparently not been returned.

SUMMER 1976: WRITING introduction to *Rock 'n' Roll Times*

Jurgen Vollmer had been one of The Beatles' closest friends in Hamburg in 1961/62; and he took some of the classic early photos of the band, clad in black leather on the stage of the Kaiserkeller, or posed around the streets of Hamburg. When he came to publish a collection of his work, initially only in Germany, he approached Lennon for an introduction. John obliged, with a short recommendation to the effect that Jurgen's photos were the best ever taken of The Beatles. This wasn't just hype: John had already used one of them on the cover of his *Rock'n'Roll* album the previous year.

On the subject of photographic collections, John and Yoko had recently announced plans to publish a book called *365 Days Of Sean* – one photo from each day of Sean's first year of life. No doubt the photos existed; the Lennons couldn't help but document their lives together. But the book never materialised.

SUMMER 1976: WRITING AND RECORDING home demos of 'Sally And Billy'/'She Is A Friend Of Dorothy's'/'Tennessee'

Not yet fully convinced that he had retired from the music business, John sporadically returned to 'Tennessee', the tribute song he'd begun at the start of 1975. He cut a series of piano demos, each one fuller and richer than the initial fragment taped the previous year. The song now worked in a number of direct references to Tennessee Williams' plays, laced with an air of nostalgic melancholy that was heightened when John changed the title of the song to 'Memories'. There was nothing quite like this in the Lennon catalogue: nothing so obviously heartfelt and composed, and yet so distant from his own emotions and experiences.

John also chose to revive an even older song around this time: 'Sally And Billy', last heard at the end of 1970 when it was little more than a tune and some improvised lyrics. The three piano takes, again backed by a drum machine, that Lennon recorded in 1976 revealed that he'd spent some time filling in the gaps in the narrative. The plot lined up like this: the beautiful, independent and artistic Sally sits in a café reading books; Billy, meanwhile, is a singer who is "playing with his mind". Both of them are over the hill, hoping Jesus will intervene and help them decide what they should do with their lives. John might have been hoping for much the same thing. As it stood, 'Sally And Billy' seemed like an unconscious metaphor for John's own lack of purpose – or, as with 'Tennessee', perhaps the result of a conscious decision to write from outside himself rather than within.

The most complete song John wrote that summer was 'She Is A Friend Of Dorothy's' – "she's gay", in New York slang. John taped seven takes of the song, playing staccato notes high on the piano as he introduced the main character, "hot lips and no shame/all fun and no game". For the chorus, which made fun of the title line, and threw in a sly reference to "the Sheik of Arabesque", Lennon speeded-up the tune of 'Aisumasen', rolling his piano chords like a New Orleans bluesman. Though the lyrics required some focus, this was a finished song, both more playful and more melodic than anything he'd written since The Beatles. But like the rest of his 1976 demos, this was work without an end in sight; and though John thought of reviving 'Dorothy' in 1979, he doesn't seem to have done any more work on the song.

If Lennon had ever played 'Sally And Billy' and 'Dorothy' to Paul McCartney, however, then the latter might have wanted to record them on the *Wings At The Speed Of Sound* album, where they would have fitted perfectly. A couple of the chord changes on 'Dorothy' were actually reminiscent of Wings' 'Silly Love Songs', by accident or design.

1976 to 1977: ILLUSTRATING Japanese phrases

In preparation for the Lennons' lengthy trip to Japan in summer 1977, John made a concerted attempt to master the language, buying a set of Berlitz instruction cassettes rather than trying to distract his wife from her Apple and Lenono business duties. To aid his learning, he filled a sketchbook with surreal and playful cartoons to illustrate particular phrases, concentrating particularly on contradictions and contrasting statements. Almost inevitably, these sketches were published as a book after his death, under the title: *ai: Japan Through John Lennon's Eyes*. The book also contained several photos that John took in Japan as a tourist, including pictures of the nation's technological pride and joy, the bullet train.

LATE 1977: RECORDING home demos of 'Mirror Mirror On The Wall'/'Real Life'/'I Don't Wanna Face It'/'I Watch Your Face'/'One Of The Boys'/'Free As A Bird'/'Whatever Happened To ...'/'Now And Then'/'I'm Ready Lord'/'When This Life Is Done (And The Angels Come)'; writing 'Emotional Wreck'

Lennon was finally awarded his green card – the badge of government approval that marked the end of his immigration battle – in July 1976, after a hearing in which a parade of notables, including Gloria Swanson, Norman Mailer and John Cage, testified on his behalf. The hearing was a formality, but this did not stop the judge from inquiring of John's solicitor – apparently in all seriousness – whether or not he might become a "state charge" and seek "national assistance". "That is most unlikely," the lawyer replied before briefly outlining John's assets. After the hearing John was amused to discover that the green card he had sought for so long was actually blue in colour.

Six months later, he felt sufficiently secure in his status to appear at President Carter's inaugural ball at the White House. Thereafter, he made no public appearances until he and Yoko called a press conference in Japan on October 4, 1977, to explain that they were concentrating on child-rearing, not business, and that they wouldn't be resuming their artistic careers until their son was five years old, in 1980.

The Lennons were then close to the end of a four-month stay in Japan, captured in the photographic portfolio *A Family Album*. But this apparent idyll was a time of some stress for John. Having exhausted the spurt of creativity that had driven him to write *Skywriting By Word Of Mouth*, he found himself drawn into a long period of depression. Lennon may or may not have dealt with this crisis by taking refuge in drugs or physical violence; you'll have to decide that for yourselves on the basis of the competing biographies that have been written over the past two decades. But towards the end of the summer, he did manage to channel that gloom into work, composing a song called 'Mirror Mirror On The Wall' while he was still in Japan, and cutting an acoustic guitar demo of the song which has sadly been destroyed.

Back at the Dakota in October, Lennon reworked the song on piano, and taped five more solo demos. The song was a weary piece of self-examination, almost self-pity: "I look in the mirror and nobody's there . . . I keep on staring, is it me?" Its descending chord sequence added to the pervading mood of sadness, and the overall feel was somewhere between 'Scared' and the as-yet unwritten 'Watching The Wheels'. It was a chilling piece of work, even in this unfinished state, and it testified to the depth of Lennon's crisis in late 1977. Two other songs from this period, 'I'm Ready Lord' and 'When This Life Is Done (And The Angels Come)', seemed to hint at a willingness on Lennon's part to see his life come to an end.

The sheer act of writing about his misery seems to have lightened it, however, and over the next few weeks Lennon composed a sheaf of new songs, almost all of which he taped for posterity – the exception being 'Emotional Wreck', a 'Watching The Wheels' prototype. In itself, this last song was significant. In his promotional interviews for *Double Fantasy* in 1980, Lennon made great play of the fact that his new songs had arrived almost without invitation. "They were inspired songs," he claimed, "and there were none where I had to sit down and make a dovetail joint." And he dated them precisely, to the Bermuda holiday he took with Sean in June 1980, when he supposedly began to write his first new compositions since *Walls And Bridges* in 1974.

As Lennon's carefully preserved composing and demo tapes reveal, that was simply a line for the press, something to make *Double Fantasy* sound like a work of inspiration rather than craftsmanship. In fact, the songs on that album, and on its companion piece, *Milk And Honey*, evolved over a period of three years or more. And with the exception of 'Woman', and maybe 'Dear Yoko', none of them emerged fully-formed from the chrysalis: they were painstakingly constructed from a series of run-throughs and rewrites, only assuming their final form after they'd undergone numerous changes of title and lyrics. That doesn't detract from their art, or devalue their emotional impact: it simply means that, like any of his public comments, Lennon's explanation of the roots of *Double Fantasy* has to be approached with caution.

Besides 'Emotional Wreck', John began work on a song called 'I Don't Wanna Face It' in late 1977. He built the song around a two-chord acoustic guitar riff, and used its fragmentary lyrics to explain to himself – there was no other audience – why he couldn't resume his place in the world. And he also offered a glimpse of why he was sometimes so hard to live with: "I can dish it out/but I just can't take it".

'I Watch Your Face' was a far less painful exercise, a hillbilly song which had something of the flavour of Buddy Holly's 'Raining In My Heart', even a hint of a far less likely source, The Applejacks' 1964 beat group hit, 'Tell Me When'. And Lennon ended his first demo with a brief suggestion of the intro of another song he had yet to write – '(Just Like) Starting Over'. The song, such as it was, seems to have been inspired by his son: "While you are sleeping/No one told me life was so worth keeping". But that was as far as the lyrics were ever taken.

'Free As A Bird' took off from a basic doo-wop chord sequence, taking in some of the stately changes of 'Grow Old With Me' as it progressed. This was another tune of great promise, which Lennon either forgot about or didn't bother to return to. Despite its incomplete lyrics, it had an air of majesty that deserved further attention. The words explored different ways of conveying the metaphor in the title, which may have been inspired by getting his green card the previous year and finally being at liberty to travel outside the United States. Quite clearly it was the concept rather than any particular lyrical phrase which had been the initial inspiration, and nothing Lennon sang on this tape quite did the title justice.

As the vehicle for The Beatles' reunion in 1995, 'Free As A Bird' underwent more scrutiny than any of Lennon's other home demos from this period. Sensibly, perhaps, Yoko chose not to use any of three piano versions of the song on the *Anthology*, as that would have revealed how unfinished John's rendition was, and also how much the other Beatles had added to his blueprint, both lyrically and melodically.

Yoko also passed The Beatles Lennon's home recording of 'Now And Then' from the same period. This was the mysterious 'third song' which was intended to lead off the group's *Anthology 3* collection, but in the event it was never completed – apparently because George Harrison didn't think the track was good enough. Lennon's original tape was marred by a persistent buzz, which must have presented severe problems to The Beatles and producer Jeff Lynne. But the song was promising enough, despite joining the ranks of mournful Lennon ballads expressing regret and guilt. Lennon's performance was erratic, as the middle section stretched his vocal range beyond its limits, and he'd probably have been mortified at the idea of McCartney and Harrison ever hearing this tape. Yet the potential was there for 'Now And Then' to become a genuinely impressive song. What we'll never know is whether it was inspired by a marital feud with Yoko, or perhaps longing for Lennon's previous girlfriend, May Pang.

Like 'She Is A Friend Of Dorothy's' from the previous year, 'Whatever Happened To. . .' (a phrase that also began the middle section of 'Free As A Bird') saw Lennon making a rare excursion into writing in the third-person

– creating characters rather than analysing his own. Just two takes of the song existed: the first broke down during the guitar intro, but the second was complete. Lennon had loved the strident rhythm guitar-work of Richie Havens in the late Sixties, and 'Whatever Happened To...' was in a similar style, with barrages of chords punctuated by dramatic pauses.

"She used to be an artist but she threw away the key ... whatever happened to the woman we once knew": well, maybe John was writing obliquely about himself after all. Either way, these demo takes were merely documents of work in progress, as John experimented with chord inversions for maximum impact; but once again he never bothered to return to the song in later sessions. The fact that several of the songs from this period vanished from his repertoire forever, while other less promising material was revived in 1979-80, suggests that Lennon might simply have mislaid the tape on which they were written.

Finally, 'One Of The Boys' offered a less intense view of the artist at 37. The faintly tropical flavour of this guitar-based tune reflected the humorous acceptance of the lyric; John might be growing older, "no longer a garcon fatale", but "they say that he's aged very well, he's still one of the boys". There was a double joke here, of course: 'the boys' was how Beatle aides always referred to the group in the Sixties. This mild self-mockery took some achieving in late 1977, but it was a sign that Lennon had written himself back into something approaching good humour. The next step was to find a project into which his restored creative powers could be directed.

LATE 1977/EARLY 1978: CREATING *Mind Movies*; drawing *Real Love* cartoons

Elliot Mintz had first interviewed the Lennons in late 1971; then in 1972 he'd lost his job as a DJ when he aired their *Some Time In New York City* album in its entirety, profanities and all. Six years on, he was one of the couple's few confidants: a trusted aide who doubled as friend and adviser, a role he continues to play for Yoko Ono today. In the late Seventies, he was in constant contact with John; and it was Mintz to whom Lennon sent his taped *Mind Movies*. These were bizarre playlets which John taped at home, mixing dialogue from TV and radio dramas with Lennon's own invented characters, foremost amongst whom were The Great Wok and Maurice Dupont, *Agent Provocateur du jour*. Under the guise of The Great Wok, Lennon announced his intention to "renounce completely everything but complete luxury and self-indulgence". That confession aside, however, these tapes didn't have a great deal of relevance; but like the collage art that

Lennon was creating around the same time, they were a sign of an imagination with too much freedom on its hands.

Elsewhere, that freedom was turned to good parental purpose, as Lennon entertained and educated his toddler son by drawing cartoons of animals and encouraging him to come up with titles for them: "a small pig is a happy pig", "a cat napping", and so on. Hand coloured under Yoko's supervision after John's death, these illustrations were compiled into a slim but attractive volume entitled *Real Love*. For once, Lennon's caricatures exuded affection, rather than the distortion and disgust that had always been his trademark when he was creating purely for his own amusement.

MID-1978: PREPARING songs, and writing programme notes, for *The Ballad Of John And Yoko*

With Lennon writing a steady stream of (albeit unfinished) new material, one might have expected him to begin work on a follow-up to *Rock'n'Roll* and *Shaved Fish*. Instead, he and Yoko supposedly made tentative plans to write a Broadway musical, based on their own relationship, and called – what else? – *The Ballad Of John And Yoko*.

Several of the songs John had already written were supposedly set aside for the project, like 'She Is A Friend Of Dorothy's', 'Whatever Happened To . . .', 'Mirror Mirror On The Wall', 'Free As A Bird', and 'Real Love' (not yet written at this point, however). Yoko composed 'Every Man Has A Woman Who Loves Him' around the same time; some of her other *Double Fantasy* material may also date from this period.

The couple didn't seem to have considered the problem of writing a script to link their songs, although more recently Yoko has succeeded in transferring their myth into a piece of musical theatre. And, of course, they didn't mention the proposed show in their 1980 interviews, because that would have ruined the illusion that John had spent five years steadfastly ignoring the guitar hung on his bedroom wall. But when Yoko compiled *Skywriting By Word Of Mouth* in 1986, she included what was claimed to be an essay John had written for the theatre programme, though that seemed rather premature.

Whatever its origins, *The Ballad Of John And Yoko* was a remarkable document – written in prose of such clarity that it was difficult to identify it with the creator of *In His Own Write* or *Skywriting*. For once, Lennon was entirely serious: any humour was strictly sardonic.

This autobiographical testament began with the search for the ultimate woman, and the realisation that he'd found her in Yoko. So the *Ballad* began, "just in time for me to avoid having to live with my ex-wife's new nose". Lennon recounts the racism the couple experienced in Britain; the hypocrisy of the British press, and of his fellow Beatles; and then the madness and magic of the Bed-Ins, the peace campaigns, the 'revolutionary period', the move to New York, and the eventual birth of their first child.

There was no mention of the 1973 separation; precious little of John's musical career; and the essay ended with Lennon admitting: "I've already 'lost' one family to produce what? *Sgt. Pepper*? I am blessed with a second chance. Being a Beatle almost cost me my life, and certainly cost me a great deal of my health ... I will not make the same mistake twice in one lifetime ... If I never 'produce' anything more for public consumption than 'silence', so be it."

It was a powerful piece of writing, though surely a strange offering for a theatre programme; more like an artistic suicide note than a warm-up routine for a Broadway audience. There was more to *The Ballad Of John And Yoko*, perhaps, than met the eye; but whenever it was written, and why, it put into clear English the underlying message of the 'house-husband' years: Lennon was tired of living his life to others' expectations.

In the end, what was perhaps most intriguing was the chasm between the mature self-confidence of this essay, and the blatant indecisiveness revealed in the songs that dated from the same period.

LATE 1978: WRITING and recording home demos of 'People'/'Stranger's Room'/'Everybody's Talkin'', 'Nobody's Talkin''

According to Yoko's astrologer, John Green, Lennon spent around 15 months after the couple's return from Japan in his bedroom, watching TV and losing weight. According to Yoko, the couple were planning a Broadway musical. According to Lennon's tape boxes, he was writing new songs – at least three of which have survived, and were reworked during the couple's *Double Fantasy* sessions in the autumn of 1980.

'People' was merely a reworking of 'Emotional Wreck', which John had begun the previous year – another step on the road to 'Watching The Wheels'. The chorus hadn't yet evolved, but John had hit upon the circular piano riff which underpinned the finished record, and the basic verses – a wry comment on public expectations, an apologia for his lack of activity in recent years.

When he did put his mind to new material, what emerged was in the same tradition as songs like 'Rock And Roll People' and 'Move Over Ms L'. He wrote 'Everybody's Talkin', Nobody's Talkin' ' around the same time as 'People', and cut a rough demo on acoustic guitar. When John wrote a new chorus, the song became known as 'Nobody Told Me'. In this form, it shared that song's chaotic rush of images, as scattered as if Lennon had been flipping the channels on TV – which was as likely an inspiration for the song as any. Without a hookline, the original chorus ran, "You can't tell no one nothing no way never", and there was no way never that was going to survive.

'Stranger's Room' was more obviously a tale from the heart – as confirmed by John's comments about its eventual incarnation, 'I'm Losing You' on *Double Fantasy*. On his composing tape, Lennon had just one verse, which he repeated over and over again, feeling his way towards the phrasing he wanted.

There was no chorus, as such, merely a lonely lyric of alienation that could have been narrated from another woman's room, on a casual fling away from Yoko. Internal evidence was slight, however, and the atmosphere of the song was more important than the setting.

DECEMBER 1978: RECORDING phonecall with Tony Cox

One of the most bizarre recorded artefacts of Lennon's entire life comprised a series of phone calls between two of Yoko Ono's husbands: Tony Cox, and the man who supplanted him, John Lennon. Seven years after the two men had been involved in a bitter court dispute, stretching around the world, over the custody of Yoko's daughter Kyoko Cox, they shared a phone call. Their aim was to hammer out a compromise deal whereby the Lennons and Cox would share custody. Typically, as two artists were involved, the conversation was taped for posterity – not by Lennon, who would only resume chronicling his life on tape the following year, but by Cox, who had clearly not forgotten his Fluxus roots.

"I often thought about you," Lennon told Cox during the encounter, "good thoughts." "We really went through hell," Cox replied. Lennon agreed, noting that without Kyoko, "there was always a hole in our lives." Referring to both sides of the dispute, he asked: "How did we do it? If we're supposed to be so damn bright." "We both have more honesty and objectivity in our lives," Cox concluded. But the two men's cautious optimism was misplaced, as negotiations soon broke down, and Lennon never saw his stepdaughter again.

LATE 1978 to EARLY 1979: DRAWING self-portrait cartoons

Most of the cartoons that illustrate *Skywriting By Word Of Mouth* were drawn within a period of months around the end of 1978. They portray the artist as a loner, a dreamer, head in the clouds, above and outside the corporeal world – as worthy a metaphor for the times as any of Lennon's lyrics of alienation. "Every day in every way I'm getting better and better," ran the caption for the mirror image of a dubious face. Another portrait named the problem without offering any solution: "And then I took it TOO seriously."

MAY 27, 1979: PUBLICATION in London, New York and Tokyo of 'A Love Letter From Yoko And John To People Who Ask Us What, When And Why'

What When and Why indeed. It was a surprise, to say the least, to open the London *Sunday Times* in May 1979 and find a page devoted to a paid advertisement bearing not an invitation to sample a new Porsche or a fine wine, but a message to their friends and fans from the reclusive Lennons. Stranger still, the message advertised no forthcoming project, not even the hint of a new album or tour. As with their peace campaigns of the late Sixties, the message justified itself: this was a worldwide event to rank alongside the poster blitz of December 1969.

Peace was the subject a decade later as well, though this time it was inner and spiritual. John and Yoko were thriving, we were told, in the simple, faintly poetic prose we'd come to recognise as Yoko's. Sean was wonderful; so were the cats; so was the world, if we'd only look to see. Magic could achieve everything: wish and it was yours. The Lennons loved us. And there was a postscript: "We noticed that three angels were looking over our shoulders while we wrote this". The 'John and Yoko' signature was unmistakeably in Ono's hand, please note, not Lennon's.

Any news of the Lennons was welcome in 1979 – a time when, if you believe their detractors, the couple were sliding further apart, and towards the spectre of drug addiction. So was their 'love letter' another piece of wish-fulfilment – the Lennons putting their own theory to the test, hoping that by saying the garden was rosy it would become so? Were they expecting to lead the world towards spiritual renewal, the substitution of hope for pessimism and distrust? And who were the three angels? The other Beatles? The Three Stooges? No one was saying, then or now. The letter went unexplained during their comeback interviews, and remained one of the weirder episodes in the disjointed history of the couple's final years.

SEPTEMBER 5 & OCTOBER 10, 1979: RECORDING audio diary

One of the stranger subplots that arose in the aftermath of Lennon's assassination was the fate of his diaries. These were reported stolen by Yoko, until it was revealed that they had been removed by former Lennon aide Fred Seaman immediately after the murder. He claimed that he had been instructed by John to pass them to his son, Julian, if anything should ever happen to him. Eventually Seaman returned them to the Lennon estate, but along the way the 1980 diary passed into other hands, and at last report it was still believed to be missing – although Yoko may have a photocopy of the manuscript in her possession. Seaman made no direct references to the diary when he wrote his fascinating account of life with Lennon, *Living On Borrowed Time*. But two books published in 2000, Geoffrey Guiliano's *Lennon In America* and Robert Rosen's *Nowhere Man*, seemed to depend on their authors having (at the very least) caught a brief glimpse of Lennon's journal.

The plot was complicated when two extracts from a Lennon audio diary passed into collectors' hands. Similar tapes by Yoko from 1968 documented her sexual fantasies and insecurities. Lennon's recordings, by contrast, were soaked in weariness, bitterness and misery. This was no happy house-husband, baking bread and counting his cows, but a desolate, desperate man who sounded as if he was on the verge of suicide.

"Take one in the ongoing life story of John Winston Ono Lennon," began the September 5, 1979 tape. He began by talking about his childhood, but soon became bored. Instead, he laid into his long-time nemesis Bob Dylan. "The singing was pathetic and the words are just embarrassing," he complained of Dylan's Grammy-winning 'Gotta Serve Somebody'. Then he widened his assault: "So here we sit, watching the mighty Dylan, and the mighty McCartney, and the mighty Jagger, slide down the mountain, with blood and mud in their nails." He admitted that he'd once been sent into a state of panic any time any of his contemporaries made a record, but now he didn't even bother to listen to their albums. "There doesn't seem any point now," he muttered in a voice that was flat-lined with depression. Returning to the attack, he accused McCartney and the others of being "company men", and said that his main pleasure in hearing their records these days was that "it's all a load of shit".

Then he changed tack again, and was off into a bizarre fantasy about his mother's breasts, and how he felt when he walked in on her giving her boyfriend, 'Twitchy', a blow job. Most revealingly, perhaps, he bemoaned the fact that his sex drive was likely to continue well past the point when he would be able to indulge it. From his tone of voice, it sounded as if he'd have been quite happy to sacrifice his libido there and then.

The October 10, 1979 tape, recorded the day after his 39th birthday, was even darker. It echoed the self-destructive tone of his wife's song, '(Aged 39) Looking Over From My Hotel Window'. He recalled how he'd spent his birthday "wondering whether to jump or get back into bed, so I got back in bed". Once, staying in bed had been a conceptual art exercise aimed at inspiring world peace. A decade later, it was a refuge for a man who was scared of himself, and life.

LATE 1979: WRITING and recording home demos of 'Not For Love Nor Money' (alias 'Illusions')/'That's The Way The World Is'/'My Life'/'Beautiful Boy'/'I'm Crazy'/'Many Rivers To Cross'/'My Girl'

Throughout the so-called 'house-husband' years, Lennon was unable to resist the lure of the guitar pinned on his bedroom wall. Little of his work during the late Seventies was complete, or would have been remotely suitable for release; but his unfinished songs and half-aired melodies were still the major source of inspiration for *Double Fantasy* in 1980, despite his claims otherwise.

Often it was the most unpromising material that was milked for the finished album. One such example was 'My Life', which Lennon cut three times on piano towards the end of 1979, then a further four on guitar. In its simplest form, Lennon sang the skeleton lyrics in falsetto; the later takes used a lower register, and an acoustic guitar riff that wouldn't have been out of place on a John Denver record. The words were equally banal, and also rather eerie, in the light of later events: "This is my life/take it, it's mine to give . . . do what you will/I dedicate it to you". They were set around a tune close to the opening section of the song that became 'Starting Over' a year later; while another line, "Life is something that happens while you're making plans", was subsequently transferred to 'Beautiful Boy'. Lennon was often distracted away from the work at hand while he was cutting these demos, usually choosing to busk his way through an old rocker or one of his own compositions. But one demo of 'My Life' ended up in the unlikely realms of The Little River Band's 1978 hit, 'Reminiscing'.

'Beautiful Boy' also began to emerge around this time, though its title alternated with 'Darling Boy' until Lennon combined them both on *Double Fantasy*. May Pang wrote in her book *Loving John* that she had heard the tune as early as 1974. Then again, she also thought that 'Tennessee' shared the same tune as 'Watching The Wheels', so she was maybe not an ideal witness. But it was also quite possible that in composing a lullaby for his son, John retrieved a finished melody that he'd had in storage since *Walls And Bridges*. Either way, the tune was fully formed on his first double-tracked demo, as were most of the poignant lyrics, though there were some slight changes to be made: "Hold my hand before you cross the street," Lennon sang, "The traffic's slow but you never know who you're gonna meet."

Another song, known variously as 'Illusions' and 'Not For Love Nor Money', borrowed some of the feel of 'Beautiful Boy', seasoned with a dose of 'Mucho Mungo'. Lyrically, it listed the illusions that Lennon had shared and then seen through – sex, drugs, fools' gold among them – and then veered into a delightful chorus that sounded as if it belonged on one of George Harrison's Seventies solo albums. (That comparison is meant as a compliment, although Lennon wouldn't have regarded it as such.)

'That's The Way The World Is' was a strangely Harrisonesque title, ironically, for a song that marked the first step towards 'Real Life'. In its earliest incarnation, on the Dakota piano, it married the eventual verse of that song with the lines that would become the middle section of 'I'm Stepping Out' the following year.

A similar process of self-cannibalization had spawned 'I'm Crazy', the third title for the song which was now close to becoming 'Watching The Wheels'. The earliest surviving home recording of the song dated from this period, and contains another reference to "the traffic flow" that John could see from his sixth-floor bedroom window. Cut on piano, the song lacked a pay-off line to the chorus, but the eventual verses were more or less there, and John ad-libbed his way through an additional set of lyrics which suggested that he had retained his sense of irony: "People say I'm stupid/giving my money away/They give me all kinds of names and addresses/designed to save me financially".

For light relief between his new compositions, Lennon occasionally turned to some of his favourite oldies. Among them was the Jimmy Cliff tune he'd recorded five years earlier with Harry Nilsson, 'Many Rivers To Cross', which eventually meandered into Smokey Robinson's 'My Girl', while threatening to turn into Bob Dylan's 'I Don't Believe You' along the way.

CHAPTER 15

January to December 1980

The dawn of 1980 brought no immediate resolution to the lingering discontent in John Lennon's life. Terrified of returning to rock stardom, but aware that he was frittering his time away at home, he continued to cut demos and write songs at the Dakota, without any specific project in mind.

JANUARY to MAY 1980: WRITING and recording home demos of 'Serve Yourself'/'Don't Be Crazy'/'Baby Make Love To You'/'Real Life'/'Watching The Wheels'/ 'The Worst Is Over'/'Beautiful Boy'/medley of 'Beautiful Boy'-'Memories'- 'Across The River'/'Across The River'/'India'/'The Happy Rishikesh Song'/'Help Me To Help Myself'/'Mr Hyde's Gone (Don't Be Afraid)'/'It's Real'

The previous summer, Bob Dylan had announced his advocacy of evangelical Christianity with a forthright declaration of faith, the *Slow Train Coming* album. Its key song, for which he won a Grammy, was 'Gotta Serve Somebody' — a tongue-in-cheek piece of gospel which insisted that between the Lord and the Devil there was no space to hide. Lennon's spiritual beliefs did not confine him to any God or prophet; he increasingly accepted the power of the unconscious, as a substitute for political, people-powered change. So the strict moralism of Dylan's album shocked him: "I was very surprised when Bobby boy went that way," he told David Sheff in

291

1980, "very surprised. But I'm not distressed by the fact that Dylan is doing what Dylan wants to do."

The sense of betrayal was somewhat stronger earlier in the year, when Lennon struck back at Dylan's beliefs – perhaps having seen him perform 'Gotta Serve Somebody' at the Grammy Awards in February. John's riposte was 'Serve Yourself': a vitriolic attack on those who claimed to have found the meaning of life in God or religion. "You've got to serve yourself," Lennon ranted in the chorus, "Ain't nobody gonna do it for you." In all, he cut no fewer than twelve takes of the song, most of them as a piano blues, New Orleans-style, complete with mock-serious monologues about creationism and the power of masturbation. "There ain't no room service here," he quipped, before ad-libbing a verse about man's descent from monkeys or visitors from outer space.

Consistency was not one of Lennon's dominant qualities during his final months. So perhaps it's not surprising that while he was eager to lampoon Dylan's religious beliefs, he was also enjoying nostalgic memories of his own spiritual enlightenment, under the guidance of the Maharishi. Maybe Lennon had dreamed about The Beatles' stay in India; more likely he caught a glimpse of the Maharishi on one of the Dakota's many TV sets. But whatever the direct inspiration, he penned two songs in the early months of 1980 that looked back fondly on the episode that he'd once satirised so caustically in 'The Maharishi Song' and 'Sexy Sadie'.

'The Happy Rishikesh Song' had the same mantra-like simplicity as The Beach Boys' meditation songs, themselves the product of time spent with the Maharishi. Lennon's demo had a lightness of touch missing from most of his work, as he worked through the repetitive guitar chords and a set of lyrics that parroted the Maharishi's slogans without real understanding. Lennon's irony surfaced with the recognition that despite meditation, "everybody needs a woman". And the final lines of the song revealed his realisation that blind acceptance of TM was just another drug: "swallow this, that's all you've got to do". Significantly, one of this song's lines was borrowed from that blast at unthinking faith, 'Serve Yourself'.

On 'India, India', however, there was not a hint of irony and distance. This was memory as a love letter to the past, set to the same melody line that Lennon had already used for 'Tennessee' and 'Memories'. He pictured himself in 1968, sitting at the foot of his guru by the River Ganges, caught up in the mystic magic of the moment. But at the same time he realised that "I left my heart in England with the girl I left behind". He meant Yoko, who had dominated his thoughts in the spring of 1968. Perhaps he felt he'd been closer to her then, several thousand miles apart, than he was in 1980, when they were sharing the same apartment.★

A third slant on religion came on 'Help Me To Help Myself', a plea for support from a deity whose existence the singer still rather doubted. This beautiful tune was steeped in the gospel tradition, with a piano part that was reminiscent of Billy Preston's playing on 'God' a decade earlier. Lennon admitted that "deep inside I was never satisfied", but confessed that "the angel of destruction keeps on hounding me". There was even an allusion to George Harrison's spiritual ballad, 'The Light That Has Lighted The World'. But there would be no space for emotions this dark on the album the Lennons would cut later in the year.

That spring, another self-examination, 'I'm Crazy', became 'Watching The Wheels'. Having worked up the song on piano, Lennon switched to electric guitar for his next demo, playing a boogie rhythm and some apparently random chord changes behind the familiar tune.

Among the other songs Lennon had left incomplete the previous year was 'Beautiful Boy'. In the early months of 1980, he made another attempt, accompanying his electric rhythm guitar with a simple drum machine and working round and round the changes until the final lyrics came. One take lasted ten minutes or more: another became a medley, moving from 'Beautiful Boy' to the long-abandoned 'Memories', then into another song called 'Across The River', an easy-paced boogie, and back through 'Memories' again. Lennon also demoed 'Across The River' by itself, revealing a piece of vaguely mystical meandering set to skiffle-style guitar and drum machine. On another occasion, 'Beautiful Boy' led Lennon into an unfinished song fragment entitled 'She Runs Them Round In Circles', set to a melody that was reminiscent of the "all the lonely people" chorus of The Beatles' 'Eleanor Rigby'.

No song received more of Lennon's attention in 1980 than the piece that had already emerged under the title 'That's The Way The World Is'. Under its new name of 'Baby Make Love To You', it returned as Lennon sat at his piano and tried to find a structure, and a set of words, that would suit the verse he'd already composed. A few weeks later, the song matured into 'Real Life', with a lyric that saw John coming to terms with existence, rather than shying away from its implications. John reworked this

---

★ This song was unveiled publicly for the first time in 2005, as part of the score of the Yoko-authorised musical about her life with John. The same show also included the otherwise undocumented Lennon original, 'I Don't Want To Lose You'.

tune constantly till the end of his life, frequently stealing part of its structure for another song. The initial take, for instance, had a verse which ended up in 'I'm Stepping Out', and a hint of the eventual chorus to 'Watching The Wheels' along the way. Vamping at the piano, John improvised lyrics – "Picked up the paper/read the daily news/nothing doing anyway" – before returning to the simple message of the chorus: "Just gotta let it go/it's real life". There followed a semi-classical piano interlude, before the take collapsed, with Lennon slapping his own wrist: "Oh rock yer balls, you bum".

What was left of the tune after he had distributed the parts elsewhere turned into 'Real Love' (sometimes known as 'Girls And Boys'), a gentle acoustic ballad for which John cut a set of near-identical demos. They captured the fragility of this slightly melancholy glimpse of a man removed from the world, yet trying to regain touch with his emotions. Title similarity aside, none of that had anything to do with the cheery wordless ditty included on *Anthology* under the title of 'It's Real', which could have dated from any of the post-1975 demo sessions.

That mood of optimism survived, albeit shakily, on 'Don't Be Crazy', itself a reworking of 'My Life' from the previous year. Using the same structure – that later became the middle of 'Starting Over' – Lennon threw in an adapted line from Buddy Holly's 'It's So Easy' ("Where you're concerned/the lessons have been learned"), and contrasted the general message of bonhomie with a pointed suggestion: "Why don't they leave us alone/we cannot fill the empty sky for you".

Gradually that spring, 'Don't Be Crazy' became 'The Worst Is Over', closer still to the final feel of 'Starting Over'. With his primitive drum machine in support, Lennon was still considering lyrical variations: "The worst is over now, it's all downhill," he sang, "relax and take it easy". Suitably inspired, Yoko turned the same thought into 'Hard Times Are Over'.

The same easiness of mind prompted 'Don't Be Afraid', which was given the more tangential title of 'Mr Hyde's Gone' for its appearance on *Anthology*. This perky piano tune, which threatened to break into some Fats Domino rhythm and blues at the end of every verse, may have been written as another lullaby for his young son. That would explain the reference to strange noises in the Dakota, which turned out to be nothing more than "the cats at play/they do it night and day". And so was Lennon, by this point, cranking out demo after demo, as he edged closer to ending the creative drought that had disturbed him ever since he'd stepped off the showbiz merry-go-round in 1975.

JUNE 1980: WRITING 'Woman'/'(Forgive Me) My Little Flower Princess'/'Grow Old With Me'/'Cleanup Time'; recording demos of 'Real Love'/'Beautiful Boy (Darling Boy)'/'Woman'/ 'I'm Stepping Out'/'Watching The Wheels'/'Dear Yoko'/ 'I Don't Wanna Face It'/'Borrowed Time'/'I'm Losing You'/ 'Serve Yourself' in Bermuda

Here's where reality and myth finally take flight. Time and again in his final interviews, Lennon explained how he'd taken Sean on holiday to Bermuda, visited a rock disco, heard The B-52s performing 'Rock Lobster', and realised that the world had finally caught up with the Lennons' experimental work from a decade earlier. He was fired to compose a series of new songs, cracking an artistic impasse that had lasted five years or more, and inspiring his wife to write her own songs when she heard John's down the phone at the Dakota.

John certainly went to Bermuda in June 1980; he did write several songs there, including 'Grow Old With Me', '(Forgive Me) My Little Flower Princess' and 'Cleanup Time'. But, as we've seen, the preparatory work for the other songs he demoed there had already been carried out in New York during his supposed retirement from creative composition. What seems more likely is that during the late spring of 1980, the Lennons had agreed to launch a comeback in the summer. Lennon went to Bermuda for a holiday, but dragged along his guitar, tape deck and drum machine, in the hope of cutting listenable demos of his work in progress. He may have played these down the phone to Yoko; in turn she may have sung her contributions to the project, some of which dated back to the Broadway musical of 1978, others even further ('I'm Moving On', for instance, was first attempted during the *Feeling The Space* sessions in 1973).

So the Bermuda myth wasn't quite gospel. What was certain, however, was that the Lennons entered the *Double Fantasy* sessions five weeks later with no fewer than 22 songs complete, while more emerged during the recording process. At least four of these were probably written, or at least perfected, in Bermuda.

The Bermuda demos were a remarkably homogeneous batch, sharing some of the acoustic richness of the pre-'White Album' Beatles demos from late May 1968. Another link between them was that they were all solo blueprints for the recording sessions to follow. There was no more rewriting or editing on these songs; this was the way Lennon expected his records to sound, albeit with the instrumental spice that session musicians would bring. Most of the cuts had double-tracked vocals and guitars – slightly

295

erratic in places, but still performed with a confidence entirely missing from the tentative Dakota demos of recent years.

Even if the whole exercise reeked of PR spin, then the fact that it produced 'Woman' made this a memorable moment in Lennon's career. There were no documents of work in progress here: 'Woman' seems to have emerged fully-formed, a remarkable tribute to Yoko and to womankind, for recognising "the little child inside the man" – a rare piece of self-perception. Its clarity of thought also marked it out from the other *Double Fantasy* material: for once, Lennon was able to pay homage to his wife without falling into self-abasement.

'Dear Yoko' was an obvious continuation of the same theme, though without any of the melodic grandeur. Instead, Lennon updated his favourite Buddy Holly changes, producing a song of simplicity to rank alongside the equally positive 'Oh Yoko' from the *Imagine* sessions. Lennon captured two performances of the song on his video recorder, sending the tape back to Yoko (and her mother) in New York as a token of love.

'Borrowed Time' assumed an eerie significance in the light of Lennon's murder. Hearing him naively talking of "living on borrowed time/without a thought for tomorrow", and recounting the joys of getting older, took on a tragic air after the events of December 1980. Again, the aura of optimism was tangible – as if Lennon's spirit had been lightened by the decision to return to work.

Which made 'I Don't Wanna Face It' all the more ironic. The skeleton of the song dated back to 1977; Lennon performed it in Bermuda as a frantic rocker, boiling over with fear and resentment at being asked to play a public role. It contrasted with another new song, 'I'm Stepping Out', which had been developed from the early lyrics of 'Real Life', again from Lennon's composing sessions in 1977. Far from dreading the public eye, the narrator of this song couldn't wait to get back on the streets and in the clubs.

Also taped in Bermuda were 'Beautiful Boy' and 'Real Love', both cementing the arrangements that he'd arrived upon in New York; and 'I'm Losing You', an extension of 'Stranger's Room' from 1978. Finally, there was 'Watching The Wheels' – completed at last after three years of intermittent work. Lennon had patched up the chorus, and given the song a Dylanesque guitar part that didn't survive onto the record. As it stood, the song settled the delicate balance of the new material – divided between nervous acceptance of the real world, and a determination to stand back from the lure of fame. In truth, these Bermuda demos were a giant step towards the world, a commitment that Lennon's five years of retirement were drawing to an end. By the time he had assembled the *Double Fantasy* band in early August, all traces of the tentative, reclusive Lennon were invisible; instead he took on the trappings of his role, as the elder statesman of rock returned to offer an example to his peers.

Yoko made only a brief appearance in Bermuda while her husband was there, though it was long enough to inspire Lennon into one of the funniest, most driven performances of his life. Obviously hoping to amuse his wife, he careered through 'Serve Yourself' with relentless acoustic guitar back-up and a Scouse accent he hadn't exposed since the days of 'Polythene Pam'. Between verses, he showed off his command of the dictionary of slang. The sheer venom of this performance was unmatched by anything since 'How Do You Sleep?', and it added extra bite to his admission that "there's only one thing missing in this god almighty stew/and that's your mother" – one last act of Oedipal worship amidst the slaughter of prophets and gurus. That was a rare moment when the Lennon that the world remembered surfaced during the Dakota years. Imagine the impact if he'd come back in 1980 with an album like that, rather than a set of love songs. . .

LATE JULY/EARLY AUGUST 1980: RECORDING home demos of 'Life Begins At 40'/'(Just Like) Starting Over'/'Forgive Me My Little Flower Princess'/'Cleanup Time'/'Grow Old With Me'

Having made the decision to re-enter the commercial world, John and Yoko booked the Hit Factory studios in New York for two months from the beginning of August 1980. They had yet to select an outlet for their new recordings; but the mere act of arranging sessions was enough to unlock another seam of Lennon creativity.

He continued to work on a new tune he'd begun to write in Bermuda, optimistically called 'Cleanup Time'. It was an admission that 1979 had been a year of private excess, but that the new decade promised a fresh broom. Several piano demos of the song have survived, each with a vague gospel feel, and soft, almost spoken vocals. "Show those mothers how to do it," Lennon whispered in the chorus, before satirising the set-up in the Dakota: "The queen is in the counting home/counting out the money/The king is in the kitchen/making bread and honey". The similarity to 'Cry Baby Cry' from 1968 can't have been accidental, nor the sly dig at Yoko's reliance on tarot card readers and fortune-tellers: "The oracle has spoken/we cast the perfect spell".

John had already agreed to contribute to Ringo Starr's forthcoming album, which was set for release early in the New Year. By November he was ready to offer Ringo four new songs – one of which was 'Life Begins At 40', written as a joint present to himself and Ringo in honour of their birthdays in October and July respectively. "Age is just a state of mind", John sang in an exaggerated hillbilly drawl, in a song which he introduced as coming from "the Dakota country and western club". Like other songs for Ringo – 'Cookin', 'Goodnight Vienna' – this was merely an extended joke, though none the less amusing for that.

'Starting Over' was altogether more serious in intent. The song acted as a theme for the Lennons' return to the music business, and as a restatement of their commitment to each other (or, at least, Lennon's to Yoko). Cut around the same time as 'Life Begins At 40', to the same guitar/rhythm-box accompaniment, 'Starting Over' built on the rickety foundations of 'My Life', 'Don't Be Crazy' and 'The Worst Is Over', combining the strongest melodic elements of all three. Even this close to the *Double Fantasy* sessions, however. Lennon still hadn't finalised the lyrics. "Why don't we take off alone/spend a weekend in an old hotel/a little place without a phone/a second honeymoon would do us well", he sang in the middle section without a hint of irony. Another rejected line suggested that he was regaining his powers of self-mythology: "The time has come, the walrus said/for you and I to stay in bed".

No such confidence inspired 'Forgive Me My Little Flower Princess'. Lennon never completed the song to his satisfaction: the studio take cut early during the *Double Fantasy* sessions was only a reference recording, so John could return and rewrite the lyrics. They needed it: as it stood, this was Lennon back down on his knees in front of Yoko, apologising for "crushing your delicateness" with his "utter selfishness". Strange that a return to creative activity should automatically produce a naked admission of guilt...

Which brings us neatly to 'Grow Old With Me'. According to Yoko's sleeve-notes on *Milk And Honey*, this song was written in Bermuda as an answer to her own 'Let Me Count The Ways' – betraying the couple's apparent obsession with the relationship between the poets Robert Browning and Elizabeth Barrett. Lennon's stately song, based on hymnal piano chords he'd already mined on his demos of 'Memories' and 'Free As A Bird', certainly began from Browning's poem of the same name, before simplifying the poetic sentiments into one single line: "God bless our love". The song maintained the Lennons' principle of wish-fulfilment, as one key line ran: "Grow old along with me/The best is yet to be". But life at the Dakota was not destined to be that simple.

AUGUST 6 TO OCTOBER 13, 1980: RECORDING '(Just Like) Starting Over'/'Kiss Kiss Kiss'/'Cleanup Time'/'Give Me Something'/'I'm Losing You'/'I'm Moving On'/'Beautiful Boy (Darling Boy)'/'Watching The Wheels'/'I'm Your Angel'/'Woman'/'Beautiful Boys'/'Dear Yoko'/'Every Man Has A Woman Who Loves Him'/'Hard Times Are Over'/'Borrowed Time'/'Forgive Me My Little Flower Princess'/'Nobody Told Me'/'I'm Stepping Out'/'I Don't Wanna Face It'/'Nobody Sees Me Like You Do'/'Walking On Thin Ice'/'Maggie Mae'/'Only The Lonely'/'Mystery Train'/'She's A Woman'/'Rip It Up'/'C'mon Everybody'/'I'm A Man'/'Be-Bop-A-Lula'/'Dream Lover'/'Stay'/'It's Now Or Never'/'The Three Bells'/'We've Gotta Get Out Of This Place'

Double Fantasy – the title itself said a lot. The front cover too: was the fantasy the fact that two 40-somethings had defied the odds and willed their relationship to survive; or that they were pretending passion for the cameras? In their publicity interviews, the couple heralded their album as a statement of intent, as a source of inspiration to their generation, a message from beyond the barriers of middle age. And the record was programmed as a dialogue, 'A Heart Play', as the subtitle had it, between a married couple – alternating songs of love and despair, longing and gentle companionship.

The actual state of the couple's marriage at this point has been questioned by so-called 'insiders', some of whom claimed that John was about to leave Yoko, others that Yoko was tired of life with John. Little of that surfaced during the sessions, or overtly in the songs: the one directly negative piece, Yoko's 'I'm Moving On', dated back to 1973, a time when the marriage was definitely in disarray. The other tunes had their moments of tension, but only within a determination to resist the forces of time and the great ennui, as Mike Nesmith once put it.

One thing was certain: Lennon revelled in the opportunity to play with other musicians. At the suggestion of producer Jack Douglas, and without the initial knowledge of John and Yoko, the entire sessions were recorded from the control booth. The 115 hours of session tape revealed that from the first, Lennon was in his element – utterly confident, disarmingly articulate about what he wanted from his musicians, encouraging them through the creative process, but still willing to criticise constructively to sting one last take out of them.

On the first morning of sessions at the Hit Factory, on August 6, Lennon played the band some of his Bermuda demos, and then led them into rough arrangements of several of the songs. 'I'm Stepping Out' was first to be taped, with Lennon rejoicing over the intro that he "finally gets the kids to bed and gets into his own space," and coaxing Hugh McCracken into the guitar solo by muttering "let's begin the beguine". After calling for some expresso, he quipped: "We don't want to turn into The Grateful Dead, do we?" The next order was for sushi, so the band wouldn't get bloated and slow up. Once he'd settled their metabolisms, and burst into impromptu versions of oldies such as 'It's Now Or Never' and 'The Three Bells', he was ready for another take, which ended with Lennon romping into The Animals' mid-Sixties oldie, 'We've Gotta Get Out Of This Place'. Then they finally hit the take that was edited down for the posthumous *Milk And Honey* album. Next, Lennon began work on 'Borrowed Time' – again not attempting to make a record, merely breaking in the band by schooling them in reggae, Wailers style. He'd even brought in a copy of 'Get Up, Stand Up' for his musicians to hear.

Over the next two days, Lennon schooled the band through two more songs that were released on *Milk And Honey*, the superb rocker 'Nobody Told Me' and the equally impressive 'I Don't Wanna Face It'. After an aborted shot at Yoko's 'Nobody Sees Me Like You Do', it was time for the first of the songs earmarked for *Double Fantasy*: 'Starting Over' and 'Woman'. In front of other people, Lennon played the role of masterful husband. When Yoko said that he was sounding like a Beatle, he snapped back: "An ex-Beatle, you cunt!" But he admitted the similarity, referring to 'Woman' as "early Motown/Beatles circa '64, ballad" in his instructions to the band.

After a weekend break, Jack Douglas tried a different approach, bringing in two key members of the band Cheap Trick, Bun E. Carlos and Rick Nielsen, to tape Yoko's 'I'm Moving On' and Lennon's 'I'm Losing You'. The results were electrifying, as the version of the latter included on *Anthology* revealed, with its reprise of the vintage 'Cold Turkey' feel that had been missing from Lennon's work for years.

In between those two sessions, Lennon steered the band through 'Cleanup Time', including one take that ended with a line or two from Leon Russell's 'Magic Mirror'. The tepid '(Forgive Me) My Little Flower Princess' followed the next day, though Lennon told the band that he'd have to rearrange it as it sounded too much like Philly soul band The Stylistics. 'Dear Yoko' was next on the agenda, before the woman herself was finally allowed to cut the remarkable track for 'Walking On Thin Ice'. 'Watching The Wheels' and 'Give Me Something' were laid down a few days later, and by August 19, the Lennons had basic tracks laid down for every song they were considering for the album.

Overdub sessions began three days later, and by August 25, the couple had prepared a provisional running order for the album, which at this stage was scheduled to include 'Walking On Thin Ice' and the two tracks recorded with Cheap Trick. But John clearly felt that their contributions to the album were too abrasive, and both songs were re-cut a day later with the house band. Early September was the time set aside for vocal and horn overdubs, the former stretching right through the month. "I feel like I'm still in the fucking Beatles with this track," Lennon declared as he worked on 'Woman'. The next day, as he prepared to tackle 'Starting Over', he told the engineer: "Make me magnificent, Lee, make me the man of my dreams. I want Elvis Vincent." Later in that session, he teased Yoko as she wheezed her way through 'Every Man Has A Woman Who Loves Him': "Start writing ones that you can sing from now on." And he recalled how difficult 'I Should Have Known Better' had been to sing back in 1964: "I never wrote one like that again."

On September 22, the day that Lennon cut his final vocals for 'I'm Losing You' and 'Dear Yoko', the couple finally signed a record deal for the first time in five years, with Geffen Records. The last vocals were added the next day, before work switched to the Record Plant East, and finally back to the Hit Factory, for the mixing process. The album's master tape was assembled, with all the sound effects intact, on October 20, the same day that the '(Just Like) Starting Over' single appeared. Less than a month later, the album itself was in the shops. And exactly three weeks after that, John Lennon was dead.

The relentness progress of the sessions proved that the game-plan for *Double Fantasy* was laid out in advance. No other Lennon or Ono songs were taped during these two months: the only out-takes in existence were either alternate takes, early mixes, or else impromptu jam sessions on rock-'n'roll oldies between takes. One such set of recordings was made during the filming of a promo video at the end of August, documenting the band trying to persuade Lennon to play McCartney's Beatles' B-side, 'She's A Woman' – only for Lennon to outwit them consistently by falling into his own favourite oldies. Another had John busking Roy Orbison's 'Only The Lonely' between takes of 'Starting Over', and toying with the guitar chords of an as-yet unfinished song, 'Gone From This Place'.

Double Fantasy mixed seven of John's songs with seven of Yoko's, and equal care went into the recording of each. In the event, several critics claimed to prefer Yoko's incisive accounts of married life to Lennon's more

301

sentimental offerings, and the no-nonsense ultimatum of 'I'm Moving On', or the directness of 'Beautiful Boys', was far more honest and worldly than Lennon's romantic daydreams on 'Starting Over' or 'Dear Yoko'. 'Beautiful Boys', ostensibly an answer-song to Lennon's own 'Beautiful Boy', pinned Lennon exactly, with its reference to "all your little ploys", and its telling summary, "You got all you can carry/and still feel somehow empty". This to a man who was telling her "I'm forever in your debt".

Elsewhere, Yoko ventured into reggae on the tentative 'Hard Times Are Over;' wandered a little too close to 'Makin' Whoopee' on 'I'm Your Angel;' explored sexual paranoia and desire on the new wave rocker 'Kiss Kiss Kiss', which ended with a violent orgasm, in stereo; and returned to the sterility of relationships on 'Give Me Something'. In reviving 'Every Man has A Woman Who Loves Him' from the proposed Broadway musical, Yoko put her own love into question: "Why do I roam when I know you're the one?/Why do I laugh when I feel like crying?". From her standpoint, this was no romantic fantasy; what was startling, in retrospect, was how far her lyrics were removed from the idealism that supposedly inspired the project.

In his way, Lennon was equally honest – 'Starting Over' was a straight-from-the-heart admission of need for his wife, while 'Woman' mixed a trib-ute to the female sex with his customary confession of failure in his relationship. Look closely, in fact, and you'll find that even the most open-hearted Lennon songs on *Double Fantasy* were invested with a sense of loss. "I miss you when you're not here," he sang on 'Dear Yoko'; "however dis-tant, don't keep us apart" in 'Woman'; "why can't we be making love ... don't let another day go by" on 'Starting Over'. And then, of course, there was 'I'm Losing You' – in which John placed the loneliness and paranoia of 'Stranger's Room' into context, inspired by his inability to reach Yoko on the phone during his holiday in Bermuda. For once, the song showed him willing to stand his ground, as the music cut close to the savagery of the 10-year-old *Plastic Ono Band* album: "I know I hurt you then/But hell that was way back when/Do you still have to carry that cross?"

The inner tension of *Double Fantasy* suggested that Yoko might just have written the album's theme in 'I'm Moving On' back in 1973, with its sear-ing denunciation of Lennon's character: "You know I'll see you through your jive ... You're giving me your window smile ... You're getting phoney."

So the *Double Fantasy* songs weren't as one-dimensional as they first appeared. Their apparent romanticism owed much to the lushness of the production, to the care of the arrangements – and to the fact that any spark in the original run-throughs was effectively dampened by Lennon's over-dubs. Typically, he double-tracked his vocals throughout the album and agreed to unnecessarily soft backing chorales for 'Starting Over' and 'Woman'. Elsewhere there were moments of magic, however: the merry-go-round jangle of the chorus of 'Watching The Wheels', arranged like another *Plastic Ono Band* out-take; the majesty of the lead vocal on 'Woman', the warmth of 'Beautiful Boy'; and the snatches of 'found sound' that cropped up across that song, 'I'm Your Angel', 'Watching The Wheels' and 'Cleanup Time'.

Overall, though, *Double Fantasy* was the work of a man feeling his way back into a career – substituting craft and experience where he had once relied upon inspiration. The album began with the tinkle of a wishing bell – a sound that not only mocked the funeral tolls of 'Mother', but also stood as Lennon's testament of faith in the strength of his relationship, and the return of his creative powers. What finally made *Double Fantasy* so affecting was not just hindsight in the wake of tragedy. It was the realisation that in its frailty and occasional lack of direction, it was as authentic a picture of the slightly bewildered Lennon as *Imagine* had been of an altogether more certain artist nine years earlier.

NOVEMBER 1980: RECORDING home demos of 'Grow Old With Me'/'Gone From This Place'/'She Runs Them Round In Circles'/'Dear John'/'You Saved My Soul'/'Pop Is The Name Of The Game'

On September 22, John and Yoko signed a one-album deal with Geffen Records. Within days, the couple's first 'comeback' interview was published, in *Newsweek* – the same day that they completed a major interview stint with David Sheff of *Playboy*. A couple of weeks later, they were filmed in Central Park for ABC's *20/20* news show – recordings that cropped up in the promo video for 'Woman', and were used for the introduction to Yoko's song, 'It Happened' early in 1981. In mid-October 'Starting Over' was issued as a single in the States; a week later in Britain too. And a month later, *Double Fantasy* itself was issued – together with a promo disc that rekindled memories of the *Wedding Album* by including a short burst of John and Yoko calling out each other's names.

In the midst of this activity and media attention, John began work on his final songs. He and Yoko were already planning their next album, prospective title *Milk And Honey*; in fact, they told the press in early December that it was almost completed, which certainly wasn't true. And they had already asked their studio band to set aside time in the spring for a major concert tour – a sweep through Japan, Europe and the United

303

States, with at least one American show being fed by satellite live around the rest of the world.

One might have expected, then, that Lennon's final work would reflect his rediscovered superstar status. Instead, this batch of songs, none of which progressed further than home demos, sent out a dubious batch of signals to the troops. 'Gone From This Place' was pleasantly melodic, though the surviving takes were composing tapes rather than demos. Take one boasted just one line: "Well I won't be satisfied till I'm gone from this place". Take two embellished it, and hinted at a middle section as well, from which only the eerie whisper, "I don't wanna die" could be distinguished. A third take found its way back to the same fragment of 'She Runs Them Round In Circles' that had interrupted work on 'Beautiful Boy' back in early summer.

Death was also a preoccupation in 'You Saved My Soul', a remarkably brazen act of self-exposure that surely not even Lennon could have considered for release. Cut with reverbed electric guitar backing, it starred Lennon as a psychological victim, for the last time, indebted to Yoko's strength for pulling him through. The first verse described how he nearly gave his soul to a TV preacher before Yoko saved him from "that suicide". The second took the metaphor seriously, with its admission that only Yoko's intervention had stopped him from throwing himself out of an apartment window on the West Side of New York – not a million miles from the Dakota, one suspects, and a clear reference back to his diary tape from September 1979. In one last irony, John ended this song of spiritual subjection by bursting into a chorus of 'Serve Yourself' – something that 'You Saved My Soul' suggested was still a motion or so away.

It would have been fitting if 'Dear John' had actually been Lennon's final composition – not just because it dealt with his favourite subject, himself, or because like so much of his output in the Seventies, it was unfinished. Its title referred to the letters received by GIs away at the war, from sweethearts who had deserted them at home. Its lyrics, just one repeated verse (apart from a tongue-in-cheek improvisation over the final chords), stood as a more encouraging message than that: "Don't be hard on yourself, give yourself a break," he sang, before telling himself, "the race is over, you've won." Whether the race was to the top of the charts, where *Double Fantasy* was already headed, or whether it referred to some darker struggle of the soul, we'll never know. Either way, this last piece of self-analysis represented a victory of sorts: at least John didn't attribute all his success at remaining afloat to Yoko.

What was ironic was that Lennon wasn't able to plan a grand final statement. All the evidence suggests that his final recording of new material was dubbed on top of a demo of 'You Saved My Soul' which he'd taped on November 14, 1980. So the last known Lennon composition was entirely trivial. 'Pop Is The Name Of The Game' was a New Orleans-flavoured R&B chant, which lasted for only a few seconds. As endings go, this one soon went.

EARLY DECEMBER 1980: REMIXING 'Kiss Kiss Kiss'/'Open Your Box'/'Every Man Has A Woman'; overdubbing and mixing 'Walking On Thin Ice'

The final week of Lennon's life was as hectic as any seven days from the height of Beatlemania. Day after day he and Yoko submitted themselves to lengthy interrogation from the media. *Rolling Stone* magazine and several radio stations were all granted lengthy interviews. The couple also posed for photo sessions with Annie Leibovitz, under commission for *Rolling Stone* – one photo from which, chosen for the front cover of the magazine's tribute issue in early January, showed a naked Lennon curled in foetal fashion atop a clothed, distant Ono.

The pose made uneasy viewing in the wake of Lennon's more self-destructive songs from this period; and in view of the apparent cynicism which led them to be filmed simulating sexual intercourse for Allan Tannenbaum's video camera – short clips from which were incorporated into Yoko's videos the following year. If Albert Goldman and Fred Seaman were to be believed, this session mocked the true state of the Lennons' relationship, which both sources stated was on the verge of complete collapse. Even if this speculation was exaggerated, then the *Rolling Stone* cover shot, with Lennon as child, Ono as his disinterested mother, still seemed to creep close to some psychic truth.

In that light, it was perhaps appropriate that Lennon's final work in the recording studio should see him planning solo releases by his wife – a disco-mix promo single which would include club versions of songs from the *Double Fantasy* set plus an updated mix of 'Open Your Box' from 1971; and a brilliant new single, 'Walking On Thin Ice'.

Like so many of Yoko's songs, as far back as 'Mrs Lennon' and 'Mind Train', 'Walking On Thin Ice' reeked of impending tragedy – from its title image to the doom-laden fairy tale she recited midway through. It appeared on a single with 'It Happened', a song that seemed to be an obvious reference to the murder – until one discovered that Yoko had written and recorded it seven years earlier, as part of the sessions for the unissued album eventually released as *A Dream*.

In Lennon's eyes, 'Thin Ice' opened up "a new era of Lennon/Ono music". "*This* is the direction," he apparently told Yoko at their final session. What's sad is that it was true. For the first time since *Fly* in 1971, John and Yoko had succeeded in regaining a place in the avant-garde – only this time their experimentation was allied to a precise feel for contemporary tastes, which allowed the record to become Yoko's only hit single in 1981. John's production gave it an eerie, glacial feel. He hammered his electric guitar to echo Yoko's wails of pain with sharp bolts of noise, and gave the track a percussive base that was always shifting under your feet, powered by a riff that suggested that the ice was about to crack.

And so it did, on December 8, as Lennon fell in the entrance to the Dakota, scattering rough mixes of 'Walking On Thin Ice' on the ground as he sagged under the weight of Mark Chapman's bullets. It was an abrupt, breath-taking ending to a life and a career, neither of which was close to resolution. The timing added to the sense of waste: not just the human loss, of a father, husband and friend, but the awareness that Lennon's future had been precariously in the balance, that 'Walking On Thin Ice' might have heralded an artistic rebirth, or that the tortuous self-analysis of 'You Saved My Soul' might have led Lennon down another dead end. The lack of an orderly climax to the story led many observers to invent one: but the real man was more interesting, and maddening, than that. Rather than succumb to the stereotypes – the saint, the peacenik, the moptop, the victim, the bigot, the aggressor, the junkie – we should celebrate the reality of the work, as one man's struggle to make sense of his life, and the times into which he was born. In a world where only flux and fate are certain, we can all learn from his battles, his defeats, the delicate balance in his work between life and death.

Appendix 1

INTERVIEWS

Both as a member of The Beatles and as a solo artist, John Lennon gave literally hundreds of interviews to the national and local press, specialist music publications, and to television and radio, in Britain, America and around the world. What follows is a selective list of major Lennon interviews, broadcast or otherwise, which add flesh to the John and Yoko myth, or to the art and music surveyed in the rest of this book.

OCTOBER 27, 1962: Of all the Beatles interviews issued on record since 1963, this was one of the most fascinating, simply because it was the earliest. It predated the group's national success, coming less than a month after the release of 'Love Me Do'. Taped for hospital radio by Monty Lister in Port Sunlight, it offered no great insight into the group — bar the admission by all four that John Lennon was their leader. But it did capture The Beatles before stardom turned the process of being interviewed into a battle of wits and puns. The interview was included on a flexidisc in Mark Lewisohn's 1986 book, *The Beatles Live!*

MARCH 27, 1964: To mark the publication of Lennon's first book. *In His Own Write*, he appeared on the BBC TV feature programme *Tonight*, reading extracts from the book and being interviewed by Kenneth Allsop. It was on this occasion, as noted elsewhere in this book, that Lennon was asked why he did not turn the verbal imagination obvious in the book to use in his songs – with notable consequences.

OCTOBER 28, 1964: *Playboy* magazine honoured The Beatles by adding the group to the long list of luminaries and celebrities who had been interviewed in its pages. The Beatles managed to make some allegations about former drummer Pete Best that attracted a libel suit, while Lennon looked forward to later controversies by making mildly blasphemous comments.

APRIL 11, 1965: Lennon appeared alongside playwright Wolf Mankowitz on ITV's *The Eamonn Andrews Show*, and for the first time the outside world caught a glimpse of the Fab Beatle at his most aggressive. Admittedly under some provocation, he laid into Mankowitz with unrestrained sarcasm.

MARCH 4, 1966: "How does a Beatle live?" asked Maureen Cleave in an interview published in the *London Evening Standard* on this date – a piece which had far-reaching repercussions, as the source of the infamous "more popular than Jesus" quote that marred The Beatles' final American tour. In retrospect, however, Cleave's insightful and sympathetic article was more notable for the way in which it pinpointed the hollowness at the heart of Lennon's existence before Yoko – life in the suburbs surrounded by his millionaire playthings, searching for a role and a purpose between Beatles commitments.

AUGUST 12, 1966: With the Beatles' US tour on the verge of being cancelled, Lennon was forced to say sorry at a Chicago press conference to any Christians who had been offended by his remarks comparing the group with Jesus. Extracts from this interview later appeared as an unofficial single, entitled 'I Apologise'.

OCTOBER 7, 1966: Marooned in Spain during the filming of *How I Won The War*, Lennon told interviewer Zdenko Hirschler: "I am doing a lot of thinking about what is going to happen when The Beatles are no longer together."

SEPTEMBER 29, 1967: Lennon and Harrison appeared on *The Frost Programme* to announce that they had renounced drugs and were living their lives according to the spiritual teaching of the Maharishi Mahesh Yogi. Public reaction to the show was so intense that the two Beatles were invited back on October 4 to continue the conversation. "I've got more energy and more happiness," Lennon explained. "I'm just a better person."

MAY 13, 1968: In New York to publicise the launch of their Apple company, John Lennon and Paul McCartney came face to face with the cream of the American press. The naive, simplistic Beatles emerged the losers, having had the gaping holes in their idealistic vision of a 'Western Communism' exposed by the comparatively stringent questioning. Along the way, McCartney exchanged phone numbers with photographer Linda Eastman: John and Paul found the first chink in their joint armour when they disagreed publicly about how Apple would be run; and John announced that he had just begun work on the script for a movie based on his first two books.

SEPTEMBER 18, 1968: As the leaders of the American rock press, *Rolling Stone* magazine had a special relationship with Lennon. His picture, shorn-headed for the *How I Won The War* movie, adorned the front cover of their inaugural issue: and then a year later, Lennon gave his longest and most searching interview to date to Jonathan Cott, which appeared in *Rolling Stone* on November 23, 1968.

Among the subjects under discussion were black power, Jean-Luc Godard, Bob Dylan and Lennon's own creative process. Throughout, Lennon did his best to remain a loyal member of The Beatles, whilst his every statement hinted at his growing distance from his colleagues.

JANUARY 13, 1969: At the height of The Beatles' turmoil during the *Get Back/Let It Be* sessions, with George Harrison still refusing to return to the group, Lennon incited more trouble by telling *Disc* editor Ray Coleman that Apple was on the verge of financial collapse. "If it carries on like this, all of us will be broke in the next six months," he claimed.

MARCH 21, 1969: Lennon told reporters in Paris after his wedding to Yoko Ono: "We shall be doing everything together. But it doesn't mean I shall be breaking up The Beatles, or anything like that."

APRIL 1, 1969: Note the date. Among the April fools when John and Yoko were interviewed on the British independent TV channel's discussion show *Today* by host Eamonn Andrews, were Yehudi Menuhin, Rolf Harris and Jack Benny. Whilst the Lennons set out their views on bags, peace and acorns, their fellow guests shuffled their feet in embarrassment, and the audience broke into gentle barracking. For the first time, the Lennons were exposed to the distaste of the British public for their life, their morals and their beliefs.

SEPTEMBER 14, 1969: This was supposedly the date on which John, Yoko and George Harrison were taped in conversation with the Indian mystic Swami Bhaktivedanta – a dialogue published in book form after Lennon's death as *Lennon '69: Search For Liberation*. The conversation was less mystic than mystifying, as Lennon and Harrison sought in vain to understand the complex spiritual beliefs of the Swami, who expounded his own particular interpretation of Krishna consciousness. "We should go to a true master," Lennon noted at one point, "but how are we to tell one from the other?" One relevant thing to remember: on September 14, 1969, the Lennons were actually in Toronto after playing the Rock And Roll Revival show the previous day.

DECEMBER 17, 1969: At the Ontario Science Hall, John and Yoko announced the Toronto Peace Festival, a multi-media event to be staged the following summer. They told the Canadian press that they had decided to call 1970 'Year One AP (After Peace)', and promised that their next album would be a record of laughing and whispering. Little came of any of these plans: within weeks. John was writing 'Have We All Forgotten What Vibes Are?', his vitriolic response to the collapse of the Toronto Festival.

JANUARY 5, 1970: Now in Denmark, where they had gone to discuss the Peace Festival and the custody of Yoko's daughter. Kyoko, with her ex-husband Tony Cox, the Lennons held a small-scale press conference to announce that all their future record royalties would be channelled into their peace campaign. Like other contemporary promises, this seems to have been quietly ignored when they made their next record.

FEBRUARY 4, 1970: In a public ceremony at the Black House in London, the Lennons gave their support to the campaign to defend the black rights leader Michael X against murder charges. They swapped a bag containing their hair, which had been cropped short in Denmark, for a pair of bloodstained boxing shorts once worn by Muhammed Ali. The British press chose to ignore the entire episode.

DECEMBER 8, 1970: The Lennons' lengthy conversation on this date with *Rolling Stone* editor Jann Wenner provided the most momentous interview of John's entire career – spread over two issues of the magazine early in 1971, and subsequently published in book form (without Lennon's permission) as *Lennon Remembers*. Still burning with unleashed emotion after the course of Primal Therapy and the recording of *John Lennon: Plastic Ono*

Band; Lennon embarked on a crash course in rewriting Beatles history, lambasting his former colleagues and aides, exposing many long-cherished Beatle myths, and spewing invective in all directions. In its way, this *Rolling Stone* interview was as important a confessional document as the *Plastic Ono Band* album itself. (It also provided the raw material for National Lampoon's satirical Lennon tribute, 'Magical Misery Tour', which comprised choice quotes from the interview set to a pastiche of *Plastic Ono Band* music.)

FEBRUARY 21, 1971: The British equivalent to the *Lennon Remembers* interview was an equally lengthy conversation between John and Yoko and the political activists Tariq Ali and Robin Blackburn, for the Trotskyist paper *Red Mole*. The political bias of their interlocutors made this less of an interview, more of a dialogue, and Yoko's attempt to shift the focus away from immediate political objectives proved more interesting than Lennon's enthusiastic adoption of left-wing tactics.

MARCH 27, 1971: In a belated plug for the *Plastic Ono Band* album, issued three months earlier, Lennon was interviewed at Apple by his old friend Kenny Everett, then working for Radio Monte Carlo. During the course of a lengthy conversation, he revealed that he would be happy to work with George Harrison and Ringo Starr in the future, but (by implication) not with Paul McCartney.

SEPTEMBER 8, 1971: Having arrived in New York a week earlier, John and Yoko took over the full 90 minutes of the top-rated ABC-TV talk forum, *The Dick Cavett Show*. Chain smoking throughout, the two did not perform but did explain the concept of Bagism to a bemused Cavett and plugged their latest film ventures with clips from *Fly*, *Erection*, and 'Mrs. Lennon' and 'Imagine' from *Imagine*.

SEPTEMBER / OCTOBER 1971: During their research for the book *Apple To The Core*, authors Peter McCabe and Robert D. Schonfeld were granted a series of interviews with the Lennons, newly ensconced at the St. Regis Hotel in New York. Never intended for separate publication, the tapes were eventually printed in book form as *John Lennon: For The Record* in late 1984. The conversation was most interesting for its insights into Lennon's difficult relationship with Messrs Harrison and McCartney, and for exposing one of Lennon's periodic, short-lived vendettas against a friend – the unfortunate victim this time being Derek Taylor, former Beatles and Apple press officer.

FEBRUARY 14 to 18, 1972: As noted elsewhere, this week saw the Lennons co-hosting *The Mike Douglas Show* on American TV (though the five shows had been pre-recorded a week or two earlier). Between musical segments, they engaged in generally fruitless conversation with Douglas and a variety of guests, the most entertaining of whom included activists Bobby Seale and Jerry Rubin, comedian George Carlin, and consumer affairs monitor Ralph Nader.

APRIL 16, 1973: In one of their final interviews together before their 18-month separation, the Lennons spoke to DJ Elliott Mintz about their idealistic hopes for the future. "1973 is our year." John announced. "The whole ball game changes now. Yoko is becoming herself again." Little did he realise that becoming herself would also entail kicking him out.

LATE OCTOBER 1973: Throughout the mid-Seventies, Lennon remained on better terms with the British rock paper *Melody Maker* than with any other publication. In early November, they published an interview carried out in Los Angeles by US Editor Chris Charlesworth in which Lennon discussed his new *Mind Games* album, his relationship with the other Beatles and the possibilities of a reunion, and hinted at a few difficulties in his present relationship with Yoko. *Melody Maker* subsequently published informative Lennon interviews, by Ray Coleman and Charlesworth respectively, to mark the release of *Walls And Bridges* in 1974 and *Rock'n'Roll* in 1975.

DECEMBER 9, 1973: Lennon placed a transatlantic phone call to Radio Luxembourg's DJ, Tony Prince. The aim was to publicise *Mind Games*, whet Europe's appetite for his album of oldies, and deny that he was having a relationship with his personal assistant, May Pang: "May happens to know about copyright, and she handles the copyright situation."

SEPTEMBER 27, 1974: Listeners to the breakfast show on radio station KHJ in Southern California were treated to a rather manic John Lennon as their guest DJ. Lennon cued up a succession of tracks from his new *Walls And Bridges* album, took requests for Beatles songs, and engaged in surreal conversations with teenage phone-in callers.

SEPTEMBER 28, 1974: The following day, at the other end of America, a considerably more relaxed Lennon was the guest of Dennis Elsas on the afternoon show at WNEW in New York. This was John's most enjoyable radio appearance, showing him at his most witty and urbane – reading adverts, satirising the weather forecasts, and talking humorously about the prospects for a Beatles reunion and the making of his new album. Lennon also took along some of his favourite singles to play on the air – among them Bobby Parker's 'Watch Your Step' and Derek Martin's 'Daddy Rolling Stone' – and once again previewed the *Walls And Bridges* album.

EARLY OCTOBER 1974: Back in California the following week, Lennon guested on KSAN-FM in San Francisco with the king of American DJs, the late Tom Donahue. Another warm and witty dialogue ensued, with John comparing the use of tape echo on Carl Perkins' 'Blue Suede Shoes' and Ike And Tina Turner's 'River Deep Mountain High'; admitting how much work he had put into splicing together Harry Nilsson's 'Subterranean Homesick Blues'; and playing obscure oldies like Rosie And The Originals' 'Angel Baby' and The Move's 'Brontosaurus'. Along the way, he gave still more exposure to *Walls And Bridges*. On the same day, KSAN broadcast Lennon's tape of 'Too Many Cooks', a track he had produced for Mick Jagger earlier in the year, its one and only official public airing.

FEBRUARY 1975: A few days after moving back in with Yoko at the Dakota, Lennon gave a major interview to Pete Hamill for *Rolling Stone* – which allowed him to announce the couple's reunion, plug the *Rock'n'Roll* album, and update America on the current state of his immigration case.

FEBRUARY 13, 1975: Lennon's old friend Scott Muni hosted a three-hour radio show on WNEW-FM in New York, on which John plugged the *Rock'n'Roll* album, and revealed to eager listeners: "John and Yoko are back together again. Our separation was a failure."

LATE MARCH 1975: On April 18, 1975, BBC TV broadcast an interview with Lennon carried out by the show's host, Bob Harris, in New York a few weeks earlier. In a country starved of Lennon TV appearances, the show was a godsend – especially as it included the performances of 'Stand By Me' and 'Slippin' And Slidin' ' discussed elsewhere in this book. Lennon merely repeated familiar stories about his reunion with Yoko and his problems with Phil Spector during the *Rock'n'Roll* sessions, however, and the interview was more interesting for its demonstration of Lennon's good health and humour than anything else.

APRIL 8, 1975: Likewise this TV interview (broadcast April 28), carried out by the deadpan Tom Synder for the *Tomorrow* chat show. Synder's prurient, lethargic questioning was constantly outshone by the wit of his guest, who still managed to remain polite and good-humoured throughout. The pair were joined for the second half of this programme by Lennon's immigration lawyer, Leon Wildes, there to make sure that his client didn't break the slander or contempt laws.

APRIL 10, 1975: London independent radio station Capital scooped the BBC to an exclusive interview, billed as *An Evening With John Lennon*. Besides the usual promotional duties and an update on his immigration situation, Lennon reassured his fans: "I miss a lot of you ... But I know Britain won't float away, so I'll see you when I see you. I'll just look a little weirder, probably."

JANUARY 1, 1976: Less than three months after the birth of their son, Sean, John and Yoko were interviewed at the Dakota by their friend, Elliott Mintz, for the Earth News service. Most of the conversation revolved around Yoko's difficulties with the birth, and the couple's delight at having finally succeeded in bringing a child to term.

OCTOBER 4, 1977: At the end of several months' vacation in Japan, the Lennons held a press conference in Tokyo, at which they confirmed their plan of remaining out of the public eye until their son was five years old. Surprisingly, the event went unreported in the British press, and this final media contact for almost three years passed almost unnoticed outside Japan.

SEPTEMBER 9 to 28, 1980: When John and Yoko finally broke media silence during the recording sessions for *Double Fantasy*, they chose the men's magazine *Playboy* as their vehicle rather than the rock press. Interviewer David Sheff spent three weeks with the Lennons, attending sessions and video shoots as well as sharing time at home in the Dakota. The result was the longest and most detailed conversation since the *Lennon Remembers* encounter of 1970 – and in its way every bit as revealing as that epochal confessional. The *Playboy* interview appeared in the January 1981 issue of the magazine just days before Lennon's death, and was subsequently printed in book form in a fuller version. It captured Lennon the publicity man, selling the story of the miraculous artistic comeback after five years' silence, and presenting himself as a cleansed, refreshed artist and human being. The text represented the strongest case for the defence in the dispute about Lennon's true state of mind in 1980. Among many highlights it included a detailed breakdown of who-wrote-what of the Lennon/McCartney songs.

MID-SEPTEMBER 1980: During the *Playboy* interviews, Lennon also gave time to Barbara Graustark of *Newsweek*, who with their shorter deadlines were able to rush a heavily edited version of the conversation into their September 29 issue. The interview was superseded by the *Playboy* text, even in the longer form published in the book *Strawberry Fields Forever.*

DECEMBER 5, 1980: Jonathan Cott completed a circle by carrying out both the first and last *Rolling Stone* interviews with John Lennon. He found a man of short temper with no time for fools, and the tapes of the conversation display an entirely different persona to the man on the *Playboy* tapes. Not surprisingly, the story Lennon was selling was the same: Cott merely sought to question it more closely than Sheff had done.

DECEMBER 6, 1980: The following day, it was the charming and humorous Lennon who surfaced in a four-hour interview with Andy Peebles of BBC Radio One. Peebles chose to take the Lennons through a survey of their solo career, keeping strictly to his script and apparently missing many of Lennon's asides. The painstaking questioning did keep the dialogue at a low ebb, but some of John and Yoko's comments on their early artistic collaborations showed that not all of their avant-garde spirit had departed them.

DECEMBER 8, 1980: On the final afternoon of his life, Lennon went through the tale of his artistic rebirth one more time, for RKO Radio. Completing a triptych of personalities in four days, this Lennon sounded as if he was speeding, babbling his way through lengthy avowals of his spiritual faith and his belief in life after death, and impatiently knocking aside most of the interviewer's attempts to interrupt. That conversation and a final photo session for *Rolling Stone* complete, Lennon went downstairs to the Dakota entrance, signed a copy of *Double Fantasy* for Mark Chapman, and proceeded with Yoko to a mixing session at the Hit Factory Studios downtown.

Appendix 2

LETTERS

As with the interviews, researching every letter John Lennon ever wrote would be a job for a bored academic with endless funds. Various items of family correspondence and replies to letters from fans have been auctioned at rock memorabilia sales in Britain and America over the last 25 years, but with few exceptions they offer little insight into the man who wrote them.

The same can't be said for the extract from a letter to ex-Beatle Stu Sutcliffe that was reprinted in Hunter Davies' authorised biography, *The Beatles*. Explicit in its language and self-pity, it revealed the empathy the pair of former Liverpool Art College students shared; there was little hint here, as elsewhere in Lennon's early prose, that he had anything to hide from his correspondent.

Throughout the Sixties, The Beatles made a point of sending postcards – usually in Lennon's hand – to the editors of the London music papers when the group were on tour. Friendship aside, and there's no doubt that The Beatles did consider some journalists as their friends, the exercise had the effect of making the group seem more approachable and human in the eyes of the public, as the correspondence was guaranteed a prominent position in the next available issue. The postcards that Lennon wrote reveal some of his simple word-play, but nothing that would surprise readers of *In His Own Write*.

It was only in the late Sixties and early Seventies that Lennon began to use the letter columns of the music press – primarily *Melody Maker* in London and *Rolling Stone* in San Francisco – as a vehicle for his own arguments. His open letter to Paul McCartney, following Paul's interview in *Melody Maker* on November 20, 1971, was a classic of its kind. Lennon's comments had to be censored "in deference to the laws of libel"; he blasted McCartney for his middle-brow views and lack of political commitment, accused him of doing his best to obstruct a legal settlement of The Beatles' court battle, and ended up advising his former partner to "Join the Rock Liberation Front before it gets you!" Around the same time, he also fired a barrage at George Martin, after The Beatles' producer was interviewed in the paper.

Lennon employed similar tactics against Todd Rundgren in 1974, again in response to a *Melody Maker* interview. Rundgren had accused Lennon of irrelevance in the modern age; Lennon replied that most of Rundgren's music was heavily influenced by The Beatles, and that Todd was simply miffed because Lennon hadn't recognised him in a Los Angeles club.

Another *Melody Maker* letter from the Lennons, in October 1971, replied to accusations from two readers in the *Mailbag* column that John and Yoko were simply spouting revolutionary rhetoric from the safety of their capitalist enclave, Apple. "Apple was/is a capitalist concern," Lennon wrote. "We brought in a capitalist to prevent it sinking ... I personally have had enough of Apple/Ascot and all other properties which tie me down, mentally and physically – I intend to cash in my chips as soon as I can – and be FREE."

Similar defences of their lifestyle and beliefs can be found in the pages of *International Times* and the other British underground press; and in early Seventies issues of *Rolling Stone*. But the most valuable sources of Lennon correspondence, and the most poignant, were unveiled by two of his closest friends. Ringo Starr's book *Postcards From The Boys* brought together a collection of missives he'd received from Lennon, Paul McCartney and George Harrison. Lennon's messages were usually brief, but they testified to his affection for The Beatles' drummer. Writing from India in 1968, he told Ringo: "We've got about two LPs' worth of songs now, so get yer drums out." In 1979, he suggested that Ringo should record the Les Paul/Mary Ford hit, 'How High The Moon', in the style of Blondie's 'Heart Of Glass' – adding "disco, natch". But an earlier card, sent from Japan in January 1971 while Paul McCartney's court case against the other Beatles was being heard at the High Court in London, said simply: "Who'd have thought it would come to this ..."

Former Apple press officer Derek Taylor reproduced many items he'd received from Lennon in his limited edition autobiography, *Fifty Years Adrift*.

An inveterate keeper of correspondence, cuttings and the trivia which made up everyday life, Taylor had preserved his postcards and letters from Lennon, mostly written from New York between 1973 and 1975. They showed little difference between the prose style of the public and private Lennon; the letters were full of word-play, involved puns, private jokes and *non sequiturs*, broken only by the occasional item of news: "I meself have decided to be or not to be for a coupla years? Boredom set in . . . how many back beats are there? I ask meself. Am thinking of becoming a magician", Lennon wrote early in 1975.

And later that same year, as the couple awaited the birth of their son, Lennon wrote to Taylor: "I ain't in a hurry to sign with anyone . . . or do anything . . . am enjoying my pregnancy . . . thinking time . . . what's it all about time too. I'll outlive the bastards in more ways than one (whatever their age) . . . My head and body are as clear as a bell . . . some nice window pane . . . and some incredibly LEGAL MUSHROOMS." Writing, at last, for private not public consumption, to a friend who had shared the mayhem and magic of Apple and Beatlemania, Lennon had no need to disguise the truth. Like his home demos, Lennon's personal correspondence cut through the fog of image and public expectation, and allowed us close to the man behind the art.

Appendix 3

THE LENNON LEGACY

When Lennon was murdered, his widow inherited a vast but tangled empire. Personal grief aside, she had been placed in an unenviable position, as the artistic guardian of a man whose fans felt as if they owned him – precisely the tricky relationship that led to his death.

In the immediate aftermath of the killing, concern over the work that Lennon had left behind was far from the forefront of anyone's mind. His final act was to complete – bar some subtle remixing – Yoko's 'Walking On Thin Ice' single, which duly appeared a few weeks later as he would have wished. But in the interviews he conducted just before his death, Lennon boasted that he and Yoko had virtually completed their follow-up to *Double Fantasy*. As soon as the initial shock faded, public pressure grew on her to release what were assumed to be his last recordings.

Had Lennon lived, there is no guarantee that more than one or two of the songs that eventually appeared on the 1984 album, *Milk And Honey*, would ever have been released – at least by John. Several of them had already been earmarked for Ringo Starr's next album, after all. And virtually all of Yoko's material on *Milk And Honey* was recorded after the murder. However it appeared, and when, that *Double Fantasy* follow-up would have been very different from the record that Yoko released.

Not that anyone was complaining in 1984, when Yoko was congratulated for her refusal to cash in on her husband's death. Having broken the psychological barrier of dealing with Lennon as a posthumous artist, she

319

declared her intention to release as much of his work as she considered worthy of his name. 1986 brought two flawed but still valuable albums: *Live In New York City*, a rather clumsily remixed edit of the *One To One* concerts from August 1972; and *Menlove Avenue*, a strange but wonderful mixture of 1973 and 1974 out-takes and rehearsals.

By then, work had already begun on a film designed to be Lennon's testament. *In My Life* – or *Imagine: John Lennon*, as it eventually appeared – was intended to mix Lennon's own reminiscences of his life with the best footage that could be assembled from throughout his career. The finished movie was something of a triumph – poignant, revelatory and only occasionally reflecting over-heavy use of the censor's hand. The most enticing segments were filmed during the recording sessions for the Imagine album, although their novelty value has been reduced by the use of the same material in the DVD release, *Gimme Some Truth: The Making Of John Lennon's Imagine Album.*

Other posthumous video/DVD projects have included a faithful reproduction (in Sixties avant-garde style) of the footage shot during the couple's Montreal peace demonstration in 1969 (*Bed-In*); and a series of compilations of Lennon's promo videos. These have not always been exactly what they seem, as Yoko has commissioned new 'collage' videos for tracks that didn't originally have promo films. In some cases – notably 'No. 9 Dream' – this has allowed her to illustrate a song about John's feelings for May Pang with clips of herself and John, a canny piece of historical rewriting. The most recent of these anthologies is *The Very Best Of John Lennon*, the audio content of which features unfaded versions of some songs – and different video concoctions to those included on previous videos and DVDs.

In the absence of a more thorough round-up of Lennon visual material (as provided, inevitably, by the bootleggers), *Imagine: John Lennon* remains the best single representation of the man's life and times. It was premiered in 1988, the same year when Yoko unleashed a mighty American radio series entitled *The Lost Lennon Tapes*. This ran for several years, and in its dying months, it descended into a hell of irrelevancies and stale repetitions. But in its original form, it represented something entirely new in the field of rock history: a weekly, syndicated radio show devoted to uncovering and presenting the unreleased riches of the Lennon archive. Yes, it would have been very different – shorter and infinitely better presented – if the series had been made by a non-commercial broadcaster such as the BBC. But for all its faults, not least the grating narration, *The Lost Lennon Tapes* allowed the outside world to hear dozens of hours of rare recordings and interviews. Ironically, the only living rock star to respond to the spirit of the series was

Paul McCartney, with his enjoyable but much less revealing *Oobu Joobu* series for the same US radio network, Westwood One.

The radio series was intended to lead up to the release of a Lennon CD retrospective filled with unissued material. Beatles historian Mark Lewisohn compiled such a set, but the project was then postponed until after the *Beatles Anthology* albums appeared. Eventually a different track listing was used for Lennon's own *Anthology*. By the time it reached the shops, bootleg versions of much of the material had been on sale for the best part of a decade. The compilation also suffered from some bizarre choices of material (one track featured comedian Jerry Lewis reflecting on a Lennon performance not included in the box), erratic and misleading sequencing, and poor annotation. But its many musical highlights offered much compensation.

Apart from the *Anthology*, there were no 'new' Lennon albums until 2004, when Yoko rifled through John's archive of home demos to produce a record that pleased few people with its mix of familiar and bootlegged material. The poorly presented *Acoustic* maintained a long tradition of slightly disappointing CD releases stretching back a decade, and involving new editions of some of the jewels of the Lennon back catalogue. *Live Peace In Toronto* suffered from some 'creative' remixing; *John Lennon Plastic Ono Band* was marred by the use of inappropriate bonus tracks; while both *Double Fantasy* and *Mind Games* offered little in the way of valuable new material. At least they were remastered, though, a process that still awaits *Sometime In New York City* and *Walls And Bridges*. Most maddening of all, however, was the reissue of *Rock 'n' Roll*, which not only missed the opportunity to round up all the out-takes from the sessions, but also created a 'new' track out of a snippet of the same performance of 'Just Because' that was included in edited form elsewhere in the set. Only the fact that few people cared about its contents prevented a similar outcry from fans when *Two Virgins* was released on official CD for the first time, with its final 30 seconds chopped off without explanation.

No area of Lennon's posthumous artistic life has attracted more adverse comment, however, than the treatment of his drawings and other artwork. Under the auspices of Yoko's Bag One Arts company, a company entitled Legacy Productions have been charged with mounting exhibitions and exploiting Lennon's work commercially. Much of the resulting cash has been directed towards charities – either directly, to programmes such as Adopt A Classroom and various food banks, or indirectly, via the Lennons' own mysterious Spirit Foundation. But much has also reached the coffers of Lenono, the holding company for the Lennon/Ono archive.

"At the time of his death," reads a typical publicity blurb for Lennon's artwork, "John had saved and preserved several hundred drawings that he considered important. His drawings are whimsical yet poetic and are a commentary on his everyday life, his wife Yoko and their son." And so it continues, lauding Lennon's status as "a loving husband", "a dad" and "a renaissance man" – all of which is true, and yet far from the full story. Much the same goes for the presentation of Lennon's work, which has been organised into categories and under titles that he wouldn't have recognised. Limited edition prints are a common way of making money in the art game, though usually they are signed by the artist. In Lennon's case, that wasn't possible, although Legacy Productions and Bag One Arts have done their best to compensate. "Each limited edition fine art print is authenticated by John Lennon's embossed signature," so another blurb has it, "the embossed printer and publisher's mark, Yoko Ono Lennon's hand signature, and John's personal chop mark." That may not add up to authenticity, but it's no stranger or more devious than the process whereby artists such as Salvador Dali and Andy Warhol handed over the creative process of some of their own work to their staff. Certainly the price of Lennon's prints is designed to place him in that upper echelon of the fine art milieu, with individual items selling for anything from a few hundred dollars to more than $8,000 for choice pieces such as 'Imagine All The People' and 'Multiple Self Portrait'.

Many of Lennon's drawings have been 'colorised' (ugly spelling for an ugly concept) before publication or sale. Back to the blurbs: "Yoko Ono chose colours that she felt would enhance the meaning of the original drawings." She herself has explained rather vaguely: "I wanted to make sure that John's original drawings were kind of standing out and that the colour was just to enhance it or something, delicately." The technique was applied to all the illustrations Lennon drew for his son, Sean, which were collected in the book *Real Love* – one of several posthumous collections of his artwork. The results were attractive enough on the eye, but as true to Lennon's original intention as a 'colorised' version of a classic black-and-white movie.

Much more controversy – especially amongst the extended Lennon family – was provoked when Yoko sanctioned the use of John's images on a variety of artefacts, from a Rickenbacker guitar to mugs and even children's clothing. John's son Julian Lennon was particularly outspoken about what he saw as the "cheapening" of his father's memory. Once again, the verdict has to be ambiguous. It is possible to share Julian's outrage, and at the same time to appreciate that commercial exploitation is an inevitable part of modern art. Lennon himself, for example, was happy to issue his *Bag One* lithographs in an edition that was way beyond the financial reach of his fans. Had he lived, it's not impossible to imagine him joining George Harrison in publishing books via the exquisite but exclusively expensive process used by Genesis Publications, who regularly charge several hundred pounds per signed, leather-bound volume.

Ultimately, Yoko Ono seems to have exerted more restraint over the Lennon industry than others might have done in her position. Whatever one's disagreements with the way in which individual projects have been handled, and with the concept of 'creating' new Lennon limited editions, it's hard not to sympathise with her defence, spoken in 2000 but still relevant today: "I don't think I'm merchandising John aggressively at all. If John's stuff is not out there, people forget about him. I have to protect his work. And this is the only way I could do it." When you compare her methods with the unseemly scramble for gold that followed the deaths of other musical icons, such as Elvis Presley, Jimi Hendrix, Jerry Garcia and Bob Marley, Yoko seems to have handled her position as 'keeper of the flame' with more dignity than she's sometimes been credited with.

THE LIMITED EDITIONS:

Reproduction prints of Lennon's handwritten lyrics for the following songs have been issued in limited editions: 'Beautiful Boy', 'Borrowed Time', 'Cleanup Time', 'Day Tripper', 'Dear Prudence', '(Forgive Me) My Little Flower Princess', 'Grow Old With Me', 'I'm Losing You', 'I'm So Tired', 'I'm Stepping Out', 'Imagine', 'In My Life', 'Instant Karma', 'Julia', 'Lucy In The Sky With Diamonds', 'Nowhere Man', 'Real Love', 'Revolution', 'The Continuing Story Of Bungalow Bill', 'Watching The Wheels', 'When I Get Home', 'Woman', 'Working Class Hero' and 'Yer Blues'.

Bag One Arts has also authorised limited edition prints of many pieces of Lennon artwork, including the full set of *Bag One* lithographs and John's *Real Love* drawings for Sean. Listed below are the other major series that have been made available so far. Some of them were titled by Lennon himself; others were named by Yoko and her team of artistic advisers.

ANTHOLOGY: The Hole Of My Life/Freda Peeple/Borrowed Time/Family Tree/He Tried To Face Reality/Peace, Brother

DAKOTA DAYS: Aisumasen (I'm Sorry)/No. 9 Dream/Beautiful Boy/Dada Mama/Feeling Good/Free As A Bird/Jazz, Man/Nothing Is Impossible/Once Upon A Time/One Day At A Time/Peace On

Earth/Power To The People/Remember Love/Suitors/Samurai/Sleepless Night/Two Virgins/Watch The Holes, Yoko

JAPAN: Jibun/Musician/Poet/Saki/Taste

KARUIZAWA: Afternoon Tea/Daydream/Face/Karuizawa 77/Look/ Love/The First One/Tokyo Summer Of 77/Visit To Japan/What's Wrong With This Picture?

MY STORY: A Day In The Life/Baby Grand/Back Off Boogaloo/Bagism/Eiffel Tower/Embrace/Everyday In Every Way/It's Only Rock'n'Roll/Looking Back/Magic Birds/Manhattan Diary/Mind Games/Morning Coffee/Multiple Self Portrait/Oh My Love/On The Telephone With Family/Peace And Love/Real Love/Self Portrait Suite/Smile/Suddenly 38/The Ballad Of John And Yoko/The Exile/The Family/The Hug/The Lennons/Two Is One/We Made Our Bed/Whatever Gets You Through The Night/Why Me?/Why Not?

Appendix 4

DISCOGRAPHY

THE BEATLES: ORIGINAL UK SINGLES

MY BONNIE/THE SAINTS (both sides by Tony Sheridan and The Beatles)
(Polydor NH 66–833) January 1962

LOVE ME DO/P.S. I LOVE YOU
(Parlophone R 4949) October 1962

PLEASE PLEASE ME/ASK ME WHY
(Parlophone R 4983) January 1963

FROM ME TO YOU/THANK YOU GIRL
(Parlophone R 5015) April 1963

SHE LOVES YOU/I'LL GET YOU
(Parlophone R 5055) August 1963

I WANT TO HOLD YOUR HAND/THIS BOY
(Parlophone R 5084) November 1963

SWEET GEORGIA BROWN/NOBODY'S CHILD (both sides with Tony Sheridan)
(Polydor NH 52–906) January 1964

WHY/CRY FOR A SHADOW (A-side with Tony Sheridan)
(Polydor NH 52–275) February 1964

CAN'T BUY ME LOVE/YOU CAN'T DO THAT
(Parlophone R 5114) March 1964

AIN'T SHE SWEET/IF YOU LOVE ME BABY (B-side with Tony Sheridan)
(Polydor NH 52–317) May 1964

A HARD DAY'S NIGHT/THINGS WE SAID TODAY
(Parlophone R 5160) July 1964

I FEEL FINE/SHE'S A WOMAN
(Parlophone R 5200) November 1964

TICKET TO RIDE/YES IT IS
(Parlophone R 5265) April 1965

HELP!/I'M DOWN
(Parlophone R 5305) July 1965

DAY TRIPPER/WE CAN WORK IT OUT
(Parlophone R 5389) December 1965

PAPERBACK WRITER/RAIN
(Parlophone R 5452) June 1966

YELLOW SUBMARINE/ELEANOR RIGBY
(Parlophone R 5493) August 1966

PENNY LANE/STRAWBERRY FIELDS FOREVER
(Parlophone R 5570) February 1967

ALL YOU NEED IS LOVE/BABY YOU'RE A RICH MAN
(Parlophone R 5620) July 1967

HELLO GOODBYE/I AM THE WALRUS
(Parlophone R 5655) November 1967

LADY MADONNA/THE INNER LIGHT
(Parlophone R 5675) March 1968

HEY JUDE/REVOLUTION
(Apple R 5722) August 1968

GET BACK/DON'T LET ME DOWN
(Apple R 5777) April 1969

THE BALLAD OF JOHN AND YOKO/OLD BROWN SHOE
(Apple R 5786) May 1969

SOMETHING/COME TOGETHER
(Apple R 5814) October 1969

LET IT BE/YOU KNOW MY NAME (LOOK UP THE NUMBER)
(Apple R 5833) March 1970

TWIST AND SHOUT (live)/FALLING IN LOVE AGAIN (live)
(Lingasong NB 1) June 1977

SEARCHIN'/MONEY/TILL THERE WAS YOU
(Audiofidelity AFS 1) October 1982

BABY IT'S YOU/I'LL FOLLOW THE SUN/DEVIL IN HER HEART/BOYS
(Apple R 6406/CDR 6406) March 1995

FREE AS A BIRD/CHRISTMAS TIME (IS HERE AGAIN)
(Apple R 6422) November 1995

FREE AS A BIRD/I SAW HER STANDING THERE/THIS BOY/CHRISTMAS TIME (IS HERE AGAIN)
(Apple CDR 6422, CD) November 1995

REAL LOVE/BABY'S IN BLACK
(Apple R 6425) March 1996

REAL LOVE/BABY'S IN BLACK/YELLOW SUBMARINE/HERE THERE AND EVERYWHERE
(Apple CDR 6425, CD) March 1996

THE BEATLES: UK EPs

MY BONNIE (with Tony Sheridan)
My Bonnie/Why/Cry For A Shadow/The Saints (Polydor H 21–610) July 1963

TWIST AND SHOUT
Twist And Shout/A Taste Of Honey/Do You Want To Know A Secret/There's A Place
(Parlophone GEP 8882) July 1963

THE BEATLES' HITS
From Me To You/Thank You Girl/Please Please Me/ Love Me Do
(Parlophone GEP 8880) September 1963

THE BEATLES NO. 1
I Saw Her Standing There/Misery/Anna/Chains
(Parlophone GEP 8883) November 1963

ALL MY LOVING
All My Loving/Ask Me Why/Money/P.S. I Love You
(Parlophone GEP 8891) February 1964

LONG TALL SALLY
Long Tall Sally/I Call Your Name/Slow Down/ Matchbox
(Parlophone GEP 8913) June 1964

EXCERPTS FROM THE FILM *A HARD DAY'S NIGHT*
I Should Have Known Better/If I Fell/Tell Me Why/ And I Love Her
(Parlophone GEP 8920) November 1964

EXCERPTS FROM THE ALBUM *A HARD DAY'S NIGHT*
Anytime At All/I'll Cry Instead/Things We Said Today/When I Get Home
(Parlophone GEP 8924) December 1964

BEATLES FOR SALE (NO. 1)
No Reply/I'm A Loser/Rock And Roll Music/Eight Days A Week
(Parlophone GEP 8931) April 1965

BEATLES FOR SALE (NO. 2)
I'll Follow The Sun/Baby's In Black/Words Of Love/I Don't Want To Spoil The Party
(Parlophone GEP 8938) June 1965

THE BEATLES' MILLION SELLERS
She Loves You/I Want To Hold Your Hand/Can't Buy Me Love/I Feel Fine
(Parlophone GEP 8946) December 1965

YESTERDAY
Yesterday/Act Naturally/You Like Me Too Much/It's Only Love
(Parlophone GEP 8948) March 1966

NOWHERE MAN
Nowhere Man/Drive My Car/Michelle/You Won't See Me
(Parlophone GEP 8952) July 1966

MAGICAL MYSTERY TOUR (double EP set)
Magical Mystery Tour/Your Mother Should Know/I Am The Walrus/The Fool
On The Hill/Flying/Blue Jay Way
(Parlophone MMT 1, mono: SMMT 1, stereo) December 1967

THE BEATLES: ORIGINAL UK LPs

PLEASE PLEASE ME
I Saw Her Standing There/Misery/Anna/Chains/Boys/Ask Me Why/Please
Please Me/Love Me Do/P.S. I Love You/Baby It's You/Do You Want To Know A
Secret/A Taste Of Honey/There's A Place/Twist And Shout
(Parlophone PMC 1202, mono; PCS 3042, stereo) March 1963

WITH THE BEATLES
It Won't Be Long/All I've Got To Do/All My Loving/ Don't Bother Me/Little
Child/Till There Was You/Please Mr Postman/Roll Over Beethoven/Hold Me
Tight/You Really Got A Hold On Me/I Wanna Be Your Man/Devil In Her
Heart/Not A Second Time/Money
(Parlophone PMC 1206, mono; PCS 3045, stereo) November 1963

THE BEATLES' FIRST (with Tony Sheridan)
Ain't She Sweet/Cry For A Shadow/My Bonnie/If You Love Me Baby/Sweet
Georgia Brown/The Saints/ Why/Nobody's Child (plus 4 tracks not by The
Beatles)
(Polydor 236 201) June 1964

A HARD DAY'S NIGHT
A Hard Day's Night/I Should Have Known Better/If I Fell/I'm Happy Just To
Dance With You/And I Love Her/Tell Me Why/Can't Buy Me Love/Any Time

At All/I'll Cry Instead/Things We Said Today/When I Get Home/You Can't Do
That/I'll Be Back
(Parlophone PMC 1230, mono: PCS 3058, stereo) July 1964

BEATLES FOR SALE
No Reply/I'm A Loser/Baby's In Black/Rock And Roll Music/I'll Follow The
Sun/Mr Moonlight/Kansas City; Hey Hey Hey Hey/Eight Days A Week/Words
Of Love/Honey Don't/Every Little Thing/I Don't Want To Spoil The
Party/What You're Doing/Everybody's Trying To Be My Baby
(Parlophone PMC 1240, mono; PCS 3062, stereo) December 1964

HELP
Help!/The Night Before/You've Got To Hide Your Love Away/I Need
You/Another Girl/You're Gonna Lose That Girl/Ticket To Ride/Act
Naturally/It's Only Love/You Like Me Too Much/Tell Me What You
See/Yesterday/Dizzy Miss Lizzy
(Parlophone PMC 1255, mono; PCS 3071, stereo) August 1965

RUBBER SOUL
Drive My Car/Norwegian Wood/You Won't See Me/ Nowhere Man/Think For
Yourself/The Word/Michelle/What Goes On/Girl/I'm Looking Through You/In
My Life/Wait/If I Needed Someone/Run For Your Life
(Parlophone PMC 1267, mono: PCS 3075, stereo) December 1965

REVOLVER
Taxman/Eleanor Rigby/I'm Only Sleeping/Love You To/Here There And
Everywhere/Yellow Submarine/She Said She Said/Good Day Sunshine/And
Your Bird Can Sing/For No One/Dr Robert/I Want To Tell You/Got To Get You
Into My Life/Tomorrow Never Knows
(Parlophone PMC 7009, mono; PCS 7009, stereo) August 1966

A COLLECTION OF BEATLES OLDIES
She Loves You/From Me To You/We Can Work It
Out/Help!/Michelle/Yesterday/I Feel Fine/Yellow Submarine/Can't Buy Me
Love/Bad Boy/Day Tripper/A Hard Day's Night/Ticket To Ride/ Paperback
Writer/Eleanor Rigby/I Want To Hold Your Hand
(Parlophone PMC 7016, mono; PCS 7016, stereo) December 1966

SGT. PEPPER'S LONELY HEARTS CLUB BAND
Sgt. Pepper's Lonely Hearts Club Band/With A Little Help From My
Friends/Lucy In The Sky With Diamonds/It's Getting Better/Fixing A
Hole/She's Leaving Home/Being For The Benefit Of Mr Kite/Within You
Without You/When I'm 64/Lovely Rita/Good Morning Good Morning/Sgt.

Pepper's Lonely Hearts Club Band (reprise)/A Day In The Life
(Parlophone PMC 7027, mono; PCS 7027, stereo) June 1967

THE BEATLES (double album)
Back In The USSR/Dear Prudence/Glass Onion/Ob-La-Di, Ob-La-Da/Wild
Honey Pie/The Continuing Story of Bungalow Bill/While My Guitar Gently
Weeps/Happiness Is A Warm Gun/Martha My Dear/I'm So
Tired/Blackbird/Piggies/Rocky Raccoon/Don't Pass Me By/Why Don't We Do
It In The Road/I Will/Julia/Birthday/Yer Blues/Mother Nature's
Son/Everybody's Got Something To Hide Except For Me And My
Monkey/Sexy Sadie/Helter Skelter/Long Long Long/Revolution 1/Honey
Pie/Savoy Truffle/Cry Baby Cry/Revolution 9/Goodnight
(Apple PMC 7067/8, mono; PCS 7067/8, stereo) November 1968

YELLOW SUBMARINE
Yellow Submarine/Only A Northern Song/All Together Now/Hey Bulldog/It's
All Too Much/All You Need Is Love (plus six tracks by George Martin and his
Orchestra)
(Apple PMC 7070, mono: PCS 7070, stereo) January 1969

ABBEY ROAD
Come Together/Something/Maxwell's Silver Hammer/Oh Darling/Octopus's
Garden/I Want You (She's So Heavy)/Here Comes The Sun/Because/You Never
Give Me Your Money/Sun King/Mean Mr Mustard/Polythene Pam/She Came
In Through The Bathroom Window/Golden Slumbers/Carry That Weight/The
End/Her Majesty
(Apple PCS 7088) September 1969

LET IT BE (boxed set with book)
Two Of Us/Dig A Pony/Across The Universe/I Me Mine/Dig It/Let It
Be/Maggie Mae/I've Got A Feeling/The One After 909/The Long And Winding
Road/For You Blue/Get Back
(Apple PXS 1) May 1970

THE BEATLES AT THE HOLLYWOOD BOWL
Twist And Shout/She's A Woman/Dizzy Miss Lizzy/Ticket To Ride/Can't Buy
Me Love/Things We Said Today/Roll Over Beethoven/Boys/A Hard Day's
Night/Help/All My Loving/She Loves You/Long Tall Sally
(EMI EMTV 4) May 1977

LIVE AT THE STAR CLUB, HAMBURG, GERMANY, 1962 (double LP)
I Saw Her Standing There/Roll Over Beethoven/Hippy Hippy Shake/Sweet
Little Sixteen/Lend Me Your Comb/Your Feet's Too Big/Twist And Shout/Mr

Moonlight/A Taste Of Honey/Besame Mucho/Reminiscing/Kansas City; Hey Hey Hey Hey/Nothin' Shakin'/To Know Her Is To Love Her/Little Queenie/ Falling In Love Again/Ask Me Why/Be-Bop-A-Lula/Hallelujah I Love Her So/Red Sails In The Sunset/Everybody's Trying To Be My Baby/Matchbox/ I'm Talkin' 'Bout You/Shimmy Shimmy/Long Tall Sally/I Remember You (Lingasong LNL 1) May 1977

THE COMPLETE SILVER BEATLES
Three Cool Cats/Crying Waiting Hoping/Besame Mucho/Searchin'/The Sheik Of Araby/Money/To Know Her Is To Love Her/Take Good Care Of My Baby/Memphis Tennessee/Sure To Fall/Till There Was You/September In The Rain
(Audiofidelity AFELP 1047) September 1982

LIVE AT THE BBC (Double LP/Double CD)
Beatle Greetings/From Us To You/Riding On A Bus/I Got A Woman/Too Much Monkey Business/Keep Your Hands Off My Baby/I'll Be On My Way/Young Blood/A Shot Of Rhythm And Blues/Sure To Fall/Some Other Guy/Thank You Girl/Sha La La La La!/Baby It's You/That's All Right (Mama)/Carol/Soldier Of Love/A Little Rhyme/Clarabella/I'm Gonna Sit Right Down And Cry (Over You)/Crying, Waiting, Hoping/Dear Wack!/You Really Got A Hold On Me/To Know Her Is To Love Her/A Taste Of Honey/Long Tall Sally/I Saw Her Standing There/The Honeymoon Song/Johnny B. Goode/Memphis, Tennessee/ Lucille/Can't Buy Me Love/From Fluff To You/Till Thre Was You/Crinsk Dee Night/A Hard Day's Night/Have A Banana/I Wanna Be Your Man/Just A Rumour/Roll Over Beethoven/All My Loving/Things We Said Today/She's A Woman/Sweet Little Sixteen/1822/Lonesome Tears In My Eyes/Nothin' Shakin'/The Hippy Hippy Shake/Glad All Over/I Just Don't Understand/So How Come (Nobody Loves Me)/I Feel Fine/I'm A Loser/Everybody's Trying To Be My Baby/Rock And Roll Music/Ticket To Ride/Dizzy Miss Lizzie/Kansas City-Hey Hey Hey Hey/Set Fire To That Lot/Matchbox/I Forgot To Remember To Forget/Love These Goon Shows/Ooh! My Soul/Ooh! My Arms/Don't Ever Change/Slow Down/Honey Don't/Love Me Do
(Apple PCSP/CDPCSP 726) November 1994

ANTHOLOGY 1 (Triple LP/Double CD)
Free As A Bird/Speech: John Lennon/That'll Be The Day/In Spite Of All The Danger/Speech: Paul McCartney/Hallelujah I Love Her So/You'll Be Mine/Cayenne/Speech: Paul McCartney/My Bonnie/Ain't She Sweet/Cry For A Shadow/Speech: John Lennon/Speech: Brian Epstein/Searchin'/Three Cool Cats/The Sheik Of Araby/Like Dreamers Do/Hello Little Girl/Speech: Brian Epstein/Besame Mucho/Love Me Do/How Do You Do It/Please Please Me/The One After 909/Lend Me Your Comb/I'll Get You/Speech: John

Lennon/I Saw Her Standing There (live)/From Me To You (live)/Money (live)/ You Really Got A Hold On Me (live)/Roll Over Beethoven (live)/She Loves You (live)/Till There Was You (live)/Twist And Shout (live)/This Boy/I Want To Hold Your Hand/Speech: Morecambe & Wise/Moonlight Bay/Can't Buy Me Love/All My Loving/You Can't Do That/And I Love Her/A Hard Day's Night/I Wanna Be Your Man/Long Tall Sally/Boys/Shout/I'll Be Back (take 2 & 3)/You'll Know What To Do/No Reply (demo)/Mr Moonlight/Leave My Kitten Alone/No Reply/Eight Days A Week (take 1 & 2)/Kansas City-Hey Hey Hey Hey (Apple PCSP/CDPCSP 727) November 1995

ANTHOLOGY 2 (Triple LP/Double CD)

Real Love/Yes It Is/I'm Down/You've Got To Hide Your Love Away/If You've Got Trouble/That Means A Lot/Yesterday/It's Only Love/I Feel Fine (live)/Ticket To Ride (live)/Yesterday (live)/Help! (live)/Everybody's Trying To Be My Baby (live)/Nowhere Man/I'm Looking Through You/12-Bar Original/Tomorrow Never Knows/Got To Get You Into My Life/And Your Bird Can Sing/Taxman/Eleanor Rigby/I'm Only Sleeping (rehearsal)/I'm Only Sleeping/Rock And Roll Music (live)/She's A Woman (live)/Strawberry Fields Forever (demo)/Strawberry Fields Forever (take 1)/Strawberry Fields Forever (take 7)/Penny Lane/A Day In The Life/Good Morning Good Morning/Only A Northern Song/Being For The Benefit Of Mr Kite (take 1)/Being For The Benefit Of Mr Kite (take 2)/Being For The Benefit Of Mr Kite (take 7)/Lucy In The Sky With Diamonds/Within You Without You/Sgt. Pepper's Lonely Hearts Club Band/You Know My Name (Look Up The Number)/I Am The Walrus/Fool On The Hill (demo)/Your Mother Should Know/Fool On The Hill/Hello Goodbye/Lady Madonna/Across The Universe (Apple PCSP/CDPCSP 728) March 1996

ANTHOLOGY 3 (Triple LP/Double CD)

A Beginning/Happiness Is A Warm Gun/Helter Skelter/Mean Mr. Mustard/Polythene Pam/Glass Onion/Junk/Piggies/Honey Pie/Don't Pass Me By/Ob-La-Di, Ob-La-Da/Good Night/Cry Baby Cry/Blackbird/Sexy Sadie/While My Guitar Gently Weeps/Hey Jude/Not Guilty/Mother Nature's Son/Glass Onion/Rocky Raccoon/What's The New Mary Jane/Step Inside Love-Los Paranoias/I'm So Tired/I Will/Why Don't We Do It In The Road/Julia/I've Got A Feeling/She Came In Through The Bathroom Window/Dig A Pony/Two Of Us/For You Blue/Teddy Boy/Medley: Rip It Up-Shake, Rattle & Roll-Blue Suede Shoes/The Long And Winding Road/Oh! Darling/All Things Must Pass/Mailman, Bring Me No More Blues/Get Back/Old Brown Shoe/Octopus's Garden/Maxwell's Silver Hammer/Something/Come Together/Come And Get It/Ain't She Sweet/Because/Let It Be/I Me Mine/The End (Apple PCSP/CDPCSP 729) October 1996

LET IT BE – NAKED (LP with seven-inch single/Double CD)
Get Back/Dig A Pony/For You Blue/The Long And Winding Road/Two Of
Us/I Got A Feeling/The One After 909/Don't Let Me Down/I Me Mine/Across
The Universe/Let It Be
Fly On The Wall: numerous conversation snippets, plus fragments of Sun King-
Don't Let Me Down/Because I Know You Love Me So/Taking A Trip To
Carolina/John's Piano Piece/Child Of Nature/Back In The USSR/Every Little
Thing/Don't Let Me Down/All Things Must Pass/She Came In Through The
Bathroom Window/Paul's Piano Piece/Get Back/Two Of Us/Maggie Mae/I
Fancy Me Chances With You/Dig It/Get Back
(Apple 5954380/5957132) November 2003

MISCELLANEOUS BEATLES RECORDINGS

MY BONNIE/THE SAINTS
Germany only; Beatles' first appearance on record, with Tony Sheridan (Polydor
24 673) June 1961

THE BEATLES' CHRISTMAS RECORD
UK; Fan Club flexi-disc December 1963

KOMM GIB MIR DEINE HAND/SIE LIEBT DICH
Germany only; German-language versions of I Want To Hold Your Hand and She
Loves You
(Odeon 22671) March 1964

ANOTHER BEATLES CHRISTMAS RECORD
UK; Fan Club flexi-disc December 1964

THE BEATLES' THIRD CHRISTMAS RECORD
UK; Fan Club flexi-disc December 1965

THE BEATLES' FOURTH CHRISTMAS RECORD
UK; Fan Club flexi-disc December 1966

CHRISTMAS TIME IS HERE AGAIN!
UK; Fan Club flexi-disc December 1967

THE BEATLES 1968 CHRISTMAS RECORD
UK; Fan Club flexi-disc December 1968

NO ONE'S GONNA CHANGE OUR WORLD (various artists LP)
UK; includes original version of Across The Universe
(Regal Starline SRS 5013) December 1969

THE BEATLES SEVENTH CHRISTMAS RECORD
UK; Fan Club flexi-disc December 1969

FROM THEM TO US
UK LP: Fan Club record including previous Christmas flexi material
(Apple LYN 2154) December 1970

THE BEATLES' CHRISTMAS RECORD
US LP: Fan Club record including previous Christmas flexi material
(Apple SBC 100) December 1970

SESSIONS
Come And Get It/Leave My Kitten Alone/Not Guilty/I'm Looking Through
You/What's The New Mary Jane/How Do You Do It/Besame Mucho/The One
After 909/If You've Got Trouble/That Means A Lot/While My Guitar Gently
Weeps/ Mailman Bring Me No More Blues/Christmas Time (Is Here Again)
Slated for release early in 1985, this album of unissued and alternate Beatles tracks
was withdrawn at the request of Apple. Also postponed was a single, which would
have coupled 'Leave My Kitten Alone' with an alternate take of 'Ob-La-Di, Ob-
La-Da'.

JOHN LENNON: UK SINGLES

GIVE PEACE A CHANCE/REMEMBER LOVE (by The Plastic Ono Band)
(Apple 13) July 1969

COLD TURKEY/DON'T WORRY KYOKO (MUMMY'S ONLY LOOKING FOR HER HAND IN THE SNOW (by The Plastic Ono Band)
(Apple 1001) October 1969

INSTANT KARMA!/WHO HAS SEEN THE WIND (B-side by Yoko Ono)
(Apple 1003) February 1970

POWER TO THE PEOPLE/OPEN YOUR BOX (B-side by Yoko Ono)
(Apple R 5892) March 1971

HAPPY XMAS (WAR IS OVER)/LISTEN THE SNOW IS FALLING
(B-side by Yoko Ono)
(Apple R 5970) November 1972

MIND GAMES/MEAT CITY
(Apple R 5994) November 1973

WHATEVER GETS YOU THROUGH THE NIGHT/ BEEF JERKY
(Apple R 5998) October 1974

NO.9 DREAM/WHAT YOU GOT
(Apple R 6003) January 1975

STAND BY ME/MOVE OVER MS. L
(Apple R 6005) April 1975

IMAGINE/WORKING CLASS HERO
(Apple R 6009) October 1975

(JUST LIKE) STARTING OVER/KISS KISS KISS (B-side by Yoko Ono)
(Geffen K 79186) October 1980

WOMAN/BEAUTIFUL BOYS (B-side by Yoko Ono)
(Geffen K 79195) January 1981

I SAW HER STANDING THERE/WHATEVER GETS YOU THROUGH THE NIGHT/LUCY IN THE SKY WITH DIAMONDS (all with Elton John)
(DJM DJS 10965) March 1981

WATCHING THE WHEELS/I'M YOUR ANGEL (B-side by Yoko Ono)
(Geffen K 79207) March 1981

NOBODY TOLD ME/O SANITY (B-side by Yoko Ono)
(Polydor POSP 700) January 1984

BORROWED TIME/YOUR HANDS (B-side by Yoko Ono)
(Polydor POSP 701) March 1984

BORROWED TIME/YOUR HANDS (by Yoko Ono)/NEVER SAY GOODBYE (by Yoko Ono)
(Polydor POSPX 701. 12-inch) March 1984

I'M STEPPING OUT/SLEEPLESS NIGHTS (B-side by Yoko Ono)
(Polydor POSP 702) July 1984

I'M STEPPING OUT/SLEEPLESS NIGHTS (by Yoko Ono)/LONELINESS
(by Yoko Ono)
(Polydor POSPX 702. 12-inch) July 1984

EVERY MAN HAS A WOMAN WHO LOVES HIM/IT'S ALRIGHT (B-
side by Sean Lennon)
(Polydor POSP 712) November 1984

JEALOUS GUY/GOING DOWN ON LOVE
(Parlophone R 6117) November 1985

JEALOUS GUY/GOING DOWN ON LOVE/OH YOKO
(Parlophone 12R 6117, 12-inch) November 1985

IMAGINE/JEALOUS GUY
(Parlophone R 6199) November 1988

IMAGINE/JEALOUS GUY
(Parlophone RP 6199, picture disc) November 1988

IMAGINE/JEALOUS GUY/HAPPY XMAS (WAR IS OVER)
(Parlophone 12R 6199, 12-inch) November 1988

**IMAGINE/JEALOUS GUY/HAPPY XMAS (WAR IS OVER)/GIVE
PEACE A CHANCE**
(Parlophone CDR 6199, CD) November 1988

**IMAGINE/HAPPY XMAS (WAR IS OVER)/GIVE PEACE A
CHANCE/IMAGINE (video)**
(Parlophone CDR 6534, CD) December 1999

**HAPPY XMAS (WAR IS OVER)/LISTEN, THE SNOW IS FALLING
(B-side by Yoko Ono)**
(Parlophone R 6627) December 2003

**HAPPY XMAS (WAR IS OVER)/LISTEN, THE SNOW IS FALLING
(B-side by Yoko Ono)**
(Parlophone CDR 6627, CD) December 2003

JOHN LENNON: UK LPs

UNFINISHED MUSIC NO. 1: TWO VIRGINS (with Yoko Ono)
No tracks listed
(Apple APCOR 2, mono: SAPCOR 2, stereo) November 1968

UNFINISHED MUSIC NO. 2: LIFE WITH THE LIONS (with Yoko Ono)
Cambridge 1969/No Bed For Beatle John/Baby's Heartbeat/Two Minutes
Silence/Radio Play.
(Zapple 01) May 1969

WEDDING ALBUM (with Yoko Ono)
John And Yoko/Amsterdam
(Apple SAPCOR 11) November 1969

LIVE PEACE IN TORONTO 1969 (by The Plastic Ono Band)
Blue Suede Shoes/Money/Dizzy Miss Lizzy/Yer Blues/Cold Turkey/Give Peace
A Chance/Don't Worry Kyoko (Mummy's Only Looking For Her Hand In The
Snow)/John John (Let's Hope For Peace)
(Apple CORE 2001) December 1969

JOHN LENNON: PLASTIC ONO BAND
Mother/Hold On/I Found Out/Working Class Hero/Isolation/Remember/
Love/Well Well Well/Look At Me/God/My Mummy's Dead (Apple PCS 7124)
December 1970

IMAGINE
Imagine/Crippled Inside/Jealous Guy/It's So Hard/I Don't Want To Be A
Soldier, Mama, I Don't Want To Die/Gimme Some Truth/Oh My Love/How Do
You Sleep/How/Oh Yoko
(Apple SAPCOR 10004) October 1971

SOME TIME IN NEW YORK CITY (double album, with Yoko Ono)
Woman Is The Nigger Of The World/Sisters O Sisters/Attica State/Born In A
Prison/New York City/Sunday Bloody Sunday/Luck Of The Irish/John Sinclair/
Angela/We're All Water/Cold Turkey/Don't Worry Kyoko/Well (Baby Please
Don't Go)/Jamrag/Scumbag/Au
(Apple PCSP 716, 2 LPs) September 1972

MIND GAMES
Mind Games/Tight A$/Aisumasen (I'm Sorry)/One Day At A Time/Bring On
The Lucie (Freda Peeple)/Nutopian International Anthem/Intuition/Out The
Blue/Only People/I Know (I Know)/You Are Here/Meat City
(Apple PCS 7165) November 1973

WALLS AND BRIDGES

Going Down On Love/Whatever Gets You Through The Night/Old Dirt Road/
What You Got/Bless You/Scared/No. 9 Dream/Surprise Surprise/Steel And
Glass/Beef Jerky/Nobody Loves You When You're Down And Out/Ya Ya
(Apple PCTC 254) October 1974

ROCK 'N' ROLL

Be-Bop-A-Lula/Stand By Me/Rip It Up; Ready Teddy/You Can't Catch
Me/Ain't That A Shame/Do You Wanna Dance/Sweet Little Sixteen/Slippin' And
Slidin'/Peggy Sue/Bring It On Home To Me; Send Me Some Lovin'/Bony
Moronie/Ya Ya/Just Because
(Apple PCS 7169) February 1975

SHAVED FISH

Give Peace A Chance/Cold Turkey/Instant Karma! (We All Shine On)/Power To
The People/Mother/Woman Is The Nigger Of The World/Imagine/Whatever
Gets You Through The Night/Mind Games/No. 9 Dream/Happy Xmas (War Is
Over)/Give Peace A Chance (live)
(Apple PCS 7173) October 1975

DOUBLE FANTASY (with Yoko Ono)

(Just Like) Starting Over/Kiss Kiss Kiss/Cleanup Time/Give Me Something/I'm
Losing You/I'm Moving On/Beautiful Boy (Darling Boy)/Watching The Wheels/
I'm Your Angel/Woman/Beautiful Boys/Dear Yoko/Every Man Has A Woman
Who Loves Him/Hard Times Are Over
(Geffen K 99131) November 1980

THE JOHN LENNON COLLECTION

Give Peace A Chance/Instant Karma! (We All Shine On)/Power To The People/
Whatever Gets You Through The Night/No. 9 Dream/Mind Games/Love/Happy
Xmas (War Is Over)/Imagine/Jealous Guy/Stand By Me/(Just Like) Starting
Over/ Woman/I'm Losing You/Beautiful Boy (Darling Boy)/Watching The
Wheels/Dear Yoko
(EMI EMTV 37) November 1982

HEART PLAY (AN UNFINISHED DIALOGUE) (with Yoko Ono)

Interview material
(Polydor 817 238–1) December 1983

MILK AND HONEY: A HEART PLAY (with Yoko Ono)

I'm Stepping Out/Sleepless Night/I Don't Wanna Face It/Don't Be Scared/
Nobody Told Me/O Sanity/ Borrowed Time/Your Hands/(Forgive Me) My Little
Flower Princess/Let Me Count The Ways/Grow Old With Me/You're The One
(Polydor POLH 5) January 1984

LIVE IN NEW YORK CITY
New York City/It's So Hard/Woman Is The Nigger Of The World/Well, Well, Well/Instant Karma! (We All Shine On)/Mother/Come Together/Imagine/Cold Turkey/Hound Dog/Give Peace A Chance
(Parlophone PCS 7301) February 1986

MENLOVE AVENUE
Here We Go Again/Rock And Roll People/Angel Baby/My Baby Left Me/To Know Her Is To Love Her/Steel And Glass/Scared/Old Dirt Road/Nobody Loves You When You're Down And Out/Bless You
(Parlophone PCS 7308) October 1986

THE LAST WORD
Interview material
(Baktabak BAK 2096) July 1988

IMAGINE: JOHN LENNON – MUSIC FROM THE ORIGINAL MOTION PICTURE
Real Love/Twist And Shout/Help!/In My Life/Strawberry Fields Forever/A Day In The Life/Revolution/The Ballad Of John And Yoko/Julia/Don't Let Me Down/Give Peace A Chance/How?/Imagine (rehearsal)/God/Mother/Stand By Me/Jealous Guy/Woman/Beautiful Boy (Darling Boy)/(Just Like) Starting Over/Imagine
(Parlophone PCSP 722, 2 LPs) October 1988

LENNON LEGEND
Imagine/Instant Karma! (We All Shine On)/Mother/Jealous Guy/Power To The People/Cold Turkey/Love/Mind Games/Whatever Gets You Through The Night/No. 9 Dream/Stand By Me/(Just Like) Starting Over/Woman/Beautiful Boy (Darling Boy)/Watching The Wheels/Nobody Told Me/Borrowed Time/Working Class Hero/Happy Xmas (War Is Over)/Give Peace A Chance
(Parlophone 8219541, 2 LPs) October 1997

WONSAPONATIME
I'm Losing You/Working Class Hero/God/How Do You Sleep?/Imagine/Well (Baby Please Don't Go)/Oh My Love/God Save Oz/I Found Out/Woman Is The Nigger Of The World/'A Kiss Is Just A Kiss'/Be-Bop-A-Lula/Rip It Up-Ready Teddy/What You Got/Nobody Loves You (When You're Down And Out)/I Don't Wanna Face It/Real Love/Only You/Grow Old With Me/Sean's 'In The Sky'/Serve Yourself
(Capitol 4976391, 2 LPs) November 1998

IMAGINE (remixed)
(Parlophone 5248581) February 2000

JOHN LENNON: UK CDs

MILK AND HONEY
(Polydor 817 160-2) January 1984

LIVE IN NEW YORK CITY
(Parlophone CDP 7461962) April 1986

DOUBLE FANTASY
(Geffen K 299131) October 1986

MENLOVE AVENUE
(Parlophone CDP 7465762) April 1987

IMAGINE
(EMI CDP 7466412) May 1987

ROCK 'N' ROLL
(EMI CDP 7467072) May 1987

SHAVED FISH
(EMI CDP 7466422) May 1987

SOME TIME IN NEW YORK CITY
(EMI CDS 7467828, 2 CDs) August 1987

MIND GAMES
(EMI CDP 7467692) August 1987

WALLS AND BRIDGES
(EMI CDP 7467682) August 1987

JOHN LENNON PLASTIC ONO BAND
(EMI CDP 7467702) April 1988

IMAGINE: JOHN LENNON
(Parlophone CD-PCSP 722) October 1988

THE JOHN LENNON COLLECTION
Bonus tracks: Move Over Ms L/Cold Turkey
(Parlophone CD-EMTV 37) October 1989

LENNON
CD1: Give Peace A Chance/Blue Suede Shoes/Money/Dizzy Miss Lizzy/Yer Blues/Cold Turkey/Instant Karma! (We All Shine On)/Mother/Hold On/Working Class Hero/Isolation/Remember/Love/Well Well Well/Look At Me/God/My Mummy's Dead/Power To The People/Well (Baby Please Don't Go)
CD2: Imagine/Crippled Inside/Jealous Guy/It's So Hard/Give Me Some Truth/Oh My Love/How Do You Sleep?/How?/Oh Yoko/Happy Xmas (War Is Over)/Woman Is The Nigger Of The World/New York City/John Sinclair/Come Together/Hound Dog/Mind Games/Aisumasen (I'm Sorry)/One Day At A Time/Intuition/Out The Blue
CD3: Whatever Gets You Through The Night/Going Down On Love/Old Dirt Road/Bless You/Scared/No. 9 Dream/Surprise Surprise (Sweet Bird Of Paradox)/Steel And Glass/Nobody Loves You (When You're Down And Out)/Stand By Me/Ain't That A Shame/Do You Want To Dance/Sweet Little Sixteen/Slippin' And Slidin'/Angel Baby/Just Because/Whatever Gets You Thru The Night (live)/Lucy In The Sky With Diamonds/I Saw Her Standing There
CD4: (Just Like) Starting Over/Cleanup Time/I'm Losing You/Beautiful Boy (Darling Boy)/Watching The Wheels/Woman/Dear Yoko/I'm Stepping Out/I Don't Wanna Face It/Nobody Told Me/Borrowed Time/(Forgive Me) My Little Flower Princess/Every Man Has A Woman Who Loves Him/Grow Old With Me (Parlophone CDS 7952202; 4–CD box set) October 1990

JOHN AND YOKO – THE INTERVIEW
1980 interview material
(BBC BBCCD 6002) December 1990

TESTIMONY
1980 interview material
(Thunderbolt CDTB 059) December 1990

LIVE PEACE IN TORONTO 1969
(Apple CDP 7904282) May 1995

TWO VIRGINS
Bonus track: Remember Love
(Rykodisc RCD 10411) May 1997

UNFINISHED MUSIC NO. 2: LIFE WITH THE LIONS
Bonus tracks: Song For John/Mulberry
(Rykodisc RCD 10412) May 1997

WEDDING ALBUM
Bonus tracks: Who Has Seen The Wind?/Listen The Snow Is Falling/Don't Worry
Kyoko
(Rykodisc RCD 10413) May 1997

LENNON LEGEND
(Parlophone 8 219542) October 1997

IN MY LIFE
Interview material, plus Sweet Georgia Brown/Cry For A Shadow/Why/Take
Out Some Insurance On Me Baby by Tony Sheridan & The Beatles
(Dressed To Kill DTKBOX 92) June 1998

ANTHOLOGY
CD1 (Ascot): Working Class Hero/God/I Found Out/Hold
On/Isolation/Love/Mother/Remember/Imagine/ 'Fortunately'/Well (Baby
Please Don't Go)/Oh My Love/Jealous Guy/Maggie Mae/How Do You
Sleep?/God Save Oz/Do The Oz/I Don't Want To Be A Soldier Mama/Give
Peace A Chance/Look At Me/Long Lost John
CD2 (New York): New York City/Attica State/Imagine/Bring On The
Lucie/Woman Is The Nigger Of The World/Geraldo Rivera-One To One
Concert/Woman Is The Nigger Of The World/It's So Hard/Come
Together/Happy Xmas (War Is Over)/The Luck Of The Irish/John Sinclair/The
David Frost Show/Mind Games (I Promise)/Mind Games (Make Love Not
War)/One Day At A Time/I Know (I Know)/I'm The Greatest/Goodnight
Vienna/Jerry Lewis Telethon/'A Kiss Is Just A Kiss'/Real Love/You Are Here
CD3 (The Lost Weekend): What You Got/Nobody Loves Me (When You're
Down And Out)/Whatever Gets You Through The Night/Whatever Gets You
Through The Night/Yesterday/Be-Bop-A-Lula/Rip It Up-Ready
Teddy/Scared/Steel And Glass/Surprise Surprise (Sweet Bird Of Paradox)/Bless
You/Going Down On Love/Move Over Ms L/Ain't She Sweet/Slippin' And
Slidin'/Peggy Sue/Bring It On Home To Me-Send Me Some Lovin'/Phil And
John 1/Phil And John 2/Phil And John 3/'When In Doubt, Fuck It'/Be My
Baby/Stranger's Room/Old Dirt Road
CD4 (Dakota): I'm Losing You/Sean's 'Little Help'/Serve Yourself/My
Life/Nobody Told Me/Life Begins At 40/I Don't Wanna Face It/Woman/Dear
Yoko/Watching The Wheels/I'm Stepping Out/Borrowed Time/The Rishikesh
Song/Sean's 'Loud'/Beautiful Boy (Darling Boy)/Mr Hyde's Gone (Don't Be
Afraid)/Only You/Grow Old With Me/Dear John/The Greak Wok/Mucho
Mungo/Satire 1/Satire 2/Satire 3/Sean's 'In The Sky'/It's Real
(Parlophone 8306142, 4-CD box set) November 1998

WONSAPONATIME
(Parlophone 4976392) November 1998

IMAGINE (remixed)
(Parlophone 5248582) February 2000

WE ARE ALL TOGETHER
Interview material from 1969
(Delta 47034) June 2000

JOHN LENNON PLASTIC ONO BAND
Bonus tracks: Power To The People/Do The Oz
(Parlophone 5287392) October 2000

DOUBLE FANTASY
Bonus tracks: Help Me To Help Myself/Walking On Thin Ice/Central Park Stroll (dialogue)
(Parlophone 5287402) October 2000

BEDISM
Interview material from 1969 bed-ins
(Dressed To Kill DRESS 155) December 2000

MIND GAMES
Bonus tracks: Aisumasen (I'm Sorry) (home version)/Bring On The Lucie (Freda People) (home version)/Meat City (home version)
(Parlophone 5424252) October 2002

THE LEGENDS COLLECTION
Interview material 1963–1969, plus Take Out Some Insurance On Me Baby with Tony Sheridan & Beatles
(Magic TOPAK 523) May 2003

MILK AND HONEY/DOUBLE FANTASY
(EMI EBX 23, 2-CDs) September 2004

ROCK 'N' ROLL
Bonus tracks: Angel Baby/To Know Her Is To Love Her/Since My Baby Left Me/Just Because (reprise)
(Parlophone 8743292) September 2004

ACOUSTIC
Working Class Hero/Love/Well Well Well/Look At Me/God/My Mummy's Dead/Cold Turkey/Luck Of The Irish/John Sinclair/Woman Is The Nigger Of

The World/What You Got/Watching The Wheels/Dear Yoko/Real
Love/Imagine/It's Real
(Parlophone 8744282) November 2004

RELATED UK RELEASES:

BAD TO ME/I CALL YOUR NAME by Billy J. Kramer with The Dakotas
Both sides written by Lennon
(Parlophone R 5049) July 1963

HELLO LITTLE GIRL by The Fourmost
A-side written by Lennon
(Parlophone R 5056) August 1963

I'M IN LOVE by The Fourmost
A-side written by Lennon
(Parlophone R 5078) November 1963

YOU'VE GOT TO HIDE YOUR LOVE AWAY by The Silkie
A-side written and produced by Lennon and McCartney
(Fontana TF 1525) September 1965

WE LOVE YOU by The Rolling Stones
A-side featuring Lennon's backing vocals.
(Decca F 12654) August 196

HOW I WON THE WAR by Musketeer Gripweed And The Third Troop
A-side featuring brief vocal contribution by Lennon
(United Artists UP 1196) October 1967

YOKO ONO: PLASTIC ONO BAND by Yoko Ono
Album produced by Lennon, who also plays guitar on every track except 'Aos'
Why/Why Not/Greenfield Morning I Pushed An Empty Baby Carriage All
Over The City/Aos/Touch Me/Paper Shoes
(Apple SAPCOR 17) December 1970

TANDOORI CHICKEN by Ronnie Spector
B-side (to Try Some Buy Some) features backing vocals by Lennon
(Apple 33) April 1971

GOD SAVE US/DO THE OZ by Bill Elliott And The Elastic Oz Band
Both sides produced and written by Lennon, who also sings lead on the B-side
(Apple 36) July 1971

MRS LENNON/MIDSUMMER NEW YORK by Yoko Ono
Both sides produced by Lennon
(Apple 38) October 1971

FLY (double album) by Yoko Ono
Album produced by Lennon, who also plays guitar on some tracks
Midsummer New York/Mind Train/Mind Holes/Don't Worry Kyoko/Mrs
Lennon/Hirake/Toilet Piece/O'Wind/Airmale/Don't Count The
Waves/You/Fly/Telephone Piece
(Apple SAPTU 101/2) December 1971

MIND TRAIN/LISTEN THE SNOW IS FALLING by Yoko Ono
Both sides produced by Lennon
(Apple 41) January 1972

ELEPHANT'S MEMORY by Elephant's Memory
Album produced by Lennon, who also appears on several tracks
Liberation Special/Baddest Of The Mean/Cryin' Blacksheep Blues/Chuck And Bo/
Gypsy Wolf/Madness/Life/Wind Ridge/Power Boogie/Local Plastic Ono Band
(Apple SAPCOR 22) November 1972

POWER BOOGIE/LIBERATION SPECIAL by Elephant's Memory
Both sides produced by Lennon
(Apple 45) December 1972

APPROXIMATELY INFINITE UNIVERSE by Yoko Ono
Album produced by Lennon, who also appears on two tracks
Yang Yang/Death Of Samantha/I Want My Love To Rest Tonight/What Did I
Do/Have You Seen A Horizon Lately/Approximately Infinite Universe/Peter The
Dealer/Song For John/Catman/What A Bastard The World Is/Waiting For The
Sunrise/I Felt Like Smashing My Face In A Clear Glass Window/Winter
Song/Kite Song/What A Mess/Shirankatta/ Air Talk/I Have A Woman Inside My
Soul/Move On Fast/Now Or Never/Is Winter Here To Stay/Looking Over
From My Hotel Window
(Apple SAPDO 1001) February 1973

DEATH OF SAMANTHA/YANG YANG by Yoko Ono
Both sides produced by Lennon
(Apple 47) May 1973

RINGO by Ringo Starr
Lennon wrote and appears on one track, I'm The Greatest
(Apple PCTC 252) November 1973

FEELING THE SPACE by Yoko Ono
Lennon appears on three tracks: She Hits Back, Woman Power, Men Men Men
(Apple SAPCOR 26) November 1973

MEN MEN MEN by Yoko Ono
B-side features Lennon
(Apple 48) December 1973

PUSSY CATS by Harry Nilsson
Lennon produced the album, and co-wrote Mucho Mungo; Mt. Elba
Many Rivers To Cross/Subterranean Homesick Blues/Don't Forget Me/All My
Life/Old Forgotten Soldier/Save The Last Dance For Me/Mucho Mungo; Mt.
Elba/Loop De Loop/Black Sails/Rock Around The Clock
(RCA APL 1–0570) August 1974

MANY RIVERS TO CROSS/DON'T FORGET ME by Harry Nilsson
Both sides produced by Lennon
(RCA 2459) September 1974

ONLY YOU by Ringo Starr
A-side features Lennon
(Apple R 6000) November 1974

GOODNIGHT VIENNA by Ringo Starr
Album features title track composed by Lennon, who also appears on Only You
(Apple PCS 7168) November 1974

**LUCY IN THE SKY WITH DIAMONDS/ONE DAY AT A TIME by
Elton John**
Both sides written by Lennon, who also appears on A-side
(DJM DJS 340) November 1974

SAVE THE LAST DANCE FOR ME/ALL MY LIFE by Harry Nilsson
Both sides produced by Lennon
(RCA 2504) January 1975

JOHN DAWSON WINTER III by Johnny Winter
Lennon wrote Rock And Roll People
(Blue Sky 80586) February 1975

I SAW HER STANDING THERE by Elton John Band
B-side features Lennon on vocal and guitar
(DJM DJS 354) February 1975

YOUNG AMERICANS by David Bowie
Lennon appears on two tracks, Across The Universe and Fame, both of which he
either wrote or co-wrote
(RCA RS 1006) March 1975

FAME by David Bowie
Lennon co-wrote and appears on A-side
(RCA 2579) July 1975

RINGO'S ROTOGRAVURE by Ringo Starr
Lennon wrote and appears on Cookin'
(Polydor 2382 040) September 1976

WALKING ON THIN ICE/IT HAPPENED by Yoko Ono
Lennon produced and appeared on both sides
(Geffen K 79202) February 1981

IT'S ALRIGHT by Yoko Ono
Never Say Goodbye includes recording of Lennon's voice
(Polydor POLD 5073) December 1982

WALKING ON THIN ICE by Yoko Ono
Contains following tracks produced by or featuring Lennon
Walking On Thin Ice/Kiss Kiss Kiss/Yang Yang/Death Of Samantha/Midsummer
New York/Kite Song/Give Me Something/Woman Power
(May 1992) Rykodisc RCD 20230

PLAYGROUND PSYCHOTICS by Frank Zappa & The Mothers Of Invention
Contains alternate mix/edit of live Lennon/Ono/Zappa material
Well (Baby Please Don't Go)/Say Please/Aaawk/Scumbag/A Small Eternity With
Yoko Ono
(Zappa CDDZAP 55, 2 CDs) October 1992

YOKO ONO: PLASTIC ONO BAND by Yoko Ono
CD adds three Lennon-produced bonus tracks to original LP, Open Your Box,
Something More Abstract & South Wind
(Rykodisc RCD 10414) May 1997

FLY by Yoko Ono
CD adds two Lennon-produced bonus tracks to original LP, Between The Takes
& Will You Touch Me
(Rykodisc RCD 10415/16) May 1997

APPROXIMATELY INFINITE UNIVERSE by Yoko Ono
CD adds two Lennon-produced bonus tracks to original LP, Dogtown & She
Gets Down On Her Knees
(Rykodisc RCD 10417/18) May 1997

FEELING THE SPACE by Yoko Ono
CD adds Coffin Car (live) featuring Lennon on guitar
(Rykodisc RCD 10419) May 1997

ONOBOX by Yoko Ono
Includes following tracks, produced by or featuring Lennon
No Bed For Beatle John/Mind Holes/Oh Wind/Why/Why Not/Greenfield
Morning I Pushed An Empty Baby Carriage All Over The City/Touch Me/Paper
Shoes/Mind Train/Open Your Box/Toilet Piece/Don't Worry Kyoko/Telephone
Piece/Midsummer New York/The Path/Don't Count The Waves/Head Play/Is
Winter Here To Stay/Yang Yang/Death Of Samantha/What Did I
Do/Approximately Infinite Universe/What A Bastard The World Is/Catman/I
Want My Love To Rest Tonight/Shiranakatta/Peter The Dealer/I Felt Like
Smashing My Face In A Clear Glass Window/Winter Song/Kite Song/Now Or
Never/What A Mess/I Have A Woman Inside My Soul/Move On Fast/Looking
Over From My Hotel Window/Waiting For The Sunrise/Angry Young
Woman/Potbelly Rocker/She Hits Back/Men Men Men/Woman Power/It's
Been Very Hard/Let's Turn The Right Turn/Walking On Thin Ice/Kiss Kiss
Kiss/Give Me Something/I'm Movin' On/Yes I'm Your Angel/Beautiful
Boys/Every Man Has A Woman Who Loves Him/Hard Times Are Over/Have
You Seen A Horizon Lately/We're All Water/Sisters O Sisters
(Rykodisc RCD 10224-10229) May 1997

PUSSY CATS by Harry Nilsson
CD adds two Lennon-produced bonus tracks to original LP, Down By The Sea &
The Flying Saucer Song
(Camden 74321950252) October 2002

THE BEST OF CILLA 1963-78 by Cilla Black
Includes promotional message 'John Lennon Introduces It's For You'
(EMI 5841242, 3 CDs) May 2003

JOHN LENNON'S JUKEBOX by various artists
Compilation of tracks found on jukebox owned by Lennon during the sixties
(Virgin TV VTDCD 608, 2 CDs) March 2004

THE BEATLES: US SINGLES

MY BONNIE/THE SAINTS (with Tony Sheridan)
(Decca 31382) April 1962

PLEASE PLEASE ME/ASK ME WHY
(Vee Jay VJ 498) February 1963

FROM ME TO YOU/THANK YOU GIRL
(Vee Jay VJ 522) May 1963

SHE LOVES YOU/I'LL GET YOU
(Swan 4152) September 1963

I WANT TO HOLD YOUR HAND/I SAW HER STANDING THERE
(Capitol 5112) January 1964

MY BONNIE/THE SAINTS (with Tony Sheridan)
(MGM K 13213) January 1964

PLEASE PLEASE ME/FROM ME TO YOU
(Vee Jay VJ 581) January 1964

TWIST AND SHOUT/THERE'S A PLACE
(Tollie 9001) March 1964

CAN'T BUY ME LOVE/YOU CAN'T DO THAT
(Capitol 5150) March 1964

DO YOU WANT TO KNOW A SECRET/THANK YOU GIRL
(Vee Jay VJ 587) March 1964

WHY/CRY FOR A SHADOW (A-side with Tony Sheridan)
(MGM K 13227) March 1964

LOVE ME DO/P.S. I LOVE YOU
(Tollie 9008) April 1964

SIE LIEBT DICH/I'LL GET YOU
(Swan 4182) May 1964

SWEET GEORGIA BROWN/IF YOU LOVE ME BABY (with Tony Sheridan)
(Atco 6302) June 1964

AIN'T SHE SWEET/NOBODY'S CHILD (B-side with Tony Sheridan)
(Atco 6308) July 1964

A HARD DAY'S NIGHT/I SHOULD HAVE KNOWN BETTER
(Capitol 5222) July 1964

I'LL CRY INSTEAD/I'M HAPPY JUST TO DANCE WITH YOU
(Capitol 5234) July 1964

AND I LOVE HER/IF I FELL
(Capitol 5235) July 1964

SLOW DOWN/MATCHBOX
(Capitol 5255) August 1964

I FEEL FINE/SHE'S A WOMAN
(Capitol 5327) November 1964

EIGHT DAYS A WEEK/I DON'T WANT TO SPOIL THE PARTY
(Capitol 5371) February 1965

TICKET TO RIDE/YES IT IS
(Capitol 5407) April 1965

HELP/I'M DOWN
(Capitol 5476) July 1965

YESTERDAY/ACT NATURALLY
(Capitol 5498) September 1965

DAY TRIPPER/WE CAN WORK IT OUT
(Capitol 5555) December 1965

NOWHERE MAN/WHAT GOES ON
(Capitol 5587) February 1966

PAPERBACK WRITER/RAIN
(Capitol 5651) May 1966

YELLOW SUBMARINE/ELEANOR RIGBY
(Capitol 5715) August 1966

PENNY LANE/STRAWBERRY FIELDS FOREVER
(Capitol 5810) February 1967

ALL YOU NEED IS LOVE/BABY YOU'RE A RICH MAN
(Capitol 5964) July 1967

HELLO GOODBYE/I AM THE WALRUS
(Capitol 2056) November 1967

LADY MADONNA/THE INNER LIGHT
(Capitol 2138) March 1968

HEY JUDE/REVOLUTION
(Apple 2276) August 1968

GET BACK/DON'T LET ME DOWN
(Apple 2490) May 1969

THE BALLAD OF JOHN AND YOKO/OLD BROWN SHOE
(Apple 2531) June 1969

SOMETHING/COME TOGETHER
(Apple 2654) October 1969

LET IT BE/YOU KNOW MY NAME (LOOK UP THE NUMBER)
(Apple 2764) March 1970

THE LONG AND WINDING ROAD/FOR YOU BLUE
(Apple 2832) May 1970

THE BEATLES: US EPs

THE BEATLES
Misery/Ask Me Why/A Taste Of Honey/Anna
(Vee Jay VJEP 1–903) March 1964

FOUR BY THE BEATLES
Roll Over Beethoven/All My Loving/This Boy/Please Mr Postman
(Capitol EAP 2121) May 1964

FOUR BY THE BEATLES
Honey Don't/I'm A Loser/ Mr Moonlight/Everybody's Trying To Be My Baby
(Capitol R 5365) February 1965

THE BEATLES: US LPs

INTRODUCING THE BEATLES
I Saw Her Standing There/Misery/Anna/Chains/Boys/Love Me Do/P.S. I Love
You/Baby It's You/Do You Want To Know A Secret/A Taste Of Honey/There's A
Place/Twist And Shout
(Vee Jay VJLP 1062) July 1963

MEET THE BEATLES
I Want To Hold Your Hand/I Saw Her Standing There/This Boy/It Won't Be
Long/All I've Got To Do/All My Loving/Don't Bother Me/Little Child/Till
There Was You/Hold Me Tight/I Wanna Be Your Man/Not A Second Time
(Capitol T 2047, mono; ST 2047, stereo) January 1964

INTRODUCING THE BEATLES
Reissue of earlier album of same title, with Ask Me Why and Please Please Me
replacing Love Me Do and P.S. I Love You
(Vee Jay VJLP 1062) January 1964

THE BEATLES WITH TONY SHERIDAN AND THEIR GUESTS
My Bonnie/Cry For A Shadow/The Saints/Why (plus eight tracks not by The
Beatles)
(MGM SE 4215) February 1964

JOLLY WHAT! THE BEATLES AND FRANK IFIELD ON STAGE
Please Please Me/From Me To You/Ask Me Why/Thank You Girl (plus eight
tracks by Frank Ifield)
(Vee Jay VJLP 1085) February 1964

THE BEATLES' SECOND ALBUM
Roll Over Beethoven/Thank You Girl/You Really Got A Hold On Me/Devil In
Her Heart/Money/You Can't Do That/Long Tall Sally/I Call Your Name/Please
Mr Postman/I'll Get You/She Loves You
(Capitol T2080, mono: ST 2080, stereo) April 1964

A HARD DAY'S NIGHT
A Hard Day's Night/Tell Me Why/I'll Cry Instead/I'm Happy Just To Dance With You/I Should Have Known Better/If I Fell/And I Love Her/Can't Buy Me Love (plus four tracks by George Martin and his Orchestra)
(United Artists UAS 6366) June 1964

SOMETHING NEW
I'll Cry Instead/Things We Said Today/Anytime At All/When I Get Home/Slow Down/Matchbox/Tell Me Why/And I Love Her/I'm Happy Just To Dance With You/If I Fell/Komm Gib Mir Deine Hand
(Capitol T 2108. mono; ST 2108, stereo) July 1964

THE BEATLES VS. THE FOUR SEASONS (double album)
Contains one album with same tracks as the second issue of INTRODUCING THE BEATLES, plus one album by The Four Seasons
(Vee Jay VJDX 30) October 1964

AIN'T SHE SWEET
Ain't She Sweet/Sweet Georgia Brown/Take Out Some Insurance On Me Baby/Nobody's Child (plus eight tracks by The Swallows)
(Atco SD 33–169) October 1964

SONGS, PICTURES AND STORIES OF THE FABULOUS BEATLES
Same tracks as second issue of INTRODUCING THE BEATLES
(Vee Jay VJLP 1092) October 1964

THE BEATLES' STORY (double album; documentary)
On Stage With The Beatles/How Beatlemania Began/Beatlemania In Action/Man Behind The Beatles: Brian Epstein/John Lennon/Who's A Millionaire?/Beatles Will Be Beatles/Man Behind The Music: George Martin/George Harrison/A Hard Day's Night – Their First Movie/Paul McCartney/Sneaky Haircuts And More About Paul/Twist And Shout (live)/The Beatles Look At Life/Victims Of Beatlemania/Beatle Medley/Ringo Starr/Liverpool And All The World!
(Capitol STBO 2222) November 1964

BEATLES '65
No Reply/I'm A Loser/Baby's In Black/Rock And Roll Music/I'll Follow The Sun/Mr Moonlight/Honey Don't/I'll Be Back/She's A Woman/I Feel Fine/Everybody's Trying To Be My Baby
(Capitol T 2228, mono; ST 2228, stereo) December 1964

354

THE EARLY BEATLES
Love Me Do/Twist And Shout/Anna/Chains/Boys/Ask Me Why/Please Please Me/P.S. I Love You/Baby It's You/A Taste Of Honey/Do You Want To Know A Secret (Capitol T 2309, mono; ST 2309, stereo) March 1965

BEATLES VI
Kansas City; Hey Hey Hey Hey/Eight Days A Week/You Like Me Too Much/ Bad Boy/I Don't Want To Spoil The Party/Words Of Love/What You're Doing/Yes It Is/Dizzy Miss Lizzy/Tell Me What You See/Every Little Thing (Capitol T 2358, mono; ST 2358, stereo) June 1965

HELP!
Help!/The Night Before/You've Got To Hide Your Love Away/I Need You/Another Girl/Ticket To Ride/You're Gonna Lose That Girl (plus six tracks of incidental music)
(Capitol MAS 2386, mono; SMAS 2386, stereo) August 1965

RUBBER SOUL
I've Just Seen A Face/Norwegian Wood/You Won't See Me/Think For Yourself/The Word/Michelle/It's Only Love/Girl/I'm Looking Through You/In My Life/Wait/Run For Your Life
(Capitol T 2442, mono; ST 2442, stereo) December 1965

YESTERDAY AND TODAY
Drive My Car/I'm Only Sleeping/Nowhere Man/Dr Robert/Yesterday/Act Naturally/And Your Bird Can Sing/If I Needed Someone/We Can Work It Out/What Goes On/Day Tripper
(Capitol T 2553, mono; ST 2553, stereo) June 1966

REVOLVER
Taxman/Eleanor Rigby/Love You To/Here, There And Everywhere/Yellow Submarine/She Said She Said/Good Day Sunshine/For No One/I Want To Tell You/Got To Get You Into My Life/Tomorrow Never Knows
(Capitol T 2576, mono; ST 2576, stereo) August 1966

THIS IS WHERE IT STARTED
My Bonnie/Cry For A Shadow/The Saints/Why (plus six tracks not by The Beatles)
(Metro MS 563) August 1966

THE AMAZING BEATLES AND OTHER GREAT ENGLISH GROUP SOUNDS
Ain't She Sweet/Take Out Some Insurance On Me Baby/Nobody's Child/Sweet Georgia Brown (plus six tracks not by The Beatles)
(Clarion 601) October 1966

SGT. PEPPER'S LONELY HEARTS CLUB BAND
Same tracks as UK release
(Capitol MAS 2653, mono; SMAS 2653, stereo) June 1967

MAGICAL MYSTERY TOUR
Magical Mystery Tour/The Fool On The Hill/Flying/Blue Jay Way/Your Mother
Should Know/I Am The Walrus/Hello Goodbye/Strawberry Fields
Forever/Penny Lane/Baby You're A Rich Man/All You Need Is Love
(Capitol MAL 2835, mono; SMAL 2835, stereo) November 1967

THE BEATLES
Same tracks as UK release
(Apple SWBO 101) November 1968

YELLOW SUBMARINE
Same tracks as UK release
(Apple SW 153) January 1969

ABBEY ROAD
Same tracks as UK release
(Apple SO 383) October 1969

HEY JUDE (also pressed as THE BEATLES AGAIN)
Can't Buy Me Love/I Should Have Known Better/Paperback Writer/Rain/Lady
Madonna/Revolution/Hey Jude/Old Brown Shoe/Don't Let Me Down/The
Ballad Of John and Yoko
(Apple SW 385) February 1970

IN THE BEGINNING–CIRCA 1960
Same tracks as UK THE BEATLES FIRST album
(Polydor 24–4504) May 1970

LET IT BE
Same tracks as UK release
(Apple AR34001) May 1970

THE BEATLES AT THE HOLLYWOOD BOWL
Same tracks as UK release
(Capitol SMAS 11638) May 1977

THE BEATLES LIVE AT THE STAR CLUB, HAMBURG, GERMANY, 1962 (double album)
I'm Gonna Sit Right Down And Cry/Roll Over Beethoven/Hippy Hippy

Shake/Sweet Little Sixteen/Lend Me Your Comb/Your Feet's Too Big/Where Have You Been All My Life/Mr Moonlight/A Taste Of Honey/Besame Mucho/Till There Was You/Kansas City; Hey Hey Hey Hey/Nothin' Shakin'/To Know Her Is To Love Her/Little Queenie/Falling In Love Again/Sheila/Be-Bop-A-Lula/Hallelujah I Love Her So/Red Sails In The Sunset/Everybody's Trying To Be My Baby/Matchbox/I'm Talking About You/Shimmy Shake/Long Tall Sally/I Remember You
(Lingasong LS27001) June 1977

THE COMPLETE SILVER BEATLES
Same tracks as UK release
(Audio Rarities AR 2452) September 1982

THE SILVER BEATLES VOL. 1
Three Cool Cats (extended)/Memphis Tennessee (extended)/Besame Mucho/The Sheik Of Araby/Till There Was You/Searching (extended)/Sure To Fall (extended) (extended tracks were re-edited for this release)
(Phoenix-10 PHX 352) September 1982

THE SILVER BEATLES VOL. 2
Searching (extended)/Take Good Care Of My Baby (extended)/Money (extended)/To Know Her Is To Love Her/Three Cool Cats (extended)/September In The Rain (extended)/Crying, Waiting, Hoping (extended tracks were re-edited for this release)
(Phoenix-10 PHX 353) September 1982

LIVE AT THE BBC
Same tracks as UK release
(Apple CDP 8-31796-2) November 1994

ANTHOLOGY 1
Same tracks as UK release
(Apple CDP 8-34445-2) November 1995

ANTHOLOGY 2
Same tracks as UK release
(Apple CDP 8-34448-2) March 1996

ANTHOLOGY 3
Same tracks as UK release
(Apple CDP 8-34451-2) October 1996

LET IT BE – NAKED
Same tracks as US release
(Apple CDP 5-95227-2) November 2003

JOHN LENNON: US SINGLES

GIVE PEACE A CHANCE/REMEMBER LOVE (by the Plastic Ono Band)
(Apple 1809) July 1969

COLD TURKEY/DON'T WORRY KYOKO (MUMMY'S ONLY LOOKING FOR HER HAND IN THE SNOW) (by The Plastic Ono Band)
(Apple 1813) October 1969

INSTANT KARMA!/WHO HAS SEEN THE WIND (B-side by Yoko Ono)
(Apple 1818) February 1970

MOTHER/WHY (B-side by Yoko Ono)
(Apple 1827) December 1970

POWER TO THE PEOPLE/TOUCH ME (B-side by Yoko Ono)
(Apple 1830) March 1971

IMAGINE/IT'S SO HARD
(Apple 1840) October 1971

HAPPY XMAS (WAR IS OVER)/LISTEN THE SNOW IS FALLING (B-side by Yoko Ono)
(Apple 1842) December 1971

WOMAN IS THE NIGGER OF THE WORLD/ SISTERS O SISTERS (B-side by Yoko Ono)
(Apple 1848) April 1972

MIND GAMES/MEAT CITY
(Apple 1868) October 1973

WHATEVER GETS YOU THROUGH THE NIGHT/ BEEF JERKY
(Apple 1874) September 1974

NO. 9 DREAM/WHAT YOU GOT
(Apple 1878) December 1974

STAND BY ME/MOVE OVER MS. L
(Apple 1881) March 1975

SLIPPIN' AND SLIDIN'/AIN'T THAT A SHAME
(Apple 1883, release cancelled) June 1975

(JUST LIKE) STARTING OVER/KISS KISS KISS (B-side by Yoko Ono)
(Geffen GEF 49604) October 1980

WOMAN/BEAUTIFUL BOYS (B-side by Yoko Ono)
(Geffen GEF 49644) January 1981

WATCHING THE WHEELS/I'M YOUR ANGEL (B-side by Yoko Ono)
(Geffen GEF 49695) March 1981

NOBODY TOLD ME/O SANITY (B-side by Yoko Ono)
(Polydor 817 254–7) January 1984

I'M SETTING OUT/SLEEPLESS NIGHT (B-side by Yoko Ono)
(Polydor 821 107–7) March 1984

BORROWED TIME/YOUR HANDS (B-side by Yoko Ono)
(Polydor 821 204–7) May 1984

EVERY MAN HAS A WOMAN WHO LOVES HIM/ IT'S ALRIGHT (B-side by Sean Lennon)
(Polydor 881–378–7) October 1984

JEALOUS GUY/GIVE PEACE A CHANCE
(Capitol B-44230) October 1988

JOHN LENNON: US LPs

UNFINISHED MUSIC NO. 1: TWO VIRGINS (with Yoko Ono)
Same tracks as UK album, but retitled Two Virgins Nos. 1 to
10/Together/Hushabye Hushabye
(Apple T 5001) November 1968

UNFINISHED MUSIC NO.2: LIFE WITH THE LIONS (with Yoko Ono)
Same tracks as UK release
(Apple ST 3357) May 1969

WEDDING ALBUM (with Yoko Ono)
Same tracks as UK release
(Apple SMAX 3361) October 1969

LIVE PEACE IN TORONTO 1969 (with the Plastic Ono Band)
Same tracks as UK release
(Apple SW 3362) December 1969

JOHN LENNON: PLASTIC ONO BAND
Same tracks as UK release December 1970
(Apple SW 3372)

IMAGINE
Same tracks as UK release
(Apple SW 3379) September 1971

SOME TIME IN NEW YORK CITY (double album, with Yoko Ono)
Same tracks as UK release
(Apple SVBB 3392) June 1972

MIND GAMES
Same tracks as UK release
(Apple SW 3414) November 1973

WALLS AND BRIDGES
Same tracks as UK release
(Apple SW 3416) September 1974

ROOTS
Be-Bop-A-Lula/Ain't That A Shame/Stand By Me/ Sweet Little Sixteen/Rip It
Up/Ready Teddy/Angel Baby/Do You Want To Dance/You Can't Catch Me/
Bony Maronie/Peggy Sue/Bring It On Home To Me/ Send Me Some Lovin'/
Slippin' And Slidin'/Be My Baby/Ya Ya/Just Because
(Adam VIII A 8018, release withdrawn) January 1975

ROCK 'N' ROLL
Same tracks as UK release
(Apple SK 3419) February 1975

SHAVED FISH
Same tracks as UK release
(Apple SW 3421) October 1975

DOUBLE FANTASY (with Yoko Ono)
Same tracks as UK release
(Geffen GHS 2001) November 1980

THE JOHN LENNON COLLECTION
Give Peace A Chance/Instant Karma! (We All Shine On)/Power To The People/
Whatever Gets You Thru The Night/No. 9 Dream/Mind Games/Love/Happy
Xmas (War Is Over)/Imagine/Jealous Guy/(Just Like) Starting Over/Woman/I'm
Losing You/Beautiful Boy (Darling Boy)/Dear Yoko/Watching The Wheels
(Geffen GHSP 2023) November 1982

HEARTPLAY (AN UNFINISHED DIALOGUE) (with Yoko Ono)
Same materials as UK release
(Polydor 817-238–1 Y-1) December 1983

MILK AND HONEY: A HEART PLAY (with Yoko Ono)
Same tracks as UK release
(Polydor 817–160–1Y–1) January 1984

REFLECTIONS AND POETRY
Interview material and poetry readings
(Silhouette SM 10014) June 1984

LIVE IN NEW YORK CITY
Same tracks as UK release
(Capitol 746196–1) February 1986

MENLOVE AVENUE
Same tracks as UK release
(Capitol 746576–1) October 1986

IMAGINE: JOHN LENNON – MUSIC FROM THE ORIGINAL MOTION PICTURE
Same tracks as UK release
(Capitol C1-90803) October 1988

LENNON LEGEND
Same tracks as UK release
(Parlophone 8219541) February 1998

JOHN LENNON: US CDs

MILK AND HONEY
(Polydor 817 160-2) January 1984

LIVE IN NEW YORK CITY
(Capitol CDP 7461962) April 1986

DOUBLE FANTASY
(Geffen 2001-2) September 1986

MENLOVE AVENUE
(Capitol CDP 7465762) April 1987

SHAVED FISH
(EMI CDP 7466422) May 1987

IMAGINE
(EMI CDP 7466412) February 1988

MIND GAMES
(EMI CDP 7467692) March 1988

JOHN LENNON: PLASTIC ONO BAND
(EMI CDP 7467702) April 1988

WALLS AND BRIDGES
(EMI CDP 7467682) April 1988

ROCK 'N' ROLL
(EMI CDP 7467072) April 1988

IMAGINE: JOHN LENNON
(Capitol CDP 7908032) October 1988

THE JOHN LENNON COLLECTION
(Capitol CDP 7915162) January 1990

SOME TIME IN NEW YORK CITY
(EMI CDS 7467828, 2 CDs) May 1990

LIVE PEACE IN TORONTO 1969
(Apple CDP 7904282) July 1995

TWO VIRGINS
(Rykodisc RCD 10411) June 1997

UNFINISHED MUSIC NO. 2: LIFE WITH THE LIONS
(Rykodisc RCD 10412) June 1997

WEDDING ALBUM
(Rykodisc RCD 10413) June 1997

LENNON LEGEND
(Parlophone 8219542) February 1998

ANTHOLOGY
(Capitol C2 8306142, 4-CD box set) November 1998

WONSAPONATIME
(Capitol CDP 4976392) November 1998

IMAGINE (remixed)
(Capitol CDP 5248582) February 2000

JOHN LENNON: PLASTIC ONO BAND (remixed with bonus tracks)
(Capitol CDP 5287402) December 2000

DOUBLE FANTASY (remixed with bonus tracks)
(Capitol CDP 5287392) December 2000

MIND GAMES (remixed with bonus tracks)
(Capitol CDP 5424252) November 2002

ROCK 'N' ROLL
(Capitol CDP 72438 7432925) November 2004

ACOUSTIC
(Capitol CDP 72438 7442825) November 2004

RELATED US RELEASES:

BAD TO ME/I CALL YOUR NAME by Billy J. Kramer with The Dakotas
Both sides composed by Lennon
(Liberty 55626) September 1963

HELLO LITTLE GIRL by The Fourmost
A-side written by Lennon
(Atco 6280) November 1963

I'MIN LOVE by The Fourmost
A-side written by Lennon
(Atco 6285) February 1964

YOU'VE GOT TO HIDE YOUR LOVE AWAY by The Silkie
A-side written and produced by Lennon and McCartney
(Fontana 1525) September 1965

WE LOVE YOU by The Rolling Stones
A-side features Lennon's backing vocals
(London 905) August 1967

YOKO ONO: PLASTIC ONO BAND by Yoko Ono
Album produced by Lennon, who also plays guitar throughout. Same tracks as
UK release
(Apple SW 3373) December 1970

TANDOORI CHICKEN by Ronnie Spector
B-side (to Try Some Buy Some) features backing vocals by Lennon
(Apple 1832) April 1971

GOD SAVE US/DO THE OZ by Bill Elliott And The Elastic Oz Band
Both sides written and produced by Lennon, who also sings lead on the B-side
(Apple 1835) July 1971

FLY by Yoko Ono
Album produced by Lennon, who also appears on several tracks. Same tracks as
UK release
(Apple SVBB 3380) September 1971

MRS LENNON/MIDSUMMER NEW YORK by Yoko Ono
Both sides produced by Lennon
(Apple 1839) September 1971

THE POPE SMOKES DOPE by David Peel and The Lower East Side
Album produced by Lennon, who also appears on several tracks
I'm A Runaway/Everybody's Smoking Marijuana/F Is Not A Dirty Word/The
Hippie From New York City/McDonald's Farm/The Ballad Of New York City –
John Lennon Yoko Ono/The Ballad Of Bob Dylan/The Chicago

Conspiracy/The Hip Generation/I'm Gonna Start Another Riot/The Birth
Control Blues/The Pope Smokes Dope
(Apple SW 3391) April 1972

ELEPHANT'S MEMORY by Elephant's Memory
Album produced by Lennon, who also appears on several tracks. Same tracks as
UK release
(Apple SMAS 3389) September 1972

LIBERATION SPECIAL/MADNESS by Elephant's Memory
Both sides produced by Lennon
(Apple 1854) November 1972

NOW OR NEVER/MOVE ON FAST by Yoko Ono
Both sides produced by Lennon
(Apple 1853) November 1972

LIBERATION SPECIAL/POWER BOOGIE by Elephant's Memory
Both sides produced by Lennon
(Apple 1854) December 1972

APPROXIMATELY INFINITE UNIVERSE by Yoko Ono
Album produced by Lennon, who also appears on two tracks. Same tracks as UK
release
(Apple SVBB 3399) January 1973

DEATH OF SAMANTHA/YANG YANG by Yoko Ono
Both sides produced by Lennon
(Apple 1859) February 1973

WOMAN POWER/MEN MEN MEN by Yoko Ono
Lennon appears on both sides
(Apple 1865) September 1973

FEELING THE SPACE by Yoko Ono
Lennon appears on three tracks, as on UK release
(Apple SW 3412) November 1973

RINGO by Ringo Starr
Lennon wrote and appears on I'm The Greatest
(Apple SWAL 3413) November 1973

MANY RIVERS TO CROSS/DON'T FORGET ME by Harry Nilsson
Both sides produced by Lennon
(RCA PB 10001) July 1974

PUSSY CATS by Harry Nilsson
Album produced by Lennon. Same tracks as UK release
(RCA CPL 1–0570) August 1974

**SUBTERRANEAN HOMESICK BLUES/MUCHO MUNGO;
MT.ELBA by Harry Nilsson**
Both sides produced by Lennon, who also co-wrote B-side
(RCA PB 10078) October 1974

ONLY YOU by Ringo Starr
Lennon appears on A-side
(Apple 1876) November 1974

GOODNIGHT VIENNA by Ringo Starr
Lennon appears on Only You and title track, cowriting the latter
(Apple SW 3417) November 1974

**LUCY IN THE SKY WITH DIAMONDS/ONE DAY AT A TIME by
Elton John**
Lennon wrote both sides and appears on A-side
(MCA 40344) November 1974

JOHN DAWSON WINTER III by Johnny Winter
Lennon wrote Rock And Roll People
(Blue Sky PZ 33292) November 1974

LOOP DE LOOP/DON'T FORGET ME by Harry Nilsson
Both sides produced by Lennon
(RCA PB 10139) December 1974

I SAW HER STANDING THERE by Elton John Band
B-side features Lennon
(MCA 40364) February 1975

YOUNG AMERICANS by David Bowie
Lennon appears on Across The Universe and Fame, both of which he wrote or
co-wrote
(RCA APL 1–0998) March 1975

GOODNIGHT VIENNA by Ringo Starr
Lennon wrote and appears on A-side
(Apple 1882) June 1975

FAME by David Bowie
Lennon co-wrote and appears on A-side
(RCA JB 10320) June 1975

RINGO'S ROTOGRAVURE by Ringo Starr
Lennon wrote and appears on Cookin'
(Atlantic SD 18193) September 1976

WALKING ON THIN ICE/IT HAPPENED by Yoko Ono
Lennon produced and appeared on both sides
(Geffen GEF 49683) February 1981

IT'S ALRIGHT by Yoko Ono
Never Say Goodbye features Lennon vocal
(Polydor PD-1–6364) November 1982

NEVER SAY GOODBYE by Yoko Ono
A-side features Lennon vocal
(Polydor 810 556–7) January 1983

THE BEST OF BILLY J. KRAMER & THE DAKOTAS by Billy J. Kramer & The Dakotas
Includes previously released Lennon compositions, plus I'm In Love, featuring
brief Lennon vocal
(Imperial CDP 7960552) October 1991

JOHN LENNON FOR PRESIDENT by David Peel & The Super Apple Band
Includes Amerika, produced by Lennon & Ono
(Orange 005) November 1980

ONOBOX by Yoko Ono
6-CD box set including multiple tracks produced by, and featuring, Lennon
(Rykodisc RCD 10224-10229) January 1992

WALKING ON THIN ICE by Yoko Ono
CD including multiple tracks produced by, and featuring, Lennon
(Rykodisc RCD 20230) March 1992

PLAYGROUND PSYCHOTICS by Frank Zappa & Mothers Of Invention
2-CD set including remix of 1971 live performance by Lennon/Ono
(Rykodisc RCD 10557) October 1992

YOKO ONO: PLASTIC ONO BAND by Yoko Ono
CD adds three Lennon-produced bonus tracks to original LP, Open Your Box,
Something More Abstract & South Wind
(Rykodisc RCD 10414) 1997

FLY by Yoko Ono
CD adds two Lennon-produced bonus tracks to original LP, Between The Takes
& Will You Touch Me
(Rykodisc RCD 10415/16) 1997

APPROXIMATELY INFINITE UNIVERSE
CD adds two Lennon-produced bonus tracks to original LP, Dogtown & She
Gets Down On Her Knees
(Rykodisc RCD 10417/18) 1997

FEELING THE SPACE
CD adds Coffin Car (live) featuring Lennon on guitar
(Rykodisc RCD 10419) 1997

Index